Experiments in Mystical Atheism

∴

Experiments in Mystical Atheism

∴

GODLESS EPIPHANIES FROM DAOISM
TO SPINOZA AND BEYOND

Brook Ziporyn

THE UNIVERSITY OF CHICAGO PRESS

CHICAGO AND LONDON

The University of Chicago Press, Chicago 60637
The University of Chicago Press, Ltd., London
© 2024 by The University of Chicago
Published 2024
Printed in the United States of America

33 32 31 30 29 28 27 26 25 24   1 2 3 4 5

ISBN-13: 978-0-226-83132-9 (cloth)
ISBN-13: 978-0-226-83526-6 (paper)
ISBN-13: 978-0-226-83525-9 (e-book)
DOI: https://doi.org/10.7208/chicago/9780226835259.001.0001

Library of Congress Cataloging-in-Publication Data

Names: Ziporyn, Brook, 1964– author.
Title: Experiments in mystical atheism : godless epiphanies from
    Daoism to Spinoza and beyond / Brook Ziporyn.
Description: Chicago : The University of Chicago Press, 2024. |
    Includes bibliographical references and index.
Identifiers: LCCN 2024002416 | ISBN 9780226831329 (cloth) |
ISBN 9780226835266 (paperback) | ISBN 9780226835259 (e-book)
Subjects: LCSH: Atheism. | Mysticism. | Irreligion. | Monotheism.
Classification: LCC BL2747.3.Z57 2024 | DDC 211/.8—dc23/
    eng/20240205
LC record available at https://lccn.loc.gov/2024002416

♾ This paper meets the requirements of ANSI/ NISO Z39.48-1992
(Permanence of Paper).

You see, control . . . can never be a means to anything but more control . . . like junk.

—WILLIAM S. BURROUGHS, *Naked Lunch*

Just this is divinity: that there are gods but no God.

—FRIEDRICH NIETZSCHE, *Thus Spoke Zarathustra,*
translated by Graham Parkes

The mind controlling the energy, called strength, I call the same: strong-arming.
心使氣曰強

—LAOZI, *Daodejing*, translated by Brook Ziporyn

The Ministry of Love was the really frightening one.

—GEORGE ORWELL, *1984*

Contents

Preface

"I've always hated the idea of God," someone once told me—and then added, almost immediately: "but for a long time I couldn't figure out exactly why." It was a passing remark made many years ago, but since then it has often come to mind. The speaker was a man named Pawel, the captain of an international freighter ship, the *T. Wenda*, which sailed under the Polish flag. Though a citizen of Poland, he had a British mother, who had mainly raised him; his English was precise, idiomatic, and rather elegant, British to my ear but seasoned with a slight continental skew. It was late at night and we were far out at sea on the Indian Ocean, toward the middle of a forty-day journey from Yokohama to Hamburg. At this late hour, relieved of duty until morning, he would indulge in his small daily allotment of high-end duty-free scotch, a ritual that often provoked him to seek some convivial company. As the only commercial passenger on the ship, and as the one other native speaker of English onboard (albeit of the cruder colonial variant), I was often singled out for this honor, which apparently was not to be lightly bestowed on his crew.

Staring at the eerily limpid and star-pierced sky that night, Pawel waxed cosmic. I was surprised by his turn of phrase, his reflectiveness, and his outspoken irreligion, of which I'd seen no previous sign. I allowed, tentatively, that the idea of God had caused a lot of confusion and turmoil in the world—is that what he meant? He shook his head slowly and then said something like, "I was always vaguely aware that many atrocities had been committed in the name of the idea of God, and that it rested on quite shaky intellectual foundations. But neither of these really explained why I've always found it so . . . so distasteful, so definitively and so intensely so." He compared it, with a certain light-hearted perversity that was characteristic of him, to the revulsion many people feel when they see a cockroach in their food or hear tell of a particularly heinous sociopathic crime: a disgust that is sharp, nonnegotiable, and imbued with a sense of deep conviction. "It was rather: you say someone created and controls the universe? You say we are living in a *planned* universe, that existence is attributable to *an intention*, that it was made *for a purpose? This must not be!*" He allowed himself to laugh a little at his own dramatization: "That was my instinctive reaction to the idea when I first really took it in." He paraphrased Kingsley Amis, an author he often quoted when in his cups: "I mean, I understood why I hated the idea, thanks, but why did I hate it *so much?*"[1]

At that I probably surrendered a noncommittal chortle or nod. In any case, we soon turned to other topics. But I had immediately registered the sentiment he expressed with a kind of muted shock: it turned out I knew exactly what he meant. It was that unsolicited remark many years ago, I now feel in retrospect, that was the seed that grew into this book. For I noticed, to my surprise, that I too had often felt an obscure twinge of instant but weirdly unshakable disaffection when faced with God-talk of any kind, a distaste that was as unplumbed and unexplained as it was unmistakable and undissuadable. Whether it rose to the level of "hate" is debatable; but without question there was something odd about the clarity and intensity of this antipathy toward the idea of God. It would be one thing if I were someone who was committed wholeheartedly to science and pragmatism and materialist Enlightenment rationalism, like modern secular persons, and thus inclined to simply dismiss all nonempirical speculation, all metaphysical tale spinning, all faith-based hypotheses and counterintuitive system building as pernicious nonsense, and to include the God idea as simply one more sordid item in the wild catalogue of discredited human superstitions. But that was not the case with me: I loved all that stuff, loved thinking about it, always found my horizons unproblematically expanded by these precious bits of human spiritual ingenuity—the more outlandish the better—whether I "believed in them," or even "approved of them," or not—with one glaring exception: the idea of God, in the sense of a purposeful creator or director of the universe. To put it naively and pathetically: my youthfully earnest good-faith search for expansive horizons of thought and spiritual kinship, my joyous excitement in discovering the profound riches brought forth by the great minds and spirits of the Jewish, Christian, and Islamic pasts and their Greek and Roman forerunners, was repeatedly thwarted, because just when things were getting good, just when the spirit began to gather and new visions to galvanize, I found to my disappointment that this idea of God, in some form or other, kept popping up to ruin everything. In every case, when that notion entered any of these strange ancient or modern visions of the cosmos, even as a mere thought experiment, that vision immediately went dead for me. It lost its magic, its salutary buoyancy and power to inspire, its opening up of new vistas toward thoughts I *might* actually come to embrace or else simply find it profitable to entertain or develop. But why?

This book is an attempt to answer that question. It entails no claims about the objective falseness or perniciousness of the idea in question, the God idea. It is rather an attempt to excavate what it is that certain contingent persons, like myself, find so off-putting about it. Given that one discovers this antipathy existing in oneself, should it be regarded as merely a narrow childhood prejudice, the outgrowing of which would bring no intellectual or spiritual cost and perhaps considerable gain? Is it perhaps no more than a failure to understand for what it is a harmlessly convenient metaphor for exactly the kind of thing one would otherwise joyfully embrace and explore? Might it even be no more than a feeble cover story for a guilty sinner desperately fleeing his righteous judge? Or might this antipathy instead have some more substantive import, in terms of other intuitions and commitments with which it is inextricably interconnected—some worthwhile philosophical or spiritual implications that can be excavated and examined and developed with some degree of rigor? It is a question of what *alternate* values and vistas might be foreclosed when the idea of God is entertained, and why. The motivation is thus admittedly very much rooted in this given dispositional fact, whatever its causes may be, rather than objective considerations about what is rationally justified or what is universally good. To pretend otherwise, or to leave this natural fact unaddressed and unavowed, would be not only disingenuous but also a serious obstacle to taking what follows in the spirit intended. Without pride and without shame, it must be owned up to: a kind of allergy, like lactose intolerance, that affects profoundly what one may or may not find digestible, however hungry one might be, and that brings with it certain other orientations and potentials, to be explored in depth in what follows. Some of us are just God-intolerant. This book is not meant to *convince* any who do not share this disposition, though it does seek to provide them with a thoroughgoing view of how the other half thinks, as a salutary beginning to further dialogue. But it is written primarily in the hopes of speaking to and with others among the mystically minded but God-intolerant, regardless of their numbers, now or in the future, and as a way of rigorously tracking down and charting the entailments and possibilities of such an orientation to the world.

Having said all that, and thus introduced this unavoidably (and perhaps slightly cringeworthy) personal dimension to the framing of this writing, I must report also another peculiar condition that informs it, lest it be even more radically misunderstood. I think it is undeniable that for some of us, this distaste for the core monotheist conception of God, and its various aftermaths, is something so axiomatic that it feels central to our very sense of identity, to our ability to recognize ourselves. But at the same time, we might sometimes have an uncanny awareness, perhaps concomitant to the imaginative space opened up by this axiomatic Godlessness, of at least one stratum of sentiment that lies even deeper: a certain attraction to the shifting of perspective on one's own prejudices, a strong suspicion at times that one could just as easily have found oneself on the other side of every determinate issue and still feel more or less the same. In certain moods, under the right conditions, it can happen: the dawning of a gentle but vivid empathetic identification, a felt surmise of what it might be like to be a conservative rather than a liberal, a woman rather than a man, an extrovert rather than an introvert, an ascetic rather than a libertine—or a pious Christian or Jew or Muslim rather than a militant atheist. In such a mood one can well imagine feeling just as strongly about all those ways of being in the world— feeling just as much at home in them, feeling just as passionately about them, thinking through their implications with the same excitement and epiphany—and gazing across the great divide at the other kind of person with amazement and incomprehension. We find ourselves seeming to have some sense of what it would be like to be there in that skin, assuming all those things to be just self-evident ways of being, feeling grateful to inhabit them, feeling the joy of working through all the details and implications of those stances, feeling just as snugly situated in those forms of existence. We may at those times begin to understand from inside how many of our characteristic ticks and stylistic features—a certain pace and rhythm of response to stimuli, say, or a way of putting sentences together, a certain tilt of irony and sarcasm and skepticism, but aimed at other objects—could nonetheless still be the forms of deportment we would comfortably inhabit, unchanged default ways of moving through the world in spite of completely altered explicit commitments. This does not imply the existence of some determinate unchanging essence, somehow rising above the particulars of our existence, which would be numerically the same as the essence of that other person if all the particulars were replaced. Rather, it is a feeling that the ever-changing and endlessly renegotiated *style of being* we currently inhabit and recognize and continue to riff through, the distinctive rhythm of the advances and retreats by which we have learned to juggle whatever is incoming, could easily be continued with other props and would feel the same to ourselves and to the people who know us in spite of replacing all the particulars of our commitments. At those times, something feels a bit contingent and irrelevant about the things we care about, even though we care about them deeply.

This sort of intuition has been something that has itself informed much of my intellectual work in the past: a sense of the ambiguity of identities, which has developed into a theorization of how such a thing could be possible—not due to the assumption of a fixed identity underlying these changing particulars, which does not seem philosophically coherent to me, but due to somewhat more exotic ontological premises having to do with the status of and relationship between sameness and difference per se.[2] In what follows I will occasionally touch on some of those more esoteric ideas, which obviously require extensive philosophical unpacking, but that is not my central concern in this book. Nevertheless, as I write this antimonotheist screed I occasionally imagine myself writing the opposite book, as that opposite me: a passionate defense of neoorthodoxy, of Trinitarian theology, of Christology, of total devotion to the one true god as the only possible form of meaning—on the glories of the Incarnation or the Resurrection or the exact fulfillment of Torah or the prophetic spirit or the ecstatic agony of waiting for the unknown messiah or the true meaning of Jihad. And I imagine I would feel this just as deeply, and naturally spin up intensely intricate swarms of interconnected ideas with complete conviction, and these would mean plenty to me, would have deep and wholesome existential resonances in my life. I should add that if there is someone else out there who can write that kind of book, I would not only encourage it and be glad to see it, but in some strange way I would even feel like I had written it. From a certain meta perspective, I want both books—even though as the me I am now, I would probably never stop throwing up if I had to read that book. Indeed, the only thing that would make me unable to sustain this imagined self-recognition in that alternate me as monotheist polemicist would perhaps be his inability or unwillingness to recognize himself in his imagined atheist alter ego that I currently am—and this is, perhaps, the real core of the structural tensions queried in the rest of this book. I offer this book both to those like my younger self who felt in need of someone to assure them they are not insane or evil to hate the very idea of God, and also to those on the other side of the aisle to aid them in imagining and empathizing with what life is like over here, so perhaps both of us can sometimes imagine being the other. I am hoping that even committed and dyed-in-the-wool monotheists will find something valuable about having the opposite point of view, which might well seem mysterious or just plain perverse to them, spelled out unreservedly and down to the last consequence. Like a long nineteenth-century novel, a full-throated and detailed depiction of the inner life of another type is a good way to temporarily feel what it's like to be someone else. And that seems to me something intrinsically valuable—for good Spinozistic atheist reasons to be explored at length in what follows.

This book is an attempt to excavate the "offending" premises of monotheism (only for those so offended) and also to look at some possibilities that open up if we suspend those premises. I see this first and foremost as a question of something that came to happen in the way human beings related to their experiences of *purpose* and *control*—namely, the absolutizing of them into general ontological structures, a tendency found already in the animistic assumption that whatever happens anywhere must be understood to have occurred in order to satisfy someone's Will, and was under the control of some conscious being whose deeds are meant to achieve some specific purpose. What came to happen with this raw intuition was its elevation into the idea of intelligence (*Noûs*) as the first cause (*Arché*) of all things, implying a universal single-order teleology that applies to whatever exists. The smoking gun seems to go back to Greek thinkers like Anaxagoras and Socrates rather than the Bible—followed by Plato and Aristotle, who did so much to set the parameters for Jewish, Christian, and Islamic theology throughout various periods of their histories, but also to define the terms of the humanistic rebellions against them. My focal point, then, is the paradoxical question of *the ultimate status and value of purpose as such.* And it is here that Chinese thought becomes crucial for properly taking in the scope and implications of this question, for it was the early Daoist and Confucian thinkers who first made the decisive breakthrough on this question, the stunning suggestion that both human life and the universal process are ultimately grounded in what they call *wuwei* 無為, nondeliberate activity, rather than planning, purpose, or *anyone's* mental control.[3] It is the ontological and axiological *ultimacy* of *wuwei,* a motif that informs almost all later Chinese thought in one way or another, that underlies my claim that Dao is, in the relevant sense, the *opposite of God.* The fundamental question before us is the meaning of the supposition of either a planned or an unplanned cosmos, and whether human purpose itself is therefore a revelation of the deepest ontological fact or rather an epiphenomenal detour that expresses, instantiates, or even intensifies a deeper value and a deeper source: purposelessness.

This opens up some interesting perspectives on many questions, and on alternate possibilities for human life, even for "religious" life. Increasingly I see this as a sort of *atheist mysticism*: not the humanistic rejection of religion, but the religious rejection of God. This idea may still sound counterintuitive or implausible to some. This book is an argument for its existence and its importance.

In part I, I attempt to get back to the origins of those premises I was just talking about: universalized and monolithized animism as the ultimate principle of causality, *Noûs* as *Arché.* This will lead to some consideration of the idea of "personality" and what happens to the universe if we make it the ultimate self-standing basis of reality rather than an embedded, embodied, mediated dimension of reality. The focus here is the *absolutization* of choice, exclusion, judgment, dichotomization, accountability, tool-being, work, purpose. These are not just aspects of a particularly bad personality; even a loving and open personality will end up saturated with such absolutization if that personality is ultimately grounded in personality (its own or Another's) rather than in something beyond or beneath or transversing personality, because this is the nature and etiology of personality as such. Then I'll talk about what *else* I think might be behind the desire for transcendent ideas, the mystical impulse, and how God gets in the way of this alternative.

This will also involve a view of some of the things that are usually seen as opposed to God in postmonotheist cultures as disguised avatars of the basic premises behind God, including not only the Anaxagorean *Noûs* as *Arché* but also the Parmenidean dichotomy between Being and Nonbeing: things like freedom to the exclusion of causal conditioning, autonomous agency to the exclusion of passivity, truth to the exclusion of falsehood, goodness to the exclusion of badness, meaning to the exclusion of meaninglessness, being to the exclusion of nothingness. These are part of the same package as the idea of God, transferred and inverted in some cases but spinning in the same cul-de-sac.

Part I is the "diagnostic" part of this discussion, where I draw on the critiques of monotheist premises found in Spinoza, Schopenhauer, Nietzsche, and Bataille, as well as various Daoist and Buddhist thinkers, in analyzing the entailments of the monotheist cultural complex. In part II and in online appendix B, "World without Anaxagoras," some of these same thinkers are examined to work through their positive proposals for alternatives: priority is given here to thinkers who have ceased to dichotomize freedom and determinism, agency and passivity, truth and falsehood, and the rest of these apparent binaries, grasping the limitations of the idea of God in which they all culminate, and how profoundly this radical undermining of what have become commonsense consequences affects their view of the world. For this reason, the real center of gravity of the book is chapter 5, on Spinoza, who is uniquely important in this discussion because it was he who broke the back of teleology *from within* the tradition that had for so long obsessively embraced it, using its own premises and procedures, as opposed to the relevant figures in the Asian traditions discussed in online appendix B, who never had to contend with any such tradition and thus also never had to break free from it. To fully explore the intricacies of this momentous event, the Spinoza section is much longer, more elaborate, and more detailed than the treatment of the other figures in this book. In a certain sense, it is what everything else here orbits around.

Here and there I have also referenced an online supplement for digressive examples and deep dives into topics that, while not necessarily essential for sustaining the through-line of the exposition, nevertheless can hopefully help fill out the conceptual and historical picture. The unlimited and interactive online space provides an opportunity also for ruminations that can be both more granular and more expansive, as well as less carved-in-stone; some more adventurous and tentative explorations can take shape here while remaining alive to real-time revisions and real-world responses in the future.

I want to make clear at the outset that I am not claiming that these Godless systems cannot be oppressive, violent, stupid, burdensome, ridiculous, entrapping, morally repugnant, sinister, and so on. Though I find Jan Assmann's carefully stated assessment of the "propensity" for violence (not the necessitation of violence) inherent in the very idea of monotheism rather persuasive both conceptually and historically, this kind of consequence is not what concerns me here.[4] For all I know, burdensomeness of one form or another is going to be a common result of almost any ideology. Though I too will identify some of the rather ugly psychological and conceptual consequences that I see as inescapably entailed by the monotheistic idea, which perhaps are describable as a propensity or even necessity for impoverishment or self-crippling of human experience, I am not in a position to say whether these little tragedies on the individual level of the soul are good or bad for society or for humankind at large. I share Nietzsche's view—at least as he saw things when in one of his moods—that many of these unpleasant human states, depressing as they may be to behold, can be regarded as sickness in the sense that pregnancy is a sickness: uncomfortable states of long incapacitation that lead to glorious later outcomes. And then again, taking a further step, the blessed, adorable child born from this difficult pregnancy may turn out to be a disaster to various other things, and on and on it turns. Maybe intolerance is good for some things. And maybe the things it's good for are bad for some other things. There's no way to assess the final value of any particular stage in the process at the maximal macrolevel. The most I'd say on a social or historical level is that, assuming for the sake of argument that all worldviews can inevitably lead to uses or abuses that are highly obnoxious, at least in the Godless systems the *extra* obnoxiousness of God is removed.

The idea here is thus not that God has bad social or moral consequences for the world; it is rather that rejecting God and all the concomitants of the idea of God is what alone makes possible a particular type of experience of the world, an experience that for some of us is the only thing that makes life worth living, and that I will unhesitatingly call mystical. The claim is that certain spiritual maladies of humankind are better seen, not as a result of a lack of God, but as insufficiently thoroughgoing atheism. Our problem is that we have hitherto had only a choice between either God or a halfway atheism. Thoroughgoing atheism—exceptionless atheism, *deep* atheism— though difficult to reach, is what resolves the impasses of both God and everyday Godlessness. This is the idea of atheist mysticism. These are mystical visionaries not in spite of their atheism but because of it—because of the depth and thoroughness of their atheism. My main examples are Spinoza, middle-period Schelling and Hegel, Nietzsche, Bataille, and the Daoists and Buddhists, very much including the seemingly ridiculously credulous Mahāyāna Buddhists with all their transcendental deity-like bodhisattvas and buddhas (which are especially bounteous in their Chinese versions), and finally the ground zero of the whole thing, the ancient Chinese Confucians and, mainly, the so-called Daoist thinkers Laozi and—above all— Zhuangzi, whom I credit with first glimpsing the liberating possibility I will call Emulative Atheism: a beatific vision of an ultimately purposeless life in an ultimately purposeless cosmos.

With petals like onyx and pistils like jade
they alight one by one on the pond here below.
I ask where they come from, how flowers are made;
the god of the springtime himself doesn't know.
瓊英與玉蕊 片片落前池
問著花來處 東君也不知

—YU ZHONGWEN 虞仲文 (1069–1123), "Snowflakes" 「雪花」,
translated by Brook Ziporyn

THE WEIRD IDEA

For the past several thousand years a peculiar idea has been afoot: the idea
of God. This is of course not the only bizarre idea we come upon in scru-
tinizing the annals of our species, if we are inclined to judge them according to prevailing rationalistic standards of common sense. The belief in,
say, astrology, extraterrestrial espionage, the Loch Ness monster, Bigfoot,
personal survival after death, the existence of invisible ghosts and spirits,
geomancy, karma, reincarnation, witchcraft, and so on also may seem unjustifiable and strange to many of us raised under the auspices of modern
secular reason and the demands of empirical evidence. But in this book I
want to suggest that the idea of God—not the idea of a multitude of unseen
forces and deities, but that of a single, sovereign creator deity who is omnipotent and omniscient—is peculiar to a unique degree, and problematic
in a distinctive and particularly important way. That is, this book might be
construed as a history of ecstatic repudiations of the entailments of the notion of a monotheistic God, what I will call the "big G God," but not against
gods in general, nor against some form of immortality or transcendence,
nor indeed against irrational or unjustifiable beliefs as such.

My main purpose here is not to offer the usual arguments against belief
in the existence of God. I will be trying to demonstrate neither that the idea

1

of God is objectively *false* nor that it is objectively *bad*. I am not trying to show either its factual falsity or its historical destructiveness. Rather, my intent is to show the ways in which atheism as such—precisely the rejection of this conception of a single sovereign creator God—has served as a lynchpin for doctrines and experiences of something we might call, following Nietzsche, "redemptive," or more broadly, "mystical," in the works, and presumably in the experience, of several individuals through history.[1] What motivates me here is thus not the desire to pile on denunciations of all religion, nor even denunciations of God, in favor of a complete dismissal of all unjustifiable beliefs in unverifiable structures or forces or dimensions of reality, though as it happens I'm not a believer in those either. Rather, the topic just involves pointed repudiations of any monotheistic notion of God, and just for what I will loosely call religious or mystical, rather than secular, reasons and purposes. Atheism can be, and has been, a certain kind of *epiphany*, by which I mean that it discloses something radically other than the world presented to us by what we call common sense, something radically different from the socially endorsed vision of reality, from the concerns of the "world" defined as the world of history, of work, of social and financial and artistic success, of shared community goals, and thus of all that is properly called "secular"—atheism precisely as a *religious ideal*.

This requires an adjustment of our usual assumptions about the default state of human consciousness and what elements are superadded to it in special cases. For if atheism is something that has to be disclosed, something that is not simply the prior absence of the addition of this weird idea from outside, and if this disclosure produces a radical change in consciousness, this implies that our common sense may inadvertently be saturated with the undetected traces of this idea of God, even when it is called something else; it implies that this idea is more difficult to eradicate than is usually assumed, and above all that this eradication is far more rare than usually supposed.

Such a suggestion is not unusual. Nietzsche famously suggested that "we are not getting rid of God because we still believe in grammar."[2] His point was that the subject-predicate form of Indo-European sentences required the addition of an agent, a "doer," for every effect: for example, the sentence, "Lightning flashes." The grammar of this particular family of languages requires a redoubling of the event, reifying the doer, "lightning," and separating it from its action, "flashing," but actually the same thing has just been labeled twice and divided by a preexisting grammatical requirement. The by-product of this form is the felt necessity for every event to be done by someone or something, by a cause or agent. Users of those languages end up with a constant intuition that since something is happening in the universe, there must be something who is doing it. This would mean that such persons would be expected to have a genuine and persistent sense "deep down," when they search their "souls," that God really must exist—and thus speakers of these languages would be able to discover the presence of God in their own hearts if they would only look deep within and be entirely honest with themselves.

Somewhat similarly, we can find the suggestion among psychoanalysts that everyone believes in God "unconsciously," and many theologians have made similar assertions, though in a different sense and with very different overall aims. Freud had regarded the attachment to the monotheistic God as the infantile longing for the lost absolute father, the father imagined in early childhood as an omnipotent protector but also as a hated rival. This is complicated by his intriguing and bizarre notion of a repressed phylogenetic murder of this father repeatedly reenacted by the rebellious hordes of brothers in early human protosocieties: the admired but resented father was killed by the brothers, who were then forever haunted by guilt for this deicidomorphic patricide, of which they were also, however, very proud. The idea of the father-like monotheist God of absolute power is thus forever set into the human psyche, replete with its heady stew of love, hate, guilt, submission, rebellion, and ambivalence. The polytheist world was, according to Freud, a brief interregnum, an exceptional moment of respite, an interim period during which the compromise truce of the brothers briefly prevailed, with their grudging nonaggression treaties and their attempt at a civil society; the irresistible appeal and triumph of the monotheist idea is no more and no less than "the return of the repressed," now decked out with various attempts to handle the torques of guilt and law and submission in variously shuffled ways.[3] For Freud, then, there will always be this longing for the single dominant, maximally powerful Father God in human beings, although this is, of course, the opposite of evidence for either the existence of God or the desirability of believing in it.

The brilliant weirdo and mountebank Jacques Lacan upped the ante on Freud and likewise declared himself an atheist nonetheless by modifying the meaning of this claim in a particularly intriguing way: given the ineradicable unconscious belief in God, true atheism lies in comprehending, not that God does not exist, but that this God in whom we cannot help unconsciously believing is himself unconscious.[4] That is to say, I take it, that God can go ahead and "exist" as much as he wants, and as much as any theist may desire, but that still won't be any help for the real problem. Whatever God there may be is in the same situation as we are: transversed by unruly, alternative torques of causality and desire that are nonetheless unrenounceably his own, which are even his own deepest self, but this self, like all selves, is devoid of unity, constantly eliding, divided against itself, without any single

purpose, impossible to bring to full consciousness and incapable of ultimate coherence. Indeed, in this formulation, God is even a little worse off
than we are: we may be undercut by our own unconscious, but at least we
also have consciousness as well; God, on the other hand, is in a coma or a
swoon, being just a cauldron of his own conflicted drives and the endless
metonymic drift of his unconscious symbolizations.

A similar move is made in early Buddhism, which freely admitted all the
gods proposed by alternate traditions but sarcastically added that those gods
are tragicomically misguided about their own ontic condition. Glued to the
treadmill of karma and ignorance and egoism like the rest of us and yet boast-
ing of their sublime status, some of them jump to the false conclusion that
they are free creators of the universe on the basis of some deceptive circum-
stantial evidence and a *post hoc, ergo propter hoc* logical fallacy, and therefore in the final analysis they are quite a bit worse off than human beings.[5]

Parries such as these reject, not the existence of unseen forces, nor even
that of undetectable personal beings with great power; rather, they assert
that this is not the question that matters. What matters is rather the larger
point that seems to be assumed here: that in principle, nothing is completely in control of itself; that there is no possibility of total control on
the part of any being, no matter how exalted. In Buddhist terms, this is
called the problem of "self," which is defined as a consciousness mistakenly
and disastrously conceived as an independent entity that is the unilateral
controller and sole cause of its own deeds and experiences. God is self writ
large. God is self projected to the cosmic level and absolutized to the point
of inescapability. Far from being a solution to the problem of selfhood in the
form of a mighty counterweight to our own petty struggles for control, God
is here seen as more of the same problem, but weaponized and locked into
a position of unsurpassable ultimacy, an exacerbation and inverted metastasis of the problem that makes it a trillion times worse. For the problem,
on this view, is not who in particular is in control but the very idea of control itself.

In at least one relevant sense, "total control" would seem to be a contradiction in terms: "control" implies nontotality. To be in control means
to be in relation to something that is being controlled; but if that thing is
completely controlled, it has to be considered part of the controller rather
than the controlled, for on this view, "control" is the essential criterion for
what among all experienced content counts as oneself. If everything were
perfectly controlled, there would be no more relationship of control. The
same consideration can be applied, *mutatis mutandis*, to consciousness: inasmuch as consciousness is always consciousness *of* something, it requires
something at least minimally other to any given consciousness in order to

be conscious—even if that object is only another instance of consciousness at another point in time, or present consciousness itself in the mode of
object-of-consciousness: the relation of mind as knower to mind as known
requires some minimal distinction between them. This would mean that
no mind can know itself perfectly in real time—that even in the seemingly
magical self-relation known as self-consciousness, some form of opacity
to itself pertains to consciousness per se, even if only in the form of the
requirement to check and verify its present knowledge against future ret-
rospection, as is imposed by the serial temporality of conscious events. By
this reasoning, knowing as such requires that whatever exists in any form
is always shadowed or even permeated by *otherness*, that no spirit can exist without being shackled to an otherness (for example a "body" and a
"world" and a "past" and a "future"), a nonself other-self that is nonetheless
itself, and/or a perpetual obstacle to its own action and knowledge that
nonetheless is, precisely qua obstacle, essential to its existence.

Though this claim is argued for vigorously (and, in my view, convincingly) in some modes of thought such as those touched on just now, it is
not self-evident. But neither is it, *prima facie*, at all shocking. After all, no
consciousness has ever been empirically discovered that isn't linked to a
corresponding body, and no wakefulness has ever been observed that does
not function by alternating with a state of sleep, namely, by periodically
wearying and losing control of itself, by succumbing to its own opposite. If
we cannot help imagining a superconsciousness as audience for the drama
of our histories, it would be natural to regard it as a superconsciousness
with the identifying characteristics of all known consciousness, embedded
in body and shot through with sleep, sometimes losing the thread and having to scramble to recover it while never entirely sure if it's got the whole
picture. Indeed, why not a consciousness so deeply fragmented and rent by
patches of opacity that we might better describe it as many minds rather
than one, a host of conflicted divinities joined at the hip of their embeddedness in some larger unconscious structure? In that case, the *ens realissimus*
would be unconsciousness rather than consciousness—or better, a kind of
ambiguous and unstable mixture of consciousness and unconsciousness
hovering around their interface. We will see some such idea in those polytheist systems that posit a nonconscious substratum from which the personalities of the gods emerge and into which they are subsumed again: the
Absolute as something that is neither devoid of personality nor possessed
of only *a single particular* personality, but as productive and destructive of
infinite personalities.

The slumbering almighty, the restlessly dreaming God, may be a more
profoundly atheist conception than the outright denial of God (which, as

we'll see, has difficulty avoiding an implicit repositing of God at a higher level as the guarantor of the initial God's literal nonexistence). For the idea of God is correlative to a certain conception of our own agency, of self-hood per se. Thus we will be considering traditions that radically rework the concept of human agency and consciousness—early Daoism with its conception of *wuwei* and Buddhism from its foundational "nonself" move forward, even into its most extreme reaches of mythology and religiosity—as the most thorough and important heroes of a genuinely atheist revolution of consciousness. In a certain important sense, a Mahāyāna Buddhist kneeling and praying to a cosmic bodhisattva for supernatural assistance, or endeavoring to see himself as seen by an eternal omniscient mind that is not a purposive creator and controller and judge but *exactly the opposite*, is a more thorough and fundamental atheist than a scientific rationalist or a secular humanist who continues to think of himself as a transparent rational agent, a consciousness that directs and controls his own actions according to clearly conceived purposes, in a universe "governed" by natural "laws." This book is an attempt to explore that "certain important sense."

GOD AS DEFAULT?

Perhaps the idea of God in some form or other—even if only in the vague Alcoholics Anonymous form of "a higher power"—can be considered a built-in structural possibility or tendency of the human machine, which is activated by certain kinds of accidental environmental switches or social arrangements and very hard to eradicate once it has kicked into gear. After all, it is hardly controversial that there exists a power "higher" than ourselves, assuming that higher means more powerful: a truck that runs us over or a swirling supernova or airless void that threatens to consume the planet would equally qualify. The question is what this higher power is like. In what sense is it "higher"? And in what sense is it "a" higher power (i.e., singular)? Even granting that many of us (at least in certain historical and cultural contexts) have some instinctive sense of being "watched" by some other consciousness or consciousnesses—a perpetual authoritatively knowing eye hovering over our shoulders—what does this signify?

In Lacan's view, God is not only unconscious, but is also one way of concretizing "the Other," sometimes denoted in English recountings as "the Big Other," namely, the intersubjective symbolic order as a whole, the system of meanings and identities into which every speaking subject is plugged by virtue of the intersubjective referentiality built into language itself, with its constantly deferred but constitutive promise of consistency. The Other has some view of me, sees me, and judges me, and my identity as such is constituted by both the supposition of this truth about myself as seen by the Other and also my inability to grasp, confirm, or understand it. Baked into this sense of being watched and identified is a need to be seen as acceptable by this Other, who is more powerful than me and on whom I am dependent—the composite face of the shadow community of powers-that-be that preexist my birth and set the parameters for my continued existence. If so, then as long as "I" exist, this unconscious notion of the more or less omnipresent, omniscient, omnipotent viewer and judge, the one who knows what I really am and gets to decide whether to continue to support what I am—God—will probably exist too. To see that the Big Other does not exist—true atheism—is to see that the Big Other itself is in fact not consistent, not free of contradictions, not fully constituted (for who is the other Big Other that would establish and guarantee the Big Other's identity?). Hence it can have no genuine consistent judgment of who or what I am nor consistent agenda about what is to become of me. God is unconscious. This realization, in one period of Lacan's musings, is precisely the traversing of the primal fantasy constitutive of the ongoing misrecognition called our identity, and the cure for neurosis. But this is very difficult to achieve: we find that we are always playacting, posturing, engaged in a performance for the benefit of the imagined audience, the God who sees and knows us, even in our disavowals of his existence: even in assuming the consistent identity as an "atheist," we are assuming a God as spectator and judge.

The slide toward God could be viewed as a kind of endemic and stubborn design flaw, something genetically predetermined though radically false, some expression of which is an inevitable temptation even in cultures that have not been subjected to enforced claims of revelation from charismatic epileptics speaking in God's name, a kind of natural detritus produced by the human experience, an attractive optical illusion that always "rings true," like the flatness of the earth. To really understand what it means for there to be no God would then require a Copernican revolution of our own sense of identity: one would have to somehow learn to intuit that it is the earth moving around the sun rather than vice versa, although all one's senses and all our entrenched animal bearings continue to tell the opposite story. To root out this unconscious belief and all of its unnoticed entailments would then be a kind of religious quest in its own right, something very difficult, which, if accomplished, would thoroughly change all our prior beliefs, affects, and orientations, the tone and implications of our perception, our volitions, our aspirations, the whole of our experience.

And indeed, if we cast our eye back over the history of human activities, we find that there have been more than a few figures who have not only rejected the idea of a sovereign creator and ruler of the universe—who bestows on it a meaning and a purpose with an interest in the welfare of his creatures, with whom one might have a relationship, whom one may please or displease, whom one may obey or disobey, holding a plan and a purpose and meaning for the lives of those creatures—but they have also experienced this rejection as the crucial premise, not just for making human life a bit better, but for bringing about a thorough and, in their own opinion, profoundly desirable transformation of experience. Atheism had become, for these thinkers, the essential adventure, a quest for something more than the "given," at the opposite pole from atheism in its more familiar incarnation, as a scoffer's skewering of all the impudent claims to undermine what is plainly before us, plainly sensible, and plain to our eyes and ears.

There are and have been here among us humans some who object strenuously to the given as given by common sense but find the idea of God, in spite of all its fanciful extravagances, to be *not* the unsettling of that world of the given, but precisely its firmest *anchor*, rooted at its perspectival vanishing point. This way of putting it can be misleading because there is a paradox built into our relation to the given and what might be beyond it, as we will see. For one unexpected result shared by almost all the figures to be discussed here—all manner of Buddhists and Daoists; European heretics like Spinoza, Nietzsche, and Bataille; freaky transcendental philosophers like the early Schelling and Hegel; perhaps even their bastard American son (via pious, rambling Coleridge) Ralph Waldo Emerson—is that the given, the unquestioned prosaic world of common sense is maintained by positing something radically *other* beyond it: an ideal, a source, a justification, an alternative. Fully accepting it—radically accepting that there is no possible escape from it, that there is nothing else—is ironically what alone can undermine it, transcend it, destroy it, electrify it, redeem it. Strangely enough, it might be only when we are convinced that there is nowhere else to go that we can ever get out of here. What follows is an examination of the forms taken by this necessarily crooked and zigzagged quest for something, arguably, that all of us do want in one form or another, because it is what wanting as wanting wants. For what does wanting want? It wants something other than *this*. It wants *something else*.

PREACHING TO THE CHOIR

In directing this discussion not against irrational beliefs or nonsecularism as such but only against the belief in a monotheistic God, I am taking a position distinctly opposed to that of a recent spate of popular books in defense of atheism. I have in mind here the works of such figures as Richard Dawkins, Sam Harris, and Christopher Hitchens. All these books argue against irrational beliefs in general, among which they number monotheism of the traditional Abrahamic faiths a particularly pernicious example. Atheism is here presented as a simple entailment of rationalism—which is itself viewed as just good sense systematized and made aware of itself as a consistent method. It is a part of the general rationalist and scientific project of the Enlightenment, which, as such, contributes to making life here on earth somewhat more pleasant: it contributes to scientific progress, hence to useful technology and knowledge, and protects against the horrors of theocratic politics. I applaud and enjoy these books, although I am not in agreement with their basic premises.

Of the three, Sam Harris is closest to what I'm doing here in the sense that he makes a sharp distinction between some nontheistic religious claims, such as those of Buddhist meditative traditions, and the theistic claims for faith in a God of the Abrahamic faiths. Harris regards the claims of meditative texts as being in some way potentially verifiable through empirical methods, as contrasted to the call for faith in the absence of empirical evidence or reasons as he sees it presented, and indeed extolled, in the scriptures and theologies of the Abrahamic religions.[6] I am in strong sympathy with Harris in seeing a difference not just of degree but of kind between the monotheistic religions and the nonmonotheistic religions. But oddly enough, in a certain sense I find Harris to be perhaps the most insufferably wrongheaded of these three authors—the least interesting, the most narrowly unimaginative about first principles, the most cluelessly preaching to the choir.

Dawkins is to be applauded for providing actual new ideas and arguments; he is the most genuinely creative and insightful of the New Atheist horsemen and a practicing scientific theorist. And Dawkins has, in books like his *Unweaving the Rainbow: Science, Delusion and an Appetite for Wonder*, tried to develop his own version of what might be called a mysticism of reason: invoking the mystery and grandeur of the materialist universe as science now presents it to us. But in most of his arguments, like Harris, he labors with an unfortunate circularity: essentially, they are both trying to reason people into accepting the sole authority of reason.

Hitchens, who is quite as caustic about Buddhism as about Christianity, is far more narrow-minded than the other two on many counts, but in my judgment his work is more meaningful for being less reasonable and less profound: it is much more amusing, persuasive, and in some ways more consistent. There is a style of life invoked more in his rhetoric than in his reasonings, drolly cantankerous and somewhat comic, which inadvertently plants a foot in values other than those of pure utility and sensibleness. The reasonings themselves, however, use the same approach as the other two: reasonable arguments for accepting reason.

To reason someone into accepting reason is preaching to the choir. If they don't already accept the authority of reason, your efforts are futile. But of course, the implicit structure of the endeavor is not quite this simple-minded. For the assumption is that everyone, without exception, is always using some form of reason, indeed depending on it to make all their practical choices, all day every day. The premise here is that the canons of reasonableness—parsimony, empiricism, experiment, assessment of probabilities—are just crystallizations of what a living creature is always doing, more or less efficiently, and must do in order to stay alive. When crossing the street, one doesn't say, "Although my senses and past experience and reasoning from the laws of physics tell me that there's a car speeding toward me, I have faith that there isn't one." Nor does one say, "It's possible that God is just manifesting the appearance of a car in speeding toward me, and since God loves me, there is nothing to fear." One applies parsimony, Occam's razor. Although there are millions of *possible* explanations for why it *seems* that there is a car speeding toward me, I believe the one that requires the fewest unproved assumptions: namely, that there really *is* a car speeding toward me. The rationalist arguments against God are an attempt to say, "Look, you're already committed to reason in a thousand ways; it's just that you don't apply the same standards to the question of God." We have plenty of reasons, applying the very same tests you use all the time when crossing the street, to conclude that there is no omnipotent God who created the universe.

But this slightly subtler version of the argument doesn't really get us anywhere either. There is no question that, in fact, we do make practical decisions on the basis of inductions and deductions that can be described by appeal to parsimony; but it's equally a fact that we can and do preserve a degree of provisionality in the conclusions we draw in this way and that we have the ability to step beyond any and every conclusion we have already drawn. Parsimony comes with a built-in cancellation clause because temporality is inextricable from it: there's always a next moment coming. (To put it more pretentiously, Openness is intrinsic to Being.) Both the positing and the stepping-beyond are facts of experience, and neither reasoning nor practical decision-making could work without both. Why privilege one at the expense of the other?

Objectivity in the metaphysical sense is an unwarranted absolutizing or sedimentation of half of a two-step process. The philosophical worldview of objectivism is read off from an aspect of this process and made into a doctrine about metaphysics, when in fact it's just *one of many tools* in the hands of a hungry animal. So even though it may be the case that, to the extent that we are admitting reasoning at all, the monotheist God can be disproved, there will always be Tertullian, that fascinatingly volatile and wickedly histrionic Church Father, who blurted out the unsurpassable final word on this issue way back in the early third century: I believe *because* it is absurd, said Tertullian.[7] And no amount of reasoning will be of any use in convincing someone who has declined to accept the ultimate authority of reason. It is no use saying, "Look, Tertullian, you're already using reason, you tacitly admit it, so how can you exempt this one issue from application of the same standard you use when you cross the street?" Why must he have only one standard? Should he do it because it's reasonable? But he's already shown he's willing to eschew reason when he feels like it. If we think of beliefs as tools, this sort of move becomes unremarkable: why should I have only one tool that I use on every kind of material? A hammer for pounding nails, a nail-clipper for clipping nails—for not all nails are the same. We call all things "things," but not all things are the same or require the same type of treatment. The illegitimate step lies in assuming that there must be a single standard applied at all times, for all types of situations, regarding every type of subject matter. Why assume that there is any unity of this kind applying to the world, that all existence must form one single system with a single set of laws and rules applying to all of it? That too is part of the circular assumption of the sole universal authority of Reason—an assumption that, I would argue, ironically has deep roots precisely in the idea of God.[8]

Some rationalists will argue that this unity is actually entailed in the very notion of reason as such. We find something like this expressed most forcefully perhaps in Kant. And there is some truth in this argument in the sense that we can always push back behind any diversity to find the field in which both are situated, which makes possible even their contrast, being the "condition of possibility" of their very difference from one another. In this sense there is indeed a built-in primacy of a kind of unity. But as I have argued elsewhere, the full thinking-through of this unity ends up effacing the type of unification that would entail the application of a literal sameness for all members contained within it: this irreducible unity is equally describable as an irreducible diversity.[9] The presupposition that the unity of Reason can be represented as a set of consistent and universally applicable laws with a positive content is, on the contrary, *a holdover precisely from raw monotheistic intuitions*. It implicitly posits the God's-eye point of view, a *unified purposive consciousness* and therefore a *single-focused consciousness*, which embraces everything at once and for which everything is a definite object, a definite tool, a definite work. And the irony, of course, is that the religious argument has always rested on asserting that the type of object we are considering when we consider God is radically unlike any other type of object—infinite as opposed to finite—and thus cannot be made subject to the canons of reason designed for handling the relations between finite things. But to whatever extent this infinite, radically other something is considered a *mind*—a *purposive* mind, a *single-purposed* mind, a *single-minded* mind—it has been the very essence of finitude, of the enforcement of finitude, as I will try to show. And it is only in this sense, I claim, that the word *God* can properly be used, in opposition to, say, the Plotinian *One* or the Daoist *Dao* or the Buddhist *Dharmakāya*, which may well be metaphysical absolutes but are not purposive minds. If it ain't a purposive mind, it ain't God. And God, the universal purposive mind, is the problem.

LET'S ASSUME A BRAIN TUMOR: FUTILE ATTACKS ON MONOTHEISTIC FAITH

A consistent rationalist account of the origin of the Abrahamic faiths would probably have to unflinchingly accept either some form of mental illness or conscious chicanery on the part of their founders. It would certainly be easy on naturalist grounds to think the key letter-writers and revelation-receivers of originary Christianity and Islam—I won't name names—were clinical epileptics. If we push this materialist supposition to its ultimate blasphemous conclusion, we should say that what "God" actually refers to in the discourse of these figures is, say, a mental disturbance erupting in the right half of P or M's brain, perhaps a brain tumor that caused them to hear voices and see visions. I myself have no difficulty at all accepting this, and though it is rarely stated in polite company, this really would be the conclusion to which Occam's razor would lead us: it is the simplest explanation, the one with the fewest extra assumptions, the minimum multiplication of explanatory entities and premises, the most consistency with what we otherwise observe.

Believers in these religions typically react to such a suggestion with horror and outrage, or worse. But the point I want to make here is that there is no reason for this outrage. Even if we could prove beyond a shadow of a doubt that a brain tumor were the proximate cause of everything written in the Bible and the Quran, this would be of no avail at all in arguing against the truth of those revelations. Once you've assumed God, you have, quite literally, an answer for everything. You can simply say that when God wants to reveal himself to someone, he plants a tumor in him. A tumor is the means by which God manifests himself. A tumor is the way God implants the epileptic effervescence in a human body by means of which alone he can shine through it, a sign recognized correctly by the spirits of the believers who flock irresistibly to the entumored visionary. And given the premises of the argument, this is absolutely a legitimate rejoinder.

The same can be said of any argument trying to show the historical background of religious ideas and beliefs, the low purposes they serve, the selfish material interests they protect. All this may perfectly well just be the means God chooses to reveal himself. The same may be said of individual present-day appearances of well-known divinities. Someone who has a personal relationship with Jesus, who has felt his presence and continues, day after day, to receive his promptings, engaging in continuous conversation with him, believes that this is actually Jesus, the same entity who appeared two thousand years ago in the flesh in Palestine, who is speaking with him. A skeptic may say these are psychological projections, engagements with aspects of the believer himself taking an externalized or slightly hallucinatory form, or manifestations of unconscious archetypes—and this may be viewed as either a fine form of self-therapy or a dangerous delusion. A Mahāyāna Buddhist may say this is Avalokitśvera bodhisattva appearing in the form most suited to this person so as to enlighten them as appropriate to their level of receptiveness, namely, in the culturally conditioned, comfortable form of Jesus. But, in fact, none of us know where this experience *ultimately* comes from, even if we know the proximate cause. The Christian believer, like the Buddhist, should not be at all disturbed by the skeptic's claim; even if this is a mental illness or demonstrably a result of brainwashing or a brain lesion, these would be perfectly legitimate ways for God or Jesus or Avalokitśvera to manifest to someone. That's just the nuts and bolts of how they go about setting up communication with human minds. Hence, none of these are decisive adjudicators of the status and value of these experiences. My claim in this book is that what matters instead is the actual content of the revelations, as tweaked by their linkage to their respective textual and institutional traditions of doctrine and praxis.

A similar consideration applies to all attempts to show how harmful particular religions have been in human history—how many wars they have caused and how instrumental they have been in creating every kind of human exploitation, servitude, and misery. Even if it were proved incontrovertibly that every single pope, preacher, rabbi, and imam had been a conscious charlatan, a self-confessed fraud motivated purely by self-interest and without the slightest belief in the wares he was selling, any real believer worth his salt would be well within his intellectual rights to simply say, "Yes, but that is the *human* misuse of revelation, probably misled by the cunning of Satan. All of that was done by Man, not God. It is only to be expected that sin will try to take hold of the Truth and endeavor to distort and exploit it. Thus does God spread his word, *even if a single pure believer has not yet appeared in human history*. This is how God sets things up for a better future, provides opportunities for holiness, waiting patiently for righteous human beings of the future who will truly adopt His revelation and make themselves pure through it. Onward!" This should be sufficient to show why the Harris-Dawkins-Hitchens approach is entirely futile.

ATHEISM POSTMONOTHEIST AND NONMONOTHEIST: AGAINST AND AFTER NANCY

At the opposite extreme from this proscience, antireligion atheism, we have lately begun to see another variety of atheism arise, especially in continental Europe: a humanist postmonotheist atheism that endeavors to affirm the value of the idea of God as a glorious precursor to the unique achievements of modern European *atheist* enlightenment. The monotheist God is viewed here as a kind of first step away from pagan polytheism and toward the rationalist modern world. In truth, this view is not far from that of Hegel or Feuerbach, and it is echoed by atheist Marxist thinkers like Slavoj Žižek and Alain Badiou as well as in a different way by non-Marxist (and ostensibly nonatheist) theorists like René Girard, all of whom admire Christianity not so much for the God it posits as for its tricky way of undermining prior cultural institutions—whether narrow local loyalties or the pagan scapegoating of sacrificial victims or the unilateral authority of an uninflected, uncrucified, nontriune Father God—to pave the way to the universalism of Enlightenment and the Rights of Man.

One can certainly understand the impulse to find something worthwhile in close to twenty centuries of obsession, after the initial period of vilification has passed—as in a difficult breakup with a lover in whom one has become thoroughly disillusioned, the passionate repudiation and self-hatred needed to extricate oneself are succeeded by the calm perspective of distance and nostalgia: you start to remember some of the good things that attracted you in the first place. And it can't be pleasant to have to recognize that one was fooled by a ruthless mountebank, or that for two millennia one's entire culture was hijacked by an insane apocalyptic death cult: finding something of value there is a way of retrospectively saving face. But from afar it is certainly an uncanny thing to witness the European mind veering again Godward: an unsympathetic observer may have to suppress the inevitable dog-returning-to-his-vomit adage (Proverbs 26:11) that springs to his lips. Be that as it may, as already hinted, the type of atheism at stake here does remain deeply beholden to the Christian past: and this atheism, no less than the scientistic New Atheism, we also want to repudiate.

Jean-Luc Nancy is perhaps the primary exemplar of this trend. In a spate of lectures and articles, which were collected in two recent books translated into English under the titles, *Dis-enclosure: The Deconstruction of Christianity*, and *Adoration: The Deconstruction of Christianity II*, Nancy has developed these central claims about Christianity and its relation to what he makes bold to call "the West." Of particular interest is the link he draws between Christianity and modern European atheism as a defining achievement of Western culture, going so far as to assert, "Not only is atheism an invention specific to the West, but it must also be considered the element in which the West invented itself as such."[10] Side by side with this claim comes the suggestion that the monotheistic God of Christianity (and also Judaism and Islam), far from obstructing this atheism, is in fact the precondition and, as it were, the prototype of it, the very "trial or process of atheism itself in its most rigorous proceedings."[11] Christianity is, on this view, the means whereby atheism, the defining destiny of the West, came to be; Christianity is atheism-in-the-making. Essentially, it is the first shot (or perhaps the second, after Platonic protomonotheism) in the war that won its way to atheism as a specifically Western achievement of "disenchanting and alteriorizing" the world. It is this distinctively Western monotheist-atheism in various disguised forms, that now overruns the world under the names of modernization and globalization, and from which there is no escape, since all alternatives are already submerged into and transformed by it—any attempt to recover non-Western alternatives to monotheist-atheism, on this view, can only be Eurocentric Orientalist distortions. Hence, Nancy says, the solution to the peculiar impasses embedded in monotheist-atheism-occidentality must be sought *within* it, thus justifying a sympathetic reconsideration of the roots of monotheism as a possible resource for its solution.[12] I would like to consider these claims here and raise some objections to both their premises and their conclusions on the basis of a contextualization against the backdrop of some non-Western traditions of atheism, in particular the forms that are central to certain Chinese philosophical and religious traditions.

Nancy claims that the monotheistic move, beginning with Plato's indefinite references to "the deity" (*ho theos*), "in the singular and lacking a proper name," was, above all, a way of *removing* a preexisting saturation of divinity in the world, draining the world of a prior presence of gods and converting the idea of divinity instead to one of a transcendent and prior *principle* rather than a presence. The definite divine "sense" that had previously been *in* the world was now taken *out* of it, resulting in the "evaporation of all divine presences and powers, and the designation of a principle that no longer has as 'divine' anything but the name—a name dispossessed of all personality, and even the ability to be uttered;"[13] and the only deity left now is "without figure and name."[14] The elevation of this God is a demand for absolute *alterity*, which Nancy reads as the opening up of the world to an omnipresent but inaccessible otherness, an unconditional alienation. Thus the monotheistic God, even the hybrid Christian god that comes from the wedding of this nameless, narrativeless Platonic God to a very specific narrative, personality and name, is for Nancy a precursor and initiator of the complete "dis-enclosure" of all alleged worldly closures, including not just those of mythology but those of cosmology and physiology as well. At the same time, as the exceptionless priority of a principle, with its fingers no longer merely in some occasional visitations but necessarily at the basis of every pie, this absent God also becomes more inescapable, given the constant presence of its own absence, as opposed to the occasional and intermittent presence of the old gods as beings that come and go in the world. The positing of this nameless, narrativeless God in place of the troop of gods who had been man's partner and counterpart in the world is for Nancy a "dual positing of a radical alterity (god and man are no longer together in the world) and a relation from the same to the other (man is called toward god)."[15]

Nancy's argument here rests on his assertion that the "other world" that was effectively used as a lever to perform this feat was never really a second world, that instead it was merely "the other of every world."[16] As such, the transcendent God is not something that "exists" in the normal sense, but is rather construed as something that does not exist but that "defines and mobilizes" existence. God, on this view, is not the highest that can be thought but rather a word for the "ordeal of thought immersed in its inability to escape what is beyond any and all thought"; this is the limitation of thought itself, presented, however, in this misleadingly positive form.[17] God is here taken as a name for the unclosability of any finite or knowable being, presented in the form of their groundedness and powerlessness before something that is itself discoverable nowhere among beings.

In the background of this wildly counterevidential claim is perhaps Nancy's intuition that this positing of a phantom other world is the *only way* to posit this otherness to any world, that, to use a Buddhist phrase, a thorn must be used to remove a thorn—that the expedient of an alternate transcendent divine presence was necessary to remove the prior immanent divine presences. We should be alert to this premise as it appears often, in one form or another, in assessments of various historical doctrines; for example, the assumption in the ancient world that the threat of postmortem punishment or reward at the hands of a deity was the *only* way to ground a morality tends to make one more indulgent in one's assessments of those ancient moralists that lean heavily on this premise, which in turn can make us assume that, since such highly esteemed figures have always deployed this threat, it must be something profoundly true, even if stripped of its ancient mythological setting. The discovery that there are alternate ways, dating back to ancient times, of talking about such matters that do not resort to this premise will radically alter our assessment of both the promulgators of such theories and the need to read demythologized versions of them back into nature. Nancy's claim here contains an implicit reference to what is *not* the West: it is in contrast to some imagined non-Western traditions that Nancy is imagining the essence of the Occident as lying in its *unique* achievement of atheism. His assumption is, therefore, that atheism could *only* be achieved by this seemingly contradictory monotheist move since monotheism itself is a far more obvious candidate for what is distinctive about the West. The acknowledgment of other forms of atheism elsewhere in the world that developed without requiring any such transitional monotheism will therefore destabilize the claim. Nancy's first reference point is, of course, the ancient Greek and Roman religions, which were the direct target of the Christian revolution, but in the claim that atheism is a specific achievement of occidentality, the assumption is made that the world untouched by the West was in the grips of the kind of religious saturation that made it unable to achieve atheism.

I consider this claim to be not only historically unsupportable and highly misleading, but also as a specific post-Christian distortion of the nature of real atheism, an inadvertent confirmation of Nancy's thesis that modern European atheism is just Christianity in a new guise—but not in a good way! The two willful smear campaigns so crucial to the sources of Western monotheism continue to reign here: the willful incomprehension of polytheistic ritual, anathematized as "idolatry," that is found in the biblical prophetic tradition and the willful bad-mouthing of poetry and art that goes hand in hand with Platonic protomonotheism. What do these two repudiations have in common? They claim to be rejections of the adequacy of any appearance to completely embody the relevant transcendent content, thereby honoring its status as beyond all concrete representation: the inadequacy of any particular concrete expression is presented as equivalent to the unreachable transcendence of that content. But looked at from a neutral vantage point, they seem rather to be rejections of an alternate way of presenting this incompleteness of every concrete expression of the divine: polytheist worship and nonrationalized art express this inadequacy in the unlimited proliferation of *alternate* appearances, each approaching the elusive content from a different angle. Every idol is a particular presencing of a god who can appear as an infinite number of other idols, as infinite alternate material or immaterial presencings. The expansive transcendence of the god is present in this inherent, unfinished ambiguity, which links each concretization implicitly to its ability to concretize otherwise in other times and places. We glimpse here two different ways of guarding against taking any specific appearance as adequate to the divine—the monotheist prohibition of any representation and the polytheist encouragement of infinite representations—with very different structures and very different implications. To the latter, at least, the former appears simply to be giving a monopoly to *one particular kind* of representation (inasmuch as "the exclusion of representation" is itself a representation; more on this to follow)—we might say, a monopoly of one particular "idol" or "art"—at the expense of all the others.

It is arguably these two specific repudiations, of idolatry and of art, that define monotheism as such, rather than the structure of "omnipresent absence that undermines all positive presences" on which Nancy focuses. For even within the Western tradition, the latter structure is really the heart of all metaphysics as such, and yet indeed also the heart of all attempts to *undermine* metaphysics. The real issue is the status of the intelligible, of knowability, which God both enables and eludes, like Plato's Sun or Plotinus's One, or indeed like Kant's transcendental categories, which both enable all knowledge and yet elude direct observation, or Heidegger's Being, which is definitionally not any particular being. For what happens in Christianity is not the creation of this interesting and important structure of thought as an omni*present* absence grounding all presences—a trope that throughout history appears sooner or later almost everywhere in the world—but the decision to wed the Platonic unnamed, narrativeless deity, which is already hostile to multiple expressions and the ambiguities of nonexclusive semiconsciousness, decisively *back* to the notion of a personal God. The alternative would have been rather to take the other option, the Plotinian option, of reading Plato atheistically and metaphysically, that is, as *calling into question the ultimacy both of purposive intelligence and of intelligibility itself*—and thereby, as we will see, beginning to question the ontological priority of disambiguation, of finitude, of mutually exclusivity itself.

Because the word "God" emphatically denotes a *mind*, indeed, a *purposive* mind—and indeed, a *single purposive* mind—the call beyond thought that Nancy attributes to the monotheistic God necessarily always fails; it is a blind window, not the establishment of what is beyond thought but rather the abuse and domestication, a gesture of *containment*, of what could have been a burgeoning move toward genuine dis-enclosure. This undercuts Nancy's wishful claim that the idea of God "really" means that "the world rests on nothing, and this is its keenest sense."[18] For it is not at all the case that God signifies that no etiology of the world is possible; on the contrary, God is the replacement of indeterminate beginninglessness with a definite act of *Divine Will*, with a motivation, with a mind that has preferences for some states over others, and in this minimal but crucial sense at least, with a shadowy personhood embracing some conception of the Good: God means that the world rests not on nothing, but on *purpose*. That the content of what is willed is necessarily unknown to us makes no difference: if we are saying "God" (instead of "the One" or "Being" or "Dao" or "Dharmakāya" or "Brahman" or "Necessity" or "Fate" or what have you), we are saying we *know* it to be purposive. It is not "nothing" that the world rests on here: it is some form of personality, with some form of purposive mind and some form of Will.

To be sure, the ideas of "personality" and "purposivity" and "Will" are, in a certain nonnegligible and rather deep sense, an interpretation precisely of what is beyond predictability, beyond thought, being determination—the unreifiable, a gap in the order of entities, *no-thingness*—in that a "person" or a "mind" or a "purpose" is itself not a reified presence in quite the same way that determinate material objects are. But they are interpretations that radically foreclose and cripple that nothingness: for if theism means any-thing, it means that God is specifically the *kind* of nonbeing that a *mind* is, not nonthinghood in general but a nonthinghood of a very specific type, the type of nonthinghood that belongs to *personhood* insofar as it is not a "thing." To state my central thesis: God turns nothingness and meaningless-ness into a specific meaning, the definite meaning "not-any-thing," which is really just another kind of thing: nothingness as purposive personal mind, as a mind that knows itself and acts consciously. For "thing," in its relevant signification here, means not simply a material object, nor even what is in-telligibly present as an object of thought and causally predictable, but more fundamentally, "what *excludes* other things"—any entity with a single, defi-nite identity that excludes other identities. In spite of attempts to make God all-inclusive in some sense, as long as the creator/created relation remains mutually exclusive (as it must for the creator to preexist, in any sense, the created; that is, for creation to be creation), God, like purposive mind in general, remains a "thing" in this sense: a mind that is constitutively ex-clusive of (1) other conceptions of good, and (2) other minds. The alleged nonmeaning is thus still a fully present meaning in the only relevant sense of presence: it is constituted simply by the exclusion of all other meanings, and therefore of all plurality of meanings. A true nothingness is an excess of alternatives; the enforced and intentional nothingness of God, on the contrary, in its central rejection of "idolatry" and "art," turns absence into a presence, defined simply as the ability to exclude other presences. The monotheistic God is the foreclosure of the only way that presence is ever really undermined: namely, by the possibility of illimitable *other presences* concomitant to each and every presence, and with it the illimitable *other meanings* implicit in each meaning, illimitable *other intentions* inherently concomitant with every possible intention. God is the limitation on the scope of other presences that can displace the current ones, an attempted crackdown on the proliferation of the ambiguity and expansiveness that were originally endemic to every presence. The problem with the West, in my view, is not metaphysics as many recent thinkers have claimed. Metaphysics is the good guy. The problem is God.

A truly atheist world would be a Godless world, which would mean specifically the lack of a unified, solitary mind whose ideas are the source of all facts; for example, the purposive, personal "big G" God who creates, plans, designs, and preconceives the universe, whether in the form of an Abrahamic creator *ex nihilo* or a Platonic demiurge, or indeed any interpretation of a Vedic god who creates the universe for a specific end by first planning or wanting or willing something rather than producing it as an inadvertent by-product of some other activity. The crucial question is whether or not *someone*, some mind, has an idea or intention of the world that precedes, and accounts for, the world's being as it is. "Small g" gods may exist within what I am calling the "Godless" universe, as facts that may or may not be so, like any other finite facts. There may even happen to be one of these gods who now rules the others. There may even happen to exist only one of them. Indeed, that one god might even *inadvertently* be the cause of the entire world's existence. But the existence of a "big G" God who makes the world *intentionally* would not just be a fact: it would change *what it means for anything to be a fact*. A fact would be something that exists *because* it had been planned, conceived in a mind before it occurred, and existing *only because* it was in accord with the *purpose* conceived by this mind—because it was "good" with respect to that single purpose of this single consciousness.

In contrast to the European form of godlessness, which Nancy describes, correctly I think, as merely a thinly disguised transformation of the monotheist God, a throughgoing Godlessness would be any conception of the universe as a whole that is purposeless, unplanned, and inadvertent, so that a fact within it (including the fact that there exist purposive mentations and deeds within it) is not precommitted by its manufacturer to serve some single specific purpose or, derivatively, to have a single uniquely privileged significance that fits uniquely well into a single schema. As long as the universe is not preformed to accord with a *particular consciousness* of any kind, any individual being's knowledge of it is posterior to its existence and not coextensive with its purpose for being so. In this conception, no mental act precedes and causes the existence of things. By the same token, no unified personality or mind with a specific set of purposes accounts for the existence of things. There is no being prior (whether temporally or conceptually) to the world who thinks the world before the world is. Purposive human action, where a desired state is first envisioned and then willed and executed, is not the privileged model for ontology, either explicitly or implicitly.

In my view, this has enormous philosophical consequences. In the absence of the idea of a God in this sense or some equivalent, there is no reason to assume that *any possible* mental act (or its derivative concept or proposition) can perfectly accord with (correspond to, represent, or account for) the real essence of any thing, let alone cause it. Less self-evidently but equally compellingly, there is arguably no reason to assume that any particular thing has a *single* real essence at all in the absence of a prior privileging of some one mind with the authorized "manufacturer's" view. The very concept of objectivity becomes problematic and unmotivated. Heidegger has expressed a similar point in tracing the assumptions in place, consciously or unconsciously, behind the notion of truth as the adequation of things to ideas: "*Veritas* as *adaequatio rei ad intellectum* . . . implies the Christian theological belief that, with respect to what it is and whether it is, a matter, as created (*ens creatum*), *is* only insofar as it corresponds to the idea preconceived in the *intellectus divinus*, i.e., in the mind of God, and thus measures up to the idea (is correct) and in this sense is 'true.'"[19] Without the idea of a creative Divine Intellect, it is hard to see what would impel the belief that there would be any single formula, essence, or idea that would happen to perfectly or adequately match or account for the existence of a thing in the world—and it is difficult to imagine what "objectivity" can mean if adequation between thought and idea is not considered, at least in principle, *possible*. At stake here is the fundamental ontological assumption that primary entities must be single-valenced, unambiguous, characterized by a definite and limited set of attributes, mutually exclusive of one another—in a word, that the world is composed of ultimately unambiguously *finite* (de /finite) entities.

We can better grasp the impact of this point by reminding ourselves of some likely phenomenological and conceptual roots of the animistic hypothesis, which routinely attributes observed events to purposes, and about which we will have more to say in what follows.[20] We animal beings have needs and desires, which means we act purposefully. Sometimes our purposes or desires are thwarted. Are we to view this as due to the satisfaction of *someone else's* desires to the contrary or because of a problem or limitation in the very efficacy of desire or purpose as such, whether our own or someone else's? Do things sometimes happen that are *not desired by any-one at all*, demonstrating that desire is not the only thing that makes things happen? Is purpose or desire an ultimate fact, playing a privileged role in ontology, or just an epiphenomenon, perhaps even an ethically undesir-able one? Even if we admit the ultimate ontological status of purpose, we encounter a second question: Is there some Uberpurpose that subsumes all individual purposes into some kind of unity, or are there instead conflicted purposes and desires at the root of things? That is, even if it is ultimately Will or desire that makes things happen, is this a single Will or multiple uncoordinated and conflicting Wills?

The point raised concerning "truth" here is that a version of this same question may be asked, *mutatis mutandis*, about knowledge. Human ig-norance is made evident when my views are disconfirmed. Is this because someone else's views are confirmed or because the very concept of "some-one's view of things"—a single, consistent, unambiguous, conscious con-ception of how things are, which is transparent to the thinker—is itself not an ultimate fact and has no necessary relation at all to what we experience and what happens? The question is whether the very idea of "someone's unambiguous view of things" is coherent or useful without requiring enor-mously improbable and expensive ontological assumptions. For these as-sumptions are not self-evident; if they appear to be so, we should suspect that this is a habitual effect of the long dominance of precisely the premises under discussion here. It may appear to be a simple empirical fact that there exist such things as people holding unambiguous and unequivocal beliefs that some things are so—do not we unproblematically believe that there is a glass on that table, that there is water in that glass, that the water is wet, and so on, without the slightest doubt or ambiguity? My answer is no, that this is not an empirical fact, but a complicated interpretation of a psychological situation that is truncated and distorted by certain metaphysical ideas—at the very least, the idea that "minds" are the kinds of things that could at least *possibly* exist without ever having to reconsider their views or hold their conclusions in suspense: that certainty in a mind is not a contradiction in terms. Because, on empirical grounds, it appears to be such a contra-diction: every mind ever actually empirically encountered so far has been demonstrably already *in time*, and every moment in time, to be time, has to open toward the future—the future that goes on for ever, with more future opening up with each future reached. If we did not assume the existence of any minds except those empirically encountered, every single experi-ence of which is inalienably confronted with unknown future experiences, would there be any reason to assume that any mind *could* have any view of things that is not forever subject to subsequent revision and reversal? Even certainty is only half of a more primordial certainty-uncertainty: Is there a reason we should expect or demand or strive for anything more? Human belief might turn out not to be the kind of thing that admits of a unilateral yes or no; there are reasons to think that a certain ambivalence permeates—is constitutive of—the assuming of any stance on any question at all. This line of thought has roots going back to Daoism, that is, to chapter 2 of *Zhuangzi*, but we can perhaps express its present implications more succinctly with a formula adapted from Merleau-Ponty: what makes the world coherent to us *at all*, namely the primordial orientation of our bodily existence at a specific place in the world and at a particular moment in time, is exactly what keeps it from being *completely* coherent. The power of any present moment to integrate its own past and future into a particular consistency of meaning operates only by positing other moments, past and future, from which it differs. But for those other moments to count as moments at all, as past and future presents, they must be endowed with the same power to unstitch and otherwise restitch the meanings given now.[21] The same goes, *mutatis mutandis*, for our situatedness in a specific orienting locus in space, which is a place in relation to the necessary presence of other, differing places. Concomitantly, the very thing that allows us to embrace any belief at all is the same thing that keeps us from ever believing it completely: the act of believing is accomplished only through the projection toward a future of other acts of believing, each of which can reverse it—and there are always more to come. This applies also to our present commitment or decision to keep the present faith in the future. But each such projection of possibly present-overturning future moments is happening *in the present*: just being a present is to be haunted in this way by alternate presents. Might we not think of even the clean modal separation of "actual" and "possible" as merely a dodge of this ambivalence, and even think of the clean separation of "present" and "future" likewise?

I have argued elsewhere that every belief is embroiled inescapably in its opposite, and that simply to take a stance is to be haunted and infected by the specter of the opposing stance.[22] More robust reasons to incline toward this view will hopefully become apparent in what follows—that is, the strict structural necessity and exceptionlessness of both ambiguity and ambivalence and what is logically problematic about the dichotomization that prevents fully taking in this point of view—but what is perhaps even more to the point at this stage are the reasons why we might *want* this to be the case: what is ethically and existentially problematic about the mutually exclusive dualisms that result from those dichotomizations. For some people might understandably regard this view of the ineluctability of ambivalence, even if valid, as of little significance and true only in a trivial sense: sure, one might say, there are always pros and cons and you can always change your mind, but that doesn't mean no one has an unproblematically firm conviction or that no one ever makes a decision one way or the other—and it's the convictions and decisions that are the important and interesting part. The real story, they may justifiably feel, lies in the complex ways in which the various alloys of opposing but inseparable affect may manifest as determinate differences, the how and why of our temporary and pragmatic disambiguations, the motivations behind the dodge itself, the strongly felt imperatives that makes this both/and always appear as some particular either/or. It is in these manifestations that the real point of interest for the human predicament lies. True enough; but we would also insist that these points of interest can only be properly appreciated and understood on the basis of the fundamental, ineradicable, and *ultimate* ambiguity that enables them, and that they always both resist and, in so doing, *also* instantiate. For what is a decision but a way of freezing the vagaries of the world into a totalizing either/or, casting a net of disambiguation in all directions in a constitutively unfinished attempt to posit a totalization that is at once both internally consistent and exclusive of alternate possible totalities? It is the virtual copresence of these internally consistent but mutually inconsistent totalities, the enabler of their communication and transition to one another, that is at stake in preserving the full ineradicability of core ambiguity and its attendant ambivalence. Every new decision, we might say, is a *repurposing* of previous decisions and indecisions. The question at issue here is the status of *repurposing itself* in the economy of the cosmos: is there a deep either/or, whether an unrepurposable purpose or a purposelessness that would definitely exclude all purpose, at either the source or the end of all repurposings, making them all mere inconsequential surface flickers or quixotic flailings over the ultimate ontological bedrock? Or might it be ambiguous repurposing *all the way down?*

And here we have the real twist and the real point: the true cost of monotheism, inherited also by the limited form of atheism that Nancy points to as its product (modern secularism), is that it grants absolute and ultimate ontological status to either/or bivalence, and with it the world of decisions and projects and judgments and purpose and meaning, making these the sole focus of all interest and praxis. For monotheism ends up *requiring* everyone, on threat of perdition, to deny *precisely this constitutive ambivalence.* Although you sometimes hear believers talk about the journey and the struggle of faith, the constitutive uncertainty of faith, the wavering intrinsic to the true faith experience, it is belied in this particular case because the object of faith is precisely God. In other words, it is a personality, a willer, a knower, a purposive being, and in this case alone, an instance of personality and Will that are not encumbered with a nonpersonal substratum, with a nonwilled body, with an unknown and uncontrolled dimension that might ambiguate his judgments—hence, above all therefore, a *judge uniquely free of ambivalence*—who will judge you, according to vast majority of scriptures and believers, precisely for either your deeds or for your belief or unbelief in him, constructed as an either/or determinant of two mutually exclusive postmortem fates. In the end your wavering faith or wavering behaviors will be seen by God to be either a thumbs-up or a thumbs-down, for the principle of purposivity, or personality, is precisely choice, dichotomy, exclusion—here uniquely freed of its usual ambiguating forces. In short: *when personal agency or purposive action are made ontologically ultimate, as in the belief in God, either/or is also made ultimate.*

Earlier I referenced the psychoanalytic suggestion of an ineradicable unconscious belief in God, and we may note another psychoanalytic approximation of this way of seeing the matter in Freud's remark that people are *both* more immoral *and* more moral than they think they are.[23] Whatever we may think of the concrete topographies and postulated entities additionally attributed to the Freudian unconscious, we can at least admit that there is more than meets the eye in everything pertaining to human consciousness and desire—and that would include our stated religious positions and attitudes. Would not the necessary corollary to the ineradicable unconscious belief in God, even of unbelievers, then be that everyone also disbelieves in God—even believers? The same would go for loving and hating God. From here we can start to ask even more alarming questions about us humans and our beliefs, even or especially our religious beliefs. Indeed, what are the presuppositions that prevent us from thinking that *everyone* believes in God and *everyone* doesn't believe in God—but also in woodsprites, astrology, flying saucers, and the scientific method—in short, in anything and everything that might be proposed? What image of how man should be or must be makes us assume that a person should believe the same thing *all the time*, or that she believes all her beliefs in exactly the same way? What sort of subjectivity is demanded as the correlate to this exclusive fealty—*and why?* Is this really how "belief" works, how our guiding images of what is true about the world are constructed and operate? In contrast to this "yes or no," and reflecting further on the default two-step of inseparable certainty-uncertainty noted previously, could we not distinguish, for example, varying degrees of the tentative application of working hypotheses, each of which always comes with an "escape clause," moving into place situationally, changing with the times, internested and intersubsumed in constantly shifting ways? The escape clause, moreover, need not be something added onto the content of the positive belief; it may be, rather, inherent to it. To be believing something would *just be already* to be half-disbelieving it.[24]

To enter the world of thought of our atheist mystics, we will have to learn to see at least *in what sense* we might rightly say that believers don't only believe but also disbelieve (whatever the proposed object of belief might be: God, woodsprites, whatever) and that unbelievers don't only disbelieve but also believe—and as a further consequence, that to love God is to hate God (or anyone else, including woodsprites, Mom and Pop, husband or wife, et al.), and vice versa—without at all erasing the seriousness of whatever tentative and incomplete positions are taken and their mutual differences. Our atheists can thus cheerfully assent to the common religious taunt that their disbelief really expresses an unconscious hatred of God—adding only that it also expresses an unconscious hatred of everything else—as well as an unconscious *love* of God and of everything else, including woodsprites, Smurfs, Hawaiian music, Star Wars characters, pencil shavings, and so on. Point granted, in other words: as long as you will also grant that your belief expresses a deep unconscious *hatred* of God. And further: if the only kinds of minds there are or could be are those that do not presuppose the nonempirical theistic premise, if mind qua mind is ambivalent and conflicted, then perhaps this God we cannot help believing in and disbelieving in and loving and hating must be a God who is *also* ambivalent and conflicted—toward us; a God who has no certain unambiguous view of what he wants of us or if he believes in us or whether he loves or hates any one of us, who in fact at every moment can't help both loving and hating us no matter what we do. Minds qua minds *can never be sure*. If our speculations do invite us to envisage an eternal, all-pervasive consciousness of some sort, a panpsychism or universal mind, it will then have to be a mind of this sort: one that must at once hold every possible view and every possible attitude toward every possible object, present in and as every finite mind, and at the same time transcend any and every such view and attitude through the plenitude of its equally inalienable embrace of all possible alternatives to each view; an absolutization of the kind of mind that actually exists in time, the kind that welcomes rather than eschews these essential characteristics of embeddedness in otherness, of ambiguity, of ambivalence, of multiplicity—a vision of eternity indeed, but one achieved only through the extension to infinity of all the inescapable vicissitudes and contradictions of *nonpurposive* temporality, rather than their resolution or rejection. And we will see some variants of this idea popping up among the atheist mystics, with profound implications for the forms of beatitude they inspire.

It is for these reasons too that we will find that some of our most radical atheists (Zhuangzi above all, as shown in online appendix B) are not those who declare themselves firm and committed atheists, but those who refuse to take the commanded either/or about him *seriously*. But another atheist mystical way to embrace this constitutive ambivalence, which looks superficially like the exact opposite, is the Spinoza route of absolute certainty radicalized to the point of overcoming the dichotomy: define God as the Absolute, as Infinity, so that it is literally impossible not to believe in God, and literally impossible to hate God. For then one may believe and disbelieve freely in whatever one can believe or disbelieve in, and love and hate whatever can be loved or hated, and *all of it* is *by definition* belief in and love of God. But this "God" is no longer God: it is the opposite of God.

Suspending the seemingly intuitive notion of an unambiguous God's-eye view helps us reconceive our sense of what is available to pretheorized human experience in its absence. It is sometimes assumed that the God's-eye view is precisely what opens up the closed horizon of socially determined norms and the monolithic identities they impose on things: on this view, humans are initially locked into narrow societies with normative nomenclatures enforced by social sanctions and embedded in the language, which assign a single, inviolable value and identity to all entities—and that the advent of a divine viewpoint from above and outside the purview of the consensus of ancestors, tradition, family, and elders opens up the possibility of seeing things differently, of dislodging those identities. Without God, on this view, there is no Archimedean point outside social structures by which to provide any truly new alternatives. But even if this were true—which is itself highly questionable on empirical grounds—*if* this openness, this provision of alternative possibilities, is the desideratum, this would be fool's gold, as we will explore more expansively in what follows: we have traded one system of monolithic normative identities for another, and indeed a much more inviolable and draconianly enforced one, which is literally *infinitely* more normative and *infinitely* more monolithic. Such an attempt at more openness would seem to have resulted in a much more severe closure—made worse, not better, by the constitutive deferral and imprecision of its deconcretized but unsurpassable demands. The attempt to broaden the meanings of things has backfired: the one extra identity we are granted ends up excluding more than the identity it replaced had excluded, for the one alternate viewpoint we are allowed to envision is itself infinitely more restrictive than the finite enclosure it overturns.

And here we can begin to detect in Nancy's seemingly absurd proposal a kernel of truth located in a rather remarkable possibility: what if monotheism really is an attempt to get at the disenclosing openness of deep atheism, as Nancy suggests, but one that again and again backfires tragically in the final reel? The problem is that Nancy has misidentified just what is rebelled

against in these revolts, and thus also misunderstands their results. The revolt against the unbearable proximity and concreteness and proliferation
of divine agents in the world is not solved by relocating and elevating and
unifying the divine agency. For the view that emerges from these considerations is that what is really at stake in the revolt against either gods *or God*
is not the repeal of a world saturated with polytheist divinities in favor of
a world haunted by one omnipresent but constitutively absent, ultimate,
conscious agent. What we would prefer to see in this adamant pushing upward and away of divine agency, which dissolves its presence into a vanishing point of riddles and postponements, is the obscure beginning of a
revolt, a *spiritual or religious* revolt, against the *divination of agency itself*—
against *conscious purposivity*, the *Will to Control*—as the ultimate determinant of whatever happens, the unsurpassable horizon of all existence. A
revolt against the very idea of control, against the narrowing of the world
that comes from prioritizing purposive control into an ultimate cause and
reason behind every fact, and more specifically, against *the dichotomy between control and noncontrol that is the essence of control*, whether one's own
control or another's or Another's, and the dichotimization of all facts and
entities that thus comes with the ultimacy of control—this would then be
what we see attempted in the history of religious revolutions, and here we
will find the key to understanding why this revolt generally undermines
itself, backfires, and ends up just making the problem worse.

There is thus an ironic sense in which we can assent to Nancy's outrageous claim that "atheism is the true satisfaction of the drive behind
monotheism"—but we accept the letter rather than the spirit of this pronouncement, thus giving it the opposite meaning. What we have in mind is
not monotheism as a confused but successful drive toward secularization,
a turning away from divine agency first approached through the infinite
exaltation of one particular divine agency at the expense of all the others,
as a temporary expedient clearing the way to the real terminus, namely,
as an infinite exaltation of *human* agency instead. Rather, we would see
monotheism as a confused but *failed* drive toward a genuine religious
awareness, aiming at a radical dislodging of *all* known agency of the divine
and all known divination of agency, a radical otherness to all god-playing
minds operating in the world—whether gods', God's, or humans'. And this
intuition is perhaps not so unprecedented. Feuerbach was perhaps closer
to it than Nancy when he proclaimed, "*Pantheism* is the *necessary consequence* of theology (or of theism). It is *consistent* theology. *Atheism* is the
necessary consequence of pantheism. It is *consistent* pantheism."[25] Feuerbach has in mind the development of the idea of the absoluteness of God as
"the most perfect being," the unconditioned that has nothing outside itself,

from monotheism to Spinoza to Schelling to Hegel, and finally to his own
atheism. With this development too we can concur, as long as we replace
Feuerbach's secularized atheism with the deep atheism we have in mind
here—atheism not as secularity but as a more thorough pantheism, one
that has not only made the controlling deity immanent in nature rather than
transcendent, in the form of an omnipresent world-soul or unified Logos
perhaps, but has also eliminated any trace of a purposive controller, any
definite locus of privileged executive authority, whether immanent or transcendent or even *human*. We can certainly grant that in conceptions like
those of the negative theologians, we see monotheism straining at its limits,
about to blossom into full atheist mysticism. It's just that, due to the premises that power this movement into apophaticism, the attempt to become
"true" monotheism—that is, real mystical pantheism landing in real mystical atheism—ends up in rather a different place from the kind of atheist
mysticism not beholden to the idea of any single purposive intelligence, or
even any group of the same, as the source and director of all existence.[26]

The problem then is not *the impulse toward* monotheism, insofar as it
entails a budding resistance to the overbearing proximity and presence of
any specific intentionality, whether human or divine, king or priest, that
abrogates unsurpassable authority and power to itself, claiming to exercise
unilateral control of what goes on. The problem is that the critique stops
short of the necessary scorched-earth decimation of all such claims, leaving
other, specific intentionalities similarly arrogating unsurpassable authority and power and control to themselves—supreme deity or free-willed
individual, absolute other or one's own-most self—untouched, or even
bolstered, by this revolt. This potentially liberating impulse would seem to
be thwarted or stunted before it can reach its full flowering due to certain
unexamined inheritances in the way the problem is set up in—in particular,
the idea of God itself: that is, the stubborn idea of controlling purposivity
as the *ultimate* cause of the world.

Viewed through such atheist mystic eyes, something of this impulse to
revolt is discernible even in the innovations of the great religious geniuses
and reformers who worked strictly within the horizons of monotheism—
for example, the attempt to distance and deconcretize and depopulate the
realm of divinity in the Hebrew Prophets, the attempt to prioritize inclusive
love over exclusionary judgment in the Gospels, the attempt to bring God
and man into deeper bilateral communion in the doctrine of the Incarnation of one of the Persons of an eternally triune God, the attempt to assuage
the hopeless akrasia of servitude to the divine Law in St. Paul, the attempt
to escape the threat of judgment lurking in God's demands for holiness in
Luther, and so on. In this light we can begin to see all these as laudable

repeated attempts at *increased* "detheification," each of which, however, shipwrecks tragically on the still unrenounced idea of God, predictably backfiring into exacerbations of the initial problem to precisely the degree that a purposive ultimate consciousness (i.e., God) remains in the picture. Viewed through this lens, each one shows evidence of noticing something crippling about the idea of purposive personality as unilateral ultimate controller of the world, and each introduces new tweaks to eliminate the problem while somehow retaining the God idea; but there is something about the structure of that idea itself that causes each such attempt to actually end up making the original problem worse.

We might then feel compelled to wonder what exactly might have been perceived to be so oppressive about that idea, as well as what it is about its structure that sabotages every attempt to ameliorate it, instead making it more deeply entrenched and more profoundly problematic. We might begin to see what is properly "spiritual" about each of these innovations to lie in *however much of "God" — of a singled-out locus of unilateral purposive control — each one manages to get rid of*, rather than whatever stopgap divinity it then puts in place of the Godishness it has banished. The lifeblood even of the increasingly refined conceptions of the divine would then be seen to lie in the knocking down, not in the setting up. Our task would be to excavate a point of view from which we can regard each as a well-intentioned but ultimately failed attempt to get to the mystical core of atheism, an attempt to kill off an oppressive God, which ends up backfiring into something even worse: each religion is an attempt to get less God, which cussedly turns out to yield, instead, more God. Might these pious innovations, in other words, betray a justifiably rabid and spiritually motivated *hatred of divinity*, which extends even to whatever divinity is left in the God thereby salvaged, a real *hatred of "God"* in the sense we have indicated? We would like to think so: for this would be a revolt against the idea of the ontological ultimacy of conscious purposive agency belonging to anyone at all — against the unpalatable world of unambiguous and mutually exclusive finite identities to which, as I'll try to show, it condemns us. For a case-by-case thought experiment that may serve to clarify what this might mean more concretely, the better to calibrate these lenses and see what might become visible through them, see online appendix A, supplement 2: "Monotheist Religious Innovation as Backfiring Detheology."

ATHEISM AS UBERPIETY

From here we can perhaps begin to glimpse our central question: How precisely can the eschewal of this viewpoint, of God, actually satisfy at least some of the demands that initially motivated its positing? How shall we understand these demands? How might thoroughgoing atheism function precisely as a redemptive spiritual practice, as I will argue is apparent in the case of the figures discussed in part II and in online appendix B of this book? To answer this question, we need to see that what undergirds the *desire* for God, the *motivation* for preserving a belief in God, is something that can conceivably be *better* served precisely by thoroughly excising all traces of God from our conceptual universe. This book is about those occasional figures in history who found that it is precisely deep atheism that provides what was originally wanted from theism—but does it better.[27]

The question is: What was the nature of that impulse? What exactly was wanted? Our concern here is not primarily the many social functions religion has served as a historical phenomenon, the roles it may play in motivating and sustaining community solidarity and moral compliance, or even its obvious compensatory role in cases of acute personal disappointment and hopelessness. Whatever effects are accomplished in these spheres depends on religion providing a *supplement* to what is apparent in its absence, something additional to human experience; our question concerns the deficiency that enables and motivates the acceptance of this "something more." Why are such outlandishly unverified propositions so commonly accepted and elaborated, even in the absence of obvious personal or social crisis? Would an ideal set of facts on the ground disincentivize this tendency? Would even an ideal set of facts on *and off* the ground, as it were, do so? That is, if the seen world is unsatisfactory for some reason, thus motivating the positing of an unseen world, would some ideal factual state of affairs in the seen *and unseen* together eliminate this need to posit "something more"? Our answer will be *no*. But why not?

Some thinkers have thought that existing religious doctrines answer to some kind of "religious impulse" or "metaphysical need" built into human beings because they are self-conscious creatures for whom to be is to be a question to oneself, or more simply that they are living creatures that know they will die. Humans need some narrative structure to tell them why they're here, where they come from, where they're going, what they should be doing, and so on: they need "meaning." Religions fill this need with one story or another, and thus, in some versions of this theory, are to be wholeheartedly supported even if, factually speaking, they are false. Schopenhauer, while fully accepted the notion that humans have some such need, gave perhaps the most cutting rejoinder to this suggestion: he said that religion (particularly the monotheistic religions; Schopenhauer was, of course, the first great European philosopher who declared himself a partisan of Indian religion) is not the satisfaction of the metaphysical need. It is the *abuse* of that need, its exploitation.[28] That need is used as an entry point for a wedge that sells the unsuspecting human a large number of extraneous doodads that actually have nothing to do with fulfilling the legitimate metaphysical need, but rather are designed to get the client addicted to a system of fixed ideas that entail the acceptance of some priestly authority or other. For Schopenhauer, religion is like a corporation that holds a monopoly on all iodine sales and cunningly sells it only mixed with large doses of opium. We all naturally and legitimately need the iodine to survive but now we can only obtain it in a form that is inseparable from the opium, which makes us all addicts at the mercy of the monopoly that alone can provide it.

A more radical approach to this question is detectable in both Marx and Nietzsche and deeply informs the modern atheist critiques discussed earlier: there is no metaphysical need as such that pertains unchangeably to human nature. Instead, we've just gotten *used to* having a metaphysical story about ourselves and now feel lost if it is taken away. Again the trope of addiction comes quickly to hand here, as in Marx's famous dictum about religion serving as the opiate of the people. For Marx, this meant an illusory happiness cunningly applied to drown out the need to remedy *actual* unhappiness, which he identified not only with various material conditions and the unequal distribution of wealth under capitalism but concomitantly with man's alienation from his own labor, his own action. This distinction between "illusory" and "actual" happiness, however, presents a myriad of problems, so that we are committed to the odd and interesting position that a human being is the kind of creature who can be unhappy *without knowing it*. This may be so—in fact, as certain of my remarks before and to come may suggest, I'm very sympathetic to this suggestion—but accepting it will at the same time wreak havoc with some of Marx's other presuppositions, indeed with his entire program of reform, his whole notion of practical desiderata. For how can we ever be sure our experienced happiness in the proposed socialist utopia won't also secretly be a kind of misery, unbeknownst also to us, and even to Marx? Our loss of recognizable misery may end up being the worst intensification of our own unconscious misery. This is a question for Marxists to answer, which they sometimes do in extremely interesting ways.

In Nietzsche's case, though, we have instead a call for the overcoming of this long addiction as a means to opening up *new vistas*, new possibilities for human experience—emphatically not for the sake of greater "happiness," much less for "real happiness" as opposed to "illusory happiness," the latter possibly being the only kind there is. Sometimes Nietzsche will present this as having something to do with "health"—the addiction is bad for us. This idea can be closely aligned with that of Marx, and many interpreters therefore adopt these critiques together as prototypes of the modern rationalist attack on religion. But taken literally, this is the least interesting aspect of Nietzsche's critique; and viewed in the total context of his thought, it is clear that "health" is a much more complex concept than a simple correspondence with some kind of positive "happiness" would suggest. The openness that comes with the elimination of God is the hallmark of this health, which takes the form of the taste for danger and even for perishing, and a new delight in riddles and ambiguity, in chance, in the infinity of possible interpretations. As Nietzsche puts it, "Objection, evasion, joyous distrust, and love of irony are signs of health; everything absolute belongs to pathology."[29] This is what makes Nietzsche one of our prime atheist mystics and separates him sharply from the rationalist atheists, as we will see in detail in part II. And it is this step that reconfigures the question for us here. This requires us also to amend Schopenhauer's point. It is not that the metaphysical need of humans as such (i.e., to have *definitive* answers about our place in the universe) is better served by getting rid of God and his representatives. Rather than looking for definitive answers, our atheist mystics were looking for a way out of *having to have* such answers. It is precisely the closure, the definitiveness, the single-valenced nature of the experienced world, that is objected to. It is because the existence of God would enforce this closure that God had to go. It is in this spirit that I read the enigmatic assertion Nietzsche puts into the mouth of Zarathustra, which stands as one of the epigraphs of this book: "Just this is divinity: that there are gods but not God." The key point here is diversification, multiplicity, and the excessive plenitude of divinity, of creative power, of divinizing forces, of alternate conceptions and realizations of value so multifarious and inexhaustible that it is impossible for them to merge remainderlessly into a single consciousness or form of divinity. The divine is a constant upsurge of divergent, conflicting gods—of alternate points of view, each one intensified and realized to the point of divine perfection—including whatever god we might be making ourselves into, for as Zarathustra also says, "If God existed, how could I stand not to be God?" God as one to the exclusion of otherness, God as other than me, God as already complete: such a God is, ipso facto, the very negation of divinity.

From this point of view, it becomes conceivable that iconoclastic disbelief, militant irreverence, radical blasphemy, and consistent and thoroughgoing atheism are where real religious experience thrives—thus picking up on the kernel of truth in Nancy's suggestion, the unexpected proximity of monotheism and atheism, but reversing it into an implication running in exactly the opposite direction, away from both monotheism and *the peculiarly postmonotheistic* form of atheism that now dominates much of the world.

For Godlessness in the sense we mean here, and *not* in Nancy's post–Christian European sense of atheism, gives us a way to rethink monotheism as an unnecessary and tragically limiting abuse of a dimension of human experience that arguably comes to be parasitically appropriated in the development of religions: a sense of the infinite opening up behind any given presence, of Being's dimension of immanent depth and the thickness and openness intrinsic to it. For it now appears that this sense is not only *not* dependent on the belief in the "big G" God, but in fact even that such belief is an impediment to what is really central to it, to this dimension that is arguably the focus of what is called religious experience, a failed innovation that has actually backfired and made an essential aspect of religiousness impossible. The claim here is that whether we see the world as being planned or unplanned matters more for religious life than whether we believe in spooky invisible entities, whether we accept charismatic revelation, whether we are optimists or pessimists, whether we have strict or loose standards of verification, whether we are monists or dualists, whether we are empiricists or rationalists, or whether we are scientific or superstitious. As we will explore next, the issue is the persistence, extension, and *totalization of animism*, as elaborated out of preliterate belief into a theoretical form in the idea that all natural processes, without exception, are *controlled by a mind*—a *single* mind—and that they are whatever they are *for a purpose*, and are thus beholden to a *specifically teleological notion of unity*.[30]

Monotheism is *not* just the unity of a principle (or premise or sense) at the source of things that is also in some systemic way absented, leaving the world at once permeated with an absence of ultimacy and suffused everywhere with a reference to it—a universal immanent absence everywhere. thereby pointing to transcendence—as claimed by Nancy. This trait is shared by Daoism, by Mahāyāna Buddhism, by Vedanta, by Neo-Platonism, and probably by many more systems in one form or another. It emerges wherever there is some notion of the all-pervasive but indeterminate ground of existence, which permeates but exceeds any finite thing, the unconditioned as presupposed by the conditioned, the space in which spatial objects exist, the infinite in which the finite is positioned, the oceanic and encompassing that extends in all directions, the unseen from which the seen emerges, and so on. What is distinctive to monotheism is not this sense of the uncontainable, indescribable, all-encompassing oceanic, but rather its secondary usurpation and adaption into connection with specifically monotheistic notions with which it is initially very much at odds, resulting in the sharp separation of the infinite and the finite. It is a *domestication* of the oceanic, making it not only a oneness but a particular kind of oneness, as we will see at length in what follows: the oneness of personhood and purpose, which is a most peculiar candidate for oneness in that it is the anomaly of a oneness that prioritizes exclusion, that dichotomizes oneness and manyness. For our atheist mystics, even the oneness of the oceanic is left behind: the oceanic, like the ocean, is not a placid, static unity but a raging cacophony of micromotions veering and crashing in every direction, a chaotic jumble of torques and currents with no single goal, direction, controller, or character: the oceanic is a riot of un-unifiable differences constantly bleeding into one another, absorbing and rebounding with each other, swallowing each other in and spitting each other out. Its all-inclusiveness and inseparability, its nonduality, make it the opposite of a oneness; it is an enabling of all it includes and connects, not their organization into a one or their separation into a many.

But even if it *were* merely conceived as an unchanging and unitary ground of existence that in some way exceeds our ordinary knowledge and transcends the causal laws that apply to all finite things, the numinous oneness of an *impersonal* absolute is still a far cry less limiting than the oneness-versus-manyness in the specific form given it when that absolute One is also a purposive person, an intentionality that named all things with an essence before they existed, that has a specific name of its own or, even if it lacks or forbids its own proper name, that still rejects all other names as not its own name, rejecting other names, other forms, other identities as definitely *not* itself. Monotheism betokens the specific form of separation and exclusion endemic to the absolutizing of the kind of unity peculiar to personality and purpose, effecting a hostile takeover and attempted taming of the oceanic—a bizarre brand of infinity that somehow, in spite of its claimed infinity, serves to *exclude*, making an *exclusive* unity the principle of all existence. With a transcendent metaphysical oneness *not* taken over into the form of a monotheistic God, on the other hand, all names are merely negotiable names for something that is itself beyond any single name: it is the lack of an identity that opens into the infinity of identities.

An ultimately unidentifiable Absolute would be truly indistinguishable from an Absolute with an infinity of identities, something that is on no level reducible to a monolithic oneness of identity, which is also to say, in no way exclusive of any single possible identity. This will change the relationship between this Absolute and any finite identity, which gets us to what really matters for us here: *some form of infinity pertaining to all finite identities as such.* This is an intentionally equivocal phrase that can be cashed out in a number of different ways. It might mean that all finite identities are given an infinite significance or value (as in some monotheisms); on the other hand, it might mean an illimitable number of finite identities are enabled or generated by the nameless Absolute, and since it has no single identity of its own, that all these finite identities will be inseparable parts or aspects of It, so that an inexhaustible depth dimension remains the true nature within each finite thing (as in some pantheisms). And it might even mean that every finite identity itself is endowed, by virtue of this absence of a monolithically identifiable infinite Absolute, or this absolute absence of monolithic identity, with an illimitable number of alternate finite identities, and as such that each is indistinguishable from that unidentifiable infinite Absolute itself—that each is indeed an alternate name for It (as in the utmost atheist mysticisms). Or it might mean all of the above. It is convergence around this shared but ambiguous motif of infinity within finitude, however, that presents itself as a working hypothesis to answer the question posed earlier in the chapter, about what it is that religions are doing, what needs they might answer and what needs they create, what is the iodine and what the opium in this potion, what is at the bottom of the "metaphysical need," the need for meaning, the religious impulse (if there is one)—but in a way that is broad enough to cover both the monotheist and the pantheist and the atheist variants, that can explain the cravings for both the iodine and the opium and thus can answer to both Schopenhauer's need for meaning-endowing narrative and to Nietzsche's need to escape and remake all such narratives. For this seems to suggest a plausible phenomenological account of what serves as the spiritual kernel of "religious experience," for lack of a better word, in its various opposed forms, the mystical core shared by these radically divergent ways of engaging the infinite: some sort or other of paradoxical resonance of infinity attached in one way or another to finite things. Maybe a better term would be something like *spirituality* or *poetic resonance* or *mysticism* or *epiphany* or *ecstasy* or some other word. What is gestured toward with these terms, in any case, is the particular aspect of experience that is of most concern for us in these pages.

What can it mean to experience infinity by engaging a finite thing? It might mean that it points to or instantiates or is endowed with some form of infinity, whether an infinite entity, infinite value, infinite meanings, or infinite identities, to name a few. But to take a stab at the phenomenology of all such cases, we can stipulate that a transition from merely finite to finite-but-infinite in all cases will involve a dramatic experiential shift. What we have in our sights here is the outsized impact observed in human beings when certain kinds of new ideas are introduced into their minds. What is distinctive about these kinds of ideas is that, if accepted as true, they register not simply as the increase by one additional fact to what we already think we know about the world, the adding of one more fact to the unchanged prior sum of previously known facts, leaving all other facts as they were, but rather as a spreading nimbus affecting some or all other facts priorly accepted, transforming or overturning the meaning of other things previously assumed to be known and understood in a particular way. If we must offer this as a working definition of what we will mean here by religious experience (or mystical experience or epiphany or what have you), always a perilous undertaking, we do so not to claim that everything ever or anywhere called religious will empirically be found to meet this definition, but to single out an aspect of concern to us, shared by some but not all of what is called religious, but that is also detectable in experiences that are not usually so named. This is the specific dimension of experience that we are eager to preserve, which we see as a key motivating factor in the embrace of religion in both its atheist and theistic forms, and in the name of which we want to track the critiques and overcomings of monotheism considered in these pages.

A religious experience, on this working definition, is an experience that dramatically alters one's relationship to many or all *other* experiences, sometimes changing the limits and character of experience per se, but always at the very least abrogating in some way the prior interpretation and apprehension of a substantial range of finite identities (i.e., what some set of other finite things or experiences is or means) through the deliberate or nondeliberate manipulation of currently unverifiable mentations. Often these mentations are framings of more encompassing concerns, a broader context or narrative that serves to recontextualize all priorly known ideas and facts and things. This change in meaning might be to suddenly see all that one previously thought important as meaningless or insignificant in comparison to another as yet unseen world or goal, or it might be a change in one's sense of things previously seen, who one is, what things are. Similar effects might be produced not just through manipulations of unverifiable mentations, but through other means such as drugs, dance, ritual, games, sports, and so on. All these may or may not have a religious dimension, depending on whether they also involve this positing of unverifiable recontextualizing mentations that have the power to alter the apprehension of a significant swath of previously known finite identities.

In other words, any activity or idea or picture or sound or whatever that is introduced into human experience, such that the mere engagement with it not merely registers as one more fact in the world but changes what other facts mean, or indeed alters what it is for a fact to be a fact, is what we take to be the triggering of a religious experience in the relevant sense. Believing an idea that does this to be *true* will do this to an even greater degree, but even the mere entertainment of its possibility will do so to some extent; on this conception of religious experience, we see the difference between belief in the idea's truth and mere thinking about its possibility as a difference not in kind but only in degree: belief supercharges the religious effect exponentially, but the nature of the effect is the same, though less intense and thoroughgoing, even in merely contemplating these ideas as possibilities. We said that the idea of God does this in a most thoroughgoing way, in that if true it would change not only what the facts are but what it is for a fact—any fact—to be a fact. We noted that this was what distinguished it from the introduction of other new belief about as-yet empirically unverified things, about things like the Loch Ness monster or extraterrestrial espionage. Now we are able to add a nuance to this judgment, and indeed in a certain sense to reverse it. The addition of the thought that the Loch Ness monster is real will indeed change my sense of what kind of world this is, and indeed what all facts in it mean, but only ever so slightly: the addition of *any* new fact means at least that this is the kind of world in which this kind of thing can be, and to whatever extent I engage this thought, I must proportionally adjust my sense of the world to accommodate it, seeing all other facts as existing in a world where this can happen. Newly added belief in extraterrestrial espionage will perhaps do so to a somewhat greater extent, and in astrology or karma even more broadly. Some facts fit more smoothly into my preconceived schema of the world's possibilities, but let us grant that by mere virtue of a piece of information being *new* (i.e., being apprehended by a real-time *experience*), it will change our sense of everything else at least slightly, even if only as a further consolidation or confirmation of our previous beliefs. The thought of God does indeed change the meaning of *all* facts at one fell swoop; *belief* in that idea changes it even more so. For example, through belief in God, the way I treat my fellow man might be seen not just as a social or personal issue, but as something cared about by God, of infinite import and with infinite consequences; any fact in the world is not just pointing to itself, but pointing beyond itself to the intentions in the infinite mind of God. Every fact about the natural world would be similarly transformed by this idea. Though the facts are the same as before, the meaning of their facticity has changed: they are there because God intended them, planned them, willed them.

This would seem to qualify the idea of God as a perfect example of a successful religious idea, the religious idea *par excellence*. Yet my claim in this book is precisely the opposite, seeing in the idea of God rather a uniquely *failed* religious idea, one that obstructs the full development of religious experience as here defined. Further explication of the implications of this conception of religious consciousness, as developed via a radical *repudia-*

tion of the idea of God, is thus tasked with clarifying why would we suggest that although a believer in God may be said to be "religious," for us she is religious only in an *intrinsically self-defeating way*.

Religious experience on this conception may, in a sense, fit the description that is sometimes given it: a *transcendence of finitude*. But by this I do not mean the elimination of all finitude in favor of the sole reality of a featureless and undifferentiated infinity devoid of finite traits: as I'll pursue subsequently at great length, this would paradoxically end up making infinity just another kind of finitude, inasmuch as it excludes something. Rather, on the conception we are working with here, finitude is "transcended" only in the sense of suspension and supersession of the *single* finite identity or meaning priorly granted to each finite thing—the overcoming of the idea that a given thing is just what we've always thought it to be and means just what we've always thought it means, just this and nothing besides—or that it is or means just what I *could* think it is or means. But this fixing of a single meaning and identity to all things takes shape due to the unnoticed assumption of a finite given context—for example, of the presumed secular practicalities of everyday life. The suspension of the priorly assumed identity or meaning of given facts is accomplished, not by replacing them with other facts, but by adding other ideations that place them in a larger context, or simply in an alternate context, or perhaps in many or even infinite alternate contexts. This abrogation of any single finite identity via unverifiable recontextualizing mentations might replace it with an infinite identity, or else it might simply replace it with *another, alternate* finite identity. We can see how such an alternate might be associated with religion in modern renderings, since to some extent it accords with the intuitive sense of religion as either the attribution of *infinite* or *total* or merely *alternate* significance to finite things. Though there is no reference to the "sacred" or "reverence" or "redemption" or "transcendence" or what have you in this definition, the idea of *reidentification*, the actual experience of a *repurposing*, is to be viewed as the root gesture that can, in different circumstances, take these various forms. When things are placed in relation to an unseen order which provides an alternative to the previously seen and known order—whether that be a set of invisible spirits or one ultimate mind or some narrative or law that subsumes things in a way that is claimed to subsume prior ("secular" or "social") narratives or laws, including cases where this involves something "ultimate" or "total" or "infinite," as we find in various well-known definitions of religion—we have an experience that its seems at least passably intuitive to call "religious." The clearest examples do this for *all* other facts: certain ideations would change the significance of what a fact is, thus changing the significance of finite identities, of what definiteness itself is. This is what the ideas more commonly identified as religious ideas do, while those not usually called religion extend their influence to a lesser extent, employing less overarching methods. But it is, again, a matter of difference in extent rather than kind: to the extent that art undermines presupposed identities of known things and opens up new meanings by providing a relation to a hitherto unnoticed context, art would then have a religious dimension. To the extent that science does this, science would have a religious dimension. To the extent that the anticipation of a coming apocalypse or social revolution does this, thus changing the meaning of everything in the present, that predicted event has a religious meaning. To the extent that belief in extraterrestrial life does this, it is a religious idea. When I see an everyday item in a new way that grants it a hitherto unseen identity, one that overcomes the limitation of its accepted identity in the economy of everyday life, I am seeing it religiously in the sense singled out here.

Why, then, would anyone be so perverse as to say that the idea of God is a uniquely *failed* religious idea, one that obstructs the full development of religious consciousness? From what possible point of view would anyone suggest that, though a believer in God may be said to be "religious," she is religious only in an intrinsically self-defeating way—that monotheism as normally practiced is indeed, as Nancy suggests, a conduit for the most prosaic secularism, for the antireligious, and in effect a kind of stealth disenchantment? It is because the way the infinite is determined in the context of a purposive and singular creator consciousness undermines, one step later, exactly what it accomplished with respect to its first level of application: by annulling the limitation to one identity (the secular, the human, the practical), it sets up another, *even more inescapable, even more fixed, identity*. But if what is really wanted, by our definition, is the overcoming of the finitude or limitedness of *any* identity, this is a Pyrrhic victory of the highest order. What is wanted is not an "ultimate" concern, à la Paul Tillich, for that implies the finality and closure and singularity of concern, but rather a transcending of *any* finite concern. The key point is that *all "concerns," qua concerns, are finite insofar as they are definite and determinate.* This applies also to allegedly infinite concerns insofar as they have any determinate content whatsoever. Rather, what is essential to the mystical dimension of religion that matters to us here is *infinity* of contexts, and thus an infinity of identities and meanings, but it is an infinity that by definition can never be *singular* to the exclusion of plurality: it is not just that infinite *significance* is present in any putatively finite item, but rather that infinite *significances*, plural, are present in any putatively finite item. It is not that each finite thing is seen to have *an* infinite meaning; it is that an infinite meaning, to be really infinite, must also be infinite *meanings*, plural—*each* of which is infinite, and *each* of which therefore unifies and subsumes all the others in its own distinctive way: not one infinite unity, but infinite alternate, intersubsuming infinite unities.

Here in this introduction, this definition can only be presented as an admittedly obscure sketch of what is to come in the pages that follow. But it should help set the stage for what we will see in our atheist mystics: a way to think about each finite thing as simultaneously infinite in its own kind, in its own way, disclosing an infinity of alternate ways of being infinite. My claim here is that this seems wildly counterintuitive precisely because of a prior beholdenness to things having a single "meaning"—for it is the commitment to the idea of meaning *as ultimate* that makes the infinite infinitudes of each finite thing unthinkable and inaccessible. The commonsense notion of "meaning" *simpliciter* entails a concealed appeal to a concept of purpose and plan. An unplanned universe is, *ipso facto*, a meaningless universe. "Meaning" is primarily derivative of "purpose." Whatever meanings exist are therefore partial meanings, which are opposed by other meanings: they begin as functions of what some being or group of beings *wants*, or how one being or group of beings impacts on some other groups. The idea of the totality of existence per se having a single meaning is, on this view, absurd, incoherent, and possibly even self-refuting, given that there is nothing outside this totality for it to have an impact on, nothing *for which* it can have a meaning or purpose—and as long as we have no reason to deny the obvious presence within this totality of differing wants of differing beings (divine or otherwise).

This suggests that for us, the genuinely religious move would be to see the denial of a meaning and the seemingly nihilistic appeal to meaninglessness as identical to an affirmation of *infinite meanings*. An unplanned universe is one of which nothing can have only a single meaning, a single essence, a single identity—or indeed any single sum thereof, any limited scope of meanings, essences, identities; it is a universe in which nothing can be strictly *finite*. Thus it is that, in the absence of some God's-eye view, I would argue, the very meaning of "real," "true," "necessary," "contingent," "free," and "fact" have to be rethought from the ground up. And this is why, even though the idea of God is more impressively religious than the belief in the Loch Ness monster in that it undermines the prior meaning of *all* facts in one comprehensive stroke, it is also less successfully religious even than this very minor religious effect of the latter belief in that it *forecloses* any further alterations of the meaning of these key entailments of what facticity is in a way the latter does not. Belief in the one additional fact of the Loch Ness monster changes the world minimally, but it leaves many more possibilities for further revisions to the entailments of facticity and meaning, opening the way to greater fluidity of alternate identities and meanings. The idea of God changes everything about what every fact is, but it also shuts down the possibility of any possible further revision of the fundamental meaning of what a fact is. Now we know for certain this one thing: that all facts were *intended*; that all facts have *a single specific, ultimate purpose.* To be sure, to the extent that this purpose is as yet not fully known by us, or may even be constitutively unknowable by us, we may still have a small range of wiggle room to connect the dots around this idea in various ways and fill in the rest of the picture. But besides whatever determinate content we may be committed to accepting, through either revelation or natural theology, concerning this purpose that is not fully known, we have one iron restraint on all our speculations about what all things are and what they all mean: they all must have *some specific purpose*, which means *one specific identity* and *one specific meaning to the exclusion of any other.* For as we will explore at length in what follows, purposivity, now posited as the ultimate ontological principle of all possible existence, is the uniquely thoroughgoing blueprint for the *excluding of alternatives*, and this structural necessity will now infect everything, even our uncertainty.

Other ideas that change the status of every finite fact in one comprehensive stroke do not work this way. If I entertain the idea that *all things are unreal*, for example, it might seem that this transformation of how all things must now be seen, while liberating me from my prior sense of what they are, likewise merely trades whatever I was previously assuming for a single iron restraint on all further meanings and identities: whatever a thing may appear to be, I now know for sure that it is *not* what it presents itself to be, that whatever I think about its specific determinations or about its status as an independent object is wrong. But this leaves open almost everything else about these appearances: what they can do, what they can mean, how they can interact, even how much I should care about them. If I posit a still more robustly religious idea, like *all things are aspects of single Being*, say, or else *all things are predetermined by fate*, there too I have a transformation that liberates me from my prior sense of all things, but one that may seem to land me again in an equally monolithic and fixed conclusion about them all: whatever it is, in the end it will turn out to be none other than the one true Being or else fated to be so, as the case may be. But here too I have a blank check for providing meanings and purposes of these finite things—for neither oneness nor fatedness necessarily pertains to meanings or purposes; they do not even necessarily imply that my proper attitude to all things should be will-less acceptance, since even my resistance to fate would itself be seen as fated, and my erroneously taking the one infinite Being to be many finite beings itself would also be included in that infinite Being. Even if I conclude that *all things that happen to me were willed by me in a former life* or that *all things happen because some god or other wanted it to,* where all things are now seen as imbued with prior purposes—whether my own forgotten will or the mischief of some god—these are not finally binding on me. Indeed, what I have made I can unmake, and what another has made I can resist or flout or defy with new purposes and reinterpretations of my own—or, to take the more relevant case, that of the atheist mystic, I can even simply *ignore* those purposes altogether, opting instead to concentrate on what is ontologically prior to all purposes and beyond their reach. The case is different if we make purpose itself the thing that is ultimate. When omnipotent purposivity is made into the ultimate ontological horizon, the genuine religious power of infinity, the infinitely expansive power of endlessly recontextualizing ideations generating for every known fact, resulting in endless new identities and meanings—in other words, religious experience as we have just defined it—has been stamped out once and for all. What was wanted was the power of repurposing itself, the religious experience itself; however, with this one big repurposing, this very powerful religious experience, what we got instead was just one new purpose—and the end to all future repurposing, which equals the demise of all religious experience.

Albeit perhaps ironically, this conception brings us closer to Levinas's analysis of what is behind the religious dimension of experience and, in another sense, Bataille's: a desire for radical otherness. What is actually wanted is anything but *this,* anything that is not here and not like this: something entirely unlike everything I know. Simply replacing one set of facts with another is one way to get this radical otherness, but it is not nearly as thoroughgoing as proposing a new fact that has the power to change what it means for any fact (past, present, or future) to be a fact, and still less so from doing the latter in a way that enable the ceaseless rediscovering of new identities and meanings of every such fact (past, present, and future) rather than closing it down. What is felt to be objectionable is the *restrictive* sense in which everything has only the meanings already attributed to it. Perhaps we will be forgiven for characterizing this as a kind of radical boredom. But this boredom is a deeper pain even than pain: it is the inescapable confinement to pain that makes pain pain, and the same confining inescapability that can make even happiness pain. We will return to this question of pain, as well as its relation to meaning and purpose, in the conclusion, but it will be a subterranean thread guiding us through everything that comes in between. Our problem, then, is not, "Why do I exist? What is the meaning of life?" These are just local versions of the real problem, namely, "Is that all?" And religion has indeed provided this dimension for human beings: there is something else going on here besides what meets the eye, besides the fight for love and glory, besides work, profit, and loss. Here we can again see a two-step process that has been tragically abstracted to leave only its less desirable by-product. The idea of God must have been thrilling at first, appealing to precisely this need for *opening things up*: the world is not just about earning and spending, forming alliances, protecting yourself from harm, and garnering advantages. Rather, there's an entirely *different* story *also* going on here. The first will be last, our failure is a sign of God's interest, and all such random coincidences are signs of an *alternate* meaning—not a search for meaning, but a search for *another* meaning. For there is never a lack of meaning; we are, as Merleau-Ponty put it, *condemned* to meaning.[31] There's always already at least one meaning going on—at the very least, me versus you, us versus them, gain versus loss, success in the current task versus failure. Our claim is that what was really wanted here was the *otherness* itself—the *ambiguity*, the *moretoitivity*, the *inalienably immanent power of repurposing per se* that is inherent in every specific thing, meaning, and purpose. The tragedy, though, is that the alternate meaning then comes to be established as the *real* meaning, the *only* meaning. Twoness was wanted, so an extra one was posited. But then the extra one became the only one, making things that much *more* restricted, because now they are *inescapably* restricted. The impulse for reinterpretability sediments into the prohibition against any reinterpretability. This brings us closer to the heart of the matter, and to what we will mean here when we speak of "redemption," "liberation," and so on: breaking out of the *boring closure* of existence into a single meaning. To put it in a formula: Every religion begins with someone saying, "Or *this* instead." What we really want is the "or . . . instead." What we end up with, though, is usually just the "instead" without the "or"—or worse, just the "*this*."

How did such a thing happen?

PART ONE

The Sleeping Island

They once thought they had landed on an islet, when the sea was tossing them about; but behold, it was a sleeping monster!

—NIETZSCHE, *Thus Spoke Zarathustra*, translated by Graham Parkes

CHAPTER 1

Purposivity and Consciousness

NOÛS AS ARCHÉ: SEEMED LIKE A
GOOD IDEA AT THE TIME

The story of monotheism is often traced historically to the Hebrew scriptures, the account of creation via mere speech and thought in Genesis, perhaps to other Mediterranean creation myths of a supreme god who gradually assumes the role of a disembodied mind serving as the sole omnipotent, omniscient, omnibenevolent creator of all things. But modern biblical criticism has convincingly shown the gradual formation of this full-blown notion of God to have taken shape only quite late in ancient Hebrew history, certainly after the encounter with Persian religion and (especially) Greek thought, and reaching its familiar uncompromising form only in some strains of Second Temple Hebrew religion and in the byzantine Hellenistic-Hebrew hybrid that finally came to be known as Christianity. I am inclined to accept the judgment of Nietzsche, George Santayana, and Ralph Waldo Emerson,[1] that the real invention of the key ideas of monotheism, in the form that I want to target here, is found in Plato (though with some crucial modifications to be discussed in a moment—above all, the fateful joining of the idea of controlling mind with the idea of *infinity*, which is not found in Plato), which allowed a rethinking of the first verses of Genesis in a way that has since exerted a powerful fascination. It seems, in fact, that some form of high god, main god, sole god, ruler god, or creator god is a fairly common invention in the ancient world, intensifying especially wherever there is empire and modeled on the emperor who conquers and dominates smaller kings—thus becoming a "king of kings." We find something like this also in early China, in the idea of *Shangdi* (上帝) or *Tian* (天) as the sponsor of the Imperial House. The Mohists even float the idea of regarding this deity as in some way the fashioner of the things in the world, though not quite of the world itself. Some form of "Great Spirit" is indeed a common trope, which was often tried out in early cultures. What is significant about the development in the monotheistic religions is that this idea *stuck*—and that it was taken seriously by educated and literate people, provided with a justification, and applied to philosophical problems. In ancient and medieval China, the philosophical tradition went another way; the literate classes soon ceased to take the idea seriously, so much so that its consistent marginalization in subsequent intellectual life seems due less to a hard-won refutation and more to a *loss of interest* in a self-evidently implausible and unworkable bit of traditional lore. There were other aspects of the cultural inheritance that seemed to provide richer and more promising seeds for making sense of the world and man's place in it (e.g., familial bonds, ritual performance, bodily cultivation, the charting of patterns of change in shifting personal and political fortunes and in the life-giving reversals of seasonal transformation—and the golden thread of *wuwei*, nondeliberate action, running through all of them), and it was these that were thereafter developed in various ways in the mainstream philosophical and spiritual traditions. Perhaps, left to themselves, the various Hebrew and Zoroastrian ideas of a world controlled by a single purposive deity would have eventually faded into the background in some such way as well—if they had not received unexpected support from Greek philosophy, specifically Stoicism and, especially, Platonism. Two and two are put together by Philo of Alexandria, and the creators of the New Testament. Monotheism thus becomes intellectually respectable. This is the real riddle: what premises allowed this idea to take root as a serious explanation of the world?

The smoking gun seems to be Plato's *Phaedo*, where we find Socrates, on the eve of his death, telling a remarkable story about a formative experience for his own intellectual work, resulting in a radical new view of *mind and causality*:

> Then I heard someone who had a book of Anaxagoras, as he said, out of which he read that mind was the disposer and cause of all, and I was quite delighted at the notion of this, which appeared admirable, and I said to myself: If mind is the disposer, mind will dispose all for the best, and put each particular in the best place; and I argued that if anyone desired to find out the cause of the generation or destruction or existence of anything, he must find out what state of being or suffering or doing was best for that thing, and therefore a man had only to consider the best for himself and others, and then he would also know the worse, for that the same science comprised both. And I rejoiced to think that I had found in Anaxagoras a teacher of the causes of existence such as I desired, and I imagined that he would tell me first whether the earth is flat or round; and then he would further explain the cause and the necessity of

this, and would teach me the nature of the best and show that this was best; and if he said that the earth was in the centre, he would explain that this position was the best, and I should be satisfied if this were shown to me, and not want any other sort of cause. And I thought that I would then go on and ask him about the sun and moon and stars, and that he would explain to me their comparative swiftness, and their returnings and various states, and how their several affections, active and passive, were all for the best. For I could not imagine that when he spoke of mind as the disposer of them, he would give any other account of their being as they are, except that this was best; and I thought that when he had explained to me in detail the cause of each and the cause of all, he would go on to explain to me what was best for each and what was best for all. I had hopes which I would not have sold for much, and I seized the books and read them as fast as I could in my eagerness to know the better and the worse.

What hopes I had formed, and how grievously was I disappointed! As I proceeded, I found my philosopher altogether forsaking mind or any other principle of order, but having recourse to air, and ether, and water, and other eccentricities. I might compare him to a person who began by maintaining generally that mind is the cause of the actions of Socrates, but who, when he endeavored to explain the causes of my several actions in detail, went on to show that I sit here because my body is made up of bones and muscles; and the bones, as he would say, are hard and have ligaments which divide them, and the muscles are elastic, and they cover the bones, which have also a covering or environment of flesh and skin which contains them; and as the bones are lifted at their joints by the con-traction or relaxation of the muscles, I am able to bend my limbs, and this is why I am sitting here in a curved posture: that is what he would say, and he would have a similar explanation of my talking to you, which he would attribute to sound, and air, and hearing, and he would assign ten thou-sand other causes of the same sort, forgetting to mention the true cause, which is, that the Athenians have thought fit to condemn me, and accord-ingly I have thought it better and more right to remain here and undergo my sentence; for I am inclined to think that these muscles and bones of mine would have gone off to Megara or Boeotia,—by the dog of Egypt they would, if they had been guided only by their own idea of what was best, and if I had not chosen as the better and nobler part, instead of play-ing truant and running away, to undergo any punishment which the state inflicts. There is surely a strange confusion of causes and conditions in all this. It may be said, indeed, that without bones and muscles and the other parts of the body I cannot execute my purposes. But to say that I do as I do because of them, and that this is the way in which mind acts, and not from the choice of the best, is a very careless and idle mode of speaking. I wonder that they cannot distinguish the cause from the condition, which the many, feeling about in the dark, are always mistaking and misnaming. And thus one man makes a vortex all round and steadies the earth by the heaven; another gives the air as a support to the earth, which is a sort of broad trough. Any power which in disposing them as they are disposes them for the best never enters into their minds, nor do they imagine that there is any superhuman strength in that; they rather expect to find another Atlas of the world who is stronger and more everlasting and more containing than the good is, and are clearly of opinion that the obligatory and containing power of the good is as nothing; and yet this is the principle which I would fain learn if anyone would teach me.[2]

I will implicitly point to this passage again and again in what follows: it is, to me, the moment in which Plato literally dramatizes the invention of the core idea of monotheism before our eyes. It is here, rather than in Nancy's fanciful suggestions of protoatheism, that we see the real implications of the new Platonic conception of "the God." What leaps to the eye already in this astonishing passage is the fateful fusion of five concepts: (1) the Good, (2) consciousness, (3) ultimate cause, (4) purpose, and (5) unity. The key unspoken premise behind Socrates's enthusiasm here is a certain experience of conscious willing, identifying with the aspect of oneself that *knows in advance what it wants* and tries to achieve it through *unifying all its efforts*, of which it is also *fully aware*. *Purpose*, as something conceived clearly in the mind before an action is undertaken, is implicitly privileged here, being considered without ado to be what actually makes things happen. The assumption is that whenever something happens, it is due to a consciousness wanting it to happen—an intelligence choosing to make it happen. The Good—that is, a single purpose—lies at the source of all being; it gives being to beings and is what makes things as they are.

To state the thesis of this book as clearly as possible and as soon as possible: I want to claim that a certain fundamental model propounded here, albeit only as a still unrealized desideratum, is the inescapable center of gravity around which all Plato's later experiments revolve—the agenda that charts the course of such varied probings as the dialectics of the *Parmenides*, the theory of Forms in the *Republic* and other middle dialogues, the Form of the Good as what is "beyond being," and the formative actions of the hypothetical demiurge of the *Timaeus*. Moreover, this model of what philosophy is looking for, what human beings are presumed to want, will go on to haunt both the explicitly Platonic traditions and the attempted escapes from Platonism that follow—the antitranscendentalism of Aristotle and the retooling of Aristotle in Neo-Platonism, as well as the Abrahamic negative theologies and even European and post-European secular humanism.

What is this model? The idea of purpose as the primary source and guarantor of all action and all being and all value.

What is being in that case? Purposive consciousness or the results of purposive consciousness.

What is beyond being? Also purposity or the results of purposity.

What is concrete reality and life? Again, purposity or the results of purposity.

This, I claim, is the kernel, the essence of monotheism—even if the explicit omnipotent God has not yet fully formed (as in Plato) or disappears either into the immanence of a purpose-driven universe (as in Aristotle) or into a theology that goes beyond being (as in mystical negative theologies in the Abrahamic traditions), or into a rumination striving to go beyond metaphysics (as in the contemporary postmetaphysical theories of the Good or Givenness or in allegedly ametaphysical secular ethics). Striving to go beyond them—*to what?* To personhood, to purpose, to calling, to goodness, to meaning. But the point of this book is to argue that this leads to monotheism and monotheism's constricted notion of being all over again, and worse. For, to make the point as clear as possible at the outset, the Good as the beyond-being is simply *being once more*; it is something more like being, and it is *worse* than being in precisely what matters: *dualism*. The inert obstructiveness of being, where to exist is to be finite, which means to *exclude whatever one is not*, is not overcome in candidates for non-thinghood like the Good or Personhood or Purpose, but exacerbated by it. Even personhood as a mode of *inclusion* of what one is not, as some process thinkers would have it,[3] or the attempt to include God's unruly prepersonal ground within God's achieved personal existence, as some rebounds from German Idealism propose,[4] ends up under the aegis of the Good, of choice, of exclusion—which is once again the typical monotheist gesture of *using inclusion as a means to the final, ultimate exclusion*. Even the apparent upending of all such speculative subtleties in favor of hard-headed, nonpersonal, objective naturalism remains saturated with the key premise of this tradition. The "Parmenidean distinction" between Being and Nonbeing, which is the very hallmark of the dominance of being, is not overcome by the Good, nor by God, nor by post-God materialism: it is expanded and radicalized. For "the Good" in this tradition, at the ultimate definitional level, means *the exclusion of the Bad*. What I will call the key monotheist idea is this: the mutual exclusivity, at the ultimate level, of Being and Nonbeing, of goodness and badness, of purpose and purposelessness. Atheism is the nonadoption of these mutual exclusivities. Atheistic mysticism is the religious ecstasy of this vision.

For easy reference, I will adopt a shorthand term for the cocktail of ideas brought together by Anaxagoras and so enthusiastically endorsed by Socrates in the passage just quoted—the Good, ultimate cause, consciousness, purpose, and unity—and their culmination in the idea of a single unified purposive consciousness that definitionally wills the Good and thereby causes the world. I will refer to this as the idea of νοῦς as ἀρχή: *Noûs* as *Arché*. *Arché* (ἀρχή) is a Greek word meaning "beginning, origin, source," with the derivative meanings of "what is first," "having priority," and "ruling." It is the Greek root of English words such as *hierarchy, archangel, patriarch*, and *archetype*. The Latin equivalent is *principium* ("principle"), which is related to the words such as *principal* and *prince*. Philosophy is said to have begun in Greece when Thales suggested that *water* was the *Arché* of all the other elements (fire, air, earth): water came first and in some way was what underlay and explained them all. All the others *came from, were made of, were moved by, or returned to* water. Thales's student Anaximander proposed *apeiron* ἄπειρον ("the boundless," "infinity") as the origin. *Apeiron* appears to be related to primal *chaos*, to randomness, to lack of definition, measure, boundary, order. This association suggests an original implication of *apeiron* that bears a close relation both to the water motif and to what we will call *raw infinity*: the utter lack of boundaries, the absence of any possibility of exclusion of anything by anything, meaning both a lack of outer limit and a lack of any definite internal boundaries or rules, something that admits of no fixed and definite identities either as a whole or for its internal parts. But as we shall see, this interpretation quickly becomes a bone of contention, for the term would soon be usurped into a new and contrary meaning by Anaxagoras, striking the beginning of the theistic tradition. The desperately daring primal move of monotheism in all its permutations is found in this contradictory idea of an *infinity* that is also somehow *determinate*: a definite being—which is this rather than that, someone rather than no-one, thus rather than otherwise, order rather than chaos—which is somehow *also* eternal and infinite; it is an infinity that somehow *excludes*. Monotheism, I will want to claim, is seen from here as the theft and domestication of raw infinity from its natural habitat: inexhaustible chaos.

Early Chinese cosmogonies follows a similar trajectory, starting with *water* origin stories (e.g., in the recently excavated text, *Taiyi shengshui* 太一生水), but quickly settling into what came to be mainstream Daoist motifs that point to the formless, the boundless, the indeterminate as the only possible source of the determinate. *Dao*, originally a word for order and purpose, for the articulated, bounded guidance of a *path*, is seized on by the Daoists in a new reversed and ironic sense (as I've argued at length elsewhere) to indicate that this formlessness, purposelessness, and orderlessness are the real source of order and purpose. Chinese speculation of all schools continues on this basis in various complicated ways, developing a variety of conceptions of the relation of the boundless to the bounded, the indeterminate to the determinate, the orderless to the ordered—but almost without exception remaining grounded in the fundamental primacy of the indeterminate.[5] What is interesting about pre-Socratic Greek thinkers, in contrast, is how thoroughly the suggestion of raw infinity, the formless randomness at the origin of all things, is rejected, neglected, and sometimes transformed. Anaximenes, who was said to be a student of Anaximander, transforms it right away—not the raw infinite, but the most evidently boundless of the concrete elements is now put forward as the *Arché*: air, which could be regarded as condensing into concrete things and dissipating back into air when they perish. Thus far we still have an analogue in China, in the theories of *qi* (氣) as the first stand-in for the formless Dao. But hereafter the two traditions radically part ways. The annoyed Socrates is explicitly rejecting the physical elements like water and air, but also passed over here as candidates for *Arché*, for the first principle giving the most basic explanation of things, are the proto-Daoist inklings of the formless infinite *apeiron* and the constant flux and paradoxical unity of opposites of Herakleitos's Logos-fire, as well as some other more abstract, nonmaterial options, like the Love and Hate of Empedocles and the harmony/proportion of the Pythagoreans. Out of all these options, the big breakthrough, from the point of view of Socrates in this passage—and of his pupils Plato and Aristotle, and all the rest of us who have been their latter-day pupils—is Anaxagoras. Anaxagoras says that none of the finite material elements can be the *Arché*. And neither can *apeiron*, the raw infinite of Anaximander, nor the fluxing paradoxical Logos-fire of Herakleitos, be the *Arché*. It is *Noûs*, intelligence, that is the first principle.

Noûs (voῦς) is sometimes translated "mind," but a modern reader needs to be wary of this translation. We sometimes speak of "consciousness" or "awareness" as mental functions, or even as the essence of mind. But this sort of detached awareness, a kind of allowing of the presencing of whatever presents itself, is not what *Noûs* means. *Noûs* is specifically *intelligence*, as connected to the idea of *understanding* as opposed to merely perceiving, and *good sense* or *sensibleness* in activity, as opposed to foolish, aimless, reckless, or random behavior. It is also opposed to unthinking openness to events as they transpire, or daydreaming, or playful whimsy—even if any of the latter are conscious. *Noûs* is thus not consciousness, but *a specific kind* of consciousness. It does the kinds of things that are accomplished by *think-*

ing, planning, and designing. In its simplest and most direct meaning, it is mind in its purposive, active mode, when it is trying to get something done or figure something out or is guiding the actions of the body. It is mind that asks and answers the question, What should I do now to make things better, to achieve my goal, to maximize my effectiveness? It is mind as purposive designer or deliberate engineer of action, coordinating ends to means. It is mind as executive function, standing above and outside its subordinates and issuing judgments, commands, directives in order to achieve a desired end. It is mind with problems to solve, work to do, things to sort out. It is mind acting purposively, doing what makes the most sense to attain its goal, eliminating superfluities, maximizing effectiveness. It is mind in command, mind as willer, mind as arranger and optimizer and designer and disposer. In sum, *Noûs* is mind as (wannabe) *controller — of self, of situation, of the world.*

This is why Socrates immediately sees this as an explanatory principle: if *Noûs* is *Arché*, then the explanation of why anything is so is that *it is best for it to be that way.* It is that way because the intelligence that runs the world thought it would be good for it to be that way. It exists because it was wanted, because it fit the plan, because it had a specific job to do. For *Noûs* originally signifies that which coordinates effective means to achieve some stipulated goal. And if there is only one such purposive consciousness, there will be no cross-purposes: what it wills is definitionally what it regards as good, and given its singularity and its ultimacy, that will now be the only good in town.

But this is a very narrow and specific model of mind, which is rooted in one particular mode of experience. It is a *problem-solving* faculty, involved in the *confrontation* between self and world, the feeling of needing to *intervene* and *resist* and *reshape* — in short, to *do something about* the environment: the mind of planning and choice and purpose and correction. It is precisely the mode of experience in which the division between subject and object is felt most distinctly and vividly. But this is a singling out of only one occasional kind of experience, which is being inflated into the characteristic of mind as such, of experience as such, even of existence as such. What is passed over as a candidate for first principle here, if we are in the market for a single first principle at all, is not only nonsentient elements like fire, air, water, atoms, void, indeterminacy, musiclike harmony, warlike contradiction, inert stuff, and energy. Equally pushed aside are other modes of sentient experience other than that of purposive mind in confrontation with recalcitrant surroundings: aimless daydreaming, neutral idling, rapt wonder, detached curiosity, inebriated immersion, ecstatic embrace, reckless exuberance, unquestioning acceptance, exhausted submission, aesthetic awe, helpless confusion, erotic surrender, numbed disassociation, contented absorption, bumbling stupor, just to name a few—the myriad modes of experience that might instead have been projected and privileged as the ultimate source or model of all existence, if indeed any such move had to be made at all. All these are modes in which new contents emerge within subjective experience, just as frequently as willed purposive productivity and problem-solving decision-making. But some of these would perhaps have highlighted areas of experience where consciousness and the nonconscious realm surrounding it are related differently, more intimately or ambiguously—where the subject and object are more closely intertwined, or only waveringly distinguished, or not yet experienced as two different things at all. The finite conscious self in this mode is the confrontational self, choosing between possible plans of actions, making decisions in the endeavor to control, wanting to be in more control, and feeling every lack of control as a potential problem to be solved. It is this *consciously controlling executive function* that is now projected outward into the first cause of all that exists.

DESIGN VERSUS INFINITY: TWO RIVAL EXPLANATIONS FOR THE INTRICACY OF EXISTENCE

One fairly straightforward way of touching on the key issue here is as a struggle between *raw infinity* and *purpose*. For *infinity* as an explanatory principle is initially the marker of atheism—all the way back to Anaximander's *apeiron* but further developed in the thought of the atomists, of Democritus and the Epicureans: it is the *alternative* to design, to control, to mind as *Noûs*. As David Sedley summarizes, "The atomist universe is infinite, consisting of infinite void housing an infinite number of atoms. That in turn means that worlds must form not only where we are but elsewhere too: there could be no explanation of how in infinite space just one region, or even a merely finite plurality of regions, had been specially privileged in this regard. Not only, therefore, is there a plurality of worlds, but the same calculation yields the result that there be infinitely many of them."[6] The later Epicureans, Sedley tells us, inherited this Democritean idea of "the extraordinary power of infinity" and speak explicitly of it as the "*vis infinitatis*": it is found in what Epicurus called *isonomia*, "distributive equality."[7] Infinity is here singled out as a positive force, an actual reason for things being as they are.

And here is where the ancient battle begins: What explains the world we see around us? Why is there something rather than nothing? Where do these amazing things come from? What made them? How do things so desirable as those we desire and so beautifully put together come to be? The Anaxagorans, the Platonists, later the monotheists and the Stoics, and in his own way even Aristotle, say that it is due to it being *good* in some way; all but the last-named (and even he in a different sense) take this to mean that some *mind made them this way*. They were designed to be this way — they are the way they are because of *Noûs*. The atomists, on the other hand, strike what will become the distinctive atheist alternative: given infinite time and space, it would require something to *prevent* any particular configuration from appearing, *and from appearing infinitely many times*. What makes them is infinity itself, which is just a positive name for a negative: it is a way of naming the absence of limits, the failure of any limits, and the fact that nothing is there to provide a reason why anything should be any one way rather than another. Infinity is the same thing as formlessness, the impossibility of restriction to any finite shape or set of shapes or determinate definite characteristics. A godless universe is, in the absence of any reason making it otherwise, an infinite one; it is infinitely productive and infinitely diverse. Why this rather than something else? Because we are here and now rather than elsewhere and elsewhen.

In its simplest form, as we find it here, this is something like the "monkeys at a typewriter" idea — infinite monkeys typing randomly for eternity will eventually write every one of Shakespeare's plays. What should amaze us about these plays is not that they all were written, but that they are clustered so closely together in time and place — which is what required a mind, in this case the mind of Shakespeare. Why was that mind in that particular place and time? It was because by the same principle of randomness plus infinity, it was inevitable that such a mind had to occur somewhere. The ancient atomists used the image of grains of sands forming shapes on the windswept beach. The more unlikely or absurd this seems, the more one is underappreciating the real extent of infinity. The more one allows infinity to be infinite, the more its power is felt. The more distinctly one senses the infiniteness of infinity, the more secure one feels in the groundedness of any particular form in formlessness, of order in chaos. The sense of infinity and the sense of trust in infinity are directly proportional to one another. They appear together, and they grow together. To see one is to see the other. To look at an eyeball as inevitable is to see infinity in the eyeball; it is to see both infinity and eyeball, to see infinity as eyeball and eyeball as infinity. The less you assume about what may steer or limit or constrain existence, the bigger your sense of infinity becomes; the bigger your sense of infinity, the more intensely you experience it to be compressed into the very structure and being of each unlikely finite thing. This is a first glimpse of the atheist mystical sense.

The God party looks at the birds and animals and sees, at their source, a mind that wanted to make them and did so; perhaps it sees a mind that also has a love of them, care for them, surveillance of them, and appreciation of how well they do the job they were made to do (which might just be the job of knowing and loving and praising their maker). Some in this party even think that the very hairs on our heads are numbered (Matthew 10:30; Luke 12:7), as if the mind of God were a vast countinghouse where everything must be precisely accounted for. Above all, what we are seeing as we see the little sparrows innocently hopping around is the manifestation and fulfillment of a purpose, of intelligence: they were made to do a job of some sort. The atheist party, looking at these little life-forms, sees rather a concentrated concretion of *chance*, of *purposelessness*, of *nonintentionality*, of *infinity*, of *formlessness*. These very forms are infinity itself—the absence of God, of purpose, of any definiteness—walking and jumping and chirping. They are the antithesis of number; likewise, the hairs on our head are not numbered—they are the very presencing forth of numberlessness, of infinity. To look at an eyeball or a sparrow and think, "How unlikely! How redolent of the maker's hand! Because how else could so intricate a thing come to be?" is to foreclose attention to the vastness of time and space, blotting them out of consciousness, a closure to the infinity of openness that necessarily extends outward from any locus. To accomplish this foreclosure requires *work*: infinity is the default. Indeed, it arguably requires a straight-up *denial*, for it is by no means clear whether a conception of a totality that is less-than-infinity is even coherent, since every conception of a limit, insofar as it is a limit, also involves a conception of something beyond that limit. Concentrated effort and considerable ingenuity are required to come up with a conception of anything that would even *seem* to limit infinity—that is, that would make it feel unlikely that any particular thing could exist that would reduce the scope of infinite agentless creativity and instead attribute things to the specific direction of a mind. God is, we are tempted to say, a conspiracy against infinity.

Now it is true that God too is said to be "infinite." By now it may be hard to realize just how counterintuitive this would initially have been. For, *prima facie*, although we are used to hearing that God is infinite, the idea of God is directly in conflict with the idea of infinity. God is mind-as-cause, and mind here is construed not as awareness but as intelligence, as choice, as purpose, as preference for the Good: but preference is necessarily beholden to finitude. The essence of purpose and choice and preference is *the exclusion of the nonchosen, of the nonpreferred, of the nonfulfillment of the purpose*. God, intelligence as cause, is, from the first, the exaltation of finitude and exclusion over infinity and inclusiveness. And yet it is true that we find, in the opening shot of the theistic view of the world, in Anaxagoras's proposal of *Noûs* as the cause of all things, the assertion that *Noûs* itself is what is "unlimited" (*apeiron*), that is, "infinite." Yet it is also "unmixed" with anything else. Indeed, the notion of *Noûs* is precisely this seemingly impossible combination of "separation" with "unlimitedness." *Apeiron* originally means what is boundless and formless and undermines all determination; it is a threat to all form, and thus something dreaded as tantamount to destructive chaos. Anaximander's *apeiron* gave this very negative term a positive spin, conceiving it as precisely what was *common* to all diverse things, copresent in all of them and separate from none, and thus having no special nature of its own. With the older idea of *apeiron* in mind, Anaxagoras's linkage of limitlessness and separateness seems a brazen and palpable contradiction, right from the beginning. Raw infinity is either the disastrous indetermination of all separate and definite individual existences, or else it is not separate from anything—if it were, it would have to exclude that thing, and ipso facto would not be infinity. But somehow Anaxogoras attempts to find in the idea of intelligence, mind, or *Noûs* a daring combination of what have hitherto been *opposites*: infinity and separateness. How does he do so?

In Sedley's translation, Anaxagoras is reported to assert: "The other things share a portion of each, but intelligence [*Noûs*] is something *infinite and autonomous, and is mixed with no thing*, but it alone is by itself. For if it were not by itself, but were mixed with something else, it would share in all things, if it were mixed with any of them—for in each thing a portion of each is present, as I have said earlier—and the things mixed with it would prevent it from controlling any thing in such a way as it does in being alone by itself."[8]

This is as close to a smoking gun for the creation of the creator as we are likely to find. Already it is all there: mind is not awareness but intelligence, and this is the *controller* of all things, and it is for this reason that it must be *separate* from them, *beyond them* in some sense. Mind must be separate because mind must stand above all things, so as to be their controller rather than being controlled by them.

But why is this controlling intelligence then "infinite"? How, indeed, can it be intelligent (and hence exclusive of the unintelligent) and unmixed (and hence apart from and nonpresent in things) and yet be unlimited or infinite? Sedley's interpretation suggests that this notion of infinity is in fact an idiosyncratic way of talking about precisely about this unmixedness, this transcendence itself. He explains Anaxagoras's idea as follows:

> The stuffs that our bodies are made of either are (on my preferred interpretation), or at least include, pairs of opposite properties like hot and cold, wet and dry. For intelligence to be 'mixed' with these would be for it itself to have a certain temperature, a certain degree of moistness, etc.

And that would make intelligence subject to physical change, so that it could be acted upon *by* matter, being for example heated and dried in summer, cooled and dampened in winter, when the reality is that it itself controls matter. To say that intelligence is unmixed is thus Anaxagoras' way of saying that, despite being present in living things, it is in itself neither hot nor cold, neither wet nor dry, and so on for all the pairs of perceptible opposites. In short, to call intelligence unmixed is his way of saying that it is free of physical properties.[9]

Intelligence is "unlimited" in the same way: it cannot be limited to either hot or cold, because it must be unrestricted to either *so as to be able to control them.* Already, it seems, only two possible relationships are imaginable between mind and nonmind, between conscious self and world, and between intentional mind and unintentional body: "controlling" and "being controlled." Relinquishing control means being controlled. Hence, mind must be unmixed with anything else, must stand completely above anything it relates to, must always remain in control. *Unmixed* and *infinite* here mean the same thing: to be unrestricted to any finite thing so as to stand above it and be unaffected by it, so as to be instead the *arranger and controller* of it, as is required by the notion of *Noûs* not as awareness but specifically as *intelligence*—which is to say, precisely as choice maker, as purpose monger, as excluder. Here it is linked, not to uncontrollable chaos, but rather precisely to control and definite outcomes. What can be both unlimited to any form but, far from undermining all form like the chaos of the limitless *apeiron* as initially conceived, serve rather as the producer of forms? Anaxagoras has come up with a candidate for one particular way to join these antithetical ideas: *mind as purposive.* But there are other options, other roads not taken.

This is the key point. For it is indeed possible to think of mind as infinite in a way that may feel superficially similar (see part II and online appendix B of this book for some examples) if we do not keep our eye on the main issue of *purpose* and *exclusion.* But "God" is infinite mind precisely as infinite purpose and infinite personality: unequivocally present throughout all time (fully occupying every moment of time forever) but only equivocally present in all of space and all of being (present in the world but also nonidentical with physical beings in space—transcending the world and wholly untouched by physical things, wholly other to them all even if "in" them). Infinity proper is, rather, unity in the sense of inseparability, where there is always more than whatever is so far imagined, but whatever more there is must necessarily also be included—a relation of inclusion of its necessary otherness, and to every particular otherness without exception. God is infinite in the form of projection into the future forever—in continuity of means and ends, of Will and purpose, of accountability and control. This temporal infinity is a kind of oneness, a binding together of moments, but in the special form in which this is done by a conscious accountable controller: the mode of accountability and control, of joining purposes to instruments. It is nonnecessary infinity, the infinity of *freedom* in precisely the sense Spinoza will deny: God is an infinite mind in control of the world, which his infinity makes necessarily finite. The world is literally required to be finite by the conception of God and to be put into a state of subordination to purpose, now made into *infinite purpose*—an *infinite personality*, which, prima facie, would have been a contradiction in terms.

There *is* however a kind of *real* infinity that pertains to mind as such, but not to mind with an external purpose—not personal mind, not controlling purposive intelligence, not *Noûs*. As we'll see, this is what we find in Spinoza's new nonteleological version of universal mindedness, the mind of the cosmos, the mind of Spinoza's anti-God "God," the Attribute of Thought of which Intellect or Will (which are, for Spinoza, one and the same thing) is merely one among many modes. This includes much more than Intellect and Will—it is something that must be present as much in any putative absence of it as in its obvious presence, whose limitation is impossible because every putative limitation of it further instantiates it, and therefore it is something to which genuine infinity pertains. In online appendix B there are other actual examples (e.g., the nonpersonal and purposeless universal mind in some Buddhist "mind-only" doctrines, and the "Mind of Heaven and Earth" in Confucianism) that will allow us to see what is at stake here and what possibilities appear with an idea of infinite mind conceived in an entirely different mode from this universal *purposeful* and *controlling* mind derived from *Noûs*—what is otherwise known as "God."

INTELLIGIBLE GOOD/S VERSUS INFINITE W/HOLE/S IN PLATO'S *SYMPOSIUM*

Two models of existence are beginning to emerge here.

The first starts from a raw infinity, endless and unstoppable, inclusive of every possible transformation and state, which produces an infinite variety of unplanned finite entities, not because of some special drive to produce but simply because infinity, qua infinity, cannot be restricted to any particular finite (i.e., definite) form or any finite set of forms. It produces because there is nothing to stop it and because a stable nonproducing entity, with a fixed, limited set of definite characteristics—even the characteristic of definitely excluding characteristics—would be more finite, more limited, more in need of some constraining counterforce, harder to achieve, and thus less likely than the contrary. These finite entities can be anything at all precisely because they are unplanned, random, and not forced to adhere to a rule or blueprint or ideal form. Among these entities, and always embedded in a surrounding muchness that surpasses them, are those that are susceptible to need and desire, producing local purposes by placing value on what they lack and need and desire to augment or complete themselves and rooted in the power of the purposeless infinity that exceeds them.

The second model starts from an intelligence that is definitionally purposive. As such, it posits some form or other of putative goodness, which it either literally or figuratively is or embodies or seeks or produces. It then plans or creates or arranges or designs or grounds or motivates the coordination of all things toward this goodness. These things are thus themselves rooted in purpose, the productions of purpose, saturated by purpose, and thus in all their activities moved to desire this Good in some form or other and striving to attain the ideal to the exclusion of the nonideal.

There are, of course, significant differences in the various embodiments of this second model (as of the first), but for our purposes here, we will try to get to certain key entailments of both by considering all these mutations as belonging to the category of monotheist thinking, broadly construed, whether a literal creator is invoked or not. Our wager is that these various stances are diverse attempts to follow through on the same intuition, namely, the creationist intuition celebrated by Socrates in the *Phaedo* passage cited earlier: the entailments of Anaxagoras's *Noûs* as *Arché*. The diverse views of Anaxogoras, Socrates in the *Phaedo*, the demiurge theory of the *Timaeus*, the ultimate creative power of the Form of the Good in the *Republic*, Aristotle's creator-less immanent hylomorphism, and later all the *creation ex nihilo* doctrines of all the Abrahamic monotheisms are variations on the same theme: *the ultimacy of purposivity*. This is why I make bold to lump them together under the umbrella of a broadly construed "monotheism," for my concern here is to establish that it is *this* idea that is really distinctive to the Greco-European-Abrahamic traditions when compared to the speculative and metaphysical traditions of China and to some extent to India as well—this mainstream European tradition of monotheism (i.e., the granting of ultimacy to purposivity) is exactly what the mainstreams of these other traditions do not embrace. At the same time, I hope to show that the nonmainstream traditions in Europe group most intelligibly in their opposition to what is shared by those "monotheist" views, the opposition to the ultimate ontological status of purposivity—for which reason I designate them as "atheist," whether they allow for the existence of polytheist gods or not.

The entailments of these two opposed models are laid out in stark contrast already at almost the very beginning of Greek philosophy. For *both* models can be found keenly expressed in Plato's *Symposium*; in a certain way, that masterpiece has claim to being the *locus classicus* of both the atheist model and the theist model. The two models, again, are as follows:

1. The atheist model, whereby any ideas (plural) of goodness that may arise derive from desires, desires (plural) derive from determinate beings, and determinate beings (plural) derive from indeterminate being, chance, and infinity. Desire here will be found to be a drive toward greater *inclusion*.
2. The theistic model, where determinate Being derives from a single eternal Goodness, and desire *also* exists because of Goodness (aiming directly or indirectly toward the one Goodness). Desire here will be found to be a drive toward greater *exclusion*.

Model (1) is given beautiful expression in the wedding-vow-quotable passage spoken by Aristophanes on the nature of love. Aristophanes tells the famous story of a jealous Zeus dividing the original eight-limbed, two-headed humans in half. We still have a god at work here rather than aimless infinity, but what is key is that the intentions of this god have nothing to do with what we finite beings want or should want. Among the things there happen to be is this extremely powerful deity and among the things that happen to happen are his desires and actions, which implies nothing about what is ultimately good or true or real. Love experienced by finite beings is here described as the seeking of a lost wholeness, the quest for our other half. But this means that what is desirable to us is entirely dependent on *what we happen to be*. We are like broken tallies seeking what we now find ourselves lacking. All desire is fundamentally the desire to unite with more, indeed to become more, but also for what we now recognize as ourselves to become less of what we can turn out to become. This is done, not by incorporating or appropriating the other into the self, but by uniting with what is missing from the fragmentary being that one is, being driven by a vaguely expansive sense of the more comprehensive being that one perhaps once was and perhaps could again be, a larger unity of which one is presently a leftover shard. To include more in one's totality here means to become less of that totality, to be digested by the world as much as to digest it. On this model, by including something presently excluded, one is also included in something from which one was excluded. But this desire for a union with what exceeds us is directed not toward a one-size-fits-all, universal totality, but rather mapped along the broken edges of our own fragmentary being.

We become more complete by uniting with what happens to fit the contours of our specific lack—our specific wounds.

In this initial form, as presented by Plato's Aristophanes, this is a longing especially for a specific completeness that has now been lost, a particular past wholeness. Since this is thought of as some specific finite whole, this desire will have a specific end, after the attainment of which it will be satisfied once and for all. As such, the idea can easily be assimilated into the paradigm of final causes and definite purposes (and in the original version, there is, further, a male-is-better homoerotic premise). But this does not derive from the etiology of love per se as presented here. The driving force of desire is rather the quest for a kind of union with what is presently not ourselves, in such a way as to maximize inclusiveness, both to include more and to be included in more, to eat and be eaten, such that the eating is as much the preservation as the destruction of both eater and eaten. The specificity of the desired object is just a by-product of this more primal desire, which is variable as beings and wounds are variable; its value lies entirely in its relation to ourselves—it has no *intrinsic* value. There is no possibility of an objective scale of better or worse among the specific desired finite objects as such even in this initial version; what gives them value is their relation to the desirer. But to further abstract the nature of value from this model, another possibility inevitably emerges: if there is to be any objective standard of value at all, it can only be indexed to degrees of mutual inclusiveness. Spinoza, for example, will view the drive to completeness as completeness (*perfectus*) as the real essence of desire: an increase in the ability to move and think, to affected and be affected, to include more thoughts and more activities in one's repertoire, is all we really want when we want anything. As we will see in what follows, this introduces a rogue element into the dominance of purposivity itself, which can ultimately overturn it. For such a drive would have no specific stopping point in the attainment of any finite end; there will always be more to include and be included by. Following this logic to its ultimate conclusion, even "more inclusiveness" cannot be the definite goal, to exactly the extent that this implies any kind of finitude or limit, any definite content, any inclusion of anything to the exclusion of anything else, or in other words, to the extent that "inclusiveness" is thought of as anything *definite* at all—to the extent that "inclusion" is inclusion *instead of* exclusion.[10]

The atheist vicissitudes of the Aristophanes position can thus be summarized as follows:

1. Love is a rebellion against the limits set by the jealousy of the gods. It is a Promethean project.

2. Again, à la Spinoza, we do not desire the Good, but rather we call good whatever we desire, and what we desire is determined simply by what we happen to be. Deep relativism adheres to this vision.

3. Greater unity without any one-way subsumption, the overstepping of boundaries, is the only intrinsic value in a valueless universe. This will alight on specific values insofar as we are finite and are seeking to unite with something that will decrease the exclusion of something more from ourselves, and ourselves from something more. To desire is to desire more bilateral inclusion, more permeable boundaries: to come to be included in more being and doing and come to include more in one's doing and being. But there was nothing intrinsically valuable about that lost piece except its contribution in overcoming our specific case of limitation. This is the sole principle of attributing value, and when extended to its logical conclusion, it entails a deep inclusiveness. The best is the most complete, setting up the possibility that even whatever seems initially negative and undesirable must be desired and included. Monism and nondualism pertain to this vision. Desire is the quest for *nonexternality*—inclusion in all directions.

Socrates, like Plato, like Aristotle, insists on the opposite: we desire what we desire *because it is good*, not the other way around. Socrates has Diotima explicitly reject the Aristophanes theory: "And there is a story that people in love are those who are seeking for their other half, but my story tells that love is not for a half, nor indeed for the whole, unless that happens to be something good, my friend; since men are willing to cut off their own hands and feet, if their own seem to them to be nasty.[11] For really, I think, no one is pleased with his own thing, except one who calls the good thing his own and his property, and the bad thing another's; since there is nothing that men love but the good."[12] Socrates insists that love is a hybrid of poverty and plenty; it is in a state of lack and desires the Good, which expresses itself in watered-down or distorted ways when we love beautiful bodies or material goods. But in all cases, the desire for what is really and universally good—good independently of any relations—is the sole reason why anyone really desires anything.

Let us summarize the theistic implications:

1. There is no rebellion against the intention of the gods, rather a striving to obey and resemble them as much as possible.

2. There is such a thing as absolute intrinsic Goodness, and it is the cause of our desiring certain things. We desire the Good because it is good, rather than calling it good because we desire it. Apparent differences in values are

explained as degrees of expression of the one true value that pertains to all things, which is reflected in some places more than others but in all places to at least some minimal degree. Absolutism concerning values pertains to this vision.

3. Each thing in the world thus has two aspects: the part that reflects the absolute value and something else that to some degree obstructs or excludes or is excluded from it. Dualism pertains to this vision: all things have one aspect that is good (later the Form, the *telos*, etc.) and another aspect that is contravening or obstructing or failing that goodness. The Good that is already present is to be extracted from the dross that is presently joined to it, which is impeding its undistorted manifestation. Desire is, in essence, a quest to divide out the Good part of what one is already enjoying from the bad part so as to isolate the truly desired. Desire is the quest to *exclude*.

The result of this model is a description of human conation that brings to the fore a poignant ambivalence, for it both affirms and negates the object of desire. On initially encountering this idea, the natural consequence might seem to be the message, "Go ahead and desire, and enjoy what you desire! After all, it's really a way in which you desire and enjoy the true Good!" But the structural separation entailed in the idea of a controlling exclusive oneness precludes this understanding: that would be idolatry—it would be worshipping and loving and enjoying the Good or, later, God, "in the wrong form," the wrong time and place. Rather than worshipping these finite things as expressions of God, they are seen as rivals and exclusions of God, which must be abandoned or destroyed. This applies to all finite goods: the real divinity is elsewhere, having been mistakenly recognized in these idols. The multiple partial expressions *obstruct* rather than genuinely *expressing* the one true Good. So it may well be that the beautiful boys admired by Socrates are vehicles of the beauty of the Good, but they serve only as transitional objects to be quickly and decisively abandoned once one sees the real Good, as Socrates shows with his own abstinence when confronted by the beauty of Alcibiades.

Taken to its logical conclusion, it says, "The only thing that is *real* in this thing you desire is the Form, not the matter: that is all that is really there to be desired, so that is what you really desire. But this form is really just a foggy approximation of something even more definite and determinate (which also means something even more *exclusive*): whether called God, or the Form of Forms, or pure activity, something with no passivity and no obstructing matter, and thus no evil. You desire the pure goodness itself, the real Good in what you are considering good. So drop the container and seek goodness per se, namely, God, for that was the only goodness that was there in the first place, the only being, the only determinacy." What seems like an affirmation of all the possible ends up being a usurpation of absolutely everything desirable into God, which absorbs all goodness and thereby negates all alternate forms: in other words, the negation and condemnation of all finite goods.

The real affirmation of all finite ends is to be found instead in the further development of the alternate, Aristophanean model. To be sure, in its original form, desire here seeks only a specific finite completeness, excluding all else. It may seem absurd to claim that this exemplar of extreme choosiness and exclusivity could hold the key to the all-inclusive embrace of atheist mysticism—one may object that this is just the usual business of regarding something as nonnegotiably desirable, a perfect example of the usual idea of an unexchangeable good essence that is desirable, and doing so in the most obsessively narrow way possible. But we view this exclusivity wrongly if we think of it in terms of our everyday concept of teleology—a concept that has been shaped by the long dominance of the model of the Good inherited from Plato's Socrates. The total victory of this model has habituated us to see everything through its lens, to the point where it becomes hard to recognize any other understanding of the structure of desire. But because for Anaxagoras's fragmentary lovers, desire is ultimately motivated by nonexclusion per se, this model, in spite of the manifestly unbudgeable specificity of its love choice, actually sets the stage for an embrace of and by the whole and whatever is beyond any whole: Spinoza's vision of all-inclusiveness of omnipresent infinity. For if desire is rooted in this impulse to include and be included, what is really wanted is not attained completeness but the feeling of becoming *more* complete, and for any finite being—meaning any determinate being, any actual being—there will always be more, infinitely more, that it has not yet embraced. Here we might hear the objection that this is the futility of an infinite regress, such as we will soon see pertaining to purposivity—but this is just the misapprehension that we wish to overturn here: they are not the same. For here we have an infinite expansion that differs from what is set in motion by the structure of purposivity: with every new completion, what is surpassed is not replaced and left behind, much less shunned as an idolatrous lure away from the true Good. On the contrary, as this desire-as-inclusion seeks further objects, unlike with desire-as-seeking-the-Good, those lowly things are retained but also supplemented by the expanding totality of united elements that is loved in turn, thus both embraced by and embracing them.

We begin to see that what every species of the monotheist impulse has in common is a notion of ultimate *unity* that is, seemingly paradoxically, *exclusive*, and that we can trace all the way back to the exclusivity of *Noûs*—

its unmixedness—in Anaxagoras. Mind as *Noûs* also must be separate from all things, must exclude them, in order to control them. This is the model that comes to the fore in Plato, not only with the literal-minded intelligent design of the *Timaeus* and the creator-less mystical participation theory of the Form of the Good as the source of the essence of all Forms, and thereby of all reality, in the *Republic's* Parables of the Sun and the Divided Line. Such are the first groping attempts to realize the promise of Anaxagoras's proposal of *Noûs* as *Arché*, the commitment that posits the ultimacy of purpose, the causative power of the Good, and with it the idea of desire as a drive to filter, to exclude, which are now being put before us as the ultimate source and the ultimate meaning of all that exists.

In due time, to be sure, this conception of *Noûs* is refined to the point of transcending the cruder aspects of personality and finite intelligences, and thus coming to be construed not as intelligence undergoing real-time conscious thinking like a finite intelligence, but simply as intelligence per se, or even as *the intelligible* per se, which is engaged in a kind of timeless divine self-contemplation; it is the locus and actuality of the Eternal Forms, the eternal thoughts of God. As such, it no longer performs acts of judgment in time, no longer plans or foresees, no longer designs and calculates. We can see this happening in Aristotle's "demythologized" version of the causative power of the Good, which dispenses both with the creator and with the ontological independence of the transcendent Forms. But the key entailments of this orientation are not changed by this alteration. It is true that Aristotle seems already to perceive serious problems in positing intelligence and purpose in their usual sense as pertaining to the first cause, though he is unable to resist its attractions. This can be seen as motivating his attempt to rethink divine *Noûs* away from both creation and design, and also to distance this intelligence from the step-by-step process of thinking, calculating through premises to conclusions or working through means to subsequently reach ends, instead conceiving its activity as closer to the ethical ideal of *theoria*, a kind of contemplation that has no goal beyond the act of contemplating itself. But Aristotle's unmoving divine self-contemplation is still infected with the basic structure of teleological exclusivity that defines *Noûs* through the pursuit of "what is best" to the exclusion of what is less good. It is just that what is best turns out to be *Noûs* itself. We end up with thinking-thinking-thinking (*noêsis noêseôs noesis*): seeking the best itself turns out to be the best that is sought in seeking the best. It seems that Aristotle is able to conceive something exempt from the structure of subject-confronting-object implicit in all teleology only by making "the best" not free of any goal but its own goal, and therefore shot through as before with the structure of exclusive purposivity even in contemplation—*autotelic* as opposed to, say, atelic or, as with our greatest atheist mystics, *omnitelic*. Far from an escape from seeking one thing at the expense of all others, he has made "seeking one thing at the expense of all others" the one thing all things seek—at the expense of all others.

In the fully developed version of this model, Being and Goodness and Form and Determinateness are all conflated, such that Form is what alone can be said to exist and matter, as pure potentiality, has no determinate existence per se. Matter, then, cannot be "something else" that gets in the way of the expression of Form: it does not exist in its own right. Instead, it is simply the concretization of the obstruction itself, the nothingness that gets in the way of the Being and Goodness. In chapter 4, we'll delve into a further move in this direction in Plotinus, and some derivative of this can be found in many of the more sophisticated monotheistic theologies.[13] This may seem to be another step away from the crude notion of a mind, a personality, a consciousness seeking some object or goal, a teleology seeking a good outside itself. But it still puts determinateness rather than indetermination, form rather than formlessness, and definiteness rather than indefiniteness at the root of the world and at the pinnacle of all values. And as we will see, this still means exclusion, separation, prioritization of division and duality, and with it a single-ordered cosmos run on a dispositive definite teleology; even if *Noûs* itself is now regarded as autotelic, thus in some sense seeming to lift free of the subordination to the normal conception of teleology as the pursuit of something outside itself, its very nature as *Noûs* ensures that it all the more imposes a single nonnegotiable teleology on *everything else*. For with this move it entrenches the rule of monolithic purposivity over all *other* things in the world all the more inescapably. But in spite of this valiant attempt, the basic *Noûs* as *Arché* premise remains unchanged and Aristotle's attempted intervention turns out to be another in the long list of backfiring attempts to fix the bugs in the God idea.[14] The immanent monolithic teleological forms no less than the eternal transcendent Ideas of Plato are already intrinsically *normative*, and when *Noûs* is made into the closest approximation and first emanation of the oneness beyond being, even the unknowable, formless oneness of Plotinus becomes normative— that is, is taken to mean an *exclusive* oneness—as well. But this makes all the difference, as we will try to make clear in due time, in what follows.

THE HYPERTROPHY OF PURPOSIVE
CONSCIOUSNESS: ANIMISM GONE WILD

So what has happened here? This Platonic adoption of the Anaxogrean impulse to identify *intention* as the origin of whatever happens is perhaps not surprising: it is the near-universal human belief in *animism*, but now writ large, unified, radicalized, and spruced up with Socratic irony and dialectic. This animistic belief is an outgrowth of what evolutionary psychology these days calls Theory of Mind, the default attribution of intention to natural events, which once had obvious survival advantages: on hearing a rustling in the grass, it's better to assume the worst-case scenario of a lurking tiger rather than a meaningless gust of wind, just in case. When universalized, this is the belief that whatever happens does so because there is some spirit that *does* it: events require an *agent*, a *doer*. This is a kind of projection from a particular way of experiencing our own experience, our own agency. I desire to raise my hand, and my hand rises. Mind makes things happen. And why did I desire to raise my hand? To attain my purpose. Nietzsche's generalization about the mentality underlying the prehistorical relation to gods and spirits still seems plausible today:

> People in those times do not yet know anything of nature's laws; neither for the earth nor for the heavens is there a "must": a season, the sunshine, the rain can come, or also fail to appear. There is no concept whatsoever of *natural* causality. When one rows, it is not the rowing that moves the ship; rather rowing is simply a magical ceremony by which one compels a demon to move it. All illnesses, death itself, are the result of magical influences. There is never anything natural about becoming ill or dying; the whole idea of "natural development" is lacking (it first begins to dawn on the older Greeks, that is, in a very late phase of mankind, with the conception of a *moira* which reigned over the gods). When someone shoots with bow and arrow, an irrational hand and strength is always at work; if springs suddenly dry up, one thinks first of subterranean demons and their mischief; it has to be the arrow of a god whose invisible influence causes a man to drop suddenly. In India (according to Lubbock), a carpenter makes sacrifices to his hammer, his axe, and his other tools; in the same way does a Brahman handle the pencil with which he writes, a soldier his weapons of battle, a mason his trowel, a worker his plow. In the mind of religious men, all nature is the sum of actions of conscious and intentioned beings, an enormous complex of *arbitrary acts*.[15]

Nietzsche suggests that the project then becomes to somehow compel these conscious willing beings who control all nonhuman events—these spirits, each of which has purposes of its own—to cooperate with human purposes, to form some sort of livable alliance, through supplication, submission, prayers, offerings, ritual hosting, and relationships of affiliation and kinship. Ultimate causality for all events is sought in the *personal*: that is, in purpose-driven intentions, in the acts of *purposeful control* exercised by conscious beings.

Spinoza's account, in the famous appendix of part 1 of the *Ethics*, is even more caustic:

Now all the prejudices which I intend to mention here turn on this one point, the widespread belief among men that all things in Nature are like themselves in acting with an end in view. Indeed, they hold it as certain that God himself directs everything to a fixed end; for they say that God has made everything for man's sake and has made man so that he should worship God. So this is the first point I shall consider, seeking the reason why most people are victims of this prejudice and why all are so naturally disposed to accept it. Secondly, I shall demonstrate its falsity; and lastly I shall show how it has been the source of misconceptions about good and bad, right and wrong, praise and blame, order and confusion, beauty and ugliness, and the like. However, it is not appropriate here to demonstrate the origin of these misconceptions from the nature of the human mind. It will suffice at this point if I take as my basis what must be universally admitted, that all men are born ignorant of the causes of things, that they all have a desire to seek their own advantage, a desire of which they are conscious. From this it follows, firstly, that men believe that they are free, precisely because they are conscious of their volitions and desires; yet concerning the causes that have determined them to desire and will they do not think, not even dream about, because they are ignorant of them. Secondly, men act always with an end in view, to wit, the advantage that they seek. Hence it happens that they are always looking only for the final causes of things done, and are satisfied when they find them, having, of course, no reason for further doubt. But if they fail to discover them from some external source, they have no recourse but to turn to themselves, and to reflect on what ends would normally determine them to similar actions, and so they necessarily judge other minds by their own. Further, since they find within themselves and outside themselves a considerable number of means very convenient for the pursuit of their own advantage—as, for instance, eyes for seeing, teeth for chewing, cereals and living creatures for food, the sun for giving light, the sea for breeding fish—the result is that they look on all the things of Nature as means to their own advantage. And realizing that these were found, not produced by them, they come to believe that there is someone else who produced these means for their use. For looking on things as means, they could not believe them to be self-created, but on the analogy of the means which they are accustomed to produce for themselves, they were bound to con-

clude that there was some governor or governors of Nature, endowed
with human freedom, who have attended to all their needs and made
everything for their use. And having no information on the subject, they
also had to estimate the character of these rulers by their own, and so
they asserted that the gods direct everything for man's use so that they
may bind men to them and be held in the highest honor by them. So it
came about that every individual devised different methods of worshipping God as he thought fit in order that God should love him beyond
others and direct the whole of Nature so as to serve his blind cupidity
and insatiable greed. Thus it was that this misconception developed into
superstition and became deep-rooted in the minds of men, and it was for
this reason that every man strove most earnestly to understand and to
explain the final causes of all things. But in seeking to show that Nature
does nothing in vain—that is, nothing that is not to man's advantage—
they seem to have shown only this, that Nature and the gods are as crazy
as mankind.[16]

What is lampooned here is not merely the empirically unjustifiable
practice of attributing purposive consciousness to all natural causality. The
problem is not just the extension of conscious agency to all causality; the
problem, as both Spinoza and Nietzsche address elsewhere in their works,
is also the very notion of what conscious agency *is*—not just in the world,
but in ourselves. What is assumed here is a certain relationship between
consciousness and unconsciousness, a certain way of valuing them relative
to one another, and a certain way in which consciousness experiences itself
in terms of *control or failure to control*. The consciousnesses that are believed
to rule every natural phenomenon do so through a kind of ends-means purposiveness that we extrapolate from certain types of conscious experiences
of our own: the experience of deliberate voluntary control. By the same
analogy to ourselves (or rather, to a *certain part or aspect of ourselves*), we
regard them as beings with whom we can have a relationship of some personal kind (political or ritual or commercial or affiliative), whereby we can
to some extent bring their controlling deeds into the sphere of our own
influence—our interpersonal network of social controls.

This was a theme that exercised Nietzsche quite fundamentally throughout his writings, starting with his very first published book, *The Birth of
Tragedy*. There, as in *Twilight of the Idols*, from the other end of Nietzsche's
writing career, the figure of Socrates is singled out as the representative of
a profoundly new phenomenon: the idea that *all action had to be guided by
clear consciousness, directed by reason, explicitly willed*. Prior to that time,
Nietzsche thinks, *instinct* was the best guide of action, and was trusted as

such—a characteristic he thinks of as typical of everything he likes and esteems: health, nobility, joy. It is a sign of physiological and spiritual disintegration, of a kind of crisis, when the extreme measure of needing consciousness to intervene in every single action is suddenly required to avert random chaotic disaster. This "absurd overestimation" of reason, of consciousness, is an emergency measure. For consciousness itself, on Nietzsche's view, is never what is really in charge of what happens, but is rather in its essence a late and secondary addition to a preexisting function. As Nietzsche puts it in a posthumously published note written in 1888, his last year of lucidity:

> *The part "consciousness" plays*—It is essential that one should not mistake the part that "consciousness plays: it is our *relation to the outer world; it was the outer world that developed it*. On the other hand, the *direction*— that is to say, the care and cautiousness which is concerned with the inter-relation of the bodily functions, does *not* enter into our consciousness any more than does the *storing activity* of the intellect: that there is a superior controlling force at work in these things cannot be doubted—a sort of directing committee, in which the various *leading desires* make their votes and their power felt. "Pleasure" and "pain" are indications which reach us from this sphere: as are also *acts of will* and ideas.
>
> *In short*: That which becomes conscious has causal relations which are completely and absolutely concealed from our knowledge—the sequence of thoughts, feelings, and ideas, in consciousness, does not signify that the order in which they come is a causal order: it is *so apparently*, however, in the highest degree. We have *based* the whole notion of *intellect, reasons, logic*, etc., upon this *apparent truth* (all these things do not exist: they are imaginary syntheses and entities), and we then projected the latter into and *behind* all things!
>
> As a rule *consciousness* itself is understood to be the general sensorium and highest ruling centre; albeit, it is only a *means of communication*: it was developed by intercourse, and with a view to the interests of intercourse. . . . "Intercourse" is understood, here, as "relation," and is intended to cover the action of the outer world *upon* us and our necessary response to it, as also our actual influence upon the outer world. It is not the conducting force, but an *organ of the latter*.[17]

Consciousness itself is for Nietzsche what it was for Schopenhauer: a secondary phenomenon, a kind of tool in the hands of the Will, which is created by the blind Will to serve its own ends and constantly manipulated by it. Schopenhauer looked on consciousness, like the brain of which it is the activity, as "a mere fruit, a product, in a fact a parasite, of the rest of the organism, in so far as it is not directly geared to the organism's inner working, but serves the purpose of self-preservation by regulating its relations with the external world."[18] This parasitic brain is what "controls the relations with the external world; this alone is its office, and in this way it discharges its debt to the organism that nourishes it, since the latter's existence is conditioned by the external relations."[19] Consciousness is thus, in effect, the public relations office or foreign ministry of the Will: it deals with external phenomena, with transborder negotiations with the outside world, with exchanges of diplomatic gifts and gestures, but has nothing to do with determining policy, and indeed has little to no information on the domestic situation (what is really going on in the workings of the preconscious Will, inside the body that is nothing but the Will's objectification). Nietzsche further develops this hypothesis to suggest that consciousness develops only under the pressure of a need to communicate, in tandem with language, and in particular the need to cooperate, and for command and obedience, for herd and hierarchy, for dumbing down and coarsening our actual experiences away from their individual subtleties into the lowest common denominator, into exchangeable tokens, which embody the exigencies of the individual person's vulnerability and need of protection from the herd, and their subordination to the needs of the herd project.[20] Nietzsche does think, to be sure, that there is a kind of unconscious "thinking" going on in all animals, and also in man, which is automatic and unconscious (just as Schopenhauer remains beholden to the idea of the sole efficacy of teleological willing, albeit of a conflicted and unconscious kind). But by this he means the work of the constant adjustments and engagements of each instance of Will to Power itself as it fares through the world; not a globally planned and executed preconceived vision directed by a conscious executive function, but a constant process of adaptation and revision and reorienting, a tentative opportunistic rhythm of attentiveness and refocusing and reforgetting. It is the reification, metastasis, and absolutization of this process into the foundation and ultimate end of all activity, rather than one among the many means it sometimes employs, that becomes the fiction of a conscious mind directing the body, or of a conscious God directing the world. And on this view, it is only the stupidest and shallowest and most craven part of this thinking that ever becomes conscious. The role of consciousness is as servant, not master; its function is basically to wait for word from the black box of the home office, find out what has been decided on or what has already been done, and then try to smooth it over with any hostile outside forces by coming up with some rationalizing propaganda. It directs nothing but only pretends it directs, like a puppet who, after each jerk on the string, comes up with an ex post facto explanation for why it jumped or slumped in each particular case, randomly concocting a narrative to make sense of what it has, in any case, already done for reasons completely unknown to itself.

It is not consciousness itself that is objected to here, but the overestimation of consciousness, the erroneous *primacy* attributed to it. It is the *ultimacy* of intentional consciousness, treating it as the ultimate basis of whatever happens, which is not caused or supported by anything else. Consciousness is always surrounded by—preceded by, succeeded by, supported by—something other than consciousness, which consciousness *serves*. It is not an end, but a means. Indeed, Nietzsche thinks it can be a very fine tool indeed, if developed as a tool. But this is made impossible precisely by regarding it, in terms of teleology, not as means but as an end, and in terms of causality, not as effect but as cause. As Nietzsche says:

> We have believed in the will as cause to such an extent that we have from our personal experience introduced a cause into events in general (i.e., intention as cause of events—).
>
> We believe that thoughts as they succeed one another in our minds stand in some kind of causal relation: the logician especially, who actually speaks of nothing but instances which never occur in reality, has grown accustomed to the prejudice that thoughts cause thoughts—.
>
> We believe—and even our philosophers still believe—that pleasure and pain are causes of reactions, that the purpose of pleasure and pain is to occasion reactions. For millennia, pleasure and the avoidance of displeasure have been flatly asserted as the motives for every action. Upon reflection, however, we should concede that everything would have taken the same course, according to exactly the same sequence of causes and effects, if these states of "pleasure and displeasure" had been absent, and that one is simply deceiving oneself if one thinks they cause anything at all: they are epiphenomena with a quite different object than to evoke reactions; they are themselves effects within the instituted process of reaction.
>
> In summa: everything of which we become conscious is a terminal phenomenon, an end—and causes nothing; every successive phenomenon in consciousness is completely atomistic—And we have sought to understand the world through the reverse conception—as if nothing were real and effective but thinking, feeling, willing!—[21]

Consciousness is anything but a cause, anything but an origin, anything but a unity. This is why Nietzsche will remark, in *The Anti-Christ*, that the

New Testament's proposition that "God is a Spirit" (i.e., Geist, or mind) is the "low-point" in the development of the conception of God: it makes a unified consciousness the origin, in a universe where origins are always unconscious and always multiple—even the origins of consciousness itself.[22]

But this does not mean consciousness is a superfluous or useless epiphenomenon. It has an adaptive function of communication and of *incorporating* new knowledge and new habits: specific conscious purposes are temporary, self-surpassing expedients of the unconscious, instinctive Will to Power of the organism. This Will to Power, as we will see in more detail in part II of this book, must absolutely not be confused with an intentional controller pursuing a definite purpose. Rather, it is a prime exemplar of what I have identified as the key atheist motif: the idea that the conception of "the Good" is a temporary function of desire, which is itself the function of a purposeless endowment of being, rather than the cause of desire. The unconscious Will to Power has no fixed intention, nothing analogous to a conscious purpose. Rather, it posits every specific conscious purpose only as a temporary expedient—as a way to get beyond it, to no longer need it. The primal error is the transposition of purposivity as experienced in intentional consciousness (control directed toward achieving a specific preenvisaged goal, action motivated by something regarded as valuable independent of the act of valuing it, or some kind of "goodness" per se) to the kind of shifting adaptive directionality of this unconscious "Will"—which, as Nietzsche reminds us, is neither something effective nor an ability; it is, in fact, no one specific thing, "a unity only as a word,"[23] or to put it more bluntly, "just a word."[24] Consciousness is, on this view, a means of incorporating new knowledge from the outside world, perhaps adaptations to changes that are too demanding and rapid for our instincts to respond to without this emergency intervention.[25] Consciousness is a temporary detour to get to *forgetting*—that is, to reaching a position where one no longer needs to micromanage, where direction and control are no longer needed and new things can become instinctive. This is the ideal shared by atheist mystics of both the Confucian type and the Buddhist type, who advocate the deliberate use of discipline, conscious control, dualistic consciousness, and so on as a means to get beyond itself: to get to the state of "following the heart's desires and yet never missing the mark" (as Confucius says of himself at age seventy in *Analects* 2:4),[26] or of abandoning the raft and reaching the other shore where such dichotomies and conscious direction are no longer needed, as most Buddhist schools advocate. In both cases, there is a bounteous role for consciousness and control, but it is decidedly nonultimate, being subordinated causally to the nonconscious desires and sufferings and aspirations that precede and motivate it and aspirationally to the attained state of effortlessness that succeeds it. We will see that there have also existed even more radical types of atheist mysticism, notably certain Daoist trends that place the role of forgetting even closer to the center of their conception of both praxis and attainment, and certain Chinese Buddhist schools that developed in the aftermath of these Daoist moves. But in any case, a clear dividing line emerges here: the question is whether consciousness—as a purposive, controlling, unified agency, as thinking personality—is regarded as the ultimate cause of what occurs and correlatively as the ultimate purpose to which all action is to be directed or given some nonultimate role.

Monotheism takes this animistic premise to a new and exponentially more terrifying level. The animist view sees all events as ultimately controlled by a purposive, conscious being. Conscious purpose is, among other things, a method of unification, which brings varied means into the service of a single desideratum, orienting all toward a single goal that becomes their shared meaning and function and eliminating anything that contravenes it. Structurally, such a unification is centered on a very specific conception of unity: not the unity whose aim is to maximally include, but rather a unity that stresses exclusion rather than inclusion, for "conscious purpose" means choice, preferring one outcome over others and selecting the means to attain some particular end and the exclusion of all alternate outcomes. But in polytheistic animism, this means there are many such exclusive-unification projects going on at once, always potentially at odds with one another. Moreover, the existence of these multiple spiritual agents presupposes an origin in something *other* than a mind, something other than a purpose, from which these many purposive beings are somehow *purposelessly* produced. At the base of each of these exclusion-unification projects there is an *undermining* of that exclusivity. The full exclusionary mania of purposive activity is thus somewhat balanced by a diversity of alternate purposive projects, all of which are outgrowths of a larger purposelessness. Indeed, the expansion of animism could have played out in exactly the opposite way: as a feeling of kinship with all processes in nature, which extends not only to what we regard as living beings but to all things without exception. This, in turn, deepens our sense of the nonpurposivity and cross-purposivity, which always lie intertwined with our own purposivity—the nonpersonhood in our own personhood and the nonagency in our own agency; this self-overcoming of animism through its own radicalization should be remembered when we consider Spinoza's panpsychist view of conatus in part II. Monotheism goes exactly the opposite way, radicalizing animism not by expanding it to apply exceptionlessly but diversely to every grain of sand, but by grounding even the seemingly nonpurposive in a *single* soul by rolling all purposes and nonpurposes and cross-purposes into a single ur-purpose. It thereby eliminates this last loophole, this last exit from purpose. Now exclusive unification is all there is, as both the source and the goal. The principle of exclusionary unification now exclusively unifies even these alternate exclusive-unification projects. What is new and decisive in the monotheist idea is not just that events are caused by minds, as in standard animism, but that animism has been pushed to the point of exceptionlessness, of ultimacy, as premised on a specific form of unity: all things are not only caused by mind, they are all caused by one mind, not many. That means that all things are ultimately part of a single system of purposes, which is subordinated to a single purpose. The model here is the human consciousness's foreground experience of its own unity when it is intentionally pursuing a goal, a unity premised on the experience of subordinating present means to future ends. When this experience of control becomes the sole model of effectivity—and of unity, of action, of experience, and of the Good—the inference becomes inevitable: what is not in my control must be in someone else's control. Finally, all of it must be under the control of the *same being*. Only what is intended has value, but the old Euthyphro question of whether something is "good because intended, or intended because good" flips with this reversal: I am supposed to intend it because it is good, but it is good because it is intended (by the Other, the one *Noûs*, or God). The result is that any good I perceive, as well as my conscious Will, ends up being a token in negotiating my relationship to this other controller, a relation between my purpose and another purpose that is a token of interpersonal communication, and one in which the other purpose is definitionally always right. We can perhaps begin to see here how "everything being for the best" might also be, for some of us, the worst possible thing that could happen.

CHAPTER 2

Purposivity and Dichotomy

THE PURPOSE-DRIVEN LIFE? NO THANKS!

The problem of God, as we start to see, is largely a question of our relation to purpose. God as in any way personal, as in any way active in time, is first and foremost a controller, modeled on a certain mode of experiencing our own attempts at control and our own ways of unifying our actions as means toward an end. Indeed, it is in the idea of purpose as the ultimate ontological category that the idea of God lives and breathes, even when the word "God" is absent. And as we will explore in depth in this chapter, the ontological ultimacy of purpose means also the ontological ultimacy of dichotomy.

But to begin with, why does everyone care so much about people having a purpose, actions having a purpose, even life having a purpose? The reason is, in one sense, self-evident: because the idea of purpose is part of the definition of what it means to want anything, and wanting things is what we living beings are all about.

Living beings have needs and desires.

To be not only alive but also conscious means sometimes having awareness, not only of what is the case right now in actuality, but of other things that have been the case in the past or could be the case in the future. This means being able to imagine having what we don't have and having awareness that what we want is not what we have—wanting some things that are not immediately available.

So to be conscious and alive seems to require that we have some degree of an "ends versus means" mentality: since I can't stop wanting what I want and it's also not here, I ask myself how to get it. What I want is the goal; how I get it is the means. And this seems to be the matrix of the idea of purposeful action: we do *this* "in order to" attain *that*.

As we've seen, some thinkers have concluded from the definitional inescapability of this structure that whenever we wonder what to do or what is good or how to go about something, that purposefulness must reveal to us the essence of what we desire when we desire—of what is desirable as such. Inasmuch as some reference to purpose is inescapable in any definition of what we regard as desirable, to any notion of the Good, it is from there loaded into the very definition of being. On this view, purposefulness is the unsurpassable source and measure of all things that happen. Radicalized, literalized, absolutized—this is the marrow of the monotheistic idea.

Others have concluded that purposefulness is a kind of narrow foreground illusion endemic to our particular form of desiring and perception, a *by-product* rather than the source or measure of conscious animal life, which cannot be either the real ultimate root of goodness or the real ultimate source of what happens.

Some among this latter group still consider purposefulness to be the best thing there is; they wish there were more of it and try to enhance it as much as possible. Much of secular atheism falls into this category.

Some others among that latter group, though, think purpose is an epiphenomenon of purposelessness and that therefore it must always play a secondary rather than a primary role in our understanding of ourselves and our world, and in our way of being in the world. These folks think that to prioritize and absolutize purpose will distort our understanding about what is really the best part of us and of the world, and how to have there be more of it—*even the "best" part as defined by purposes, and even though no definition of "best" can make any sense without some reference to purpose.* I call these atheist mystics: some are Spinozists, some are Nietzscheans, some are Daoists, and there are also some Confucians and Buddhists, especially those working within the Daoist cultural sphere.

We can thus sketch something like a Venn diagram with some surprising connections. Roughly speaking, we can identify four models of the relation between the ultimate character of the cosmos and the relative valuing of the aspects of human existence:

1. Emulative Theism. This is the elaboration of the Socratic impulse that sees the universe as ultimately guided by purpose and holds concomitantly that the best part of human beings is the consciously purposeful part, their moral rationality, which should rightfully guide their behavior. The universe is guided by clear, conscious knowledge of the Good (including also the True and the Beautiful, perhaps), and humans should also be consciously guided by their own rational recognition of the Good. Conscious control is what it's all about, both at the macrolevel and at the microlevel, for both the world and for human beings. The slogan here might be: "Knowledge is virtue, for it is what makes us most godlike."

2. Compensatory Theism. This position goes with a more acute sense of the unknowability of God—a sense of his inaccessibility to precise human knowledge and the gulf between creator and creature. God is still stipulated to have a clear, conscious knowledge of the Good and thus a clear, conscious purpose, and that divine purpose in the mind of God is still the best thing there is, the standard of all value. But human beings can never really know God's plan, and thus they must piously accept that even what does not seem good to their own conscious knowledge might be something that God regards as good, and thus might be something that really *is* good. Humans thus need to transcend their own conscious purposes, their narrow purposivity. Whatever happens in the end must be good, so the right attitude for the human being is to humbly surrender to the Will of God, to give up trying to adjudicate or know what the Good is, to let God take them where he wishes, even if at the moment it seems terrible to the humans themselves. That means, though, that while it is still recognized in principle that conscious knowledge of the Good and conscious control are the ultimate standards of real value, for a human being it is just the opposite that is the highest possible state: the complete abrogation of conscious control, the surrender to what is beyond one's own consciousness and values, in the faith that this is the way to accord with Someone's conscious control. Control is still what it's all about, the only thing with any real value. But now the control that matters is not mine, but Thine. The world is purposeful, and for that very reason we must not be purposeful ourselves but allow ourselves to be driven wherever the wind of the spirit lists. "Not my Will but thine be done" might be the watchword of this stance in its purest form, although in practice there is no doubt that we will almost always find it combined with the previous Emulative Theist stance, which strives to find out about and incorporate the Will of God. Everyday theism is usually somewhere on the spectrum between these two pure extremes, engaged in mixing them according to a schema of the "the wisdom to know the difference" between what is in my control and what is in God's control, as the Alcoholics Anonymous prayer has it. But wherever we place the marker between faith and works, in whichever way we combine the two, we find the same ultimate evaluative stance: purpose, control, that's what it's all about. It's just a question of what's in whose control, mine or God's. The unchanged ontological primacy of control means that all entities, without exception, and including the ethical ideals and states of soul, will continue to be construed as structured by all of the entailments of "control," to be explored in what follows—above all, the dichotomization of oneness and difference and the ontology of mutual exclusivity.

3. Compensatory Atheism. Here the idea is that the world itself is purpose-

less; there is no conscious controller guiding it toward the Good, and for that very reason we humans must step up our own efforts at conscious control, at the determining of values, at purposeful activity. We must create our own values, order our societies, and cultivate our gardens. This is the attitude of some early Confucians like Xunzi, Legalists like Hanfeizi, and most atheist secular humanism in the modern world, and arguably in secular collectivist utopianisms like Bolshevism. It also appears in its most extreme and self-aware individualistic form in movements like Sartrean existentialism. Note that here, as in all the previous cases, what is really valuable is still purposive, conscious control as such. That's still the best thing there can possibly be, the sole standard of value. Like Emulative Theism but unlike Compensatory Theism, though, the best aspect of the human being is his conscious, purposively controlling aspect. That was true for the Socratic Emulative Theists but not for the pious Compensatory Theist mystics, for whom the best aspect of the human being was his faith, his ability to renounce his own conscious control and his own purposes.

4. Emulative Atheism. Here, finally, we have an entirely different alternative. The universe is purposeless, not under anyone's control, and not directed toward any conscious goal, but it is here also true that the best aspect of human experience is also purposeless, not under anyone's control, not directed at any conscious goal. Here, as in Compensatory Theism, the best aspect of the human being is seen to be a renunciation of his commitment to his own conscious control, to his own purposes as he knows them. So this position shares the view of the Compensatory Atheist about the nature of the cosmos, but it shares the view of the Compensatory Theist about the best aspect of human experience: the abandonment of beholdenness to one's own conscious purposes and controls. And it is unlike all three of the previous positions in that it alone views conscious purpose and control per se as less "valuable" than purposelessness and noncontrol, not just for humans but for the cosmos as a whole. The most valuable aspect of anything is the unconscious, purposeless, uncontrolling and uncontrolled aspect, and wisdom consists in understanding the purposeless, and understanding the rooting of our purposes and their fulfillment in the purposeless. It goes without saying that, since value itself is defined by its relation to purpose, this will entail some interesting intellectual challenges and a nondismissive attitude toward paradox to flesh out. This is what I call "atheist mysticism."

Emulative Theism is like Compensatory Theism in that both posit a purposive consciousness running the cosmos. Emulative Theism is like Compensatory Atheism in that both see conscious control as the best aspect of humanity and the principle of all ethics. Compensatory Theism and Compensatory Atheism are direct opposites, having neither aspect in common. Emulative Theism and Emulative Atheism are likewise direct opposites. But note that Compensatory Atheism and Emulative Atheism are alike in both seeing the cosmos as meaningless, purposeless, and not run by a consciousness, so both are atheist, and yet in their view of human life, Compensatory Theism and Emulative Atheism are alike in seeing the best aspect of human life as its ability to pass beyond its obsession with its own conscious purposive control, so both are mystics. Hence Emulative Atheism is what I call the atheist mysticism.

If the watchword of Emulative Theism is perhaps, "Reason is divine, and knowledge is virtue," that of Compensatory Theism, "Not my Will but thine be done," and that of Compensatory Atheism, "We must cultivate our own gardens," the watchword of Emulative Atheism in its purest form might be the description of Zhuangzi found in the thirty-third chapter of the eponymous book:

> Blank and barren, without form! Changing and transforming, never constant! Dead? Alive? Standing side by side with heaven and earth? Moving along with the spirits and illuminations? So confused—where is it all going? So oblivious—where has it all gone? Since all the ten thousand things are inextricably netted together around us, none is worthy of exclusive allegiance. These were some aspects of the ancient Art of the Course. Zhuang Zhou [Zhuangzi] got wind of them and was delighted. He used ridiculous and far-flung descriptions, absurd and preposterous sayings, senseless and shapeless phrases, indulging himself unrestrainedly as the moment demanded, uncommitted to any one position, never looking at things exclusively from any one corner.[1]

Note that the uncertainty and directionlessness of the world and those of the mind go hand in hand here. And yet precisely because the mind is as directionless and uncertain as the world, even the world's uncertainty and directionlessness are not something "known"—indeed, even the godlessness of the world is not known. It's just question after question, an open door even to "the spirits and illuminations"—that is, all manner of nonempirical spiritual beings, but not to the firm establishing of any one of them as discernibly in control or to the absence of any one or of all of them as the standard for setting a single goal, as a consciously graspable signpost of purpose. It is purpose itself and conscious knowing itself and control itself that are dismissed here, for both the universe and the person.

We should perhaps call this "Isomorphic Atheism" rather than "Emulative Atheism," since the latter term implies the paradoxical attempt to imitate the purposeless, which would itself be a purposive endeavor. Indeed, because purpose is actually ineradicable, is built in to the entire framework in which the issue can be raised (i.e., the question of values), what we actually always end up with in Emulative Atheism is some combination of the purposive and the purposeless, the conscious and the nonconscious, the controlled and the uncontrolled; what matters is simply that this combination of the purposeless, unconscious, and uncontrolled is the *ultimate* term, standing at both the source and the goal. Indeed, we may even want to say that emulation itself is ineradicable, as suggested by modern mimetic theory as well as by Spinoza (E3p27)[2]—which would highlight for us even more why the choice of the object of highest value and greatest ontological priority matters so much, since it will inevitably lead to emulation: it is the structure of purpose and purposelessness in this object, prioritizing the latter, that allows the emulation to take on a different character, in spite of its necessarily purposive motivation. (Contrast this to Compensatory Theism, where we always end up with a combination of two kinds of control, mine and God's, since I must at least willingly consent to my surrender to faith for it to count as my own faith, thus leaving no place at all for the purposeless, the truly uncontrolled.) Conscious controlling purposes may, and even must, be construed as a *means* in some form, as playing some role, but the ultimate goal or reference point or regulative ideal that informs all purposes is here purposelessness—the uncontrolled and nonconscious as the real locus, or at least the real source, of being and value.

With the idea of the monotheistic God, on the contrary, *purpose* becomes the source and end and meaning of all things; purposelessness becomes, by definition, the thing most to be despised and minimized. The idea of God means that purpose is the ultimate, the highest, the privileged and eternally unsurpassable category at the root of all things. But the unsurpassability of the idea of purpose creates a mode of relating to the world in which, literally by definition, no possible experience can be intrinsically worthwhile. Once we accept the idea that accord with a preexistent purpose is what makes something count as good or what makes things exist, we seem to have condemned ourselves to an eternal regress of dissatisfaction. This is the most obvious problem that arises when we prioritize the idea of purpose. If A's purpose is B, what is B's purpose? What is the purpose of the total whole, A plus B? Is it C? What is C's purpose? Is it D? And on it goes. It would seem that once we have started asking this question we cannot stop until we come to the largest whole or the ultimate destination. But what is the purpose of the whole or the destination? What is the purpose, the meaning, the point of, say, the universe, or human happiness, or a future utopia? What is the purpose of pleasing God? And indeed, what is the purpose of God? This is a mirror image of a problem that comes with making causality ontologically ultimate: if "to be" is to be caused by something prior, what causes the prior thing, and its own prior thing? The idea of God is engineered precisely to avert this infinite regress of purposes, as much as to avert the infinite regress of causes: the idea is that somewhere along the line there must be something that is "its own purpose," something valuable in itself, or else the entire chain of purposes would become meaningless. The only problem is that the very definition of value as purpose makes the very idea of "valuable in itself" inconceivable and impossible. This is somewhat ironic, since the whole problem only emerges because purpose has been absolutely prioritized in this way. Purpose creates the disease, and the deification of purpose is offered as the cure.

To pull off this cure, both the first link and the final link in the chain must be defined as radically different from all the others, since all the others are caused by something prior and lead to something later. Having an actual prior cause that has brought it about is usually considered a necessary condition for considering something to actually exist; leading to something later is what is usually meant by something having a purpose. But the first term and the last term cannot have being and purpose in this ordinary sense, so they must exist and be purposeful in some radically other way. The first and the last are typically conflated in theories like this and combined into one. This first and last term has to be something that can somehow mysteriously be its own cause, unlike any other being, and just as mysteriously, it must have value or purpose or meaning just in itself, also unlike any other being. We can perhaps begin to see why Aristotle's proposed solution to this problem, the autotelic as thought-thinking-thought, might have seemed attractive: the very nature of *Noûs* being purposivity itself, it can serve as what has purpose even if it serves no purpose beyond itself. Efforts would also have to be made to view it somehow as caused by no prior cause—and a certain disposition of mind, negligent of its own causal embeddedness, does indeed feel that way, as if springing up from nothing. We call it the feeling of free will or agency: mind when it intervenes and disrupts an apparent trajectory of events, believing itself to be sole cause of what happens; it is *Noûs* as the endeavor to control. Once purpose is privileged, this most purposeful thing, *Noûs*, is the only thing that will fit the bill to end the infinite regress of endless externality in both directions—which purpose itself has wrought.

Once this noncaused and non–externally purposed thing, this antithing, is thus fitted in place at the beginning and the end of the chain of causes and purposes, its removal will cause all causes and all purposes to collapse.

It must radically subordinate all the finite meanings and purposes in the chain: they have all of their purpose solely because of this mysterious item that is claimed somehow to have "purpose in itself." All things must then be aligned from top to toe to serve this final end or otherwise fail in attaining their purpose—to serve as cogs in this grand plan. They must not have other purposes, but only the ones that derive from and also lead to the purpose-giver. From here we get the idea that all knowable things were specifically made for a specific purpose, whose sole meaning was to serve the purposeful designs of something or Someone that is itself not purposeless but somehow purposeful while violating the usual definition of purpose. So, Someone creates all things with the purpose of knowing, praising, loving, serving, and obeying him.

Are there any alternatives to this arrangement, which some of us find so depressing? One would be to try to identify some of our own actual *experiences* that we actually feel to be intrinsically worthwhile, to be ends-in-themselves, which are thus experienced as breaking out of the structure of subordination of present means to future ends. Unfortunately, this privileging of certain experiences over others, regarding some as intrinsically worthwhile and others as worthwhile only to the extent that they serve the first group, will *again* have the consequence of committing us to the idea of purpose as the most important aspect of existence. This seems to be what we have in the humanistic aftermath of formerly monotheistic cultures— namely, cultures that have long regarded purpose as the ultimate category of all existence. Secular atheists in these cultures, which today compete with God-cultures for dominance of the globe, are generally themselves very much in the thrall, with a slight modification, of the main thing about God-cultures: the obsession with subordinating all existence to purpose as what matters most. In the secular, Compensatory Atheist version, purpose no longer stands at the beginning of existence, but it still stands at the end of all action and the standard of all value. The purposeful aspect of ourselves is still regarded as the best and most important aspect. When God drops out of the picture, the obsession with purpose becomes one or another form of hedonism, whether of the crude type, where we work in order to enjoy, earn in order to spend, endure in order to indulge; or else of the more refined type, where we esteem only certain achievements—cultural, social, artistic, technological, moral—and enslave all experience to their service, where life is considered good when we consciously know what we want and make attaining that good the purpose of our actions, identifying the excellences in the moral, cultural, technological, or experiential sphere, and then devoting all other things and all other times to making those things and those times happen. In either case, the structure is the same: X exists "for the sake of" Y. Subordination is the name of the game, and conscious purpose still ends up dominating everything.

A great many people seem to find this arrangement just fine or at least the best that can be hoped for, or perhaps they are just used to it and see no alternative. But some—though I don't know how many—will breathe a sigh of gratitude and relief to discover that there is another way to approach this problem, proceeding from the other end: by questioning the very structure of meaning, or purpose, or value, itself: the value of value, the point of things having a point, the purpose of having purposes as such. Though this approach pops up here and there in other places, its main source is the Daoist thinkers of ancient China, one of the few literate cultures not under the thumb of some form of the crushingly ubiquitous God-generating paradigm: the worship of purpose as the best thing about human life and what it would be best to discover at the root of all existence.

I'm referring to the Daoist concept of *wuwei* 無為, literally "nonaction," but signifying more specifically "effortless action," which is to say, "nondeliberate action," or to put the point more sharply, "purposeless action." This means action that does not proceed from a conscious embrace of a goal in advance, action that happens "spontaneously" or with no experience of doing it for any reason at all—not even "for itself." To quote the fuller elaborations of this idea from the *Zhuangzi*, it is what one is doing without realizing it (不知其然; *Zhuangzi*, chap. 2), or what is happening without knowing whereby or for what reason it is happening (不知其所以然; *Zhuangzi*, chap. 17)—moving without knowing where one is heading and stopping without knowing what one is doing or for what reason one is doing it (行不知所之，居不知所為; *Zhuangzi*, chap. 23). It is a critique of the idea that purposes as such—ideals, values—are the most basic thing about either goodness or existence. It begins with a critique of having any values or ideals or indeed, therefore, any "ethics" at all. The concept of Dao is the *ne plus ultra* of purposelessness; it is the precise opposite of the concept of God, which is the *ne plus ultra* of purpose.

The four categories in this typology are admittedly rather rudimentary, and they do not quite exhaust the possible ways in which the purpose or purposelessness of humans and those of the world might be related to each other. Where things really become interesting is in two crucial hybrid categories that root themselves in an insight into the inseparability, and indeed intersubsumption, of purpose and purposelessness. I will call these two categories Emulative Intersubsumptive Theism (Hegelianism) and Emulative Intersubsumptive Atheism (Tiantai Buddhism). But because they require a more intricate unpacking, I will postpone their presentation to online appendix B of this book.

THE GREAT ASYMMETRY: PURPOSE OBSTRUCTS PURPOSELESSNESS, BUT PURPOSELESSNESS ENABLES PURPOSES

Before becoming frightened about the alleged "nihilism" of the denial of ontological or even existential ultimacy of purpose ("nihilism" being the alarmist term often used by purpose-driven people to slander any denial of the ultimacy of purpose), we must notice one hugely consequential point. Purpose, by definition, *excludes* the purposeless: to have a purpose is precisely to prefer one outcome over others and to strive to whatever extent is possible to eliminate the unwanted outcomes. Wanting something is wanting to get the wanted thing and to avoid whatever is not that thing (of course, I may, at the same time, also have other, conflicting wants—but each will be structured in exactly the same way). But this relationship is not symmetrical: purposelessness does not exclude purpose. On the contrary, it includes, allows—and on the Daoist account, even generates—purpose. This is not a single purpose, however: it is many purposes—perhaps infinite purposes, or even a surfeit of purposes—all of which remain embedded in a larger purposelessness but not contradicted or undermined by it. The structure of purpose, and hence of personhood, is such as to exclude: it is specifically a choice, an either/or, beholden to a conception of goodness, whether individual or universal, which necessarily means the exclusion of something. Even if we make some room for the impersonal or the non-exclusive or the purposeless, a monotheist cosmos will be one in which personality, purpose, and dualism must win in the end; they must be the ultimate. The purposeless must be subordinated to the purposeful. But purposelessness subordinated to purpose is no longer purposeless: it becomes instead instrumental to purpose, pervaded completely by purpose. So a monotheist cosmos is one that ultimately forecloses entirely purposelessness, inclusiveness, nonduality, and the nonpersonal.

The reverse, however, is not true. Purpose is precisely the attempt to exclude whatever does not fit the purpose, but purposelessness is what is, by definition, not contravened by any possible outcome. Purposelessness makes no choices and excludes nothing. It is, rather, precisely the allowing of unforeseen, uncontrolled, unpredetermined outcomes. Purposelessness is openness. It allows. That means it *also* allows purpose—indeed, innumerable purposes; it cannot exclude even purpose, and it is what escapes the control of any single purpose, what splays any given attempt at monolithic control, what opens up any one purpose to alternate purpose. Purposelessness is the fecund matrix from which purposes arise, the allowing of both any given purpose and all other purposes and the further fecund purposelessness that escapes the control of any of them. The personal seeks to subordinate the impersonal; indeed, the personal really is simply the attempt to subordinate the impersonal, to completely subdue it into an instrument. But the impersonal allows both the personal and the impersonal. The question is which is the means and which the end. And indeed, "end" and "means" are categories that are only ultimate insofar as purposiveness is ultimate, since they are aspects of the idea of purpose. If the ultimate end is the purposeful and personal, all the impersonal is reduced to a means to reach the purposeful. But if the ultimate end is the purposeless and impersonal, although it will also allow the purposeful to arise, this will not ultimately be as a means to an end, but will be the purposeless allowing itself to be a means to any given nonultimate purpose for as long as that purpose obtains, and also, to that purposeful being, the allowing of the purposeless to serve its purpose and to find new purposes—indeed, even to make a purpose of finding the purposeless if it wishes. From the point of view of purpose (which is undeniably our starting point and necessarily a part of any discussion, any thought, any viewpoint), every action is a self-canceling means to an end that lies beyond it. If this point of view is applied to the ultimacy of purposelessness over purpose, purposefulness is a means to reach the end of purposelessness. But it is construed in these purposeful terms only from the point of view of the purposefulness. In fact, whatever purposes may arise are here nonultimate "means" that ultimately are not even means at all. Instead, purposes that transcend themselves toward purposelessness, or toward the multiplicity of purposes, are just additional ways in which the ultimacy of purposelessness manifests itself. We have here, not the exclusion of purpose, which is impossible, but the multiplicity and nonultimacy of all purposes.

The relation of purpose to purposelessness is thus trickier than it appears, and the great virtue, to my mind, of the concept of *wuwei* as effortless and purposeless action is that it allows us to achieve some direct reconfiguring here. The type of purposelessness involved is well illustrated by a parallel problem stumbled on in passing by Ralph Waldo Emerson in his essay, "Spiritual Laws": "I say, do not choose; but that is a figure of speech by which I would distinguish what is commonly called choice among men, and which is a partial act, the choice of the hands, of the eyes, of the appetites, and not a whole act of the man. But that which I call right or goodness is the choice of my constitution; and that which I call heaven, and inwardly aspire after, is the state or circumstance desirable to my constitution; and the action which I in all my years tend to do, is the work for my faculties."[3]

We see a strange kind of part-whole relation here. What is experienced as *devoid* of purpose—as effortless, intentionless, purposeless—could also be described as an *all-inclusive oneness* of purpose. To experience effort, choice, an end as opposed to and different from a means, or a choice of alternate means toward one end is to experience a contrast, a twoness, a doubleness, a conflict—two alternate things are appearing in consciousness, grinding and scraping against each other and battling for dominance. Some impulse in one direction is crashing against some impulse in another direction. When all factors of one's experience tend in the same way, when all have unanimously chosen one end of action, it is not experienced as a choice but as an inevitability, an unpremeditated gushing forth. What is lacking is the sense of any controlling executive function, for it is not needed. A genuinely and fully unified purpose is actually phenomenologically indistinguishable from no purpose. Under some circumstances, many diverse things can be experienced together as a single whole, as all the varying stresses and torques and directions of a pitcher's muscles may be experienced by him as the windup and release of a single pitch, a single effortless flow with no conscious choices involved once the action has begun. Once he is "in the zone," though the individual muscles may be straining in different directions and he can experience them all, he experiences them all *as* one single action, one single purpose, and to that extent, it is beyond the experience of choice, effort, or even purpose itself. Indeed, we may say that whenever many purposes are working together, this is tantamount to them being experienced as purposeless: "together" means "nonconflictually," means "no effort felt to be required." As Spinoza says (E2d7),[4] when multiple individual things collectively act as causes to a single effect, they can, to that extent, be considered a single individual thing.

My heart beats: but why? Do I beat my heart? Do I decide and choose to beat my heart? I might describe the activity of the heart as done "for a purpose" (e.g., "in order to" circulate blood in my body, "in order to" keep me alive, and so on)—to speak as Aristotle did, as Kant said anatomists still must do, as theists do, as even materialists do, albeit (allegedly) figuratively and merely as shorthand. But in doing so, I am attributing that purpose to someone or something besides myself as a purposive being: God, Nature, the body. For I don't experience myself as the one doing it, and thus, *a fortiori*, I do not experience myself as doing it with any purpose in mind. It is only my assumption, going back to the animist assumptions discussed earlier, that whatever happens is done for a purpose that forces me to speak in this way. But while my heart is beating, other "purposeless" quasipurposive activities are going on: my stomach is digesting—not done by me, not for any purpose that I consciously set, but "in order to" extract energy from my food to sustain my life. My liver is busy filtering and processing my blood—without an experience of effort or strain (if I'm not ill), without known purpose, but "for the purpose" of purifying and detoxifying to keep me alive. All these processes go on in tandem, and to the extent that they are working together as one, with no conflict between them—in equilibrium, in harmony, "healthily"—and I remain unconscious of them as effort, as work, as purpose. If my heart starts pounding or straining, I know there is something wrong, some conflict with other unintended processes. Then I may have to make it my purpose to calm my heart—to eat less sodium, for example, or to think calm thoughts, or to lie down. So to the extent that they are unknown and unconscious and are working well—together, not in conflict, and integrated as one totality—I experience the health of all my organs and their diverse purposes in and as my conscious purpose; for example, to type these words on my computer. All those diverse purposes are functioning together, qua purposeless, present only as this purpose of typing. The one I experience consciously is *where the problem is*: where effort is required, the interface between me and the world, where there is conflict and less than perfect integration. Consciousness and purpose are *frontiers*, markers of finitude, of boundaries, of conflict, of mutual exclusivity: they are the chafings of the integrated totality of purposeless-purposes and what is not yet so integrated. As Zhuangzi said, when the shoe fits, the feet are forgotten. When the mind fits, right and wrong are forgotten.[5] We only notice things when there's some problem there. Conscious purpose is a by-product of antagonism. Again we find it already in *Zhuangzi*: "conscious purposive knowing derives from struggle . . . it is basically a weapon of war" (*zhichuhuzheng. . . . zhiyezhe zhengzhiqiye* 知出乎爭. . . . 知也者，爭之器也).[6]

In this way, many purposes all included as one, integrated as one, and bundled seamlessly into the whole one's being are experienced as no purpose: purposelessness in this sense cannot only be the ground and allowing of purposes, but rather must be the actual undisturbed copresence of multiple purposes right there and then. If I do experience a purpose—as in my typing these words—it means that a bundle of multiple unexperienced, integrated activities, which would count as purposes and conflictual counterpurposes if unintegrated and thus made conscious, has hit a snag in integrating a certain activity; that alone makes it an experience of "purpose." Qua conscious purpose, all these activities would be in conflict; because they are not in conflict, not mutually exclusive, they are not experienced as purposes at all. The interface of the purposeless and the purposive is thus an interface between a nonconflictual non-mutually exclusive many— experienced not even as a one but as a none, like Zhuangzi's comfortably forgotten shoes—with a single conflictual, exclusive one. This means that the only time we experience choice, conscious action, effort, purposeful-ness, is when we actually have present to our awareness an antagonism, which is present to our consciousness as the unity of this particular pur-pose. In other words, the oneness of each conscious purpose—that is, of purpose qua purpose—is an embodied antagonism. It is the specific modal-ity of *oneness as exclusion* that pertains especially to *personality*—conscious personality as a weapon of war, as the uniquely *antagonistic form of unity*— and is the basic structure underlying the effects of the personal, purpose-driven and purpose-driving God of monotheism. The true oneness of pur-pose is experienced as purposelessness, and its morphing into another, contrary purpose is not felt as conflict. The sure sign that the oneness is not a true oneness is that the one purpose remains "one purpose," maintaining its identity as such only through its felt opposition to other purposes and to whatever resists its purposes. We have here another key entailment of the idea of God: it is the distortion of the noneness of true oneness into an exclusionary oneness that, through its exclusions, remains an identical one. Mutatis mutandis, what is said of purpose can also be said of "meaning" and "value": whatever presents itself as a single meaning is a distorting usurpa-tion of the true meaningless omnimeaning infinity of intermelding mean-ings, and whatever presents itself as a single value is a distorting usurpation of the true valueless omnivalue of infinite intermelding values.

What does life look like—what does the world look like—when lifted free of its final beholdenness to the quest for purpose, for meaning, for value? What is it like to learn to experience purposelessness, meaningless-ness, and valuelessness differently, welcomingly—perhaps ecstatically? What is it like to experience them as allowing the horizon of all purposes, as the ground from which all purposes spring, as the copresence of all pur-poses, as the inclusive field of all purposes, as the sum of all purposes, as each purpose as an alternate sum of all other purposes, as infinite alternate purposes, as infinite inclusive, purposeless totalities of all other purposes— and on and on? Shall we make it our "purpose" to find out what that would be like? There would be no contradiction in doing so. That too would be one of those infinite purposes that are not only not excluded but even en-abled and produced by the open vistas of a purposeless universe. But spe-cial forms of consciousness are needed for the quest, with special proce-dures and structures, special problems and satisfactions. When we make it our purpose to go beyond purpose, we change our relation to it: it is not the disavowal of purpose, but rather a redefinition of what purpose actually is and the range of ways in which it can be experienced.

THE GREAT ASYMMETRY REDUX, MUTATIS MUTANDIS: CHAOS AS ENABLER AND ENCOMPASSER OF ORDER

Another convenient way to frame the question we are posing here, as well as the great divide we are identifying, is to focus on the question of *order*. For something structurally parallel to the purpose/purposeless relation is going on in the order/chaos relation embedded in this question of God. To see order and chaos as dichotomous—as mutually exclusive, as sharply divided—is perhaps the first premise behind the monotheist instinct. It can easily entail the further intuition that order, which is so profoundly different from chaos, cannot possibly be generated by or from chaos; it must have its own origin, must be created by something already orderly. This in turn easily segues into the idea that order must have an orderer; it must be created or executed by someone who is himself embodied order and thus also wants or approves of order, and who chooses to fit things together in an orderly way, that is, in a way that fits under the control of an overriding purpose or design. The latter is full-blown monotheism. The Compensatory Atheist, on the other hand, may share the first assumption—the absolute dichotomy between order and chaos—but not the latter premises. What we are interested in in these pages, however, is the world of the Emulative Atheist. That orientation can be traced back to the intuition that chaos and order are not dichotomous at all. This could mean either, in the softest version, simply that order, or many orders, can emerge from chaos. And this is, of course, easily linked to the kind of asymmetry just noted concerning purpose and purposelessness: chaos can accommodate anything, given enough time and space, and so order, and many orders, should certainly not be excluded from it. But order, if made primary and ultimate, is precisely, definitionally, the exclusion of chaos. Chaos can include order, while order cannot include chaos. Any chaos included in order is, ipso facto, made into a component of order and thus loses its character as chaos. Conversely, any order included in chaos is still orderly and yet also still chaotic at the same time.

The stronger version of this Compensatory Atheist mystical orientation would claim that not only are order and chaos not dichotomous, but that all order is itself a particular kind of chaos. Put more strongly, orderliness is itself chaotic. I take this to be the view of Tiantai Buddhism, for which interested readers may refer to my discussion in *Being and Ambiguity*, in the section entitled, "'Natural Law' as Global Incoherence."[7] The basic idea, however, which should be intelligible to any student of statistics, gives a strong account of how macrocosm predictability is itself nothing more than microcosm unpredictability viewed en masse. A more direct illustration is perhaps provided by the easy intelligibility of the idea of the "Law of Averages" as something that may have actual predictive power but is really nothing more than a name for the absence of any law whatsoever; in that case, we need no disjunction between the micro- and macrolevels—the "law" is simply a metaphor for the absence of law, which is useful in some descriptions of the situation but not others. Further premises and steps are needed toward the full Tiantai view, but the basic intuition of a deeper identity between order and disorder, between chaos and pattern, between nonsense and sense, is what we should keep an eye on as identifying the shared ethos of our atheist mystics. Chaos as originary, not as something substantial but as a placeholder word for the absence of any principle at all and seen to be allowing of, as productive of, or even as coextensive with or identical to all forms of order, predictability, pattern, and reason itself—this is the starting intuition of the atheist mystics in all their variants.

This can be further restated in perhaps the broadest terms of all: it is a question of the relation between *determinateness* and *indeterminacy*. The Great Asymmetry appears here as well: when determinateness is ultimate—as source, goal, or both—it excludes, or strives to exclude, indeterminacy. Where indeterminacy is allowed to exist at all, on this picture, it too will be subordinated to the teleology of the determinate: it will be a temporary means to attain the final exclusive determinacy. But when indeterminacy is ultimate, it allows and also includes determinacies and it nonexcludes the arising of infinite determinacies—for to exclude *anything* would, ipso facto, make it determinate. The allowance of these determinacies is not due to any teleology on the part of the indeterminacy (for it has none) nor produced *in order* to instantiate or expand indeterminacy, but in fact they *do so*: each new determination that is allowed to arise in and from indetermination changes the prior determination of reality, de-determining whatever has already been determined of the world, instantiating in their very multiplicity and diversity ever more indetermination, overcoming every temporary limitation, every definiteness of reality, and demonstrating again and again that indeterminacy cannot be taken as any simple determinate blank as opposed to nonblank. When indetermination is ultimate, there is really no difference between determination and indetermination: every determination instantiates further indetermination and there is no indetermination apart from these infinite determinations. Here determination is not a means to attain an indetermination: rather, indeterminacy and determinateness *converge in every entity*. When determinacy is ultimate, on the contrary, determinateness and indetermination *diverge to mutual exclu-*

sivity. Determinacy, definiteness, differentiation, distinctions—all express God, *Noûs*. Indeterminacy, indefiniteness, indistinction, ambiguity—all express raw infinity, the very opposite of God. There we have the gist of the whole problem.

DAODEJING: THE DISCOVERY OF THE OPPOSITE OF GOD

It is in our ancient Daoist sources that we find perhaps the earliest and most relevant exploration of the implications of this opposite of God. The preference for the indeterminate is evident, not only in the ideas expressed in these texts, but perhaps even more so in the way they are expressed—and not expressed. This, of course, presents its own set of invigorating challenges and ironies when we approach this material. The story begins with the *Daodejing* (*Tao Te Ching*), a text that, famously, can be read to mean almost anything. It is arguably more ambiguous than pretty much any other known text, statement, or deed. In fact, that might be precisely the point of it. Indeed, its studied ambiguity is one of the most consistent things about it: though most likely a composite text, it displays a rather remarkable consistency of tone—omitting any proper nouns (it is the only self-standing text in the Chinese classical corpus that does this), eschewing disambiguation, and skipping steps to arrive at highly foreshortened and unexpected reversals. This common resistance to definiteness found in all its assembled motifs and pronouncements is, ironically, one of the few things that argues for the meaningfulness of treating it as a coherent text at all. Indeed, it is precisely analyzing and collating these materials with a foothold in this peculiar shared feature that allows us to wrest from them at least a minimally discernible position.

The attentive reader will quickly notice in this text, as we have it, a wide range of images and tropes that have a similar structure, a kind of rhyme scheme that echoes through seemingly very disparate topics, claims, and styles. It involves a *contrast* between two poles, and in every case these two poles are organized around an evaluative assumption, reflecting the conventional valuations prevalent in early Chinese societies. On the one hand we have terms like *being, having, name (fame), adulthood, masculinity, fullness, action, high, bright, flavorful, complete, formed*, and so on. These are all things that were, at the time, assumed (rightly or wrongly) to be *valued and sought*. I will call these valued things "category A." On the other hand we have the opposite terms, like *nonbeing, lacking, nameless, infancy, female, empty, nondoing, low, dark, flavorless, incomplete, formless*, and so on. These are all things or states that it was assumed people would *disvalue*, would try to diminish or avoid or eliminate. I will call these "category B." Again and again in this text, we find the contrast of the valued and the disvalued, in one form or another, poking through one or another twist or turn. And we will instantly notice a tendency to invert their positions: to promote the disvalued and demote the valued.[8] But why, and with what consequences?

The points made in many of the building blocks that constitute this text seem to presuppose a not-uncommon classical Chinese assumption: that being able to name and know things is a kind of ability to "cut" something out of a prior plenitude, a skill in parsing or separating something out from a larger context and finding or establishing boundaries for it.[9] This means that our notions of identities of specific cognitive objects—concrete or abstract—are derived from a mental act of cutting something out from a background. We do not do so randomly or disinterestedly: our selection of an object is motivated by a desire. How we identify the objects we apprehend and desire is conditioned by our language and the value preferences encoded in it. Whenever something is focused on and singled out, something else is left behind in the background from which the chosen object was taken. The early Daoist texts refer to this leftover as the "unhewn" (*pu* 樸)—that which is left behind by the "hewing" of chosen things out of the raw material of the world. Implicit in this conception is the denial that nature has joints at which it demands to be cut. It can be cut up in all sorts of ways, and each way will leave an unhewn residue or background. The name given to this unhewn background, as cut in any way whatsoever, is Dao (道). In earlier tradition this word had been used to mean almost exactly the opposite: a Way or Course or Guide (cognate with 導, "to guide"), which is to say, the means used when one has a set purpose to pursue, a path carved out as a way to reach a goal. "Dao" was originally a category A term *par excellence*. The biggest rhetorical move in the *Daodejing* corpus is that, for reasons to be discussed next, this most global of terms for the valued is *ironically* used to denote the entire category of the disvalued.

For this term originally means something very close to *purposive action* as such: a prescribed course to attain a prescribed goal. It is precisely something that is selected out, valued, desired; something that is kept rather than discarded. Dao, in its everyday earlier pre-Daoist sense, means a source of value: whatever it is you may regard as valuable, what you need is a *dao*—a way, a method, a purposive course of action—that will produce or procure that value, and that is the "course" you should follow. If you want good government, what is needed is a *dao* of government: it is what you should do to fulfil the purpose you have embraced. If you want to have family harmony, to become a good archer or charioteer, to become virtuous, or to be a successful merchant, you need a *dao* of that. For whatever you are carving out of the world as the target of your deliberate action, of your purposive endeavors, you need a path, a set of behaviors that will generate the sought value, a *dao*. The Daoist usage of the term *dao* turns it on its head: it is thus an *ironic* usage, used deliberately in the opposite of its literal sense—to make a point. The real way to attain value is through what we don't value; the real way is an anti-way, and the real fulfillment of purpose lies in letting go of purpose. It is like saying, "Oh great, nothing is going as I planned," and then realizing, wait, it *is* great that nothing is going as I planned, or as anyone planned—and it is "great" in the only sense in which something can be great, in that it is how I do get what I had originally wanted. This would be so, for example, if one were to become convinced that it is only because things do not follow any particular plans that there are such things as "plans," or such things as states of affairs that fulfill those plans; that my plans are followed only because nothing follows a plan; that ways that can be followed as a way are not the way things can or should proceed; that values that are valued are not what produce values and the achievement of those values. But why would anyone conclude that?

When we identify a thing and assign it an "essence," we distinguish it from other things and determine what qualities or features contrast with those of other things. But how one thing differs from others does not account for all its qualities or features, nor even for what is most "itself" among these. The alleged essence of a thing is not what makes it what it is, nor is its essence really "what it is." What is the essence of a human being— what makes a human human? Many answers have been proposed, but they all share a common structure. Some have said it is rationality, some have said morality, some have said language, some have said toolmaking. Each of these is an attempt to indicate what it is about humans that differs from other animals—what we have that the others lack, the loss of which would be tantamount to ceasing to be human. What is left out of all these definitions is what we share with other animals: functions such as respiration, digestion, and reproduction. These are not the human essence because they are not unique to us. But without them, there is no rationality, no morality, no language, and no toolmaking. A *purely* rational being, divested entirely of all that is not rationality, would not be able to live; such a being could not be any sort of animal, let alone a human or a rational one. The same would apply to a purely moral, a purely linguistic, a purely toolmaking being. Perhaps we will attempt to remedy this problem by expanding the definition to include what it left out: we may amend our claim by saying that the essence of a human being is to be a rational *animal*, thereby trying to factor in the nonrational, nonmoral, nonlinguistic, nontoolmaking elements rather than excluding them. But if we try to pinpoint the essence of "animality," we run into the same problem: we define animate beings in terms of what differentiates them from inanimate beings, from dead matter, which lacks digestion and respiration and such, being only able to do things like take up space and be composed of chemical and physical molecules. But a purely respirating being is no more possible than a purely rational being if all nonrespiration, all taking up of space and being composed of chemical and physical molecules, is removed. This same issue will reemerge whenever we try to define what anything is. When we identify things, when we try to define essences, we separate the extruding tip-top of each thing, which is easy for the eye and the mind to differentiate, from its substratum in unidentifiable, unhewn raw materials that are not unique to it, that are not part of its identity and are useless in in differentiating it from other things and thus in identifying it.

The early Daoist riffs assembled in the *Daodejing* intimate that this unhewn background is the source of the cutout figures that we call definite things. The unhewn—what is left over when the determination of any definite thing is made—is by definition indefinite. The unhewn is what gets left out whenever an entity is identified: the unhewn is whatever you are not paying attention to, whatever you have no interest in. We cut things off from their real roots when we conceive of them as too cleanly marked off from other things or from the nonthing, the indeterminate, which is the actual source of their existence and their value. For the unhewn is:

1. the unseen and unseeable *source* and *destination* of all concrete things—of whatever we are looking at, whatever we are interested in, whatever we are currently valuing—*from* which and *toward* which it flows;
2. the *course* of all things, in the sense of embodying their tendency to "return," in a bell-shaped or inverted V-shaped pattern of rise and fall, to that unseen source. The source is by definition unseen but is made evident by its function as a center of gravity toward which things return; hence its manifestation as the "course of things"; and
3. the stuff of which all things consist, as the raw material from which they are carved out and of which they are still composed.

The combination of these seemingly disparate implications depends on the view that the unseen and unattended to, the "unhewn raw material" (*pu* 樸) of the valued object, the B category, has a crucial *double meaning*. It is (a) a name for the detritus that is left over and discarded *after* the object has been carved out but *also* (b) the only available name for the whole of the unvalued, uncarved stuff that was there *prior* to the cutting. The Dao is thus the "unhewn" in these two senses simultaneously. It is both the "disvalued" and the "not yet valued or disvalued, the neither-valued-nor-disvalued." It is a catch-all term, like "garbage," that means simply "whatever I am not looking for." But garbage is always a broader category than nongarbage: it means anything and everything that doesn't fit into the category of use, of purpose, of desire, of what-I'm-looking-for in any given context. Nongarbage has a definite shape and definition, or a finite set thereof; garbage is *everything else*. So as I'm sifting through the world hunting for that one thing—that X, that flower, that letter, that name, that value—everything else is "not it, not it, not it, not it, crap, garbage, no, no, no . . ." Garbage has infinite shapes and sizes and colors and forms. Among them also is the very sources of the X I am looking for—whatever the sources of X are, they must be, by definition, Non-X, but since all Non-X is, by definition, garbage, the source of X must be garbage. It is the compost from which the desired X grows. So I can say, "Oh great, the world is all garbage"—and then I say, "Oh wait, it *is* great that the world is all garbage!" That's Daoism.

This way of thinking stands in sharp contrast to those ancient traditions that, under the auspices of the "Parmenidean distinction," which attempts to sharply dichotomize Being and Nonbeing, assume that "like begets like" and that "from nothing nothing comes," and apply this principle to the origins of all things. The upshot of those traditions is that, if there is any being or value or order in the world (anything in the "valued" category), it must be an emanation of some prior being or prior value or prior order, which ends up requiring that these must all be, in some sense, always priorly existing, not having arisen at all but always in some sense present in the eternal or infinite, perhaps in the divine. The Daoists do not think like that, partially perhaps because their ontological premises—that a "being" means a determinate being and that every determinate being is what it is relative to an indeterminate background—do not allow for an absolute ontological dichotomy between being and nonbeing. There is no definite being that does not arise, that is not contextualized by a prior not-being-that-state from which it appears, just as there is no definite being that does not appear in a context of surrounding entities that are not it. If I say that a god or a world exists, I am already presupposing some nongod or nonworld around it, *in* which it exists. If I say "the universe exists," I am already presupposing a nonuniverse *in which* it exists. Even "all that exists" must exist in something else. Even "nonbeing" or "the original void in which all arose" will have to be in something else if it can be said to exist at all, which it must to do its work of being *determinately* nonbeing (i.e., definitively excluding "being"). If there is anything eternal and omnipresent, it must thus be something in some sense other than any definite being, in some sense a formlessness.

The working out of the implications of this position obviously brings with it many puzzlements and complications of its own. But if we keep these founding premises well in view, we can begin to grasp the inner logic in some of the seemingly contradictory claims we find in this corpus. On the basis of this double meaning of B, the relation of the "disvalued" category (Dao, the unhewn, garbage) to the A category (whatever we are focusing on, valuing, and desiring) now takes on six surprising and only apparently conflicting forms, thus expanding into paradox from the relatively straightforward three senses of *source, course, and stuff* already noted:

1. The disvalued is the *opposite* of the valued, excluding the valued. This was its original meaning.
2. The disvalued is the *source* and *end* of the valued. Whatever valued thing we pinpoint, it can only have an origin in something that is disvalued. However we define value, it must originate in nonvalue (relative to that value); however we define an entity, it must originate in nonentity—there is nothing else from which it can come if it comes at all. The formed originates in the formless; the carved comes out of the unhewn raw material. That is also where it will return once it is used up, when we cease to value it: to the garbage heap.
3. As *stuff*, the disvalued actually encompasses *both* the valued and the disvalued. For the disvalued is the raw material from which the valued was cut, and the valued is still entirely made of what we now, after the cut, refer to as the disvalued. The wooden cup is still wood, so "wood" refers both to the cup and to the scraps carved away from it.
4. The disvalued is really *neither* "the valued" nor "the disvalued," as it excludes both. For we only call it the disvalued in contrast to the valued, which is the name it got only *after* the cut. By so doing, we name it "namelessness," but that becomes a name—the real namelessness is named neither "name" nor "namelessness."
5. The disvalued is actually always *more valueless* than whatever we call disvalued. Since it is neither valued nor disvalued, it is even more a negation of form and value than "the disvalued," which was supposed to be the negation of all form and value (i.e., all of the valued), but was still itself a form and a value, precisely because it had a specific delineation (i.e., contrast to and negation of the valued). It is even more "formless" than (the form we call) "formlessness," even more indefinite than (whatever we are defining as) "indefinite." The real disvalued is beyond "the disvalued," being more disvalued than "the disvalued"—indeed, it is so disvalued that we cannot even stick the label "disvalued" on it, so worthless it is not even worth noticing enough to bother to call it "worthless."
6. The disvalued is actually always *more valuable* than whatever we regard as the valued. By definition, the valued was supposed to be the reservoir of

value: where value comes from and how we get value. But it turns out that what really does serves as the reservoir is the disvalued—the course, the source, the end, the stuff of the valued. The valued means the exclusion of the disvalued, but the valued without the disvalued turns out not to be sustainable value at all. Conversely, the disvalued includes both the valued and the disvalued, so the disvalued is the only true value. Dao is a value term that is here used in a new, "disvalue" sense, which enfolds all the previous senses. Disvalue is the real value. Precisely the negation of all courses, all ways of generating value, is the real *course* of all things, whereby their value is generated. Dao that can be dao'ed is not the constant Dao. The constant Dao is the nondao Dao.

It may be helpful to think of this as analogous to the relation between a flower (A) and dirt (B).

1. Dirt is the *opposite* of flower, being what is excluded when we pick out "flower." Disvalue is the opposite of value. (We may, of course, first contrast the blossom, as the valued, to the stem and roots and sprout and seed, as the disvalued; we can also then consider this whole flowering plant as the valued and the surrounding dirt as the disvalued, and so on).

2. Dirt is the *source* and *end* of the flower, from which the flower is formed, and is what it must return to. "Flower" emerges from and returns to "nonflower."

3. Dirt *includes both* dirt and flower, as the entire flowering plant not only emerges from the dirt, but is, from seed to bloom, a transformation of what we now call the nonflower, the dirt—including some surrounding nonflower entities. This is valueless if the only standard of value is "flowerness."

4. But this dirt is thus *neither dirt nor flower*. It is not really what we call "dirt"—it includes much more than the mere exclusion of flower, which is how we defined dirt; in fact, it is what precedes the distinction between flower and dirt, not what excludes flower. So it is not flower, but it is not dirt either.

5. But that makes this dirt even more "dirty" than what we normally call "dirt"—it is even more formless and diffuse, more resistant to any particular use or structure or name.

6. But just that is what makes it more "flowery" than flower. This is because the so-called flower alone, when separated from dirt, is actually not a real flower—it is a dead flower or a plastic flower. The only real flower is the total flower and dirt system, which, as we saw in item 3, is one of the meanings of "dirt"—but *not* one of the meanings of "flower."

This last point—the asymmetry between dirt and flower, between the valued and the disvalued—is crucial here. The valued is defined precisely as the exclusion of the disvalued. But the exclusion of the disvalued, from the side of the disvalued itself, has an unexpected side effect due to the ambiguity of the disvalued as both precut and postcut. The disvalued *includes* the valued, but the valued *excludes* the disvalued. And it is here, in the Daoist corpus, that we have the originary discovery of what I've been calling "The Great Asymmetry" in its most basic form.

Perhaps we can now glimpse why we might insist that Dao is not a misty, Chinese near-equivalent of the idea of God, in either its Greek or Hebraic senses, but rather, in a very real way, the exact opposite of God. It is not the apotheosis of Form—what is cut out of the background and desired, the Good—but rather just the reverse. It is not the intensification of purposivity, but rather just the reverse. It is not the elevation of control into the ultimate cosmological fact, but just the reverse. We find in the *Daodejing* text very explicit statements that the universe has no values—but that this is just where values come from:

> Heaven and Earth are not benevolent;
> They treat all things as straw dogs.
> The sage is not benevolent;
> He sees all people as straw dogs.

> Is not the space between Heaven and Earth like a bellows?
> Empty but never thwarted,
> The more it is moved, the more emerges from it. (Laozi, *Daodejing* 5)[10]

Straw dogs were ritual effigies made of straw. That is, they were useless junk lying around, which was then bundled together in a particular form, given a name and an identity and a function and a name, worshipped and valued for awhile, and then afterward thrown away, becoming garbage again, and got trampled back into namelessness and valuelessness and uselessness. That's how we all are. We didn't exist. Now we exist. Later we won't exist again. We were worthless, purposeless. Now we have purposes, values, worth. Later we'll be worthless garbage again.

That's how Heaven and Earth treat us. They don't value the middle segment of that process, the one in which there are purposes and values and names and identities, any more than they value the first segment or the last segment. Like a bellows, the universe is empty—of intention, of values, of benevolence, of purpose. And if this juxtaposition of what were perhaps originally two self-standing aphorisms has any rationale behind it, that emptiness is suggested to be a *productive* emptiness, like the space in a bellows: inexhaustible, undefeatable, constantly spitting forth—but spitting forth what? Values, purposes, persons, things, ways. The emptiness of value in segment one is the source of the value of the temporary "straw dog" at the crest of the curve, and it is just its emptiness, its unconcern with the crest, that allows for the crest, the ceaselessness of crests, the availability of infinite crests, values, purposes.

Even more to the point, the text explicitly contrasts Dao to control. Dao is not anyone's "lord," and it does not have any desire to be known or praised:

> Vast Dao is a drifting that can go either right or left.
> All things can rely on it to get themselves born, it never refuses.
> And when it gets a job done, it does not take any credit for it.
> It clothes and feeds all things, but does not control them, does not play
>   the master, is not their lord (*buweizhu* 不為主)
> Forever having and inciting no desires, it can be called the negligible,
>   the Tiny.
> But since all things return to it, though it is not their lord,
> It can also be called the Vast, the Great.
> Indeed it is just its never taking itself as great that enables it to
>   accomplish its greatness. (Laozi, *Daodejing* 34)[11]

It is just its valuelessness—in the sense of both not embracing any values and not inciting any values, of not being valued—that makes Dao so valuable. It is just its exclusion from all that makes it include all, like "garbage." It is just its having no purpose that fulfills all purposes. It is just its not being lord that makes it vast and great. It is just because it does not control anything that it contains and nourishes everything, that all things cleave to it, that it contains and possesses all. It is just because it is the opposite of God that all things find their source in it, return to it, are sustained by it, find their purposes and values and ways in it, from it, to it. Its vastness is a drifting, a directionlessness, a both/and, a left and right, an all-inclusivity, a choicelessness, a purposelessness. Dao is the opposite of God.

In passing, it is important to recall here our distinction between Emulative Atheism and Compensatory Theism. For this Daoist emphasis on drifting—and yielding, and softness, and inclusiveness, and weakness, and lowliness—has, from the earliest days of its translation into European languages, led some unwary readers to toss out any consideration for context and see an analogue here to the teachings of the Sermon on the Mount in the Gospel of Matthew (5–7). It seemed to them reminiscent of such injunctions as "take no thought for the morrow, do not worry about what you will eat or drink; consider the lilies, they reap not neither do they sow," as well as "the sun shines on both the good and the evil," "blessed are the meek," "judge not," "resist not evil," "the last shall be first," and so on. There, too, it was claimed, we have the idea of living without purpose, without planning, without an attempt to control—of letting go of control. But one of the main points in our discussion has been that this is a surface convergence that conceals a much profounder conflict. The difference lies in *why* these things are recommended—what is different in how the two texts conceive what it is that makes the lowly and disvalued valuable, by what means and for what reason they ground or reverse into its opposite. And the difference lies in one word, whose identity should be no surprise by this point: the word is "God." The Sermon on the Mount is all about control—the total control exercised by God. It is not control itself, or purpose itself, or planning itself, or thought for the morrow itself being questioned here: it is whose prerogative it is. In fact, control is *too good* for you, as a mere creature: it is the prerogative of God. Judgment and vengeance also are *too good* for you: they are a prerogative of the creator. So when the Sermon on the Mount advises against humans having control, or showing vengeance, or judging, or worrying about the future, it interposes constant threats and promises about *judgments in the future!* For if you are *not* meek, if you *do* judge, if you *do* take thought for the morrow, if you *do* resist evil, then "what reward have ye? . . . cast into hell . . . in danger of the judgment . . . in danger of hellfire," and so forth. The point is that only God gets to do these things *because they are the best things in the universe.* The Sermon on the Mount thus is not an exception to the general elevation of purpose and control in Greco-Hebraic thought: it is perhaps its high-water mark. It belongs to the category of Compensatory Theism (indeed, it is, perhaps, its *locus classicus*), not Emulative Atheism. Purpose is divine. Control is divine. The universe runs throughout on purpose, on planning, on design: "Even the hairs on your head are numbered." Moreover, "not a sparrow falls without the Father being aware of it"; "Thy will [must] be done on earth as it is in Heaven"; and on and on. Mind, Will, purpose, control, are here intensified and elevated to such a point that mere creatures are unworthy of partaking in them. So the similar appearances in the *Daodejing* and the Sermon on the Mount of calls for weakness, for lowliness, for purposelessness, for drifting, for not judging or resisting the disvalued, for not playing the lord, conceal the most extreme difference in point of view: one is the hyperatheist rejection of the idea that conscious purpose is the real source of anything in the universe, the other is the hypertheist view that every jot and tittle is accounted for by the One conscious purpose that rules and micromanages all things, that conscious purpose is the only source, so much so that we are unable to participate in it and unworthy of doing so.

From this understanding of Dao in the *Daodejing*, we can draw a number of aphoristic implications: the more clear-cut things are, the further they are from any sustainable reality; the more clearly we know things, the less accurate our knowledge is; and the vaguer our knowledge, the more it resembles, and participates in, the reality of things. Vague knowledge is concomitant with a vague Will. Union with the Dao means not knowing exactly what you are doing and therefore not knowing exactly what you are doing it with or for. But, again, as detailed in the previous sections on "The Great Asymmetry," this does not require the exclusion of mental processes or even of directed impulsions. The *Daodejing* offers this striking and instructive image: "The infant does not yet know the union of male and female, and yet his member is erect—the ultimate virility!" (Laozi, *Daodejing* 55).[12] This infant has no mental image of the "goal" or "purpose" of his erection, has no idea what it's for, but he has an erection just the same. The infant's erection does not know what it is doing or what it wants, yet it does, in a certain sense, want—albeit vaguely, inchoately. As the first chapter of the text puts it, it is "always desiring, always desireless." But this vague, inchoate wanting without knowing is, the *Daodejing* says, the real source, the real course, the real essence of virility—of what actually gets the union of male and female and the birthing of all creatures done.

Historically speaking, the *Daodejing* might be a collection of loosely assembled verses, which is one way to explain the diversity of views found there on the A/ B relation—the relation between purpose and purposelessness, between value and valuelessness. Each can sometimes appear as leading to and from the other. But read as a whole, it presents a challenge to harmonizing these views. What one learns in trying to do so, as commentators did over the centuries, is the way in which Emulative Atheism uniquely provides a way to encompass and ground the other positions, while the reverse is not the case—again because of "The Great Asymmetry" between purpose and purposelessness, whereby the former excludes the latter but the latter does not exclude the former. We have here the *locus classicus* of Emulative Atheism as such. For what seems to characterize the text is precisely the circle of ends and means (as they might be called when seen from the side of purpose), or of the mutual generation of purposeless formlessness and purpose-bearing form (as they might be called when seen from the side of purposelessness)—their continual process of flip-flopping. It is the commitment to purpose itself that ends up being undermined in this juxtaposition of purposeful uses of purposelessness and purposeless emergences of purpose. The denial of purpose here plays out, not as the elimination of purpose, but as the allowing of purposes; it is the source from which they flow and the nourishment that allows them to flourish. What we end up with is another example of the one/none problem discussed previously, as embedded in the purpose/purposeless asymmetry. The opposite of one is not none, but many. The denial of purpose is not the excising of purpose, but the open door allowing multiple purposes. Although the purposes trotted out in the text are not particularly diverse, being the standard set of the usual human desiderata of the assumed early Chinese readership— long life, good government, harmony, order, success—their groundedness and return to what is beyond any purpose provides a way to relate different purposes to each other, just as the unity of the empty hub is equally a part of multiple opposed purposes, multiple alternate values. But that step is not taken until Laozi's empty hub at the center of the thirty spokes (Laozi, *Daodejing* 11) becomes the "Axis of Daos," the center that allows and responds to and enhances *every* possible perspective, showing its applicability to *every* possible value system and how it serves to augment each of them, no matter what they are, with the furtherance of whatever that perspective itself takes to be valuable. This is the development that occurs in the second of the great classical Daoist texts, the *Zhuangzi*, to which we have already alluded, and which we will take up again repeatedly in what follows.

THE MORAL HAZARD OF MORAL IDEALS

The idea that a consistently intelligent intentional consciousness is the real source of everything that happens is the key premise of monotheism. Our shorthand for this idea is *Noûs* as *Arché*. Quite often, the structure of this supposition is transferred directly to the microcosm of human behavior (what we have called Emulative Theism, but which is also present in any but the extreme and unmixed form of Compensatory Theism, which has perhaps never actually appeared). That results in the idea that it is our own intentional willing that is the real source of everything that we do (sometimes this is even given as a circular definition of what "doing," as opposed to mere "happening," *means*). This supposition has indeed come to be a kind of default premise of a field of human discourse called *morality*. This is where people try to formulize ideas about how people *should act*, premised on the idea that formulizing these ideas will have a causal role in making people *actually act that way*. This premise is so commonly assumed as a default that it's almost difficult to formulate. The idea is that telling people, "You should do this," or "This is what it is good to do," or even, more forcefully, "Do this!" will itself (apart from any threats or promises that might be attached to it, for that is claimed to be something other than the moral part of these claims) actually cause people to do that thing, or at least contribute to making it more likely that they do.

Empirically speaking, it cannot be said there is overwhelming evidence that this is at all true. It certainly has not been demonstrated that the conscious recognition that something is good will, in fact, cause a person to do that thing. In fact, there is considerable anecdotal evidence that in very many cases, it has exactly the opposite effect. But this is an empirical question, which I do not have the data to adjudicate here. What I want to explore instead is the alternate conception of human action that comes into view when we remove the monotheist premise and thus operate free of its application as the default model of human agency.

It is again ancient Daoism where we find the most striking examples of an alternate model. Indeed, one of the key themes of both of the two classic Daoist texts, the *Daodejing* and the *Zhuangzi*, is that moral ideals, moral preaching, and moral effort are not only of no help to improving human behavior—neither for the stated goals of encouraging people to actually act in the ways designated as moral by those very ideals *nor* in opening alternate horizons of human experience that are not limited to those ideals—but are likely to be an actual *impediment* thereto. What is at issue here is the *very idea of morality as such*: the entire idea of explicitly thinking about what should be approved or disapproved—what one should do or not do, what is good and what is bad—coming to conclusions about these matters, and then communicating them to others and trying to convince them. The *Daodejing*, in its most commonly circulated version, suggests that moral ideals like "benevolence" and "righteousness" are *symptoms* of the abandonment of something it calls "Great Dao" (chap. 18) and also *attempted remedies* to the desolate condition of human beings in the absence of the Great Dao, but they are remedies that *exacerbate* the cause of the malady rather than alleviating it, something that can only be achieved by getting rid of them (chap. 19). Conscious moral ideals and the conscious moral effort they inspire are like an addictive painkiller that only appears to solve the real problem (the loss of the Great Dao), while actually further weakening the patient and making him that much more susceptible to the illness. In effect, morality is the opiate of the people.

The premise behind this claim is the basic atheist idea that the real source of what we do is not our conscious ideals, and this includes those of our actions and states that we consider desirable or good. We do not attain the Good by means of conscious allegiance to the idea of the "the Good." But we do, sometimes, attain those things that we then, after the fact, label with the word "good." The goodnesses that emerge are part of a larger economy, netted together with other things that also emerge, as a flower is netted together with dirt and shit. "Flower" emerges from dirt, and we like it—its fragrance and appearance happen to interact with our perceptual and conceptual apparatuses in a way that is pleasing to us. So we want more of that. Why must we have so much dirt and shit too? We try to purify, to make as much as possible flowery. We judge the goodness or badness of things according to how much they resemble the flower, the part we like, and try as much as possible to eliminate anything unflowery. Ideally, we would like to have a pure flower. Our ideals are attempts to make those lucky hits, the parts of the whole spontaneous growth that happen to please us, happen *more often*. In this effort, it doesn't matter whether the ideals are moral or amoral or immoral: what is essential is an attempt to control, to single out some one type of event (whether it is universal kindness or my own fame and power) and make it happen more often. The *Daodejing* critique of morality, embodied in its claim that morality arose only when the Great Dao fell away, suggests in effect that when the flower-dirt system was no longer found to be enough, either because it was having a temporary bad year and the flower was a little meager, or because last year's standard was applied to this year as if it had some authority to be the universal standard for all years, or because in general we ceased to see the interdependence of flower and dirt, someone got the idea of remedying the situation by demanding more flower, more flower! But the Great Dao can only be restored by throwing away morality; in other words, by throwing away the demand for more flower and less dirt. The demand for more flower and less dirt has not made there be more flower, but on the contrary has undermined the very conditions of flower production; it has made the situation worse: it has made even fewer flowers grow and then demanded more, which made even fewer grow, until all we have is a plastic flower with no dirt—which is to say, no flower either. Moral ideals do not create morality; they create hypocrisy and a hostility toward certain parts of the self, a self-division that makes actual moral goods impossible to attain. The hostility to parts of the self is then projected outward, into hostility toward others who seem to exemplify or encourage the hated parts: as Nietzsche says, "Stings of conscience teach one to sting."[13] The more "pure" the demand for control in one direction rather than any other, the worse the consequence.

The *Zhuangzi* anthology contains some sections that echo and develop this general point of view (e.g., chaps. 8, 9, 10, 22, and 29). Elsewhere it develops the critique of morality in another direction. One passage in particular is worth considering in this connection, which I freely paraphrase here:[14]

> My life is at every moment grounded by its embankments. [That is, it is bound by the limits of its situation, like a current grounded and shaped

between its banks, but also shaping them with its flow.] My knowing consciousness, on the other hand, [which embraces general ideas of right and wrong and conscious controlling purposes,] is not grounded by any embankments. If the embanked flow of life is forced to follow and obey something not shaped and grounded by any embankments, [like my knowing consciousness and its ideas of right and wrong], that flow is endangered. And to meet this danger by enhancing the control of consciousness even further—that merely exacerbates the endangerment of life's flow all the more.

This embanked and grounded flow of life may do things labeled "good" [in a given community], but not so consistently or persistently that it could bring upon one any reputation [in that community, for moral virtue]. It may do things labeled "evil" [in a given community], but not so consistently or persistently that it could bring one punishment [for crime in that community]. For it tends toward the current of the central meridian[15] as its normal course. And this is what enables us to maintain our bodies, to keep the life in them intact, to nourish those near and dear to us, and to fully live out our years.

The idea here is that notions of right and wrong, of approval and disapproval, as adopted by the conscious mind and its pretended general criteria of knowledge of values, are a danger to something else in us, which this passage calls "life," a term that in the "Inner Chapters" of the *Zhuangzi* means, not a specific span of life, but the actual process of generation, including the flow of experiences, moods, and other changing states: the passage of experienced time per se. The previous chapter of this text had offered an extensive critique of the mind's ability to reach any such universal conclusion, on the basis precisely of its own embeddedness in its particular situation and perspective. The present passage offers a vivid image of this perspective and its limitations: it is every moment of life's "groundedness in its embankments." This implies a flow that goes through unpredictable twists and turns, like a zigzagging river between its banks, shaped by the line of least resistance but also thereby carving its own path, its own "Dao," into the landscape.[16] What is critiqued in the first paragraph quoted here is what Zhuangzi later (in chapter 4) calls "taking the conscious mind as master" (*shixin* 師心):[17] forcing the spontaneous and ever-changing generation of activities to follow the guidance of the mind's judgments about what is good, and its directives about what means should be employed to reach those goals. This includes not only self-interested goals but also moral goals (as shown in the dialogue between Confucius and Yan Hui in which that phrase occurs, in chapter 4). Subordinating life to moral ideals obstructs and endangers its ability to ground itself in its present circumstances, to cleave to the flow embedded in that circumstance, and to proceed to flow and carve through the landscape on that basis, as the direction of flow of water would be embedded in the topography through which a river flows. This is illustrated in the famous story that follows this passage, which recounts how Cook Ding carved up an ox, letting the contours of the animal's carcass guide the flow of the knife rather than attempting to direct the cutting through global ideas about the structure of the ox and the best ways to carve it.[18]

But the second paragraph cited here adds another dimension to this critique. "This embanked and grounded flow of life may do things labeled 'good' in a given community, but not so consistently or persistently that it could bring upon one any reputation for moral virtue. It may do things labeled 'evil' in a given community, but not so consistently or persistently that it could bring me punishment upon me for crime" (*weishan wujin-ming, wei'e wujinxing* 為善勿近名 為惡勿近刑). If we take the most usual meaning of the negative imperative *wu*, these sentences would mean literally, "In doing good, stay away from fame; in doing evil, stay away from punishment." Since this baldly assumes that the reader will sometimes "do evil" and nonjudgmentally seems to advise him on how to get away with it, blandly condoning it, this passage has caused commentators considerable worry. But what is really claimed here, as I read it, is something about the spontaneous grounded flow of life itself. Like a river, it tends to go back and forth, to twist and turn, flowing now left and now right. Precisely because it has no fixed shape or direction, it is deeply attuned to the slight changes in its environment. In the absence of any global guidance—any conscious direction, any *Noûs* choosing the Good, anyone or anything controlling it—it cannot sustain flow in any one direction for very long. So it may flicker in any direction—either toward what any given value system calls good or what it calls bad—but it cannot execute a consistent plan over a long period of time in any one direction. The commitment to the Good, to moral virtue, to some specific moral ideas, is in the same boat as the commitment to evil in that both require conscious guidance to be made consistent over time in excluding what does not accord with their guidance. If not interfered with by conscious control, it can surge left or right, "good" or "evil," but it cannot sustain either quality for long enough to lead to any fixed character of either kind, and thus to commit any action substantial enough to bring on a response from the environment based on a definite identification of the agent as either good or evil: it eludes judgment; its character is not fixed and it follows no single "way."

The implication here is, first, that it is this consistency and persistence of a particular course of action, of following some definite ideals or guidance, that produces both moral virtue and a definite maliciousness of character, as well as the blowback of both identities, good reputation and punishment. All four of these items (good character, bad character, good reputation, and bad reputation) are regarded as dangerous and noxious. The self-torture and invasive self-righteousness of moral virtue is here looked at as a problem precisely because it imposes this kind of conscious value on oneself and on others, as well as inciting envy, resentment, anger, self-blame, and so on. Zhuangzi likes to note how a reputation for virtue makes one either a target to be taken down, or an ideological smoke screen to be used by powerful people as propaganda for amoral purposes, or a way of making oneself useful and thus prone to be used and used up, or a model used to oppress those who do not meet the standard of that model, which no other flow should be expected to do since its own twists and turns are grounded in its own embankments of its own ever-changing landscapes. Similarly, the real evils are seen as those that come, not from the occasional drifts and blips toward evil that unguided life sometimes takes, but in the imposition of some consistent plan or guidance, some conscious commitment to control and constrain the wiggle of life. It should be noted that what is called evil is a consistent and unchanging direction of action is actually only possible under the guidance of an ideal of some kind, a controlling idea of the conscious mind. We may think here of large-scale evils like Hitler's Final Solution or Stalin's bloody reconstruction of the Soviet Union: without a commitment to a conscious set of values, an idea of the Good, some design and control, it would be impossible to produce the large-scale consistent evils accomplished by these regimes. The evil of the Final Solution is as much a function of its attempt to be a "solution" as its specific content, if not more so. It could function only because it was itself a morality, a deep commitment to some ideal of a good (in this case, a *Judenfrei* Europe). The real problem is absolutist morality itself: the idea that certain identifiable deeds or attitudes are good and always to be encouraged while others are evil and always to be avoided or if possible destroyed—that good and evil are mutually exclusive, and at war with one another. The real problem is *Noûs* as *Arché*. The real problem is God.

This is a thoroughgoingly atheist critique of this morality itself, in that it is rooted in the deepest premise of monotheism, namely, the idea of conscious value as the real cause of what happens. And it is in this spirit that throughout this book we can view moral idealism as an attempt at conscious control of behavior, an impulse that appears here and there all over the world and in all kinds of ideological settings but is brought to its highest pitch and given its most ontologically deeply grounded expression in the idea of monotheism, which makes conscious control the ultimate principle of the entire cosmos. Moral agency itself is what we question here, the idea that human beings should will their own actions according to conscious ideals of any kind, whether selfish or altruistic. This is also why we will not give serious consideration to any alleged moral benefits of monotheism. Many people feel that one of the best things about the well-known monotheistic religions, even if they think these religions are obviously not true, is that they propose an absolute morality and strongly enjoin people to follow it. This is for us, rather another thing that is problematic about them. The worry is not just that absolutizing morality makes it unchanging and thus prone to fanaticism and a sometimes cruel disregard for changes and the idiosyncrasies of individual situations. This is part of the critique here, but the problem runs deeper: it is the idea of the ultimacy of conscious control itself that is reinforced and exacerbated by the belief in the efficacy of moral ideals, and vice versa, and the way this harms the uncontrolled flow that is, for an atheist, *the actual source of consciousness itself and of conscious ideals themselves.*

Does this imply that there is some prior "goodness" to that spontaneous flow, some tendency toward life and productivity and the Good? It does not. This is really the heart of the question. The source of the "self-corrective" power of this flow is not that it has any preference for correctness or that any principle or value is controlling it, much less any consciousness that embraces a principle or a value. For "correctness" is here described merely as a tendency toward "centering," and centering is a function of *not* having a preference for any of the extremes, for any determinate state or direction. Water is, here as in the *Daodejing*, the default model for Dao. Water, if poured out randomly, in the absence of any tilt or torque or friction in one direction or another, tends to take the shape of a circle. This is not because circularity is a principle that someone or something has to embrace or promote or enforce or that must be secretly hidden within the water as some definite thing called its "nature." It is because circularity simply means having no reason to go one way rather than another. The absence of any constraint is called "circularity," just as the "Law of Averages" is not a positive law but rather the absence of any law. It is this sense of the power and activity of infinity, of boundlessness, of nothingness, of chaos, of formlessness, that is central to atheist mystical intuitions. The simple lack of any constraint, of any limit, manifests in an infinite number of ways because there is nothing to stop it. The generation of beings does not require the interference or intervention of any positive law or principle, and self-correction as adjustment away from imbalance requires no special values or laws. It is the absence of all laws and principles that produces all laws and principles, as temporary, nonultimate manifestations of infinity.

This is why I will not be arguing for the moral benefits of atheist mysticism either, not attributing to it some way in which it does a better job of promoting or motivating morality. At the same time, I would certainly not call for a removal of moral ideals—that would itself be a moral ideal. I call for a reinscribing of moral ideals as an epiphenomenon of something that is itself neither moral nor an ideal. Just as purposelessness does not exclude purposes, the amoral flow of life does not exclude moralities or local forms of accountability and goals. It just removes their ultimacy and their role as source, their right to be the controller of the overall direction of life. Conscious control, the knowing, judging consciousness itself, is a secondary phenomenon, an inadvertent offshoot or "bastard son of a concubine" (*nie* 孽), as Zhuangzi puts it:[19] it is not the source, not the ultimate value, not the final arbiter, and thus it allows for the proliferation and robustness of many more microcalibrated forms of morality, twisting and turning as they carve through each new landscape and grounded not in any controlling ideal but in their own zigzagging embankments. The temporary conflicts between these differing purposes are resolved in their common rootedness in the purposeless, rather than the eventual victory of one or another of these purposes over all the others—the one that manages to integrate, subsume, sublate, or simply annihilate all the others. It is only in this sense that we regard all demotions of the authority of moral ideals as real moral advances. This is another dimension of the critique of the ultimacy of purpose: the denial of the ultimacy of purpose is a liberator, rather than a suppressor, of the infinite robustness of infinite purposes. At the same time, it is a preserver of their unity, not in another, "higher" purpose—not in the unity of a conscious controller—but in the purposelessness that enables their coexistence and interrelations. But to fully appreciate the nature of these nonpurposive "interrelations" among elements that are somehow "unified" in the absence of their common subordination to a single purpose, we need to further inquire into the ambiguities of the fuzzy term "unity"—what kinds of unities can there be and how do they differ? How does the "unity" wrought by conscious purposivity—the unity that pertains to personal agency—differ from the "unity" enabled by the rootedness of all purposes in an all-allowing purposelessness? How do the "unified" elements interrelate in these different cases? It is to these questions that we now turn.

CHAPTER 3

Purposivity and Personhood

WHAT IS A "PERSON"? CONTROL VERSUS NECESSITY AND THE DICHOTOMIZATION OF ONENESS AND DIFFERENCE

We are slowly advancing toward a position that may strike many as an outrageous reversal of commonly shared intuitions about thinghood and personality, about necessity and freedom, and more broadly about objectivity and subjectivity. For it has become usual to see an opposition between mechanistic determinism and personalist freedom—seeing meaninglessness, inert objecthood, closed determinacy, and lifeless inertia on the side of mechanism, while seeing meaning, dynamic engagement, open possibility, and life on the side of personalism. The idea is that the world of inert things, of laws and facts, is a blind, lifeless mechanism of cause and effect, in which each thing is inertly just what it is, unable to transcend its own boundaries, closed off and statically determinate. If this realm of nondeliberate material entities forms any sort of "unity" at all, it is only in a weak sense, in that its elements share a common and equally inert substratum, are passively contained within a shared boundary, are made of the same lifeless stuff, or share in subjection to the rigid, deterministic laws of blind, causal push and pull. The world of persons, on the other hand, is on this view the only place where we find freedom, activity, meaning, and real unity—a transcending of the present toward the future in teleological activity, the binding together of elements into a meaningful whole through their coordinated service to their shared goal—the realm of possibility and openness, dynamical self-creation through freely willed projects, considered action due to reasons rather than the material push-pull of mere causes, openness toward the future and the world, overcoming of any fixed determinacy, the locus of creative negativity, and the transcending of boundaries.

But here I would like to suggest that just the opposite is closer to the truth, though still not quite right. For as I will try to show in detail in this chapter and the next, *both* these terms are, on my view, the product of the stranglehold of the ultimacy of purposivity and personhood: *both* inert separate things related causally through deterministic external relations *and* persons projecting toward the future and the world intentionally are by-products of the type of personhood prioritized as a result of granting ontological ultimacy to teleology. To borrow the Daoist language of the last chapter, we here view both sides of this opposition as the result of a primal cut in an unhewn something that precedes them both—a cut made by purpose, valuation, and desire. By carving values out of the unhewn, by making tools and tool-users that lock in this purposivity ultimate, the worthless, inert, leftover garbage of matter is simultaneously created at the same stroke, as a by-product. The Daoists see the detritus as the first place to look for a way back toward the precut unhewn that precedes both the chipped-away garbage and the carved-out tool, though this garbage too is misunderstood when apprehended only in terms of the cut. The alternative to both the free person and the deterministic thing is the unhewn, the one-and-many, the oceanic: this is a raw infinity, a nonmechanical necessity, a necessary inseparability of oneness and multiplicity, which is initially mistaken for mere dead, causal determinism or meaningless waste—the opposite of God, as called Dao by the Daoists. We will see the unhewn worked out through different methods, presuppositions, and emphases by Spinoza on the one hand, where this opposite of God is approached first through necessity and called precisely (*inter alia*) *God*, and by Bataille on the other hand, where it is first approached through violence and called intimacy. It is also worked out by some Buddhists who call it the Emptiness-as-Awareness and others who call it the Middle as Mutual Asness of Permanence-Impermance / Nonself-selfhood / Suffering-bliss; by early Schelling and Hegel as the convergence of necessity and freedom in the impossible / necessary in-itself / for-itself; and by Nietzsche as the moment willed wholly and thus both excluding and including all others, eternally first and eternally last, and in various other ways by our other atheist mystics to come. What they share is this golden thread: a prior third that is an alternative to both mechanism and teleology, thingness and person, freedom and determinism, the loss of which generates both of these contrasted extremes, which are then conceived as mutually exclusive opposites. And the implications of this alternative, we claim, are enormous, constituting the main thrust of this book: it will mean that the attempt to safeguard things like freedom and life and meaning and personhood and consciousness by separating them from blind, lifeless, meaningless determinism—by granting them ontological ultimacy—is bound to backfire, while the seemingly nihilistic embrace of blind, lifeless, meaningless, impersonal determinism is, in fact, the first step toward overcoming the dichotomy between the two sides. We cannot stop at this first step, to be sure; but when this "nihilistic" move is pushed to the point of exceptionless thoroughness, as with our atheist mystics, an unexpected reversal emerges that alone makes possible the excavation of a genuinely unbounded source of freedom, meaning, life, personhood, and consciousness. How does that come about?

Let us start, in this chapter, with the question of personhood. "Person" is a concept initially deriving from theater, and specifically from the masks (*persona* in Latin or *prósōpon* πρόσωπον in Greek) used to present and continuously identify a character in a theatrical narrative. It is rooted in a need to pinpoint and track a role in relation to other roles in a specific drama, something that can be traced across the narrative time of the play, so that the cause and effect of the story will make sense: the character who suffers or enjoys consequences in act V must be identifiable as the same character who performed certain deeds in act I for the narrative to cohere at all, for the narrative to be a narrative, and for the drama to succeed in being a drama. These consequences to actions may or may not be specifically moral in the sense of implying punishment and reward (although this does seem to be the dominant motif in early Greek drama, insofar as some sort of hortatory message was part of the propaganda function of the performance as a ritually required part of civic life), but at the very least, for the drama to make sense, a person must remember his relation to the other persons in the play, be able to recognize them and retain causally meaningful attitudes and obligations toward them, recall debts, and anticipate the repaying of debts to and from the other characters. A person must bind past and present together into some coherence having to do with memories and anticipations about other persons, about debts and obligations, and about the exchange of credits and debits, for these are the lifeblood of the dramatic imbalance and rebalancing that structure, the lifeblood of the narrative form.

The term *persona* is taken up into Roman law out of this theatrical background, and we can see how this would be an easy connection to make. The foregrounding of *legal accountability* is a small step from the notion of temporal coherence in a narrative, in the interaction of debts and credits among the characters and the memory and anticipation of love and hate, of obligation and gratitude. Where law has to do with punishment and reward, the idea of moral responsibility is thus given a useful carrier. That makes good narrative sense, and also good legal sense. As members of a cast of social characters with debts and obligations to one another, we all are "persons." In short, *person* becomes, above all, the locus of the notion of *responsibility*.

In drama we may wish to revel in the hopelessness and inevitability of a tragic fate, a certain deadlock in the world that can be borne bravely and nobly by the person who happens to embody it and who suffers the conflict and consequences of this inner conflict of the world itself. That may be one of the things that is offered to our aesthetic contemplation and enjoyment. In other cases, the drama may serve a hortatory function more centrally, warning citizens against certain actions by showing their unpleasant consequences and encouraging other actions that lead to happy endings. But once this dramatic notion of a person is shifted over to the juridical realm, the latter aspect, the moral aspect, inevitably comes to the fore. For now there is a question of justice, and the state legal apparatus will seem justified to exactly the extent that the punishment fits the crime. That means the culprit must be identified: the real *cause* of the crime must be in the deed of the individual and traceable no further back, for example, into the conditions of the society, for which the state apparatus, the very same entity as that proposing the punishment, would itself be responsible. For justice to seem just, we must not seek a cause of any action that goes further back than the person. Since the person is, by definition, the one who will receive the punishment or reward, justice requires that the person be the final term in the chain of causes to which an act is traced. In the context of penal law, "person" is an embodiment of the question, Where should the blame be placed? The person must be "*free*"—in other words, the first in the chain of relevant causes—for the punishment to be just. Any prior causes to the action preceding the person's deed itself must be ruled irrelevant. Of course, if the "state" in question is the inescapable Kingdom of God, we have the same problem in spades. Absolute free will is the only way to avoid the obvious implication of God's omnipotence, that is, that he is the ultimate cause of all our sins, and thus that his punishments of us are wildly unjust. The radical notion of free will as an entirely unprecedented beginning of a chain of causality in the deed of a person thus seems to have a lot to do with clearing God's name, making it possible for God to be just in spite of being omnipotent and at the same time promising dire punishments—indeed, in most forms of Christianity and Islam at least, these are *eternal* punishments. For those eternal punishments to be just, we will need a real crime, and an adequately serious crime. But the very notion of person is part of the same juridical problem. A person is someone who must be the one in *control* of his actions, who is solely responsible for his actions, for this is the only conception that gives the term the required meaning in a juridical context.

We can thus far define a person as an "accountable controller." "Control" of something means to be the cause of what happens to that something, the sole cause. It means that I will be accountable for what happens to those things: some subset of the events in which I participate are to be attributed solely to myself as cause. That is what it means to say I am the agent in control of them: they are my free acts. The notion of control implies a duality, a controller and a controlled. In the context of accountability, as traced from drama to law, it further implies *purpose and motivation*. We have noted also the time-binding aspect of purpose; it goes hand in hand with the anticipation and memory structure necessary for the coherence of drama, for the tallying of debts and credits, for reward and punishment. Something is foreseen, envisioned, projected into the future, and this experience of projecting toward the future, of anticipating, is linked to an act of Will that is singled out as the locus of responsibility, for it is credited with causal efficacy, with being the reason why something happens. In other words, someone wants something to happen in the future—he wills it—and this fully accounts for why that thing happens. This act of envisioning and de-siring and willing is what *controlled* the outcome, which means the person who did the envisioning and desiring and willing is the one responsible for it happening.

The necessary relation of dramatic character and spectating audience must be noted here. A person is not a person unless he is *watched*. The audience traces the action of the character through the narrative: the char-acter is a "person" to whom expectations are attached—but the spectator is also thus drawn into the connective expectations of this narrative time, without which he cannot do the job of tracking the character. The spectator thus also becomes a person, but necessarily a *different* person, who is *not* accountable for the deeds in the play. The person is only a person if recog-nized as such—by a person. Persons cannot exist in isolation; they emerge in the act of recognition itself, as two sides of a single relation of mutual expectation. The mutual recognition between persons as persons in this context thus signifies most directly the expectation of accountability one way or the other. It involves being responsible or not responsible for the actions unfolding in the narrative. To be a "person" caught up in this expec-tation of accountability, in this mutual recognition, requires that one must at least be someone who *could* be responsible even if in this case he is not. To be recognized as a person by another person means I can expect that he expects me to have expectations. I anticipate that he will treat me as an an-ticipating being, that is, as a being that projects toward the future, and one who can thus be held accountable for controlling certain outcomes in the future; he sees me as responsible for my actions. To be known as a person by a person is to be accounted accountable. The distinguishing feature now is cast entirely in terms of control: who is in control and who is not. The two sides, the two persons, must be sharply distinguished: they must be fully other to one another, so that accountability attributed to one is not at-tributed to the other. Personhood is, on the one hand, a kind of unity—the unity of control, of purpose, of accountable intentions of the controlling, choice-making consciousness across time that coordinates its actions into a unity in service of a preconceived future goal. But at the same time, it must differ from all other persons and from all nonperson things absolutely.

But this necessary relation of watching and being watched by another accountable person in the constitution of accountable personhood has further consequences. A strange, intensifying, chicken-and-egg feedback loop is put in place when, for whatever contingent reason, the controlling executive function that is occasionally present in human experience is singled out and elevated into the constant first principle of all that exists, that is, God. The human *Noûs* must at once emulate, witness, and conflict with this new and better version of controlling, personal *Noûs*. As we have seen, a kind of mimetic doubling is endemic to personhood, but so is accountability, the requirement of being in control—and control is, by nature, a zero-sum game. A very troubling double bind accompanies this way of organizing the relation of sameness and difference between entities, which ensues if, and only if, the entities in question are *ultimately* persons; in other words, if personhood is made into a first principle. If we grant that personhood requires a witness of consummate status, God as person likewise requires a consummately free and responsible witness to his absolute freedom and responsibility: his personhood can only be recognized by another person. But the nature of personhood itself has now been wildly inflated. The finite, conscious selfhood now must integrate this newly aggrandized version into a revised conception of itself—it too must be recognized, and must recognize itself, as a totally responsible first cause of all its actions. After being selected out of experience and projected into the position of first cause, the finite *Noûs* now sees itself as a pale reflection of what *Noûs* could and should be were it freed from all limitations: the true nature of *Noûs* as such is, by rights, to be the controller of everything that happens to it without exception. In principle it should be, not only the responsible agent at the source of all one's own actions, but the responsible agent at the source of everything, without exception. Anything not in its control must now be a problem to it. Once engaged in the mutually recognizing gaze of the projection of itself writ large (i.e., God), once watched by the eyes of God, the finite, controlling, conscious selfhood feels mimetically tasked with being as fully focused on absolute control as its putatively primordial model: it is infinitely responsible for everything it does. But for the same reason, it is required also to always battle for control with that same God—for as we've seen, the mutual recognition of personhood also requires the absolute mutual exclusivity between the persons, since it is grounded in the need for a single source of accountability: again, control as such is a zero-sum game. The finite *Noûs*, which is required to exercise absolute control, must always conflict with any other controllers, and hence with its own model—God—as well. But in this case it must also always lose this battle: this relationship comes with the absolute demand for subjugation to the other, absolute person. Formerly, the finite person could perhaps feel its own occasional sense of control simultaneously as rooted in something, not only beyond its control, but beyond *anyone*'s control—beyond control, full stop. And when it lost control, what it lost it to could also be something beyond anyone's control. Now in cases where it must relinquish control, as it is now morally required to do, it must not be to anything uncontrolled, but to what is controlled by the greater Controller: the Will of God. And it must control even its submission to the greater Controller—any failure to do so will be something for which it must be held accountable, for it is now accountable for everything that it does and everything it fails to do. The only two options are now to control or to be controlled. For man, both options are now unacceptable. In the world where personhood reigns as ultimate principle, that is, in the monotheistic world involving the existence of a sovereign, personal God, precisely this double bind, internalizing both the watcher and the watched as well as all the mimetic conflict between them, is what will be called "being a person."

And here we come to the point. For there are other ways to organize the relation between oneness and difference besides that enforced by conceptions of ultimate personality, purpose, and control. One of these is simply *necessity*. The question of atheism and atheist mysticism in one sense begins (but does not end) with this distinction between *necessity* and *control*. Why do we claim that even mechanical determinism is preferable to person-centric free will, though both fall short of the atheist mysticism we expound here? Why does the prioritizing of free will and personal meaningfulness backfire while the embrace of unfreedom and meaninglessness opens the door to infinite freedoms and meanings? Because the idea of necessity involved in determinism at least *begins* to undermine the dualism that is, on the contrary, exacerbated by the notion of free will, restructuring the one / many relation such that the very idea of control and of being controlled is instantly dissolved. How does that come about?

When we say that B is a *necessary* consequence of A, we mean that these two apparently different things or events are not ultimately two, not really self-standing, not really separable. When I say that triangles with the property of having three equal sides *necessarily* also have the property of having three equal angles, I mean that equilaterality cannot even be conceived without also entailing equiangularity; every instance of one will bring an instance of the other along with it, with zero exceptions. At the same time, it means that, for this very reason, A is not merely what it appeared to be at first—that A is not merely "A." Equilaterality *necessarily* has the property of being otherwise expressible in this alternate, quite different, way. Equilaterality and equiangularity are recognizably different, but they are also inseparably one; it is intrinsic to the inalienable nature of each that it implies the other. A property that is inalienable from a thing, which it cannot lack as long as it exists at all, belongs to the identity of that thing itself. The monolithic identity of A, as excluding non-A (e.g., B), is effaced: A is really AB, as is B. A is, in addition to being A, also more and other than A; B is more and other than B. The difference between them is as inalienable as their oneness: they must be different and they must also be one. *Necessity, thought through, is an undermining of the dichotomy of oneness and difference.*

The ordinary conception of necessity, of course, does not quite bring out the full implications of this undermining as long as it operates under the aegis of the presupposition of the dichotomy of oneness and difference. Because of this presupposition, "necessity" in its ordinary meaning remains a sort of transitional concept, a hybrid that is expressed inadequately because it continues to understand itself in terms of presuppositions that it has already begun to transcend. As long as we are still thinking in terms of two distinct entities that must be ontologically external to each other *by definition*, we can only grasp necessity as some sort of obscure bond that somehow has to join the two—which leads to all sorts of unsolvable riddles about the nature of relations, including the question of their reality or unreality, the infinite regress of relations between any two relata and their relation, the distinction between analytic and synthetic judgments and the possibility of synthetic a priori judgments, the coexistence of freedom and necessity, and so on. But this ontological assumption itself, as I'll try to show in the coming pages, is a result of the prioritizing of freedom and control over necessity, which is the ontological ultimacy of purpose—that is, of monotheism as we've defined it here. Starting from the atheist premises outlined previously, we will instead find the collapse of the twoness into a oneness, but a oneness that is equally necessarily an infinite multiplicity; in short, we'll find the collapse of the hybrid transitional concept of rational necessity into the simultaneously and necessarily one-and-many seeing of what Spinoza calls (misleadingly perhaps) "Intuition," as will become clear as we explore his thought in part II.

For control, in contrast, means that one thing and another are really distinct and one of them is dominating the other, directing it toward a particular goal, a purpose, that is not, by nature, priorly entailed by the existence of that other thing. Control means making something a means to an end that, in the absence of that control, would not result from that means.

The two things are, in their nature, genuinely two, and if left to themselves they will have no connection until one is shifted from its own trajectory under the power of the other. The thing's relation to the external is now *contingent* rather than *necessary*. Though it requires the presence of *some* externality—it must be situated in *some* environment that is external to it—*which* elements in that environment it relates to and *how* it relates to them are not determined in advance by either its own nature or the nature of the other. It *necessarily* requires an outside, but it relates to each external element variably rather than as a necessary consequence of what it is and what they are. It is a necessary relation to having an outside-as-such that, at the same time, forecloses any necessary relation to any *particular* outside. We sometimes call this "free will," decision-making, choice, agency, taking actions due to reasons rather than things happening necessarily due to causes, or something similar. It is the very epitome of what we have been calling an exclusive oneness.

Control requires purpose. In essence, control is something performed only by personalities, to the kind of continuity that demands numerical identity and responsibility across time, where the purpose must be felt to be truly distinct from the means that accomplish it. For the structure of purpose, unlike that of necessary causality, is such that it cancels itself out if the ends and means are not only distinguishable but also ultimately inseparable: if the connection is truly necessary, it simply becomes cause and effect rather than means and ends. So a real difference of the goal from both the means to reach the goal and whatever fails to reach the goal, real variability of their relations, is the very essence of choice, of purpose, which in turn is the very essence of personality. This is the precondition for control as opposed to necessity. The metaphorical application of the concept of control to nonpersonal and nonpurposive things—for example, asserting that events are "controlled" by the laws of nature or that an organ of the body "controls" the regulation of some particular bodily function—is a category mistake, and when applied globally, it can be a very costly one.

In sum, then, necessity means that the two are not *really, ultimately* two: it means that what appeared to be two are really inseparably one, and also that this one is also necessarily two: both a premise and a conclusion, both cause and effect. But since there is thus no real twoness here, no ultimate twoness, there is no control, for control always means one thing dominating another thing, one end controlling a means; control presupposes otherness, full stop. Necessity means that just by a certain thing being itself, something *else* is also going to be there without fail. It means that there is an *inseparability of oneness and twoness*. This is what frees us from the idea of control altogether, and thus from the passivity—the "suffering," in the primal etymological sense—of being controlled. In contrast, the unity or continuity that goes with personhood is of a very restricted and specific form. It is unity only in the sense that the same being must be there conceiving the purpose in advance, creating a prospective unity of moments projected into the future. Purpose implies the attempted removal of whatever is not to the purpose, unifying all remaining elements under a single goal, which is made possible only by conceiving its existing relations to *specific* external things as nonnecessary, in spite of its necessary relation to *some* outside things. It must relate to something, but not necessarily to what it is, in fact, related to. It is a principle of choice, the desiring of one result rather than another: an exclusive unity. As such, it must be the sole cause of its own actions, the one that is responsible, and must still be there in the future moment when the deed is accomplished and when the deserved result, consequence, punishment, or reward occurs. A person is a responsible controller, and the kind of unity that pertains to a person is the unity that belongs to responsible control. This is unity of purpose in a state of coping with obstacles and selectively forming alliances with other personalities: seducing, charming, fighting, recognizing, critiquing, and the like. It means choosing among alternatives as to what to ally with, what to combat, what to incorporate, what to expel. That means, again, that its relation to the external is *contingent* rather than *necessary*—no specific othernesses are now seen to be entailed simply in being what one is. It may seem that what I am is thereby *less* determined, less bounded, less finite than a being with necessary entailments would be: there is no way to know what I will do, indeed no way to identify any specific definite set of characteristics that I am, for any definitely identified characteristics would have to have necessary consequences. But this apparent gain in indeterminacy is completely overturned by the flipside: this unknown and perhaps unknowable entity, my free self, whatever it is, is now sharply delineated off from all that is not myself on purely structural grounds, since anything that it does or interacts with or produces is definitionally something other than what it is since they are variable, optional, fungible, do not belong to its essence, and are not conditions for it to be what it is. Personality and purpose are the *dichotomization* of oneness and difference.

It is only when a finite entity is considered the *ultimate* cause of anything, choosing "freely" to do what it might not have done, that we can experience its action as personal. Even if we stop short of real atheist mysticism, simply content with a vulgar determinist necessity, real gains can be found in dispelling this idea of control rooted in free choice, to anticipate a motif presented in great detail by Spinoza—the first step, but not yet the culmination, of his exposition of full-blown atheist beatitude. How do we feel about, say, an acid that burns the hand? Can we hate it as we hate a personality? Does it have the same kind of unity? No, we see transparently that it is what it is and does what it is because of all the otherness that surrounds and precedes it; it is both a necessary cause and a necessary effect—its oneness is a twoness in all directions, necessarily. As we saw earlier, the animist, the believer in personalities, reaches an opacity at which his mind's eye goes no further, and he sees no necessity in what follows from the agent's being either: to the extent that he sees it as personal, he fails to see it as necessary. If I saw a person as simply having a character from which certain actions necessarily followed, I would not see him as free, and I would be liberated from a certain kind of love and hate toward him. That is, I would be liberated from single-narrative intentionality. We are not angry at the empty boat that crashes into us, as Zhuangzi says, and our desire to kill our enemy does not extend to the wish to smash his sword.[1] But when we imagine an agent doing something "intentionally," as part of a personal narrative—taking an "attitude" toward us, with an intended *meaning*, with an imagined expectation premised on a speculation he has about us—we are affected with a peculiarly intense form of love or hate toward that agent. Animism, extended toward not only the natural world, but even to other people, *even to ourselves*, is, on this view, the cause of a great deal of irrational pain. Animism is the imputation of a soul to anything whatever— that is, the imputation of something that is the sole cause and controller of certain events that are called "its own actions." To impute a soul to another person, or to ourselves, is to impute a single controlling agent with personal intentions. Once we see that the agent did what he did, not as a free choice with no prior cause, but due to causes that made it necessary for him to act this way, our anger or hurt is dispelled—or really, it is spread across an infinity of prior causes and diluted. By seeing a prior cause working to make the agent angry, for example, I see that this effect comes from more than one source: in the simplest case. from the combination of both (1) the prior cause and (2) the agent, not from the agent alone. But these are, then, two different stories, two different meanings. One story starts with the prior cause—for example, me being in his way. The other starts with him being angry at me. It is only if I consider one of these and not the other that we have the cryptoanimist, "personal" relation, the action by a particular agent, infusing it with only one intended meaning pinned to one particular narrative. Or it may be that there are other contributory conditions and causes involved, not merely the single prior condition. Perhaps his blood sugar was low, he was hearing a voice that by random association of ideas reminded him of a great sorrow of his, or whatever. There too the angry deed is to be attributed not just to "him"—as in the animist account, the "personal responsibility" account, the "free will" account—but to several sources at once, and ultimately to an infinity of causes.

In contrast, a "person" is a unity that is neither a necessary result nor a necessary cause of anything: it is, yet again, the impossible idea of a finite unity, which is distinct and therefore must be related to some surrounding otherness, but that utterly excludes any specific *necessary* relation of its unity to any *specific* otherness. What does this really amount to? *Free, personal, intentional, meaning, narrative*—these terms all mean *oneness to the exclusion of at least some dimension of manyness*. It is the oneness that unifies into itself some diversity, but, definitionally, *not into all diversity*. It is an *exclusive oneness*, a unification of the model of responsibility and purpose, of choosing the better over the worse. It is unity as *control*. What is really at stake here is singularity of meaning, of purpose, of identity. A responsible controller is someone who is answerable to the past, who can make the past and future cohere, who chooses which things go into the sequence of actions and which are excluded, who subordinates the present to the future, and who makes his actions one, in accord with one purpose or one finite set of purposes. What this suggests is that the whole question of "personality" is really just a question of a certain form of purpose-driven construal of oneness to the exclusion of some of the available multiplicity: where we see multiplicity, we no longer see a single character, a single agent, a single intention, a single narrative, a single meaning. Control means making all the available ingredients, all the means, get in line with one purpose, one intention, one consistent meaning, to whatever extent is possible; anything that cannot be integrated or transformed accordingly is expelled or destroyed.

The tool, the thing worked on by the tool, the "person" working the tool: in a world where personhood has been made ultimate, all these become single-valenced items, which are tasked with being determinate as one definite link in a definite chain, one part of a single narrative of responsibility and not others—as one determination but not any other. They are judged, prejudged, in the logical sense of judgment: they are this rather than that; they must be one thing rather than another. They have become "things" in the deeper and more rigorous meaning of "thing" already mentioned: a thing is whatever can exclude or be excluded. A thing is what excludes another thing. As Nietzsche suggested, and as we will discuss in detail subsequently, we project thinghood in general from our misapprehension of our own psychology, from our benighted sense of ourselves as free unitary selves: personhood, and personhood alone, is what makes the world into a world of things, and vice versa. We stand here sharply opposed to the Buberian distinction of person and thing, I-Thou versus I-It, which gave the twentieth century a new way to reinstate respectability for the entailments of theism. For us, this is a choice that is no choice: "it" and "you" and "I" are all part of the same system, the God system, the purpose system, the utility system, the work system—the system of mutually exclusive identities, of "things." What interests us is rather what other alternatives there can be—especially since the very idea of "alternative" *seems* precisely to require exclusion. But does it really? We have seen that even logical or mechanical necessity at least opens up a nondichotomous relation of oneness and multiplicity. Are there other ways? If so, would they even actually be "other"?

RETHINKING PERSONHOOD AS NONULTIMATE

To find an actual model of a world whose "keenest sense" is that it "rests on nothing" of the kind Nancy claimed for the monotheistic West, we must turn to China. For, prima facie, if there is any tradition that is really marked by its consistent and thoroughgoing atheism in the sense that matters, it is the Chinese philosophical tradition. This is true of all three of the main classical traditions, Daoism, Confucianism, and Buddhism. The clearest and most paradigmatic anti-God resource in the Chinese tradition is the conception of Dao, as the term comes to be developed in what are later known as "philosophical Daoist" texts such as the *Laozi* (*Daodejing*) and the *Zhuangzi*. For as I have insisted already, though Dao has sometimes been depicted as some kind of vague or partial equivalent of the idea of God, it is better described as the *most extreme possible antithesis* of that idea. Indeed, classical Daoist thought can very well be described as one long polemic against the idea of purpose—the idea of conscious design, of intentional valuation as a source of existence, of deliberate creation, of control, of God.

What is involved in the Daoist notion of Dao is what we might call the in-principle unintelligibility of the world. The deep structure of the world is not just unknown by me, nor just unknown by all humans, nor just unknown by all beings: it is, *in principle*, unknowable. We cannot know Dao, but *Dao* cannot know Dao either. To speak theologically, it is God's own agnosticism about God, his own ignorance and indifference to himself, his own atheism, his unconsciousness. It is defined precisely as what is left out of any act of purpose-driven conscious awareness—and it is through its relation to specific *desires* that all conscious awareness is intrinsically purpose-driven, is narrowed down into definite form, and assumes a specific identity. Here, a purportedly knowing consciousness, in any usual sense (i.e., as an apprehender of definite facts), without a finite, needy, desiring animal behind it is suspected to be a contradiction in terms.

Dao, in fact, is the resistance of all existence to any possible *complete-*

ness of knowing—and therefore, the deepest exclusion of the concept of an omniscient knower or a fully determinate knowable (object, world). *Determinate* means knowable in principle, if only a skillful and well-informed enough knower were present. *Dao is unknowable even to an omniscient observer.* For Dao may be described as something like the unknown half of any possible act of knowing, the background that tacitly accompanies any foreground, the *necessary* outside that goes with every inside. It is built into the structure of knowing as knowing, and hence of the known as known, to have an unknown involved in knowing it. Dao is a concomitant of the structure of knowing as *always* involving one half dark. But these "halves" are not self-standing independent facts; instead, we have a thoroughgoingly contextualist and relational account of meaning and identity. What we end up with, then, is a constitutively half-blurry status of facts *as such*. Daoism means, in short, that omniscience is a contradiction in terms. Fully determinate order, including moral order, is a contradiction in terms. The meaning of life is a contradiction in terms. Nature following rules is a contradiction in terms. Purpose of the universe is a contradiction in terms. God is a contradiction in terms. Final, once-and-for-all sense-making of any kind is a contradiction in terms—it can only be a partial epiphenomenon.[2]

And this has radical implications for how we relate to oneness and difference, to personality and the interpersonal and the nonpersonal, to morality, to love. It means an openness to both the boundless production of selves, determinate things, persons, world, but also that no such production can be final or exclusive. Dao has no personality or intention, which means, not that it excludes personality and intention, but that it manifests in and as every personality and intention, and in the nonfinality and self-opacity of each of them, which is also their link to each other.

Zhuangzi says, "When the springs dry up, the fish have to cluster together on the shore, gasping on each other to keep damp and spitting on each other to stay wet. But that is no match for forgetting all about one another in the rivers and lakes. Rather than praising Yao and condemning Jie, we'd be better off forgetting them both and transforming along our own Way."[3]

"Our own Way" (*qi dao* 其道) is at once *the* Dao and *our own* Dao—our own Course. The rivers and lakes are here the all-encompassing and invisible oceanic medium of the activity of the fish; it is also their sustenance and support; it is also the enabler of their unfettered slip and glide and float and drift, each traveling along its own trackless way, untouched, unguided, unblocked, unconstrained. The water is to each an open channel in which it swims; to any fish, both its own Way and the opening of every Way into every other Way, the Way of all Ways and the Ways of all fish; it is what feeds them, what embraces them, what mobilizes them, and what allows them to swim either together or alone as they please, but not reliant on each other, dancing around one another but without crash or scrape: the water, the Way.

Zhuangzi is comparing our interpersonal relations, our demands for mutual accountability, to the spit of the beached fishes; barely surviving, they are choking and drooling on each other to keep each other wet. The satire touches on both our morality and our sociality, which are seen here as two sides of the same coin, part of a single package. We need each other, and we need our judgments of each other, because we are out of our element; we are trapped and grounded and immobilized and dying of thirst. We judge in order to cluster, and we cluster in order to judge. We mark out our in-group by barfing out our judgments about what and whom we approve of or despise. And yet this ridiculous thing is literally the best thing we do because it is the best we can do: in our current sorry situation, it is our only option, our only possible survival. It's disgusting and pathetic, but it's better than nothing—it's better than choking to death in the otherwise waterless world in which we find ourselves stranded.

That warm sense of mutual approval and recognition, the thin, shiny, surrounding glow of friendship and love, is our last little vestige of that vastness, the water in which we could shimmy and shake our way through and around and away from each other. We are not mistaken in feeling that this love is precious, that it is the most precious thing we have—but it is precious because it is a shabby reminder of our former unaccountable, mutual asociality, a pale and turbid shadow of the clear seas that enabled us to move toward and away.

That righteous feeling of rectitude and belonging and approval we experience when we say what is right and wrong and who is right and wrong, when we feel justified and take it on ourselves to justify ourselves and each other—that too is a last little vestige of the opposite, of being oblivious to both judging and being judged, as spit is a sort of gross but still much needed gob of what was once water, the unconstraining sea of mutual oblivion. In this pathetic and alienated state, our morality and our love for each other are indeed the most valuable things in all our experience, our only reminder and the only contact with the beyond-good-and-evil, the sovereign amorality in which we used to freely transform.

The Way, the water, is transformation. Transformation is the transformation, not only of what we are, but of what we associate with and what we approve of, our loves and our values.

Zhuangzi says elsewhere, "What makes my life good also makes my death good."[4] What makes good? What makes life? What makes death? Transformation.

Do we want love? Do we want goodness? Yes and no. Speak to me, love me, approve of me, spit on me: sadly enough, that may be the only thing keeping me alive, the only moisture available, the last gasp of ocean available in this wasteland of a shoreline.

Emerson, paraphrasing Goethe's paraphrase of Spinoza, wrote: "Hence arose the saying, 'If I love you, what is that to you?' We say so, because we feel that what we love is not in your Will, but above it. It is not you, but your radiance. It is that which you know not in yourself, and can never know."[5] It is not your spit, fellow fish, but the moisture still vaguely detectable in that spit that I love when I love you, that I approve when I approve you, that you love when you love me, that you approve when you approve me—it is the radiance of you, which you know not and can never know, the open expanse of transformation that is more you than you and more me than me, connecting us inextricably in one way or another, either in our desperate heapings here on the shore or out in the slippery, transparent depths of our boundless mutual forgetting.

Let us return to Zhuangzi: "Who can be together in their very not being together, do things for one another by not doing things for one another? Who can climb up upon the Heavens, roaming on the mists, twisting and turning round and round without limit, living their lives in mutual forgetfulness, never coming to an end?"[6]

The boundless production of selves, of determinate things, of persons, of world is also what ensures that no such production can be final or exclusive. We begin to see what is meant by saying that the lack of personality and intention of Dao means not that it excludes personality and intention, but that it manifests in and as every personality and intention, and in the nonfinality and inner multiplicities of each of them, their multifarious links to one another. Dao is the water that enables and remains present in all our disgusting, mutual spittings of personhood and purpose and accountability.

This is perhaps the reason why what we are invited to do in and with this watery Dao is not really very similar to what we are always being told to do about God or the world or Nature or Truth. The world? It's something to *deal with* and *find a place in* and *live your life in*, possibly somewhere to *make a better place*. Nature? It's something to *study* and *enjoy* and *protect* and *understand*. God? He's someone to *worship* and *obey* and *pray to* and *contemplate*, and to *have a personal relationship with* and *fear* and *love* and *be loved by*, to *be saved by* or *condemned by*, to *accept* and *be acceptable to*. The Truth? It's something to *seek* and *grasp* and *face up to* and *recognize* and *demonstrate*. The Universe? It's something to *gasp in wonder at* or *explore* or *comprehend*. The One Absolute Reality behind All Appearances? It's something to *dispel illusions so as to recognize and realize* or *to merge with* or *dissolve into* or *to recognize one's identity with.*

How about Dao? What are the verbs that we constantly find applied there? What can we do to, for, with, or about Dao?

Float. Drift. Swim. Wander.

The *Daodejing* compares Dao to water: it flows downward, naturally tending toward the despised lowest places but thereby nourishing all things at their roots; and like the flow that wears away the stone, it is a yielding softness that outlasts and overcomes the hard and rigid. Daoist writers often focus on this soft, yielding character of Dao-as-watery, stressing the adaptability and shapelessness of water, which can effortlessly assume whatever shape it finds itself situated within. Perhaps this watery Dao is thus far something to be *utilized* and *followed* or *emulated*, or perhaps *imbibed* or *fed on*, like the nourishing maternal breast in *Daodejing* 20. But Zhuangzi, in keeping with his much-favored fish metaphors, sometimes takes this shapeless, unfixable, transforming, watery Dao as something to "float on" and "drift on" and "swim in" and "wander in"; he describes it as a wavy, unstable, funhouse medium of ups and downs, of value and valuelessness, of purpose and purposelessness, providing nothing underneath for support and yet bearing all things up on its formless, quicksilver surges and drops:

> Zhuangzi was traveling in the mountains when he came upon a huge tree, luxuriantly overgrown with branches and leaves. A woodcutter stopped beside it but in the end chose not to fell it. Asked the reason, he said, "There is nothing it can be used for." Zhuangzi said, "This tree is able to live out its natural life span because of its worthlessness."
>
> When he left the mountains, he lodged for a night at the home of an old friend. His friend was delighted and ordered a servant to kill a goose for dinner.
>
> The servant said, "There is one that can honk and one that cannot. Which should I kill?" The host said, "Kill the one that cannot honk."
>
> The next day, Zhuangzi's disciple said to him, "The tree we saw yesterday could live out its natural life span because of its worthlessness, while our host's goose was killed for its worthlessness. What position would you take, Master?"
>
> Zhuangzi said, "I would probably take a position somewhere between worthiness and worthlessness. But though that might look right, it turns out not to be—it still leads to entanglements. It would be another thing entirely to float and drift along, mounted on only the Course and its spontaneous Virtuosities—untouched by both praise and blame, now a dragon, now a snake, changing with the times, unwilling to keep to any

exclusive course of action. Now above, now below, with harmonizing as your only measure—that is to float and drift within the ancestor of all things, which makes all things the things they are, but which no thing can make anything of. What could then entangle you?[7]

Worthiness is no good: you will be used. Worthlessness is also no good: you are expendable. Is the best course hunkering down somewhere between the two, half worthy and half unworthy, then? That might seem better but it isn't: it's also no good. Everything definite and constant is an entanglement. Everything unwatery entangles. This oceanic, watery Dao all around and beneath our necks and waists and feet has no one shape or form; it cannot stand still and it cannot be stood on. Yet we do not sink down under it either: we float in it, we swim in it. Things emerge from it, but it is no thing—not this, not that, not high, not low. It cannot be grasped as anything at all: it "things" out thing after thing but is never "thinged" by things (*wu wu er bu wu yu wu* 物物而不物於物). To ride it is to be likewise unthingable, ungraspable as any this or any that, unlocatable in any locus, impossible to pin down. Its instability is its lubricity, its softness and yieldingness, but also its power, its dynamism. Floating in Dao is floating in the unknowable at the bottom of all knowing, the shapeless at the source of all shape. It is not merely unknown *so far* or merely unknown by certain knowers but known by others: it is, by nature, unknowable—it would be unknowable even to an omniscient observer. But this watery shapelessness is tempestuous: it is the reckless wriggle and the reckless surrender that Zhuangzi elsewhere calls, with reckless words, the *tranquil turmoil* or the *tumultuous tranquility* (*yingning* 攖寧). Shapeless and void, yet shape-shifting and lurching forth with ever new virtuosities, here spasms the ancestor of all things, unable to settle into any one configuration—unable to stop spitting out its buoyant waves swelling upward and its pitching waves plummeting downward. To ride this tumultuous void is to transform with it, from snake to dragon and back, from straw to straw dog to straw, from valueless to value and back, from purposeless to purpose and back. That's how it is for us living beings, the same old up-down, the ancient three-step: from clueless infant to know-it-all adult to blithering senile oldster; from incompetent newbie to virtuosic top dog to over-the-hill embarrassment; from dead matter to living go-getter to decaying cadaver. That's how we get whatever gets got.

This is not something done by obeying it or loving it or worshipping it, by drowning and dissolving into its oblivion, or by knowing it or following it or using it or controlling it or accepting one's place in it. We cannot "do" the floating of us, and the water is even less a someone who is doing the floating. It carries us without intending to, and we are carried when we too forget our intention to be held on to or to hold on, to secure our specific whereabout. We float when we stop trying to keep to one particular place in the water, when we cease trying to hold our position. Who would have guessed that water, which slithers away through your fingers when grasped, is also something you can *lie down on?* Something that caressingly carries you up by letting you drop into its folded pocket, while snubbingly scurrying away around whatever it accepts into its heaving, nourishing breast? Dao dozes like the nursing mother of *Daodejing* 20, snoring softly in and out, unaware of the bite and the bliss of her rising and falling offspring, who doze and dream and loaf on her bosom, suckling absent-mindedly, as beautifully oblivious of her as she is of them.

LOVE CONTRA THE ULTIMACY OF PERSONHOOD

It is the intractable nonpersonal dimension of all personhood, the purposelessness that accompanies all purpose, that is forefronted here. And that, as we have just considered in the words of Emerson (paraphrasing Goethe who was paraphrasing Spinoza) is what is really at the basis of love: what I love is not you, but "the radiance of you." We can now elaborate on this passing trope with a weightier dictum: love is not love if it is *only* personal.

Love is a somewhat intuitive candidate for the ground of being, and an attractive one: we have seen it carefully explored by Plato in the *Symposium*, where it is concluded that love is a kind of hybrid of abundance and lack, of riches and poverty. It is the overabundant wealth that cannot help spilling over, the "bestowing virtue" as Nietzsche called it, much like the volcanically overspilling sun we will see in Bataille: it is excess and profligate generosity. But it is also poverty, need, lack, hunger. That was *eros*, of course—a combination of lack and abundance. There both sides show a certain *moretoitivity*, to use a Neo-Tiantai term, with respect to personality and purpose; neither is completely controlled by purpose. Abundance was more than could fit into any purpose, while lack was the confrontation with the recalcitrant realness of the nonpurposive, indifferent world; its failure to automatically accord with our Will, or possibly *any* Will. When *eros* is eliminated in favor of *agápē*, both the abundance side and the need side tend to lose their ability to transcend personality and purpose. In the case of *God's* love, the aspect of need or lack is eliminated altogether, leaving a pure, giving love without need, without erotic hunger; the abundance is now no longer a potlatch-style, excessive self-annihilating but self-expressive overflowing, only secondarily turned into an item of exchange, but, as a personal gift given intentionally in the proper measure and for a specific purpose (or at least as a part of a general purposivity), it is in constant danger of becoming an exchange item from top to bottom—the distribution of rewards and wages or a gift that *expects a return*; a quid pro quo gift that *indebts the receiver*. Meanwhile, the neediness that has been repressed from the side of God's love is turned instead into total dependence on the side of the receiver, the created soul, repressing the overflowing abundance side and now requiring a *commandment* to give love to other needy parties, but only as a function of the grateful love for God that is rooted in our own need.

But this idea that love is somehow at the source of all things is still powerful, for we can feel the givenness of our existence as something superfluously bestowed, as an impulse that stands at the root of our existence and takes joy in us being here and in being so. We can thus feel easily that love is the ground of being—even when the more literal and physical sense in which this is so (nonpurposive needy eros as the ground of sexual reproduction, unstoppably instinctual self-sacrificing *agápē* as parental love) is suppressed. By making the personal ultimate, monotheism usurps the feeling of love that we might indeed legitimately feel at the core of our being, strips it of its dual dimension and of the inherent doubleness of both dimensions (the simultaneous purposiveness and nonpurposiveness in the abundance as well as in the neediness). "God is love" in effect steals love from the source of being, de-eroticizes it and puts it in the service of the personal and the purposive. The result is that it becomes the best tool yet for indebtedness, responsibility, guilt, vengeance, and judgment.

For what sort of love can there be between persons if one of the personalities in question (God's) is *purely* a personality, that is, not simultaneously also expressing the impersonality, *the illimitable untamed multiplicity*, which is necessarily concomitant with all known personalities, tied as they are to animal bodies and to uncontrollable future moments? This untamed multiplicity is the traditional domain of specifically *erotic* love, as opposed to *agapic* love. Eros, though taking its cue from the undeflectable unruliness of sexual love, is no more confined to the sexual than *agápē*, taking its cue from the selflessness and unconditionality of parental love, is confined to the parental. It is the ungovernable exuberance uncontainable in any personhood but pervading the personal, a polymorphous overflowing at the root of the conscious person that is beyond both his comprehension and his control and doesn't always have his best interests (or indeed any consistent set of interests) at heart yet is most intimately cherished as crucial to his own unsettled self, and demands the utmost intimacy with other such selves and nonselves. We may remember here the story of the spitting fishes from *Zhuangzi*: of all the things we experience while stranded here on this riverbank, love is the closest approximation, the best reminder, of what it was like to swim free of one another, of the touch of the all-pervading source of our being in which we frolic and float. But by making this form final and ultimate, we are, as it were, saying the spit is the source of our being in which we float and frolic, that *spit* is all around us sustaining and bestowing our life; we are forbidden to reconvert it into water and forget our debts to the spitter. That is precisely what keeps us *out* of the ocean. The contrast between the erotic and agapic forms of boundlessness allows us to pinpoint a central tension in the idea of the *loving* God, which from this point of view appears to be another backfiring attempt to reconstitute the lost intimacy of impersonality, the water encompassing Zhuangzi's together-in-not-being-together fish or what Bataille calls the "intimacy" of "water-in-water," as we will see in the next chapter, by absolutizing personhood. If the last vestige of this intimacy is the fish-spit, that is, purely *interpersonal* love completely deprived of its subpersonal frenzy, then monotheism is the absolutization of this spit as the final horizon of existence, the interpersonal without its source and resolution in the impersonal, which crashes by clinging to the one and completely losing sight of the other—an ocean of spit, or an ocean replaced by spit, or the ocean channeled into spit and continually spat on us. In contrast, our atheist mystics discern the boundlessness of love as requiring both the embracing and the surpassing of all personalities. This is not the absolutization of personality but also not its extirpation; it is the *permeability* of all personalities, their simultaneous disclosure of what lies above and below and around and behind them, not their removal. Whatever we are seeing, we are always involved in also seeing through to something more—and since each moreness is transparent to still more, this extends out through each person and thing to a boundless expanse of others. This is a oneness that includes any and every otherness (and embracing the paradoxes for both its own identity and for the identity of otherness that this entails, as we find in Necessity but also in Dao), *not* oneness necessarily excluding at least some otherness (as we find in personality and purpose).

Again we must stress emphatically that atheist mysticism is thus *not* some kind of endeavor to see through the illusion of freedom and love to find only necessity and mechanical, lifeless impersonality. In the discussion of Bataille in the next chapter we will explore further the idea, already lightly hinted at, that both "mechanism" and "lifeless impersonality" are strictly by-products of teleological personalism and the universalized animism of theism. There we'll get a more detailed elucidation of how the mutual exclusivity of mechanistic causes and effects is a conception that can be traced entirely from teleology, as its opposed by-product. For teleology is the postponement of satisfaction to the future, the subordination of the present to the future, as embodied in work and in toolmaking, which in turn leads directly into the conception of the world as a tool (in the hands of God) and the self also as a tool (ditto). For Bataille, this teleological outlook is the primary intervention that accomplishes genuine difference and separation into a world that was originally all immediacy and continuity, "like water in water." The primary mutual externality is that of present to future, of means to ends, in the teleological world of tools and work. Once this move has been irrevocably taken, an attempt to restore the sovereignty of the world free of its subordination to purposes at first can only cling to blind mechanism. Mechanistic, purposeless, blind causality is just what happens to tools when they are abandoned, when the purpose is removed from them. But it was purpose that had posited them as separate things in the first place.

But the real point is to go a step further and reinstate the terms *freedom* and *love* in exactly the *other* direction, precisely as Spinoza does in his own critique of teleology, as we will see. "Seeing necessity" is freedom. The love of necessity, Nietzsche's *amor fati*, Zhuangzi's befriending of agentless *ming* (命)—that is, of the inextricable relation to any and all otherness that constitutes my very being—is atheist mystical love. Precisely because I am a finite being, I can never succeed in seeing myself entirely mechanistically: there will always be missing links in the chain of causality by which I try to explain my own behavior. I cannot know the specificity of necessity that actually determines me—and this is exactly why I think I am free, a personality, a responsible controller, exactly why I am motivated to seek recognition and love from another free personality. But for the very same reason, because of my finiteness and necessary ignorance, I can know at least one absolutely necessary relation to otherness: this is, for Spinoza, my relation to Substance, my inextricability from Being in general, my inseparability from the Absolute infinity that expresses itself in infinite ways, as infinite infinities. I can know *that* I am both a necessary and necessarily finite mode of the unconditioned infinite Substance and thus intrinsically related to every otherness without exception, even if I can never know exactly *how*. That is love of fate, the *ming* that Zhuangzi tells us really refers to nothing more or less than the unknowability of what or who or why,[8] the knowledge that all acts of control come with something beyond any control, that what happens always depends on what is *necessarily* outside my control and outside *any* control, that no one and nothing is in control (see online appendix B). Love of *that* is love of fate.

Keiji Nishitani, in *Religion and Nothingness*, raises a question that gets to the heart of the matter: "Can God sneeze?"[9] This is really the theological thought experiment that reveals to us the inner nature of the concept of God more fully than catechism conundrums like "Can God create a rock heavier than he can lift?" The latter concerns an inner contradiction in the notion of omnipotence per se, which applies at the logical level. But the problem we have in mind here concerns more specifically the conception of power as *control*, as structured around the idea of a *personality*—that is, a narratively accountable controller with a nonnecessary relation to all that is not himself, yet who is the sole cause of certain events, which we call "his own actions," as opposed to mere happenings in which he somehow participates. We can answer yes to the question, and thus avoid the seeming self-contradiction of God's omnipotence very simply by admitting, à la Spinoza, that God is the universe. Then God can sneeze because the universe sneezes (i.e., because some things in the universe sneeze), just as my body grows hair although it does not grow hair everywhere. Omnipotence in this sense does not face the same internal contradiction as long as it is not somehow something that belongs to personality, as long as power is not thought of as control—that is, as long as God is not a person, which is really just to say: as long as "God" in the monotheistic sense does not exist. The non-existence of God means the nonultimacy of personality, which means that all personality experiences, constitutively, its relation to the impersonality that surrounds it, grounds it, surpasses it, accomplishes it. The revelation of the interface of personality and impersonality here comes in the form of sneezes, farts, orgasms, laughter, unintended bodily functions, frenzy of any kind, or any other true, inescapable necessity that short-circuits the sense of control, of *any* agent's control; that undermines the premise of one thing controlling another and thereby excluding interference from alternate goals. It is in this way alone that infinity, as the necessary nonpersonal that surrounds and supports my personhood, comes to consciousness, forcing its way into the system of personhood. And it is this necessary relation to infinity as such that solves the problem, the essence of atheist mysticism, beyond determinism and beyond freedom, beyond love and beyond recognition: the otherness that is necessarily also myself. I am necessarily related, not merely contingently related, to *every* possible otherness. All othernesses are parts of me being what I am. The lifelessness of nonteleological, mechanistic causality overcomes itself in genuine necessity, in the overcoming of the false otherness posited by teleological personality, as Spinoza and Hegel both saw clearly. My claim here is that this is what finally fulfills what recognition, communication, love, and interpersonal recognition strive for but necessarily fail to achieve.

We can now perhaps begin to glimpse the consequences of monotheism, of reducing the relation to the Absolute to a *social relation*. As a compensation for the foreclosed relation to the extrapersonal aspects of experience (whether deemed subpersonal or suprapersonal), the best it can do is proffer the stopgap compensation of communication between one

person and another, or that of love and recognition, command and obedience, or seemingly inevitably, the worst of all, which is the combination
of all of the above: *commanded* communication, *commanded* recognition,
commanded love. But social relations as such are a *double* distortion and
foreclosure of the extrapersonal: they make of me something merely personal and similarly make of the world something merely personal, in a kind
of double animism. Atheist mysticism is not me-as-mere-person (responsible controller) relating to a personless universe, nor is it a personal god
(responsible controller) relating to a personless me. It is personlessness to
personlessness as the matrix of infinite, ephemeral persons. Monotheism
means that the personal (and hence the meaningful, the purposeful, the
teleologically unified, the disambiguated) is ultimate and foundational; it
is the source and the end of all things and of all values. Atheist mysticism
means that the personal — the responsible controller and his responsible
control, the meaningful, the purposeful, the consistently unified, the disambiguated — is always only foreground; what it emerges from is always the
impersonal, which is meaningless, purposeless, diverse, ambiguous. Value
lies in the interfaces of the personal and the impersonal, of the transitions
from control to noncontrol and from noncontrol to control. Pure control as
a steady state, completely devoid of noncontrol, is hell. Pure noncontrol as
a steady state, completely devoid of control, is also hell. But floating in the
oceanic is the interface of control and noncontrol, of person and personless, of purpose and purposeless.

For even in personal relations, what is valued are the places where the
persons bond in awe at their shared participation in and facilitating of and
withstanding of and shakenness in reaction to what is beyond their control and what undermines their control, fraying the edges of their personhood: laughter, emotions, sexual arousal, new ideas, intimacies, secrets,
music, rhythms — the personal awed by the sublimity of the impersonal.
To love another person is to love the presence of the other person as what
sparks this synergy, not merely as a communication between "persons" —
accountable controllers — where the end, the standard, is what lands in the
person, in the accountable controller, but rather as what enables them to
cling together in the lifeboat of personhood on the ocean catalyzed into
existence by the chemical reaction of their combination, which threatens
to destroy them but to which they together bear witness. A loving personal
relationship among non-God persons is always erotic. It is like a couple
seeing a horror movie or riding together on a roller coaster: what gives it
value and what each finds liberating in the relation is that it reveals to both a
shared experience of the fragility and nonultimacy of personhood, of what a
thin charade it is, of the transitions in and out of control, of the sublimity of

the release from the accountable controller (from the self, from the person) and the battered crawl back into the personhood of which the tenuousness is now exposed, that this other person occasionally somehow enables—in love, in sex, in conversation, in music. For this intimacy of love is, of course, the great exception; generally a social relation has the opposite effect: it is a demand that locks one all the more securely into the role of the responsible controller, the person, and requires that all else be excluded. To be seen socially, to be recognized as part of a society, is to be called on to control one's own behavior responsibly and not to allow any of the nonpersonal, whatever is beyond one's control and for which one is unable to be accountable, to leak through. One mustn't laugh, one mustn't belch, one mustn't drool, one mustn't fart, one mustn't sneeze, one mustn't convulse into orgasm, one mustn't weep. To be seen, as in Sartre's famous keyhole example, is to be objectified and recognized specifically as a person; that is, as someone of whom there are expectations of behavior, who is responsible for his actions, who will be called to account. This means that the other mind that sees one has a memory and an expectation, as well as a categorial scheme of judgment. It means to be drawn into duration, for present moments to be subordinated to future moments.

Now the presence of another mind is thus far ambiguous. It can be liberating if, for example, the other makes me laugh or climax or riff, if my nonpersonal spontaneity is unleashed. But this presupposes the liberation from a prior restraint into a social role, also created by the presence of other minds. It is because I have been forced to assume the role of accountable controller, who is the sole cause of certain events called "my own actions," who has to move my actions forward in time, who has to apply the means-ends schema to all moments in time—in other words, because I am already a person—that a personal relationship can be liberating. While remaining a person, I can also share with someone the opening to the dissolution of personhood into the sovereignty of laughter or orgasm. This liberating kind of personal relationship, however, thus signifies the epiphany that *personality is nonultimate*. It is not the interpersonal as the elimination of the impersonal or the full subordination of the impersonal to the personal, nor is it the impersonal as a denial of personality: it is the interpersonal triggering the collapse of the *ultimacy* of personality. The recognition that objectifies me is partially turned against itself for an aesthetic experience of maximum contrast at the interface of personhood and nonpersonhood, personhood reoriented to the nonpersonhood (the uncontrolled and unaccountable realm of no subordination of one moment to another, of spontaneity, of purposelessness, of nonresponsibility, of no control and no controller), which always surrounds and supports and vivifies it.

What, then, is the meaning of monotheism, which makes the infinite, the ultimate, the source of all things into a Person? It means the denial of any escape from personhood; it means the assertion of the ultimacy of personhood, the ultimacy of responsible control. It seems to be no accident that the monotheist God never laughs, never dances, never sobs, never farts, never jams, never cums, never sneezes. Indeed, that is a contradiction in terms: God cannot sneeze because sneezing is that aspect of the self, the body, that is beyond direct conscious control, and thus beyond the reach of the responsible controller. That is the nonpersonhood at the fringes of all known persons, but it is denied of God, who is all spirit, all purpose, all control. And that has huge consequences for the kind of personal relationship that pertains to God. For what does it mean to be seen by such a God—to be watched by, loved by God? It is not the laughing, sneezing, farting, orgasming kind of love—it is the social recognition kind of love, which pertains only between two responsible controllers, two persons, and where personhood, responsibility, and control are ultimates. That means we are forever at the keyhole, objectified as accountable controllers, moral agents, who will be. or should be, held responsible for what we do, and even for what we think. We are reduced by God's gaze entirely to the subordinate principle, to a being who is responsible, whose sole occupation is control. If God is watching, it means you are always on trial; it is demanded that you always be at work (i.e., husbanding and directing means toward ends), and your work is being monitored and evaluated at all times. God's love and mercy are only given to you *as a person*: your acknowledgment of your own failure to be really responsibly in control (confession of sins) is permissible only as recognition that *he* is the one who is *really* responsibly in control, and for this acknowledgment of the ultimacy of accountability and control, your sin is forgiven and he will love you in spite of your failure. He doesn't love you for your nonpersonhood, for your failure to control, for the fact that you sneeze, but for your recognition that he and he alone is the maker and controller of your sneeze; he is the responsible controller of your sneeze but never sneezes himself. There is literally no escape from responsible control. This makes it fundamentally unlike the loving relationship of laughing, sneezing, farting, orgasmic, frenzied creatures, where two ostensible, hitherto accountable controllers—two personal selves—glory in the mutual recognition of the universe of nonresponsible controllessness that saturates them, enlivening their persons in the thrill of what threatens and expands it, bursting through prior boundaries of expectation and planning and purpose into unsuspected new dimensions. The latter reveals a greater capaciousness of personhood that can *bear* more of the nonself, which is kept in abeyance and not yet relegated to any specific purpose. If the gods have loves that are not entirely under their own control, who love what they love without knowing why, whose purposes are rooted in nonpurpose, with whom we could sneeze or laugh or orgasm—perhaps the Greek gods, or gods who grow old and die like the Buddhist devas, or whose degree of control is merely a nonultimate means with the sole goal of revealing the opposite, noncontrol and nonself, control directed exclusively to revealing the nonultimacy of control, of selves, of responsibility, of personhood, like the Buddhist bodhisattvas—there we might have a real relationship, a real love, a real intimacy. For there we are all in the same boat, *mutatis mutandis*, as in the case of erotic intimacy: we are exploring the boundaries of the control and the uncontrolled, a double-sided situation endured not only by us but also by those gods. Contending or cooperating gods, mutually affecting gods, proliferating alternate gods, proliferating multiplicities of ways of being divine and conceptions of divinity, many clashing ideals that can combine and intertwine and conflict into infinite new alloys and hybrids and situations and possibilities—that is possible only in some form of polytheism. "Just this is divinity: that there are gods but no God," says Nietzsche.[10]

Unlike anything resembling *that* sexed-up kind of interpersonal intimacy, the relation with God, who is a responsible controller all the way through, means that any breaks in responsible control on one side are only added to the ledger of control on the other side. All noncontrol is to be read as a sign of control further along, higher up: there is no escape from control. Indeed, in a monotheism, our personal relationship with God is used precisely as a means to undermine even the appearance of noncontrol, of the nonpersonal, anywhere at all in the universe: our own failings, our own laughter, our own sins, as well as the winds that blow without purpose and every sparrow that falls, are now nothing more than signs meant to reveal purpose, control, responsibility, personhood, self, God.[11]

GOD BEYOND PERSONHOOD? NO, NOT REALLY

Before leaving the question of personhood and what might lie beyond it, we must pause to register a likely complaint. A sophisticated theist might well object to all this, saying, "What a straw man you are attacking here! What an unfairly vulgar, unsympathetic, and deflationary account of God! Everybody knows that the traditional theologies of all the Abrahamic traditions fight mightily against anthropomorphism and literalism! All of them reject the idea that God is a 'person' in any such literal sense! 'God' is clearly understood by all educated Jews, Christians, and Muslims to be a word for the ineffable ground of being, something outside the ordinary order of things, which is beyond our conception. The description of God's wisdom, consciousness and even Will are all just approximate metaphors to make this transcendent being somewhat more accessible to humans—but no one is foolish enough to think these are meant literally!"

I will leave aside the empirical part of this claim—namely, whether it is true that most educated theists understand God to be merely a metaphor for a mystery. Even if that were true, which I think is doubtful, we might still ask, Why *this* metaphor, of all possible metaphors? Could there be a *worse* metaphor for this mystery than that of a conscious, purposive creator and controller, lawgiver, and judge? Could there be a more misleading way of approaching our relationship to an ineffable boundlessness than to map it onto an interpersonal relationship between a human being and an owner, master, or all-powerful consciousness with no dark side and no bodily aspect that is beyond his conscious control?

However we may want to answer such questions, it is clear that many prominent theologians of all three Abrahamic traditions have certainly put forth some such view seeking to bracket the personality of God in favor of a metaphysical absolute that transcends all conceptualization—Being itself, or Pure Act, or the Self-Caused Ground of Being, or the Supreme Being, or the Unimaginable First Cause of All Being, or even something beyond any conception of Being or any conceivable relation to Being. In its most extreme form, this takes the form of "negative theology," which takes a fully apophatic approach to the essence of God. Does negative theology abrogate the focus of our critique here: the ontological and axiological ultimacy of purpose? Readers interested in a detailed discussion of this question are asked to consult online appendix A, supplement 8: "Monotheist Negative Theology, and Why It Doesn't Help Much."[12] Here I will state my conclusions only in the barest form: even when they abrogate the exclusive oneness of *Noûs* in favor of a divine ineffability beyond Being, claiming to transcend all being and/or include all being, when we consider how this ineffability relates to beings—imposing an inexorable, single-valenced teleology on each of them, with a hierarchy of proximity to the ineffable that continues to prioritize the determinate and the purposive—the theistic negative theologies continue to conform to the Compensatory Theist variant of the *Noûs* as *Arché* model. This is true for both the weaker model, in which God is inaccessible to human knowledge and Will but is still thought to know and will himself, albeit in a way that is ineffable to us, or in the stronger version, in which even God himself can also be said to not know or will himself. For it will turn out, on close examination, that this alleged non-self-knowledge and will-lessness are really just an *accurate and bivalent* knowledge and willing of himself insofar as he is superessential, truly and definitely beyond all determination: to know himself correctly as beyond all determination, excluding the incorrect misapprehensions of him as having an essence, is all that is meant here by his nonknowing of himself. Whether the nonknowing and nonwilling of creatures is enjoined in deference to the Uberknowing and Uberwilling of God or (more rarely) the enjoined Uberknowing and Uberwilling are claimed to be themselves a nonknowing and nonwilling on God's part, it turns out that this divine Nonbeing of God beyond "God" remains an *exclusive noneness* rather than an *inclusive* noneness. It ends up being *either* a definitive blank that *excludes* all finitude *or* an omnipresent plenum of unitary formal reality that *excludes* illusion and matter and multiplicity, rather than, like the no-thingness found in the atheist mysticisms, a shape-shifting Mobius-strip mirror that never lands unilaterally on any one side—that is infinite and/or/as finite, unitary/formal/real and/or/as illusory/material/multiple; a noneness/oneness/allness that neither excludes nor contains anything, however real or unreal. Nihilistic mainstays like purposelessness, meaninglessness, chaos, and skepticism remain definitively repudiated in the monotheist negative theologies, rather than serving as privileged conduits that can lead to their own self-overcoming into beatitude, as in atheist mysticism. The reasons for this can be found in a further consideration of the baked-in ontological models embedded in these two contrary approaches to the world, which will require further probing of the Platonic-Aristotelian-Plotinian roots of the specifically theistic forms of apophaticism and of what becomes possible when, not purposivity, but the *ultimacy* of purposivity, is overcome. We have perhaps already begun to see how difficult this conquest might be, given that we are finite, living conscious beings, and therefore, essentially needy beings who are aware of being needy, essentially purposive beings: how can there be anything beyond purpose for us? How can we care about anything more than purpose, given that our caring is itself a function of purposivity? How can we know or experience anything more than how things relate to our purposes? If we were simply finite, there would be no way. But if our assurance of being *merely* finite is itself a function of this very commitment—not to purpose but to the *ultimacy* of purpose—well, then what? But for this possibility to even make sense, we must first rethink the finite/infinite relation from the ground up, exploring how it takes shape under the aegis of the purposivity model rooted in *Noûs* as *Arché*, and how it might take shape in the absence of that model. To this we now turn, with a little help from Bataille, Schopenhauer, Plotinus, and Tiantai Buddhism.

CHAPTER 4

Purposivity and Finitude

TOOL, CONTROL, PURPOSE, THINGHOOD:
BATAILLE ON GOD AS FAILED RELIGION

In the introduction, I sketched some general themes that would occupy us in these pages: the consequences of absolutizing purposive control in the idea of a monotheistic God, its role in the construction of sharply defined and mutually exclusive entities, and its sometimes ironic relation to both the development and the foreclosure of alternative religious and philosophical visions. In subsequent chapters we tracked some of the motivations and structures of various models for approaching both purpose and purposelessness, drawing on early Greek and Chinese sources supplemented by diagnoses, from Spinoza and Nietzsche, of some of the attendant philosophical premises and problems. In the previous chapter I tried to reconstruct the origins and entailments of the related notion of personhood, along with its relations, on the one hand, to expected narrative accountability and, on the other, to interruptions of the same from the prepersonal domains of the oceanic, the erotic, and even the scatological. I can begin to bring these themes together now by taking up the more detailed and concrete, if also more daringly speculative, diagnosis offered by a third great European atheist mystic, Georges Bataille. Bataille's step-by-step reconstruction of prephilosophical relations to purposivity, which is oriented to the vicissitudes of concrete human practical activity and communal bodily life, give us a distinct but related version of the genealogy of monotheism as both an outgrowth and an obstruction to primal religious impulses—for Bataille is, as he himself says, interested in religion, not from a scientific point of view, which is a "profane" point of view, but from a religious point of view, albeit one that, he is quick to point out, is not committed to any particular religious form.[1] To engage Bataille requires a willingness to sink with him into his idiosyncratic nomenclature and peculiar obsessions, to become comfortable in a world of blood sacrifice and orgies and scatology, but this messy work is well worth our trouble, for Bataille is especially important for our current project.

We can gain an overview of his relevant contributions most concisely from the materials posthumously published under the title, *Theory of Religion*. The basic idea there can be summed up very succinctly. For Bataille, man's situation is to find himself aware of himself only as a *toolmaking* animal, and it is this, the creation of tools, that subordinates everything in his world to purpose. What begins as perhaps an innocent stumble into a slightly more efficient mode of getting wanted stuff, which all animals are always trying do, has vast unexpected consequences, completely transforming the world and the self almost at one stroke. Prior to this occurrence, the animal can only be imagined (by us, it is granted) as living in a state of what Bataille calls "intimacy," "like water in water," in a temporary, unstable, permeable, vague separation from the environment; constantly shifting, a wave slightly above the rest of the water but always continuous with it, about to splash back in at any moment, with no border really enforced. Bataille sees eating and being eaten and shitting and being shat as water flowing through water, with some slight interstitial resistance but without any positing of separate objects as genuinely "other." As he puts it, "The lion is not the king of the beasts; in the movement of the waters he is only a higher wave overturning the other, weaker ones."[2] There is no real relation of "subordination" between eater and eaten. All we have here is a porous boundary; even when an animal resists being eaten, or flees, inasmuch as (we assume) it isn't thinking about death, it therefore isn't resisting death. The pain and instinct and flight and fight are themselves part of a continuity; they are "intimate" with one another. The animal is unable to view itself as an object, from outside; it is unable to have second-order desires about its desires. The main issue is whether the animal is capable of caring about the future, transcending itself into the future—into duration, into an *accountable* relationship with future purposes: it is nothing beyond whatever is going on right now. The animal does not "transcend itself."[3] In such a world, Bataille suggests, there simply are no definite objects, no "things."

"Things," in Bataille's special sense of the word, are created by the creation of the tool. "The positing of the object, which is not given in animality, is in the human use of tools; that is, if the tools as middle terms are adapted to the intended result—if their users perfect them. Insofar as tools are developed with the end in view, consciousness posits them as objects, as interruptions in the indistinct continuity. The developed tool is the nascent form of the non-I."[4] The tool is "subordinated" to the man who uses it and to the goal for which it is designed, as a definite non-I, a definite object. Only thus do definite "objects" appear, and with this everything changes:

"The object . . . has a meaning that breaks the undifferentiated continuity, that stands opposed to immanence or to the flow of all that is—which it transcends. It is strictly alien to the subject, to the self still immersed in immanence. It is the subject's property, the subject's thing, but is nonetheless impervious to the subject. . . . The perfect—complete, clear and distinct— knowledge that the subject has of the object is entirely external; it results from manufacture; I know what the object I have made is, I can make another one like it."[5] With this, the general principle of "subordination" is let loose into the world: the ends-means relation as the fundamental category of experience. Now man finds himself in an insoluble predicament:

> At the same time [the tool] establishes the clear distinction between the end and the means and it does so in the very terms that its appearance has defined. Unfortunately the end is thus given in terms of the means, in terms of utility. This is one of the most remarkable and most fateful aberrations of language. The purpose of a tool's use always has the same meaning as the tool's use: a utility is assigned to it in turn and so on. The stick digs the ground in order to ensure the growth of a plant; the plant is cultivated in order to be eaten, it is eaten in order to maintain the life of the one who cultivates it. . . . The absurdity of an endless deferral only justifies the equivalent absurdity of a true end [i.e., an immanent, autotelic, active actuality, *entelechia*], which would serve no purpose. What a "true end" reintroduces is the continuous being, lost in the world like water is lost in water, or else, if it were a being as distinct as a tool, its meaning would have to be sought on the plane of utility, of the tools, it would no longer be a "true end." Only a world in which the beings are indiscriminately lost is superfluous, serves no purpose, has nothing to do, and means nothing: it only has a value in itself, not with a view to something else, this other thing for still another and so on.[6]

Before he has tools, man has no awareness of himself as an object, no self-awareness. But once he does have tools, he finds himself hopelessly stretched between two contrary worlds of experience. For tools are the key consolidators of the ends-means relationship, which is the necessary premise for the positing of things qua things. The tool is itself the first "thing": as made, it is something of which we must control the specifications to suit its purpose—we must know how to make it so we can make others like it. To make or even *keep* a tool is to plan and prepare for the future, to have a purpose stored in reserve, to create the continuity of a purposive self geared to a predictable goal at a later time. The tool must be formed in a certain definite way to serve its function, with definite rigid boundaries and a single

determinable and definite identity. It is thus a "thing," but it makes everything around it a "thing" as well: its end, which now becomes correlatively
fixed as a something outside the tool, must be equally definite and single
and persistent unchanged through time, equally exclusive of interference
by contrary identities. And this goes for the user of the tool as well—the
possessor of the desire or purpose for which the tool is designed: he must
become a thinglike "self" with a definite identity defined by the continuity
across time of his purposes, which suck him out of a prior continuity with
the present moment, separating him from the present and his unworried
proximity to death in his interplay and interpenetration with the external
world, "like water in water." Once tools exist, the world is instantly sucked
into an economy of ends and means. Everything is now seen as a means to
something else. Man himself knows himself as a something seen from outside and as potentially a means to an end; to see things as tools is to see that
you can also be seen as a tool. There is no end to the process. The familiar
paradoxes of futile infinite regress are present at once. Attempted solutions,
like the autotelic "true end," only reinforce the problem: on the one hand
it becomes a future end to be attained by other things that have not yet
reached the autotelic state of "flourishing," and on the other hand the ends-
means structure has, in this way, been smuggled also into the inner workings of intimacy itself: what was atelic becomes split into an internal ends-
means relation with itself in the project of maintaining its selfsame form
of autotelic activity across time. Once the ends-means structure has been
unleashed by toolmaking, it spreads to every corner of human experience.

At the same time, Bataille thinks, the success of this operation is spotty
and incomplete: the feeling of "continuity" or "intimacy" with the nonself,
with the oceanic that surrounds the wave that is temporarily himself, is still
there in man's indistinct but immediate experience. Once man exists in
the discontinuity of the world of tools and purposes and things, even nonmanufactured elements are taken as things—including ourselves, as seen
through the eyes of another, from outside. But "this bringing of elements
of the same nature as the subject, or the subject itself, onto the plane of objects is always precarious, uncertain, and unevenly realized. . . . In the end,
we perceive each appearance—subject (ourselves), animal, mind, world—
from within and from without at the same time, both as continuity, with
respect to ourselves, and as object."[7] The remaining feeling of continuity,
felt "from within," is our experience of ourselves; it is the messy continuity
of random drives crashing into and overturning each other, our internal
"water in water." In contrast, our sense of ourselves as seen from without,
as part of the objective order of chains of mutually external ends and means,
is ourself as subject-object, as user and used—at this stage, body and mind

both belonging equally in the world of things. From here on, we are always both vague intimacy and distinct thing.

Bataille is at his best when waxing poetic about this intimacy and its tension with our distinct individuality, with our identities in the world of tools and work and purpose. "What is intimate, in the strong sense, is what has the passion of an absence of individuality, the imperceptible sonority of a river, the empty limpidity of the sky . . . paradoxically, intimacy is violence, and it is destruction, because it is not compatible with the positing of the separate individual."[8] What Kant called the Sublime and what Nietzsche called Dionysus are included in what Bataille here calls the Intimate: the threat to individuality, the overcoming of separateness, the transgression of boundaries and limits, the intermixture and leakage of what was once separated into a terrifying and/or ecstatic joy that forgets self-as-opposed-to-other at the same time it forgets now-as-opposed-to-future—forgets the structure of purpose, of duration, of individuality, of personhood, of utility, of labor. This is called "violence" inasmuch as it is a breaking through of the latter, although what lies on the other side of it is the water-in-water world, which is neither violent nor peaceful. To the tool-world, this oceanic world itself may appear terrifyingly violent, or conversely, transcendently placid. To itself, it is not violent or peaceful, neither a unity nor a diversity, a constant swirl of emergence and disappearance of semientities. It is the relation between the two worlds that constitutes the violence, either as projected into the oceanic as its own threatening character, or in the requirement for violence to break through into it, though this breakthrough would not be experienced by the oceanic itself as violent. The prioritization of work and tool brings with it all these varied effects. As Bataille says:

> Work and fear of dying are interdependent: the former implies the thing and vice versa . . . man is an individual to the extent that his apprehension ties him to the results of labor. . . . He would have no anguish if he were not the individual (the thing), and it is essentially the fact of being an individual that fuels his anguish. It is in order to satisfy the demands of the thing, it is insofar as the world of things has posited his duration as the basic condition of his worth, that he learns anguish. He is afraid of death as soon as he enters the system of projects that is the order of things.[9]

Man is always both, always a purposive separate being simultaneously rooted in and destined for, drawn to and in dread of the oceanic that threatens to consume and liberate him, to explode him. This tension defines human experience. We long for the lost intimacy, but our sense of self is completely tied up with a structure—the ends-means structure, the idea of purpose, which is derived from the existence of tools—which makes that intimacy impossible or else tends to postpone it and transform it into an end; but the ends-means structure is itself inherently paradoxical and can never achieve consummation. *Religion* is what we call man's various attempts to deal with this tension.

It is from here that Bataille finds the roots of animism, which attributes the same doubleness also to the nonmanufactured objects of the world, to the animals, and even to tools themselves: all are regarded as subject-objects, users and used, as man feels himself to be. From there it is just another short step to the idea of "the supreme being," first as an immanent world-soul and thereafter as a transcendent lord ruling over the world. The doubleness endemic to tool-being is applied first to every object in the world, and then to the world as a whole, rendering it twofold: the world itself is, on the one hand, reduced to a tool and, on the other hand, to a user of the tool that is the world—that is, a world-soul, which, even if conceived as somehow immanent to the world, is separated off as the user as opposed to the used, the doer as opposed to the done, Nature's soul as opposed to Nature's body. The user, a thingified world-soul whether immanent or transcendent, a thinking thing in the role of tool-using subjectivity of the whole world as tool, has to be posited as something separate, one distinct element that exists side by side with other existences. Both the world-as-tool and the separated out user-of-the-world-tool, the supreme spirit of the world as a whole, are part of the economy of "things," that is, of duration, planning, ends-means.[10] Granting agency to the user of the world as a whole was intended as give this supreme being a value greater than the agency similarly granted to all lesser things within the world. However,

> this desire to increase results in a diminution. The objective personality of the supreme being situates it in the world next to other personal beings of the same nature, subject and objects at the same time, like it, but from which it is clearly distinct. Men, animals, plants, heavenly bodies, meteors. . . . If these are at the same time things and intimate beings, they can be envisaged next to a supreme being of this type, which, like the others, is in the world, is discontinuous like the others. There is no ultimate equality between them. By definition, the supreme being has the highest rank. But all are of the same kind, in which immanence and personality are mingled; all can be divine and endowed with an operative power; all can speak the languages of man.[11]

This is the still animistic and polytheistic cosmos, where everything is actually double. On the one side, the body-mind as thing, as subject-object in the chain of utility, as distinct object seen from outside as both an objective thing to be used as the tool and as the user of the tool—the latter being the distinct and divine personality of a distinct subjective spirit, known even to oneself only if viewed as if from the outside like a thing. On the other side, for man himself as well as for all other things as ensouled and for the ensouled world itself, there is also still the excessive and vaguely felt depth dimension of useless intimacy, beyond user and used, beyond objective body and subjective mind. Each being is endowed with both, but they are now placed side by side and separated into their respective isolated beings. The spirit of each, the user, as one distinct personality among others, is still also a thing, and this applies also to the supreme spirit of the world, which is above them all.

Once the idea of a supreme being is in hand, having been endowed with the discontinuity that belongs to all beings in the economy of purposes and tools, the stage is set to single this supreme being out from among all the others, exalting it into the thing of things, the thingiest thing of all, the *ens realissimus*. Yet this does not happen immediately. "All peoples have doubtless conceived this supreme being, but the operation seems to have failed everywhere. The supreme being apparently did not have any prestige comparable to that which the God of the Jews, and later that of the Christians, was to obtain."[12] Why was that the case? Several things had to happen first, which were at this stage just taking shape. With the establishment of the tool-world, which instrumentalizes both separated things and the similarly separate users of those things, with their past-present-future structure of purposivity, there is now a felt contrast to something else, something putatively left behind but never entirely gone: the intimate continuity of water-in-water, which mixed everything together in blood and ejaculate and ecstasy and had no future or past. This excess realm, itself the very antithesis of a separable entity, can only be felt as a separate realm at all due to this contrast, and thus only vaguely, and with a deep ambivalence, combining both attraction and terror. This simultaneously attractive and terrifying realm, which now, through this felt contrast, has been given at least a vague presence that it never could have for non-toolmaking animals (who remained submerged entirely within it), is what comes to be called *the sacred*. At first, Bataille thinks, the full exaltation of the supreme being fails whenever the felt sense of this contrasted sacred realm is still too strong, for at those times, this "reduction to an objective individuality" was felt too directly as an impoverishment of that realm to hold much attraction. As long as both body and mind were equally regarded as merely things, the supreme mind held no special religious charm. There was something more attractive: the sacred, the vaguely felt excess haunting the fringes of the thing-world of users and used, minds and bodies. But this begins to shift precisely due to the newly felt contrast, which concretizes a vaguely delineated realm of the sacred for the toolmaking animal. It is now that disembodied spirits of the dead begin to enter the picture; they are less obviously tied to any single tool, as they seem to exist (in dreams and visions) even when their primary tool, their body, has died. The antipodes to the world of things is now itself starting to take shape as a counterworld of thinglike spirits given hierarchal standing in proportion to their degree of disengagement with the world of things—that is, of specific bodies. The user side of the user-used thing begins to climb in value, precisely in proportion to its seeming liberation from the stranglehold of the one-to-one chain of ends and means; now that the realm of uselessness is vaguely separated from the realm of the useful, some of the glamor of the useless is given concrete form in the guise of spirit, as the user that is not tied to any single tool. The supreme being, due to the huge multiplicity of its tools, is likewise gradually disengaged from its tie to a body—the physical world—instead landing at the top of the hierarchy of spirits. But until the advent of dualistic morality, under the aegis of the state, the supreme being remains one more among the individual spirits, side by side with those over whom it reigns and thus lacking the religious appeal of the sacred, the realm of uselessness, which entails the freedom from ends-means purposivity altogether.[13]

Religion thereafter comprises various ways of handling the impasse between the world of utility and its ambivalent love-hate relationship with the uselessness that lies beyond it, which to some extent is now vaguely concretized as a separate realm of disembodied spirits, who are still purposeful users but not usable in the form of any definite tool; they can now only be made useful to us by appealing to their own purposes and aligning them with ours. Bataille focuses on one way of handing this in particular: *sacrifice*. This comes in many forms, but its basic feature is the destruction of something *useful*, something that was once part of the intimate oceanic world but has been worked over to become valuable in the work-tool-thing-purpose economy—a domestic animal, wealth, slaves, in any case something useful and not a luxury item—destroying the aspect of its "thinghood" only and returning the remainder of it, the matter of it, to the oceanic. However, the priest who does so, along with the community of spectators and participants in the ritual, survives this procedure, remaining in the world of purpose and work, alive. He participates in the dissolution into the oceanic *vicariously* and allows the community to do the same, but he then finds a way to consecrate this spectacle to some purpose of the community with invented narratives of magical connections to our own purposes, appealing to the purposes of the disembodied spirits, the pure unused users:

propitiation, crops, social harmony. But insofar as this deal with the spirits is successful, making it a simple alliance of separate purposeful interests, it reverts to the world of utility and things, thus losing its sacredness. The true attraction and eternal appeal of this procedure, what gives it its sacred power, actually lies simply in the vicarious destruction itself, in the violent reversion of utility to uselessness, of purpose to purposelessness. But the shift over onto a designated victim, making the death vicarious, preserves the world of utility in principle, and this is given various fanciful concrete expressions in the claims of magical efficacy. What we have here is the essence of religion: an attempted convergence and compromise of the two tendencies, putting uselessness to use within the tool-world but also putting the tool-world into some necessary relation to uselessness, and thus reaffirming, in a new, compromised form, its inseparability from and constant draining into the oceanic world of uselessness and purposelessness. Religion may be defined as the use of some kind of sacrifice to promote a livable compromise between the intimacy and the duration, between purposelessness and purpose, between eternity and time, between the world of things and work and purpose on the one hand and the world of water-in-water, the oceanic sense, on the other.

These compromises, the invocations of this tension, are what Bataille sees, in fact, in all aspects of human society, defining their properly religious dimension. He singles out Festival and War as two further compromises, limited solutions whereby man can gaze on the oceanic, and harness it partially for social purposes, aligned with the purposes of the disembodied spirits as unused users with purposes of their own, without having to surrender to it completely. We find drunkenness and dance and music at the festival, but again repurposed and contained for social solidarity or pleasing the gods, for future, for purpose. War is seen in this light as a means of turning the destructive impulse of sacrifice onto an out-group for the benefit of the in-group, effectively a division of labor of the two sides of the contradiction: the other will be sacrificed for the benefit of us. We inhabit the work-tool-purpose world and the other is the sacrificial victim, so again we have a way of being and doing both:

> The virtue of the festival is not integrated into its nature and conversely the letting loose of the festival has been possible only because of this powerlessness of consciousness to take it for what it is. The basic problem of religion is given in this fatal misunderstanding of sacrifice. Man is the being that has lost, and even rejected, that which he obscurely is, a vague intimacy. . . . Religion, whose essence is the search for lost intimacy, comes down to the effort of clear consciousness which wants to be

a complete self-consciousness: but this effort is futile, since consciousness of intimacy is possible only a level where consciousness is no longer
an operation whose outcome implies duration, that is, at the level where
clarity, which is the effect of the operation, is no longer given.[14]

Bataille sees another important social condition developing out of this
impasse and setting the stage for key further developments: the evolution
of something called *the state*. The universal state as an exceptionless system
covering all aspects of life (and with implicit claims also on all surrounding communities as prospects for conquest), but that subordinates itself to
ends that it pursues through the administration of enduring future-oriented
gratification-deferring institutions, essentially positing itself as universal
"thing," and it is this that sets the conditions for real dualism, the sacral-
ization of morality, and the full success of the Good God of monotheism
(taken as correlative with the establishment of universal states, like the Roman Empire). This is where the sacred finally breaks into two absolutely
opposed parts, the pure and the impure, God and devil, ecstasy as divine
and ecstasy as carnal:

> Originally, within the divine world, the beneficent and pure elements op-
> posed the malefic and impure elements, and both types appeared equally
> distant from the profane. But if one considers the dominant movement
> of reflective thought, the divine appears linked to purity, the profane to
> impurity. In this way a shift is effected starting from the premise that di-
> vine immanence is dangerous, that what is sacred is malefic first of all,
> and destroys through contagion that which it comes close to, that the
> beneficent spirits are mediators between the profane world and the un-
> leashing of divine forces—and seem less sacred in comparison with the
> dark deities.[15]

Human beings always lived in both these worlds at once and suffered the
tension between them. The tool-realm had already split into two, into user
and used. Now the sacred sphere of intimacy, of the excess that keeps escaping the formats of utility, is divided in two: we have two different opposite
realms *both* of which are now set up against and strictly excluded from the
profane world of work and purpose. One is deemed the holy, clean, outside
time—the eternal, which usurps what was originally the present water-in-
water moment's sovereignty and its transcendence of purpose (it has no
needs, it is subjected to no goal outside itself, and it is outside time). The
other is the filthy world of whatever exceeds any apparent use: the body in
its resistance to the control of mind, along with sex and murder and other

forms of violence and crime. The ambivalence that inevitably characterizes the tool-world's feelings about the oceanic—both dreading it and longing for it—now is tidied into two different and opposed realms of the purposeless: the holy and the demonic. The antithesis of the world of work and tool and purpose was formerly both of these together as water-in-water oceanic continuity, which was felt, in contrast to the profane world, as the sacred. Now, however, it is split in two. God and sex, the One and matter, are in reality two alternate names for the entire oceanic intimacy as such; the first is a usurpation, and the second is what's left over once that "pure" form has been abstracted from it. "Matter is to spirit as crime is to society,"[16] says Bataille. In fact, as we've already briefly brushed on and will explore in more depth presently, there is an "identity of indiscernibles" problem that we will find most glaringly in Plotinus: what is beyond words and description, beyond thinghood, is, on the one hand, the One, God, Purity, Eternity, pure Form, the holy, and on the other hand, matter, formlessness, chaos, filth, sex, death; the dissolution of all boundaries and all individuality. The sacred now becomes limited to the moral, which is opposed to intimacy, since it is all about duration, results, purpose, causality, and what some traditions call "karma." This happens when "sovereignty in the divine world shifts from the dark deity to the white, from the malefic deity to the protector of the real order."[17]

Now we have landed in a new dualism, with a pressing demand to find some kind of mediation. "The different forms of the dualistic attitude never offer anything but a slippery possibility to the mind which must always answer at the same time to two irreconcilable demands: lift [i.e., suspend] and preserve the order of things."[18] Every religion, every cultural form, perhaps even every human activity, is thus for Bataille an experiment in finding a compromise. And it is here that we see his great contribution to our inquiry about the religious implications of monotheism. Pagan religion depended on contact with the intimate, oceanic realm of pure continuity and on acknowledgment of its ultimacy, via a vicarious experience of deliberate violation, a voluntary sacrifice or festival of violence and holy transgression, of breaking through the boundaries of the tool, of all fixed identities being defined by utility and purpose, where both the destroyed animal or consecrated object and the priestly act of destruction are seen as sacred. In contrast, the ideal of the holy and purely Good God of monotheism *opposes* transgression. But if monotheism had "turned its back on the fundamental movement which gave rise to the spirit of transgression it would have lost its religious character entirely."[19] Transgression, strictly speaking, is the lifeblood of religion. The "holy" monotheist God presents an enigma in that, although we are used to regarding it as the prime exemplar of religion, it is, in this view, a paradoxical antireligious, antidivine kind of divinity, for it is committed to the absolute *denial* of the oceanic, or to be more exact, the thoroughgoing *subordination* of nondualism (oceanic intimacy of water in water) to dualism (thing, work, purpose, tool). Monotheism's distinctive wager for doing so is to conceive the enforcer of the dualistic world of work as the *sole* instantiation of nondual intimacy, to reshape the oceanic itself into the form of a "thing," now itself given the purpose of suppressing of the oceanic everywhere *else*. It is the *violent usurpation of violence*, and the forms of monotheism are distinguished by their varying treatment of the violence they deploy.

The first version of this purely holy monotheist God is, of course, the jealous, violent Lawgiver God. The violence and the lawgiving go together, for purity—holiness—is precisely a separation, an exclusion: the lawgiver claims a *monopoly* on violence. While initially the dismissal of the oceanic through tool-being was only implicitly violent, indeed an imposition but one still unperturbedly received by the oceanic, which from its side would experience just another wave of water in water rather than definite violence breaking down a real boundary, now that the oceanic itself is deployed to the exclusion of the oceanic, the relation from the God side becomes violently bloody-minded. The violence that is inherent in the oceanic has here been brilliantly repurposed: it is deployed and channeled against the oceanic itself, against idolatry, against diversity of values, against the faithless shifting of purposes from moment to moment, against the obscene act of ignoring the proper boundaries. The uncanny nature of this conception of God lies in his use of the force of violence precisely to enforce boundaries and divisions, to keep the holy cleanly separated from the oceanic violence and chaos and purposelessness and obscenity. The exclusion of violence now requires violence. The exclusion of violence is itself now a violent act, a separation, a wrenching away, a cut in being. To create the sacred nonviolent sphere where all is embraced by God's oneness, a huge rejection and cut are needed. This is the oneness of monotheism, an inclusion used to exclude.

This amounts to a *monopoly* on violence, echoing the political monopoly on violence claimed by the institutions of the sovereign state. But this is also a monopoly on the sacred, for it was violence that served as a pathway back to the lost and longed-for intimacy of the oceanic, and it retains this power and attraction even when monopolized by God. As Bataille puts it, "The good is an exclusion of violence and [yet in reality, once the world of purpose is established,] there can be no breaking of the order of separate things, no intimacy, without violence; the god of goodness is limited by right to the violence with which he excludes violence, and he is divine, open to intimacy, only insofar as he in fact preserves the old violence within him, which he does not [yet] have the rigor to exclude, and to this extent he is not the god of reason, which is the truth of goodness."[20]

There is thus an unresolved tension in the holy Good God, as Bataille sees it: the sacred originally meant the realm of the oceanic, which to a mortal, finite creature means the violent sundering of all particular separate forms. Now Reason and the Good are the exact opposite of this: complete domination of all that exists by purpose and utility. But the exclusionary relation between these two is itself a kind of violence, a kind of severing. This God violently excludes violence. The violent exclusion of the oceanic is the last vestige of the oceanic in this God. As such he has separated himself from all violence, all oceanic continuity, and all undermining of the formed and the useful except the violence he uses to exclude that oceanic continuity. The violence of the Good God is thus initially part of himself, not coming into him from outside: he is a jealous God of righteous exclusion. He violently negates all violation of himself, all unrighteousness, all false gods, all disobedience. His holiness is found only in that remaining paradoxical violence of his righteousness against all violence, and in a substitute kind of "eternity," Bataille thinks, replacing the intrinsic timelessness of the oceanic purposelessness with the putative persistence of something that is in the weird position of *owning violence*—for violence is the very antithesis of the principle of ownership. God has a monopoly on chaos: thus does he order the world.

Bataille reads the Christian development of this jealous, vengeful God as a metamorphosis into an alternate form of monopolization of the boundary-breaking oceanic: love. But insofar as this divine love is monopolized as the sole remaining legitimate locus of the oceanic transcendence of boundaries, the boundary between love itself and what lies beyond it manifests as a redoubled and transformed violence. The boundary between boundless love and the profane world of nonlove is as violently enforced as before, but the essence of the religious consummation lies in the attempt to bridge that gap—through violence. As love, the violence is now necessarily inflicted also on the God himself. This allows the old idea of divine sacrifice to make a reappearance, but this is now less a recovery of the sacred than a sham parody of it, a kind of bait and switch which seems to satisfy the original impulse but ends up subverting it. This is because now that God is defined as love, the violence is *disavowed*: it comes to the divinity *from the outside*. As always, "crime is necessary for the return of the intimate order . . . the violence of evil must intervene for the order to be lifted through a destruction, but the offered victim is itself the divinity." Since man, morality, and god are placed side by side in the order of things, no way exists for "deep communication" between them—violence is needed. In this case it's the divinity that is to be torn up and eaten by man for a return to intimacy. But the violence comes from without. This is not like the standard sacrifice of old: for there, "in the mediation of sacrifice the sacrificer's act is not, in theory, opposed to the divine order, the nature of which it extends immediately. However, [in contrast,] the crime that a world of the sovereign good has defined as such is external to the moral divinity."[21]

From here we can come to understand Bataille's disappointment in the new deployment of sacred violence in the Crucifixion, his belief that Christianity thus botched the profound meanings of sacrificial violence, in a complex and fascinating read of the meaning of the Passion:

> In reality the sacrifice of the moral divinity is never the unfathomable mystery that one usually imagines. What is sacrificed is *what serves*, and as soon as sovereignty is reduced to serving the order of things, it can be restored to the divine order only through its destruction as a thing. This assumes the positing of the divine in a being capable of being really (physically) done away with. The violence thus [both] lifts [i.e., suspends] and preserves the order of things, irrespective of a vengeance that may or may not be pursued. In death the divinity accepts the sovereign truth of an unleashing that overturns the order of things, but it deflects the violence onto itself and thus no longer serves that order: it ceases to be enslaved to it as things themselves are. In this way it elevates the sovereign good, sovereign reason, above the conservative and operative principles of the world of things. Or rather it makes these intelligible forms [i.e., the inviolable Mosaic law] that which the movement of transcendence [i.e., the violent jealous lawgiver Old Testament God] made them: an intelligible beyond of being, *where it situates intimacy*. But the sacrifice of the divinity is much more closely tied to the general exclusion of the given violences than was transcendence [of the old God], whose movement of violence was given independently of evil (in reason's being torn away from the sensuous world). The very violence without which the divinity could not have torn itself away from the order of things is rejected as something that must cease. The divinity remains divine only through that which it condemns.[22]

In the Passion, the divinity accepts violence applied to itself and dies. But what dies is actually just the divinity as *thing*. The result of this acceptance could have been to restore the oceanic nonthing realm; but instead, because the violence is disavowed and ejected from the divinity, who is presented only as innocent victim of dark, external forces of sin, the result is to remove the divinity from the order of "things," as sacrifice always did, but now it is placed *above* that order, making the divinity inviolable, absolute, as an individual being. That being is still the repudiator of violence, the repudiator of the oceanic—in other words, it is Reason, it is Logos, it is purpose, it is Goodness per se, which is now elevated beyond utility and made absolute. And there it situates intimacy—*monopolized* in a distinct, discontinuous being above the reach of the world.

But there is more. Nonviolent victimhood transfers the necessary violence now to the register of *blame*: it repudiates sin—it condemns the agents of sacrifice, the murderers of God—while also depending for its sacredness entirely on this violence. The logic of exclusive oneness, turning the intimate continuity of the oceanic against itself and into an agent of dichotomy and antagonism, here reaches its pinnacle. The oceanic violence has become completely subordinated into a tool of the moral world of utility, of Goodness. The only available ways to access the oceanic are either to sin and be condemned, or to become a fanatic and zealously condemn others. Both of these forms of violence have lost their power to break free of the realm of utility; both become tools in the hands of the moral order, roads back to the absolute *subordination and foreclosure* of the oceanic, its total one-sided subsumption into purpose. What was once, in the transcendence of the jealous God, an evenly balanced tension of the violence and holiness, of arbitrary uselessness and lawgiving goodness, resulting in the convergence and compromise satisfaction of both, is now a unilateral dominance of purpose over purposelessness. Even the purposelessness is now just a tool for purpose—and thus is no longer purposelessness at all. The crucial balance, the maintenance of the doubleness that sustained man in religion heretofore, purpose into purposeless and purposeless into purpose, has been destroyed in favor of the decimation of purposelessness entirely: the world has become thoroughly a tool, thoroughly a workplace. Intimacy—salvation—is monopolized into a discontinuous being who is *elsewhere*, the oceanic funneled into a specific person, that is, as a thing characterized by a purpose, individuality and duration, operating and accessed through the ends-means forms modeled on the social and interpersonal order of personal relationships and work. When intimacy itself is regarded as a *thing*, characterized by individuality and duration—that is, as a *person*—as in this second form of monotheism, the chaos that still survives in the holy righteous rage of the old God has been ejected from the Godhead, leaving only (1) the kind of love limited to the realm of the personal, the ocean of agapic spit, and (2) work (service of the Good). But violence is not, for this reason, eliminated—as always, it must find its place in the sacred, without which the sacred loses its sacredness. Violence now persists as violent sin and violent repentance and violent persecution and punishment for sin. The violence is of course still there, metastasized into these new forms. Among these new forms, it is only the first-named, violent sin, before it is supplemented by the equally violent repentance, that is not through and through a tool in the universal tool-being in service to the Good, to purpose. Since in the post-tool world, violence is the locus of the oceanic for Bataille—the real source of the sacred—this presents a new sort of impasse for human beings. Sin now becomes the sole remaining locus of the sacred.

In our terms, the Christian compromise amounts to a way of excluding the oceanic purposelessness entirely from *both* the divine and the world— and yet keeping the human thirst for purposeless intimacy fulfilled by means of the very deferral, the displacement, the otherness, the separation of the two worlds, as presenced in the violent opposition of the two embodied in the symbolic markers of faith. God becomes the God of purposivity par excellence. Henceforth there is no escape, no licit connection with the oceanic in any form. All that remains of it in such a world is a slight reminder in the form of criminal violence and sex seen now only as rebellion against God, as what is, by definition, excluded from the sacred. For sex and violence are always kept alive somewhere in the accursed outskirts of these monotheist societies, spurned and outside the sacred yet necessarily present as a correlative to this sanitized sacredness, since in Bataille's view humans need a substantial constant dose of the oceanic just to keep existing. Indeed, by defining the oceanic as sinful, the forever unrenounceable oceanic is brilliantly repurposed as a means of generating extreme guilt to make the violent submission to priestly forgiveness all the more necessary, thereby providing a taste of the oceanic after all.

Bataille sees that Christianity is an attempt to present the experience of continuity that is always obscurely craved by discontinuous, thinglike beings, accomplished formerly in the violence of the transcending of boundaries, and thus of personhood per se toward the intimacy of the oceanic, in the form of interpersonal love. In this version, the oceanic is no longer chaos and purposelessness. It is replaced by a surrogate: subordination to divine purpose. This is what we have called Compensatory Theism, in Bataille's, perhaps naively romantic, view, which replaces a preexisting Emulative Atheism of water in water. Bataille tries hard to honor the audacity of this move:

[Christianity] retains the essential core, finding it in continuity . . . reached through the experience of the divine. The divine is the essence of continuity. . . . Basically the wish was to open the door to a completely unquestioning love. According to Christian belief, lost continuity found again in God demanded from the faithful boundless and uncalculated love, transcending the regulated violence of ritual frenzy. Man transfigured by divine continuity was exalted in God to the love of his fellow. Christianity has never relinquished the hope of finally reducing this world of selfish discontinuity to the realm of continuity afire with love. The initial movement of transgression was thus steered by Christianity toward the vision of violence transcended and transformed into its opposite. This ideal has a sublime and fascinating quality.[23]

This is the primary redirection of the Christian monotheism: its strategy of satisfying the need for intimacy and continuity, for the oceanic, while eliminating violence and transgression: *an attempt to rethink the oceanic as goodness*. This is its greatness and its wager—but it was shipwrecked by the ultimacy of personality that constitutes monotheism.

For as Bataille proceeds to note, this redirection immediately presents the problem of "how to adjust the sacred world of continuity to the world of discontinuity which persists. The divine world has to descend among the world of things. There is a paradox in this double intention [i.e., bringing divine continuity, now in the form of divine love, into the midst of discontinuous purposive beings, but thereby also turning the divine continuity itself into a merely purposive personal being]. The determined desire to centre everything on continuity has its effect, but this first effect has to compromise with a simultaneous effect in the other direction."[24] This simultaneous countereffect is the narrowing of the human into personhood, on the level of interpersonal but de-eroticized love, which instigates a new level of fear of death—and thus also a solution to that fear, one that Bataille views as the foreclosing of the oceanic once and for all. As he puts it "The Christian God is a highly organized and individual entity springing from [what is originally] the most destructive of feelings, that of continuity." But since "continuity is reached when boundaries are crossed"—what Bataille calls "transgression" or "intimacy"—this amounts to an attempt "to make an order out of what is essentially chaos . . . [so that] transgression becomes a principle of an organized disorder. . . . Such an organization is founded upon work but also and at the same time upon the discontinuity of beings"—which is, of course, coextensive with the world of work. This is why death becomes so central a focus here, as "death is revealed in relation to the discontinuous world of labour. For creatures whose individuality is heightened by work, death is the primal disaster; it underlines the inanity of the separate individual."[25] The discontinuous, working, toolmaking, purposive being feels himself as a separate individual, and it is this individual who fears death. Bataille goes on to show how Christianity brings together two opposite ways in which the human spirit responds to the precarious discontinuity of personality: first, "the desire to find that lost continuity which we are stubbornly convinced is the essence of being"—the traditional way of transgression and sacrifice as contact with the lost, oceanic, purposeless universe, here reshaped into the mystical, self-abandoning love of God. The second, however, goes in just the opposite direction: "mankind tries to avoid the terms set to individual discontinuity, death, and invents a discontinuity unassailable by death—that is, the immortality of discontinuous beings."[26] These are two opposite responses to the same problem: the problem of death, which is only a problem for the tool-using, purposeful being, not for the animals, who are always already water in water. One is to recover contact with what transcends the discontinuity, and monotheisms maintain this in their conception of the infinity and eternity of God as beyond all finite individualities, albeit thoroughly personalized as de-eroticized love. But this is combined with the incompatible notion of the immortality of discontinuous beings, including God as a discontinuous being. In fact, what has happened is that immortality as such, originally the oceanic purposelessness revealed by transgression and sacrifice and sacred violence and eros, has been entirely usurped into one particular, discontinuous being: God. God is a purposive being, a person, yet an eternal and infinite one! What has happened here is simply that the purposeless oceanic has been swallowed up, been made use of, by purpose, by discontinuity. Monotheism is a hostile takeover of purposelessness by purpose.

Bataille zeroes in on the worrisome consequences:

The first way [i.e., contact with the oceanic continuity via transgressive violence or via contemplation of the eternity and omnipresence of God] gives continuity its full due, but the second enables Christianity to withdraw whatever its wholesale generosity offers. Just as transgression organized the continuity born of violence, Christianity fitted this continuity regarded as supreme into the framework of discontinuity. True, it did no more than push to its logical conclusion a tendency which was already marked. But it accomplished something which had hitherto only been suggested. It reduced the sacred and the divine to a discontinuous and personal God, the creator. What is more, it turned whatever lies beyond this world into a prolongation of every individual soul. It peopled Heaven and Hell with multitudes condemned with God to the eternal discontinuity of each separate being. Chosen and damned, angels and demons, they all became impenetrable fragments, forever divided, arbitrarily distinct from each other, arbitrarily detached from the totality of being with which they must nevertheless remain connected. This multitude of creatures of chance and the individual creator denied their solitude in the mutual love of God and the elect—or affirmed it in hatred of the damned. But love itself made sure of the final isolation. What had been lost in this atomization of totality was the path that led from isolation to fusion, from the discontinuous to the continuous, the path of violence marked out by transgression.[27]

Love itself made sure of the final isolation. Even the individual creator is condemned to eternal discontinuity here by that secondary form of love, love that is de-eroticized and nonviolent, which here is all that is left of the original continuity and intimacy of the contact with the oceanic. The oceanic means death to the creature, make no mistake; and romanticized nostalgia for pure submersion in the purposeless oceanic is no solution either—it too is a nightmare, but of the opposite type. In all religious forms, what we have is compromises of one kind or another, various experiments seeking a solution to this fundamental tension. The one struck on in the central trope of Christianity, the Crucifixion, is to deploy the vicarious enjoyment of human sacrifice as a vehicle of love—and even perhaps, in a stroke of genius, surreptitiously to mobilize the very hatred and hostility toward God as purposive controller, the inevitable wish to destroy him and all he sustains of the purposive cosmos into the vehicle of that love, into the endless redelectation of the liberating murder of that divinity. This could have been a brilliant way to recombine the two sundered halves, insofar as the sacrificial victim now shows himself to be the god both before and after the sacrifice, had he owned up to the love-hate convergence here and therefore embodied both the entire community as holy murderous priest and the slaughtered offering. That would have been the divinization of both of the participants in a violent erotic encounter that dissolves both of them, insofar as they are considered discontinuous tool-wielding beings, with all the purposive projections of both splattering away in the crash of water meeting water and scattering its exploded drops and mists everywhere on both sides—which could then perhaps be endlessly sustained and reenacted in ritual. Instead, it is the oceanic itself that is sacrificed and subordinated to purpose—to the idea of subordination itself.

That is how far religion fell when it became monotheistic. But religion is still, for Bataille, the only hope of a way out: "for anyone *to whom human life is an experience to be carried as far as possible, the universal sum* is necessarily that of the religious sensibility in time."[28] The real meaning of religious sensibility, thinks Bataille, has now become comprehensible in deceptively zigzagging developments through history, above all because he has cracked the meaning of *sacrifice* as a religious phenomenon, revealing monotheism to be a world-historical misstep, a misguided blind alley, into which the religious impulse cornered itself for awhile. We may say that monotheism is a failed experiment in attempting to satisfy a drive that has tried on many hats over the years—many forms of sacrifice, many forms of self-torture—but a particularly tragic one in that it fatally forecloses and obscures the impulse at its root: the copresence of the personal and the impersonal, the intimacy between persons in the purposeless, oceanic destruction grounding and superseding and connecting them, the nonultimacy of the personal as the enlivening horizon of personality and purpose. What is that like? Bataille says, "You are not any more different from me than your right leg is from your left, but that which joins us is THE SLEEP OF REASON—WHICH PRODUCES MONSTERS."[29] *That* is "intimacy," that is the monstrousness of the oceanic: where the personal bleeds into the nonpersonal in the frenzies of sex and death, where multiple consciousnesses pierce and penetrate and ooze and throb into each other with the oblivious self-forgetting erotic *violence* where they begin and end, and where purpose tangles with purpose and putrefies in the purposeless.

SCHOPENHAUER ON THE SUSPENSION OF THE PRINCIPLE OF SUFFICIENT REASON: HOW THE HALFWAY MEASURE OF "GOD" OBSTRUCTS THE ABSOLUTE (OR, THREE OUT OF FOUR AIN'T BAD)

But what Bataille explicitly advocates is not an animalistic return to this state, which is impossible for man as man, but the emergence of what he calls the "clear consciousness" of the violence, of the transgression; this is clarity concerning the unclarity at the root of consciousness itself and its role in shaping the tormented compromise of human life—no longer disavowing its own violence, even its violence toward itself. It means actually transgressing and expending and bestowing wastefully, as violence and as love and as waste, but doing so in full consciousness. Bataille's ideal is a simultaneity of real sin and real consciousness of sin *as sin*. He gives an amusing example: he is contemplating a table, bought with the money gained by his labor, on which his glass of whisky sits before him. The money is thus used to eat up the fruits of his labor in an experience of drunkenness that attains no end beyond itself, negating the table as a thing in the economy of purposes. This is labor and waste of the labor, both of which must be done, and done with full consciousness of this transformation of the table (work) in the drunkenness (waste), even as the table provides necessary support for the glass of whisky. The table and the violence toward the table (or the work embodied in the bought and owned table) enacted in dissolving it into the drunkenness are both necessary here, and both are to be brought to full consciousness. And that consciousness itself is ineluctably a product of the tool-world of purposes, and known to be so. It is not the disavowal of the destruction, nor merely the theoretical understanding of the necessity of the destruction, nor the mere recollection of the destruction in tranquility—none of these sides is to be prioritized. It is a new religious form, an alternative way of living the compromise that is human life: fully conscious assent to sin as sin, continually engaged in but without locating the sacred in a promised secondary disavowal located elsewhere—knowingly sinning (as transgression, self-violence, uncalculating waste, the individual's own assent to his destruction body and soul, the personality's participation in the destruction of personality) as the sacred itself. What exactly this practice and experience might look like will be explored at length when we consider Bataille's "Practice of Joy before Death" in part II.

But even if we can look past the seemingly naive nostalgia and intrinsic paradox of Bataille's idealization of an imagined, unmediated, nonidealizing intimacy, many questions are left hanging in his conception of the conscious dimension to be combined with it. Perhaps the most pressing of these is the issue I began to adumbrate at the beginning of chapter 3: the relation between teleological and mechanical causality, between viewing the world and ourselves in terms of purposive actions motivated by conscious reasons and viewing them in terms of push-pull events produced by blind causes. I suggested there that one of the most salient entailments of all the mystical atheist positions we will be exploring is their shared tendency to see these not as two opposed conceptions between which we must choose, but as standing and falling together, with the goal of overcoming both of these conceptions in favor of a new, third way of viewing both ourselves and the world. Both conceptions, as ordinarily deployed, must be overturned, and somewhat surprisingly, *both* are seen as deriving from the prior privileging of one of the two: from the granting of ultimate ontological status to teleology. Mechanism, which seems to be precisely what teleology is trying to supplant, is on this view actually a by-product of making teleology itself ultimate, above all in the idea of God. I will have much more to say about this in the detailed readings comprising part II of this book. But we can begin to clarify the stakes of the question already in considering the obvious problems that Bataille's effusions place before us. Like all human consciousness, on Bataille's own account, the "clear consciousness" component in this experience of sinning would seem to have to be derived from the problematic subordination of the present to the future, the subordination to purposive utility, the subjection to durably identified "things," even when it is so intimately united to its own suspension in the state of self-abandonment to a useless sovereign moment. Does this denote a special subjective state entirely devoid of any consciousness of separate things, an experienced alternative to teleology? Or is this a double vision that somehow experiences both at once—thinghood and its negation as a single event? How are either of these even possible, on Bataille's account? Does this experience also suspend the experience not only of teleological concern for the future but also of mechanical causality, of cause and effect more generally? Even if this is somehow possible, we may justifiably feel, at this stage, that whatever it is, it is merely a subjective self-blinding; that in any case, some form or other of *real-time mechanical causality* is still very much in operation here. In other words, even though the ecstatic Bataille, in his frenzy of erotic or scatological or self-immolating or drunken sovereignty may not be *aware* of any causality, or any purposes, or any "things," or may be aware of them in some mystical new way that is coextensive with their negation, we may come away from his descriptions feeling that this amounts to no more than a passing subjective illusion, itself still very much embedded in the world of spatiotemporal matter and causality, an occasionally achieved mental state that in itself would have to still be under the sway of subordination to purpose and, more generally, the conditionality of distinctly separated things leading to and from one another. The experience of timelessness still happens in time.

Bataille, of course, would claim this very supposition on our part is just another example of how thoroughly this conception of "things" has a hold on us. Here we confront what are really the ultimate stakes of Bataille's entire project, and more broadly, of atheist mysticism generally. But at this juncture we might begin to get a better purchase on the problem by approaching it from another angle, using more traditional philosophical tools. For what is at issue here is the very nature of material causality, indeed of conditionality itself: given that an experience of timelessness sees all things as untouched by the subordination of effect to cause and of means to end, of the entire causal order, which can also (at other times) itself be seen as itself subordinated to that causal order, how do we adjudicate between these two seeings? Is one true and the other false? Is there any argument to be made for understanding the experience of timelessness as a revelation of the truth, and the subordination of this experience to the causal order as the illusion? Or perhaps for both to be equally truth and illusion, or to be neither? Or for the question to be unanswerable? Further reflection on what any of these answers would even mean and what is at stake in our handling of them requires us to dig into the traditional questions of truth and illusion, and with them, questions of conditionality and unconditionality.

To begin this reflection, we now turn, first, to the earliest openly atheist metaphysician in the European tradition, the first self-declared post-Christian who is not merely a secular atheist: Arthur Schopenhauer. For Schopenhauer, with his customary thoroughness in seeking the most fundamental structure of familiar ideas, sees teleology as but one form of a broader principle, which also includes not only mechanical (efficient) causality, but also *logical entailment* and *spatiotemporal relativity*: the Principle of Sufficient Reason (PSR) itself. This is another name for what we have called conditionality. The essence of this idea is simply that the being of something is, in one way or another, determined by—made possible by, accounted for by—*something else*. Schopenhauer tells us that this principle operates in four different forms. In the case of purposive action by conscious animals, an end is attained by various means, and the means are brought about by reference to their intended end, so that actions are grounded by, made possible by, the motive that includes reference to the goal. In the case of mechanical causality, one state emerges from a prior state. In the case of logical entailment, a conclusion follows from a premise. In the case of spatiotemporal relativity, each position in time and space gives way to and is determined by, is made possible by, its relation to another position. For Schopenhauer these four are distinct, and it is important not to confuse them: each has its own proper area of application, and enormous problems arise from misapplying them, from spilling the proper form of PSR from one arena into another. This, in fact, would be the essence of Schopenhauer's own critique of theism: it illegitimately applies the PSR in the form that applies only to the actions of conscious animals, Consciousness of Motive, the idea of Purpose, to the events in the physical world, for which the proper form of PSR is mechanical causality between changing states of unchanging matter. The confusion of the two, starting with Anaxagoras, is the prioritization of consciousness over something that is not consciousness—namely, for Schopenhauer, "the Will," advanced as the Kantian thing-in-itself, *to which the PSR does not apply in any way.*

The italicized phrase is the key point for us here. This is where Schopenhauer's more traditional formal philosophical approach can help. For Schopenhauer, thinking along Kantian lines, makes clear that the transcendence of conscious purpose and conscious personality involves the suspension of the PSR entirely as it is only in consciousness, and that of the world of representations (*Vorstellungen*) that goes with it; that the Kantian a priori categories of the Understanding (*Verstand*) apply. Schopenahauer boils these down to time, space, and causality, constituting the *principium individuationis* that conditions the appearance of any objects at all to consciousness, and thus also all of our theoretical and practical activity as normally experienced (including both theoretical sense-making by means of concepts and self-interested, consciously motivated desire).

For Schopenhauer, we can experience the suspension of the PSR in three different ways, which are intertwined in a very interesting manner. We experience it, first, in the epistemological "miracle par excellence" of our own *felt act of willing*,[30] whereby we are both "inside and outside" of a causal event, both the knower and the known, the actor and the acted-on. This is our direct revelation of the Thing-in-Itself, which is still conscious and thus still filtered through the forms of the PSR that are endemic to consciousness (time, space, causality, division into individuated subject and object), but giving us a glimpse, as it were, of something that doesn't really fit the PSR that well. For here, although the category of cause is still present as it *must be* for any conscious experience, cause and caused are one and the same entity, which violates the very idea of causality, of the PSR: our voluntary action feels unconditioned to us for this reason, and we thus mistakenly name this feeling "free will." It is perhaps from this primary error that this, a free conscious person, is, in the post-Anaxagoran traditions, taken as the highest model of unconditionality: God. But there is a fatal flaw here, inasmuch as voluntary action, Will, is itself by definition precisely subordinated to something: the goal of its desire. Schopenhauer will have immense trouble because of this point: Will, which as thing-in-itself is supposed to be beyond the PSR, is nevertheless still something usually conceived of as something that is understandable only as utterly beholden to the PSR, insofar as all desire is motivated, enabled, by something other than itself: the object being sought, the desired thing, the good toward which it strives. For this reason Schopenhauer has to stipulate that the pre-PSR Will cannot have any object at all. It is fruitless and pointless and blind Will, a Will that is not a Will as we know it from conscious willing, and thus is also not unified, not consistent, not directed toward any single determinate goal. It is thus necessarily in conflict with itself, and necessarily doomed to creating and re-creating constant suffering—at least insofar as it is viewed in terms of the PSR, the principle of individuation, for its refraction into separate and mutually exclusive individuals, demanded by time, space, and causality (i.e., by consciousness itself), will necessarily construe its inconsistently multifarious infinity of goalless thrashings as conflictual: insofar as it is thought to have any goals at all, its goals will be in conflict with one another. But what if there are no goals? Beyond the PSR, the will is neither one nor many, for these categories apply only to the world of representation, as refracted through the PSR—as Schopenhauer himself notes when he is speaking strictly. Unfortunately he is not always so careful; the Will, the Thing-in-Itself, is often depicted as One in contrast to the multiplicity of representations, betokening both a compassionate oneness with all that lives and a horror at the necessary conflict embedded in this very oneness. And for this reason, I think, there are irresolvable tensions in his account of the source of the suffering of the world, of which he is such an eloquent and unrelenting chronicler: is this seemingly ineluctable suffering to be blamed on the Will itself, which therefore should be nullified through the practice of ascetic self-abnegation, or is it to be blamed on the PSR and its view of that Will? When the Will is viewed whole and entire, *sub species aeternitatis*, freed from the prejudices imposed by the PSR, might its infinite multifariousness be experienced differently, not as conflict but also not as harmony, perhaps as the harmony of their conflict and harmony, or better, the indistinguishability between their conflict and their harmony, as the unfolding of a new form of beatific experience? The latter possibility points us toward our atheist mystics, both before Schopenhauer (i.e., Spinoza) and after him (i.e., Nietzsche, Bataille), as we will see in part II of this book.

But in spite of these concerns with the limitations of Schopenhauer's own account of the source of the problem of suffering that his soteriology sets out to solve, his analysis of the PSR remains crucial in detecting both the incentives and the oversights behind the idea of God. An eternal, omnipresent, self-caused, self-grounding being like God may seem an attractive solution to the problem of inexorably willful life as experienced under the auspices of the PSR: conditionality, temporality, instrumentalization, the oppressive workaday treadmill where every cause requires a prior cause and every purpose is in need of another purpose—the infinite regress of prosaic meaninglessness. But with Schopenhauer's help we can also see exactly where it comes to grief. God qua "eternal and omnipresent" evades the PSR in the sense of temporal sequence and spatial position, which is one of its four forms. God qua "self-caused" evades the PSR in the sense of efficient causality, which is another of its four forms. And God qua "self-grounding" evades it in the sense of logical entailment, the following of a conclusion from a ground or premise, which is yet another form of the PSR. But if this eternal, omnipresent, self-caused, self-grounding being is in some sense a *person*, that is, a purposive mind, engaged in *conscious* willing of any definite object (even itself), if it is the abstract, self-knowing intelligence of eternal *Noûs*, or even if it is conceived as freedom on the model of "free will" (the sort of agency that exists in a world of things other to it and makes decisions about what state of affairs, different from itself, it wants to make happen), the enterprise *fails completely: for purposivity is merely another form of the PSR*, with the motive serving as the *cause* of teleological action. The concept of God can present itself as the Absolute, as a solution to the suffering and meaninglessness endemic to conditionality under the PSR, because it transcends three of the four forms of the PSR. But is entirely enmeshed in the fourth.

We might also say, with Schopenhauer, that mind, or consciousness, is already PSR through and through in its dependence on an object of consciousness: following Kant, he views the entire realm of phenomenal consciousness as entirely beholden to the PSR (via time, space, and causality). Consciousness per se is also conditionality writ large. Self-consciousness is even more so, for in Schopenhauer's view, self-consciousness is the mixture of Will and its first form of objectification, the eternally insatiable, other-desiring Will manifesting to itself as an object, as an other in a network of others, under the form of division into individuated subject and objects. So the well-intentioned attempt to find some alternative to causal servitude is shipwrecked on the idea of purpose. Eternity, check. Omnipresence, check. Unsupported by prior cause or premise, check. But if this eternal, omnipresent, self-grounding entity is something that acts with a purpose, and if it is a mind, however eternal and omnipresent, or if it has agency and free will, then we are still slaves to the PSR, still locked into the realm of servitude, of subordination, of infinite regress, of toolmaking and tool-using, of utility. God, insofar as the term denotes anything like an eternal Will willing the Good (unlike Schopenhauer's noumenal, purposeless, un-conscious Will), is thus a poorly-thought-through solution to the problem of finitude, of conditionality, of suffering—one that backfires violently on itself. The link to Bataille's theory of religion as outlined in the previous section should be obvious.[31]

Experiencing the world as the product of a universal purposive mind, as a manifestation of an eternal self-caused purpose, as the disclosure of the eternal divine will, can now be seen to be a failed attempt to transcend the PSR. But fortunately, according to Schopenhauer, there are at least two other types of experience that to some extent annul the experience of the PSR, but do so in an entirely different manner, which points us in another direction—toward another way of conceiving the unconditioned—the atheist way, which is closer to the possibility opened up by but narrowly bypassed in Schopenhauer's own soteriological explorations: experiencing the world not as the disclosure of an eternal, conscious, unified, will to the Good, but as purposeless, uncoordinated, infinitely multifarious willing.

One of these types is *aesthetic experience*. For Schopenhauer, the experience of *beauty* is a name for what happens when a moment is, effectively, *lifted free* of the PSR, of temporal sequence, of spatial position, of its place in a causal narrative deriving from specific antecedent historical events, from logical step-by-step entailment, and above all from the tyranny of desire, of motive, of purpose, of willing itself. It is the experience of time-lessness, but also of the blessed feeling of being liberated from the torture and tyranny of the insatiable willing of the Will: "the wheel of Ixion stops turning."[32] This liberation comes from experiencing this torture machine of the Will as it really is, that is, as thing-in-itself, and no longer subject to the PSR. This transformation from the form of conditionality to the form of unconditionality changes the selfsame content from misery to bliss: even the tragic, hopeless conflict of it all is transformed into beauty once it has been frozen into eternal form, having been lifted out of the PSR. For Schopenhauer, this transformation is accomplished through art's presen-tation of definite "grades of objectification" of the PSR-free thing-in-itself, the Will, which he equates with the timeless Platonic Forms. For to see something as beautiful, even something evil and miserable, is to see it as free of the principle of individuation (indeed, he will claim, to see in this way is to no longer be an individuated subject doing the seeing), not merely as an instantiation occurring in a particular time and place but as timeless, complete, universalizable, freed of proximate causes and ground and purposes—unconditioned, in the strictest possible sense: it is an ob-jectification of the timeless, placeless, uncaused, groundless, purposeless, universal Will itself, but transformed by this special kind of objectification in a way that changes the suffering of the self-conflicted, aimless Will to the bliss of aimless will-lessness. Kant described it as an experience of pur-posefulness per se that is simultaneously devoid of any identifiable goal, purposivity without purpose, retaining the *form* of purpose (unification of means toward a purpose) without revealing any specifiable purpose.[33] Schopenhauer's metaphysics allow him to replace the mode of unification characteristic of purposivity, means unified by shared subordination to an end, with the unity of the *whole* Will itself as objectified in some particular form—a unity that really means all-encompassing unconditionality itself, which as thing-in-itself is neither oneness nor multiplicity as they appear in phenomena through the lens of the PSR. The delight and liberation of artistic experience is the feeling of simultaneous liberation both from sub-ordination to a future goal and from subordination to a past antecedent. This break in the PSR is most simply evident in painting and poetry, lifting snapshot moments out of time into a kind of timelessness, and it is most powerful, Schopenhauer thinks, in music, which he terms the supreme art-form because it expresses the Will itself rather than its various representa-tional objectifications.

But the break can also be achieved by the imposition of an adequately forceful *alternate exemplification* of the PSR. Even when we experience a literary narrative with its own internal past and future, its own PSR of causes and effects and motives and consequences, we are experiencing the suspension of our own prior past and future narrativity, the beholdenness of our concerns to our own past and the cares of our Will about our own future. This is the liberating effect that the dramatic art of narrative can have, in spite of, or perhaps because of, all the mimetic expectations between spectator and character that it entails—as long as personhood is not abstracted from it into ultimate legal responsibility, and then finally into the absolute principle of the cosmos, as in monotheist milieus, thereby transferring the PSR, and with it the inescapable torture of the Will, to the thing-in-itself. As long as personhood remains nonultimate, this *doubling* of purpose undermines the monolithic dominance of purposivity per se; temporary nonultimate absorption into the alternate fake world of the story or the stage reveals the nonultimacy of the real world. The dreamlike alternate, dramatic time line of the narrative reveals the dreamlike timelessness of the spectator's own ephemeral dramas: another way to experience the bare form of purposivity without adding a (single, monolithic) purpose; that is, as beauty. The very contrast between two entirely disjointed PSRs is already a liberation from the PSR as a necessarily unified framework, allowing us a glimpse of the forms displayed in both the new mini-PSR world and our old PSR world in this new way. In this way purposeful action is itself experienced as beyond purpose—a huge step on the way toward atheist mystical experience of the simultaneity of the two, enabled by the "Great Asymmetry" of purpose and purposelessness already touched on earlier.

This is the experience of a kind of timelessness that we know from certain artistic experiences, but also perhaps from peak experiences of sublime natural beauty—and that is similar also, as Schopenhauer too notes, to the way *memory* appears to us: the "good old days," which in retrospect seem so magically otherworldly, even if at the time they were miserably banal. Back then they still engaged our Will, and thus the PSR in its teleological form of purposes and motives. Now that has fallen away, and since the other forms of PSR were eclipsed by a teleology that has now disappeared from our image of that time, we are left with this golden husk, which seems like a glorious eternal moment from another world. The experience some people have when doing *math* is perhaps another partial example: the contingency of and conditionality in the forms of temporality, efficient cause, and teleology fall away, and though one is left with PSR purely in the one remaining form of logical entailment, the feeling of the falling away of the others is itself a glimpse of the bliss of the unconditioned. As in the case of the beatitude experienced by some in the contemplation of God, one of the four forms of the PSR is still present; in the case of God it is teleology, and in the case of math it is logical entailment. But the falling away of the others cannot but give some taste of the true liberation from conditionality. The question is always, in each case, at what cost.

Now the specificity of the aesthetic experience remains conditional, precisely insofar as it is determinate, because of the specificity of any given "specific grade of objectification" of the Will (a notoriously woolly concept in Schopenhauer). We may feel that this respect for the definiteness embodied in the Platonic Forms is the one aspect of the old *Noûs* as *Arché* paradigm, the inheritance from his nemesis Anaxagoras, that Schopenhauer has failed to overcome. But far from being a problem signaling that conditionality, the PSR is not really overcome here, this is rather a clue toward a big advance toward understanding the problem I raised with respect to Bataille: how exactly can we imagine the coextensivity of both clear consciousness, ineluctably wedded to purposivity and thinghood, and the sovereignty that abandons it into the water-in-water thing-free purposelessness? Aesthetic experience is here seen to be precisely the simultaneity of the two, purposivity without purpose, the convergence of PSR and non-PSR, both conditioned and unconditioned at once. But in this form, it remains haunted by the doubts that beset Bataille's take on religious experience: inasmuch as it singles out certain experiences at the expense of others, the experience of beauty is fleeting and thereby is made into a cherished goal—and thus tumbles back into the arms of purposivity and the PSR. I may see something as unconditioned, but that seeing is still itself very conditioned. The experience of unconditionality is conditional. The experience of timelessness is subject to time. The Will kicks in again, time starts moving onward. Artistic bliss temporarily makes me forget my petty strivings, to see things without reducing them to their utility, as *sub specie aeternitatis* rather than historical contingencies glued to a particular time and place. But then a moment later I'm back in the old grind, wanting things, wondering what to do with my experience or with the artwork, or what to do next, where to get my next fix of allegedly unconditioned, omnipresent timelessness. The problem appears at this meta level precisely because as yet there is no way to apply it to *all experiences without exception*. This is exactly what we'll pursue in our exploration in part II of what Spinoza (whom we'll see coming to a similar conclusion on the basis of his own metaphysical premises) calls the "Third Kind of Knowing," where the distinction between the premise and the conclusion collapses into real Necessity and thereby beyond Necessity in its ordinary sense, to a short circuit of a causal link into obvious tautology, where the intrinsic moreness of both the premise and the conclusion each immediately reveal the other, and where both the twoness and the oneness are experienced at once. This is what Spinoza calls "Intuition"—the transcendence of the PSR, precisely through its radicalization, and one that can now apply to every experience without exception. For as we'll see, in Spinoza, "whole" is also "infinite" and "indivisible," and therefore "active," and thus has no simple parts from which it is built up, since none could exist apart from it and thus prior to it. This is not the case for finite wholes, for which the parts are always prior. The infinite whole is more than merely a whole of parts: every touch of it touches only the infinite whole. There is simply no thought or feeling to which at least this one "adequate idea" fails to apply (E5p4): each one is available to be experienced *sub specie aeternitatis*. This enriched notion of wholeness—this is really just an inseparability that is instantiated in every possible state, which is therefore necessary and eternal—is the point of contact with the big watershed in Kant's *Critique of Judgment*, the idea of teleology as self-instantiation of infinite unity (which Kant has excavated as the deeper meaning of the ordinary expression "causal efficacy of concepts," i.e., purposivity as such). This is the bridge from Spinoza's purpose-purposelessness to Kant's concept of beauty: purposefulness without specific purpose, a convergence of conditionality and unconditionality, like Schopenhauer's conception of beauty, but accomplished without Schopenhauer's post-Kantian metaphysical premises and without restriction only to specifically artistic phenomena, but rather in full force and available at every moment of experience, excluding none.

We might have hoped that Schopenhauer had taken something like this final step in his second example of suspension of the PSR: his own account of religious experience. But here there is, if anything, an even more stringent exclusion going on. Schopenhauer has in mind particularly asceticism, the mortification of the body, and that of the Will, which for Schopenhauer is objectified as the body. Schopenhauer holds up moral altruism as a first form of this suspension: the denial of self-interest pushed to an absolute extreme, and coupled with the compassion deriving from the problematic intuition of the "oneness" of the noumenal Will, or the less problematic "non-twoness" of the noumenal Will, manifesting in all creatures and in all their sufferings. But this is just one among many forms of the general denial of the Will, which is manifest in self-torture and voluntary pain above all. The self-mortifying saints are doing nothing but trying to find a sustainable form of the unconditioned, of this lifting free of the PSR, and in this first self-proclaimedly atheist version of mysticism in Europe (Spinoza was still obliged to deny that he was an atheist, although as we'll see, his mysticism more closely matches the atheist mysticism we have in mind in this book than does Schopenhauer's), it is self-imposed pain as the transcending of mutual externality—of ends-means relations, of control, of conditionality, of duration—that is the means. Inasmuch as these experiences are perhaps even more rare than the experiences of beauty, this is an even more severe limitation: the coextensivity of the suspension of the PSR and its presence qua determinate states is itself subjected to the PSR, full stop; there is no coextensivity on this second-order level, only the straight-up PSR of distinct moments in time, distinct experiences. The second-order construction thus remains unqualifiedly in the realm of thinghood, PSR, purposivity—it is something that has to be striven for, made into the purpose of all other moments. We are back in the clutches of the aftermath of *Noûs* as *Arché*, a world enslaved to purposivity.

The link to Bataille is strong, for there too we see a privileging precisely of violence, especially self-violence, as a form of contact with what lies beyond the subordinate relations of consciousness and personality. But the link goes through Nietzsche, who opposes these two versions of Schopenhauerian mysticism to one another, restoring the primacy of the aesthetic as the "real metaphysical activity of man."[34] We will return to these points in part II of this book, where we will explore possible solutions to this last remaining impasse—and to a reconsideration of the mystical implications of pain, in the conclusion. But for now Schopenhauer's way of setting up the problem can help us settle into a broader sense of what our options are, enough to say clearly: atheist mysticism is the experience of the unconditioned in some form *other than* those candidates for something beyond the PSR given by the theist, which fail because they are still beholden to some form of self, consciousness, or purpose, but also (in common with the theist) not settling for locating this unconditionality merely in matter, causality, narrative intelligibility, theoretical consistency, or logical order. We now have our agenda. It is to see that these two sets are not the only two alternatives, and that instead they belong within a single system, that they go together, and that moving from one to the other does not solve the deeper problem. What we are looking for in our atheist mystic heroes are those cases where some third way has been found, some experience of the unconditioned as an alternative to both mind and matter, to both conscious purpose and blind causality, to the PSR as such in all its modalities. Beauty and pain are our first clues, but our goal here is to find other possible ways of suspending the PSR, including but also going beyond both beauty and pain, inasmuch as these are still special states, which are not yet seen as applicable in all moments of experience, and which therefore simply reinstate the dominance of the PSR and beholdenness to purposivity—unless both beauty and pain are themselves seen as happening in and as every moment of experience. That is the Tiantai Buddhist solution, as we'll soon see, but it's also one we'll find approached through other means by the key figures discussed subsequently. The most important breakthrough for us, as shown in part II, will be to see the overcoming of the PSR *precisely in the radicalization of the PSR itself.* This is where necessity turns to freedom, as Spinoza saw it in the Third Kind of Knowledge, where pure logic turns into the collapse of the PSR in its very consummation. The way out of the otherness intrinsic to all determinate being is the full acceptance of the otherness intrinsic to all determinate being, the exacerbation of it; it is the embodiment of the strict necessity and inescapability of the pain of conditionality, the beatific vision of its omnipresence. To this we now turn.

TOWARD THE SYNONYMITY OF CONDITIONALITY
AND UNCONDITIONALITY: TWO ALTERNATE MODELS
OF OMNIPRESENCE, THEISTIC AND ATHEISTIC

Taking in the previous discussion at a glance, then, we have on the one hand the infinite, the Absolute, the unconditioned, eternity, omnipresence, indeterminacy, freedom from PSR, purposelessness (in the present context, these all serve as functional synonyms); and on the other hand, the finite, the relative, the conditioned, spatiotemporal limitation, determinacy, subjection to PSR—and purposiveness (also functionally synonyms here). There is reason to think that, contrary to common opinion, the establishment of the latter category as a whole—finitude of distinct objects and therefore conditionality of one finite entity by another, efficient causality as much as final causality—is to be viewed as a by-product of the basic dichotomizing premises derived only from purposiveness itself. The dichotomization of the two categories themselves thus follows from the ultimacy of purposivity, from its absolutization—what we are calling monotheism.

But attempts to overcome the dichotomization endemic to purposivity fail if they simply repeat it at a second level, that is, by positing any sort of realm of purposelessness that is beyond, *transcendent to*, the realm of conditionality, finitude, and purposivity—for this itself then becomes just another dichotomy. Hence we have begun to ask whether there is any way of thinking about the purposelessness that must pertain to the unconditioned and that does not revert to the structure of purposive consciousness and conscious unified agency, thus landing us in a dichotomy between the purposelessness and purpose, the unconditioned and the conditioned, the infinite and the finite, the transcendent and the immanent.

To find an alternate approach, let us go back to the beginning: Why would anyone care about the infinite in the first place? And why care about the finite?

Cognitively, as Kant showed, we can't help concerning ourselves with both: we live and breathe the inescapability of the PSR, but its inescapability means that it is also applicable to its own pervasiveness as a definite fact about the world: the PSR itself forces us to consider what *its own* sufficient reason could be. What grounds the need for grounding? What is the condition for the entire realm of the conditioned? We experience only the conditioned, but to consider the conditioned as conditioned is to feel conditionality itself as requiring grounding in the unconditioned: that is the infinite regress problem to which we've condemned ourselves by locking into the ultimacy of the ends-means schema of purpose, and what he have argued is its necessary shadow—the exceptionlessness of the schema of mutual exclusivity of determinate things, of their beholdenness to otherness, and thus of cause and effect—of the PSR in general.

Religiously, soteriologically, existentially, the unconditioned promises to be the only stability, the only independence, the only way to be able to withstand the undermining of ourselves that comes from without, and hence the only freedom, whether as freedom from suffering (Buddhism), as certainty, as eternity, as the only worthy object of love (Spinoza, along with various mysticisms and even with monotheism in this case), or what have you. But we need the conditioned too. Without the conditioned, there is nothing to be free or freed of, nothing to be released from suffering, nothing to enjoy the beatitude of love of the eternal, of joy in the eternal. All determinate and real entities are, ipso facto, conditioned; otherwise, they would not be determinate and real at all. Moreover, following Seng Zhao and Hegel, among many others, there is a logical contradiction in the unconditioned: it is defined as the antithesis of the conditioned, but it cannot be such as to exist only where conditionality is not, for that would make it conditioned itself—existing in any given concrete or conceptual locus only on the condition that conditionality is absent there.

The most thorough solution to the double need for both the PSR and the freedom from the PSR is the Tiantai Buddhist solution: it lies in their absolute convergence, their synonymity, their Mobius-strip relation as two sides that are one side, one side that is two sides. That requires some specific Buddhist logical and soteriological moves, along with a willingness to follow the consequences all the way to the end. For me this is still the most satisfying solution: an infinity of unconditioned-conditioneds in endless intersubsumption. Each finite phenomenon is indeed lifted out of the PSR, but precisely by means of a fuller thinking-through of the PSR itself, and in its resultant unconditionality reinstated in and as the ground and reason and setting and stuff and cause and goal of all other finite things: PSR as anti-PSR, and anti-PSR as PSR. To be any determinate phenomenon is indeed to be completely beholden to otherness, just as the PSR demands. But precisely because this is the very definition of what it is to be appearing in experience at all (even for the putative non-PSR, "the unconditioned" per se), this beholdeness to otherness is the own-most dimension of any experienceable being. Every inside has an outside, but because the outside—indeed, every possible outside, since each outside has a further outside—is *necessarily* entailed in any inside, it is intrinsic to what it means to be an inside. That means the outside is, in the most essential sense, also inside. Precisely because of the intrinsic inescapability of otherness, otherness is other but not *merely* other. Otherness per se is intrinsic to selfhood per se; Non-Xness is intrinsic to Xness. X is therefore really a name for X-plus-Non-X—which is a particular way of viewing all that exists with nothing excluded. X is an X-centered way of viewing the entirety of existence. Since conditionality as such means the dependence on what is other, this amounts to a *fuller* disclosure of X's conditionality, which reveals it to be a *synonym* for an enriched notion of unconditionality. For here the conditionality of *any* single phenomenon is seen to entail the conditionality of *every other* phenomenon. X can only occur in a particular time and place, rather than everywhere and at all times, because it is conditioned rather than unconditioned. To be conditioned is to have an outside, but it is an outside that is also essential to it, inalienably a part of it: a conditioned X is always, in truth, an X-plus-Non-X. But if any X is appearing at any time or place, all others are failing to appear there and then, so "failing to appear there" is also a conditioned state. Since all Non-X phenomena are conditioned, the instantiation of Non-Xness—the absence of Xness—is also conditioned. So Non-X is, in truth, Non-X-plus-X. Both X and Non-X are thus Both-Non-X-and-X—the same internal elements always present but appear in different configurations. When X meets Non-X, which is what is always happening everywhere, it is the entirety of existence meeting the entirety of existence. What is it that accounts for the different ways of appearing of what is, in every case, there, so that it appears variously as X or as Non-X? Given that they are, in this respect, the same, what is it that accounts for their being also different? It is necessary that there be some difference, some contrast, for there to be any appearing at all. But something must always be appearing, and this something must always be specific and conditioned—because even total non–appearance-of-everything would be a something-appearing, would itself also be a conditioned appearance, one that presupposes and even posits its contrast to its exclusion of something-appearing. Exclusion entails conditionality. Now, since conditionality applies to all without exception, there can be no particular closed sum of appearances serving as the condition for any given appearance, for this closed circle itself would then be unconditioned. The entirety of existence is not a finite set, but an unclosable infinity: when X meets Non-X, which is what is always happening everywhere, it is infinity meeting infinity. This also means that every appearance of X (which means X appearing precisely *as* X) is always susceptible to being affected by the addition of any other appearance—and there are always more available. An Xness whose appearance as X can be undermined by the presence of an additional external factor is an ambiguous Xness. Hence, whatever is "appearing conditionally" is "an ambiguous appearance." To appear as X is always only to appear ambiguously as X. This means that the appearance of X can be either as X or Non-X; in other words, there must always be appearing, but whatever is appearing is appearing only ambiguously, and conversely also that X is appearing ambiguously everywhere and Non-X is also appearing ambiguously everywhere, in that wherever X is appearing (ambiguously), Non-X is also appearing (ambiguously). When X meets Non-X, which is always happening everywhere, X precisely in being X is therefore also infinitely ambiguous, thus is itself an infinity of alternate Non-Xs. The *conditioned* ambiguous appearance of X is the *unconditioned* ambiguous omnipresence of non-X, and vice versa. In both what appears as X and what appears as Non-X, both X and Non-X are always ambiguously appearing, as both conditioned and unconditioned—as the ambiguity between conditionality and unconditionality. Both X and Non-X are thus both appearing (ambiguously) everywhere and under all conditions, which means the (ambiguous) appearance of X is unconditioned and the (ambiguous) appearance of Non-X is also unconditioned. This is the revised form of unconditionality that now applies, precisely in and through and as the conditionality of each phenomenon, in their mutual inclusion and mutual identity in and through and as their mutual exclusion. Each possible entity, precisely because it is necessarily and thoroughly conditioned, is, ipso facto, unconditioned. Unconditionality entails omnipresence, and this new kind of unconditioned omnipresence now means to be present *as* all other things and all of their possible mutually grounding and mutually undermining relations. This applies also at the second-order level, the third-order level, and so on, to infinity. That is, even the (ambiguous) failure to realize all of the above is also a form in which its realization also is (ambiguously) appearing, and so on. Each coherence, each determination, each fleeting moment of experience is, in this precise manner, unconditioned, absolute, indeed the *sole* Absolute, ineradicable from all other possible experiences, and yet as such always conditioned by and conditioning of all other possible experiences; yet each remains completely conditioned through and through. Each experience is both the unsurpassable and the always-already-surpassed. Each is the determiner of all, is beyond determination, and is determined by all. It is not just determinateness or indeterminateness that is everywhere and nowhere; rather, indeterminateness is itself just another determinateness, and every determinateness is indeterminateness, and this determinateness-*sive*-indeterminateness is everywhere and nowhere. Each This is This and the All and the None. The All is Each This and the None. The None is the All and Each This.[35]

This may sound very abstruse and insane and weird. But once we have an eye for it, we can find on all sides some gesture in this direction, a deep human need to find a way simultaneously to affirm the absoluteness of all experienced things and to deny that absoluteness, at the same stroke, affirming somehow the ineffable dimension, not only of the infinite, but also of the finite, in spite of its apparent limitedness and definiteness and knowability. This is a recognizable strand of the sort of mystical impulse we are tracking here. It is a demand that the experienced world give us a taste of what lies beyond the PSR, of the unconditioned, of the Absolute, but also that it must be transcendable, so that we are not bound down to it, do not become subjected to it. We want to participate in the palpable immediacy of that freedom from all limitations, to be energized and enlivened by its omnipresent uncontainability, and yet also not to be enslaved to it, subordinated to it, which we would be if it were the sole infinity before which we must bow and from which we cannot escape and a demand to annihilate all the riches of knowledge and determinability in the midst of which we live our lives. We need every existing presence to be experienceable as both finite and infinite, conditioned and unconditioned, relative and absolute, determinate and indeterminate, subject to and also free from PSR. This must apply also to the experiencing of this as "experienceable" and its contrary. The Absolute must be everywhere and nowhere; it must be everything and nothing—but also specifically this, specifically here, specifically now.

We must dwell a bit on this point: we have already begun to note in the history of metaphysics many instances of the "halfway" move, the *partial* or one-way suspension of the PSR: that is, when we separate out some one entity and regard it as being a *conditioner of other things* but not of being *conditioned by other things*—the unmoved mover, the cause of all that is the effect of none, or the ground of all but grounded by none. That is, rather than lifting it entirely out of the cause-effect or ground-grounded matrix, we lift it only out of being grounded in otherness or being an effect and consider it only as a cause—a first cause, an uncaused case, an ungrounded ground or the like. This is the case when modeling the exception to the PSR on an absolutized version of what is experienced as consciousness and Will, even when these determinations are ostensibly transcended when applied to the infinite—when modeling it on our tenuous human experience of our free will and autonomy, critiqued in some form by all our atheist mystics, from the Daoists to the Buddhists to Spinoza, as a primal instance of ignorance, of being aware of the effect but not the cause of a causal event, of knowing what we desire but not why we desire it. The elevation of this bogus transcendence of the PSR, free will, as rooted in our finitude and ignorance or its projection in a free-willed first-cause God, to the status of the best model of the Absolute and infinity might have been a good faith attempt to contemplate the unconditioned in some way at least, a nonthing that in some way at least is disentangled from the PSR and yet also has some presence in our immediate experience. But this is undermined, not only by its questionable psychological roots, but more importantly, by a lack of thoroughness of the move, maintaining the tyranny of the PSR all the more in making *one thing* a universal conditioner of other things, selling all other things into slavery to that one thing.

The key issue is simply the status of the alleged *otherness* stipulated as obtaining between the conditioned and the conditioner, the mutual externality characteristic of finite determinate *things*. As we saw previously, the mutual externality of conditioner and conditioned is absolutized and locked in most ineradicably if the first cause is thought of in terms of the fourth form of the PSR—the conception of *purpose*, of motive, of final cause—which is intrinsic to the idea of a personal God or even to the more shadowy derivatives of *Noûs* as *Arché*. But even more than an absolutization of another form of the PSR might do: the absolutization of purposivity, with its emphatic either/or structure of exclusion, generates endless dichotomization, not only between thing and thing, outcome and outcome, purpose and purpose, but even between the conditioned and the unconditioned.

This allows us to make a more general comparison of two deceptively forms of unconditionality, of omnipresence, which appear similar but in reality are radically different, with important differences in implication for their alignments with purposivity, and thus with the PSR more generally. For assuming that what is wanted is always the everywhere-and-nowhere of the Absolute alluded to at the beginning of this section, the convergence of the conditioned and the unconditioned, there are at least two opposite ways of hedging on omnipresence (of infinity, of the unconditioned, of reality, of the Good, of divinity, of enlightenment, of bliss, of being, of truth, or what have you)—two opposite ways of having your cake (it is everywhere) and eating it too (it is nowhere). These two opposite ways embody a recapitulation and further development of the two competing models we began to trace out in the previous discussion of Plato's *Symposium*.

Model One might be called the omnipresence of the indeterminate, of the "stuff" or raw material that exceeds any defining limit, or of unhewn Dao exceeding any determinate boundaries, of raw infinity, of spatial materiality, of consciousness as the field of awareness (as opposed to thinking of definite thoughts or the appearance of definite perceived objects), of Substance. For convenience we will call this Indeterminacy-Omnipresence, which *initially* brings with it an intuitive "whole/part" materialist conception: underlying matter (etc.), indeterminate in itself, is everywhere, is in one sense the whole of reality, but every determinate entity is then one "part" of this whole. We regard this as a weak form of omnipresence (the sought-for exceptionless affirmation), a kind of hedge: the background field of perception, or stuff, or matter, is indeed everywhere, but not *all* of it is in each locus. Its ineffability, its Nonbeing beyond all determinations of being (the equally sought-for exceptionless negation), is also initially quite weak, still thought of here as a definite indeterminacy that excludes all determinations: it is nowhere because it is present everywhere only as indetermination, and as nothing in particular.

Model Two is the omnipresence of determination, of the defined, of Form, of the existent as the thinkable. We will call it Determinacy-Omnipresence, of the kind we find most pronounced in Plato and Aristotle and in their monotheological heirs. This model, like the previous one, begins in a "determinate/indeterminate" contrast, with an omnipresence of determinacy, due to the fact that for anything to really be considered existing is for it to be determined: it is only meaningful to say something is there if some determinations can be made about it, to distinguish its being there from its not being there. Omniabsence is here initially entirely excluded, by design: there is no role for any kind of being that exceeds thought and determination, which would be a Parmenidean contradiction in terms. But an unexpected *ineffability* of the Absolute also gets a foothold here, starting with Plato's remarks in the *Republic* about the Form of the Good, the sun which cannot be directly viewed, and is brought to fruition in Plotinus (d. 270 CE), opening the way to centuries of monotheist negative theologies. But very significantly, the Nonbeing or ineffability of the Absolute begins, in this context, to be available only through the category of the causative role of the Good, of universal telos—an upshot of our old friend *Noûs* as *Arché*. We will see that in Plotinus, the ineffability, the arrival of an Absolute that is "beyond all thought, being and determination" at long last, is a consequence of a radicalization of *oneness*, where the subject-object split and the mutual contrasts to other existents necessary to determinate cognition are seen to be impossible for truly radical and foundational oneness. But this very hyperoneness, beholden as it still is to the structure of the *Noûs* as *Arché* model, is itself still conflated precisely with *telos*, with the Good, with the normativity so central to Determinacy-Omnipresence. The initial intuitive upshot of this model is not the whole/part hedge, as in the first model, but a value hierarchy where "determinate" admits of degree, which limits in a different way the robustness of both the sought-for exceptionless affirmation and the sought-for exceptionless negation. The more determinate something is, the more being it has—and "more determinate" here means more robustly able to exclude otherness, more definitely to be this *rather than* that, to be more completely unambiguous. Since everything identifiable does, ipso facto, do this to some extent, determinateness—Form, exclusivity—is present everywhere, but to varying degrees depending on the levels of robustness of definiteness and exclusion of otherness. Again both the omnipresence and the ineffability are here initially quite weak.

Each of these attempts, through the whole/part model on the one hand and the hierarchy of degrees of determinacy on the other, marks out a direction of omnipresence, which, if it is not pushed to a sort of self-overcoming via a more thoroughgoing application of its own premises, leads to a dualistic impasse, establishing only a sham omnipresence and a sham omniabsence, which is, in fact, still conditioned and limited, falling short of the convergence of omnipresence and omniabsence which, as suggested, is the true mystical desideratum motivating these reflections.

The self-overcoming of the limitations of the materialist whole/part version of the Indeterminacy-Omnipresence model into full atheist mysticism will be our focus throughout part II. Here, however, the better to grasp the contrast, it behooves us to tarry a while with the Determinacy-Omnipresence model, particularly its own reversion into a seeming overcoming of its initial limitations, an exaltation of a seeming Indeterminacy: the ineffable One. It is important to see the difference between the identical-sounding claims of ineffable omnipresence arrived at by the self-overcomings of these two opposite models, for in fact, even in its self-overcoming, the Determinacy model still continues to severely restrict the meaning of both ineffability and omnipresence. As I've suggested, the key figure here is Plotinus.

In Plotinus we have an impersonal primal ground of reality that is not characterized as a thinking thing, and which is supposed to be beyond all predication: the One or the Good. It can not be known through any categories or essences, it is beyond Being, it has no thought or intention. It is the oneness in which is possible no opposition of subject or object, no otherness of cause and effect; hence nothing like the PSR can operate with respect to it. It is itself unconditioned, and this is understood to mean it can in no way be touched by conditionality. Unlike a purposive deity, it is not beholden to the PSR even in the form of final causality: it is beyond purpose, beyond freedom, beyond even necessity—utterly ineffable. Strictly speaking, it is not even its own final cause, as in Aristotle: it is beyond the PSR entirely, since it is beyond even Being.[36]

But precisely as such, the Good serves as both primal and final cause of all the rest of existence, the source of all and the end toward which all must strive. Developing a motif found in Aristotle,[37] for Plotinus to exist is to be one, to be a unity in some sense, as an army or a body exists as such only to the extent that it is unified as this one particular identifiable thing: without some kind of oneness, no thing can exist. Things have being to the extent that they have oneness, some consistent definite determinacy—that is, to the extent that they participate to some extent in this primal unknowable oneness.

Plotinus gives us the primordial trinity of (1) this ineffable One, beyond all knowledge and description, beyond even Being; (2) *Noûs*, the eternal Intellectual Principle that emanates from it, radiating necessarily and involuntarily as light does from the sun; this is composed of all the Platonic Forms as Intellect-Intelligibles, both knower and known, eternally contemplating the Oneness from which it emanated but eternally incapable of adequately conceiving it, yet reaching the next best thing, the eternal contemplation of unity as expressed in the universal intelligible Forms; and (3) Soul, the principle of appetition and movement insofar as it is active in real time, apprehending particular objects in association with particular bodies, the soul of both of the world as a whole and of each living thing, which is in one sense indivisible at every locus but in another sense divided into individuated souls, striving but failing to adequately coincide with the unity of the *Noûs* from which it emanates, just as *Noûs* eternally strives but fails to adequately coincide with the unity of the One.[38]

Noûs is here still sometimes described as "divine" or a "divinity," but it is really a subordinate emanation of the strictly nonconscious and unknowable One. The latter is, clearly, in no sense a person. The One is so indivisible that it is utterly ineffable, beyond Being but also beyond even necessity (in the sense of a requirement of acting in a way that follows necessarily from its nature, for no such division between acting and Nature is possible in it), and for the same reason also beyond chance and beyond free will, at least when Plotinus is speaking strictly (though as we'll see, there is some telltale equivocation on this last point when he is speaking less strictly). But even the knowable aspect of the divine, *Noûs*, its first emanation, is also not in any sense a *person*, though it is the maximally One-like among all beings, and it does have a purposivity of sorts: to contemplate itself and the real unity of intelligibility in all its Forms, even the oneness of knower and known in Itself, and thereby to always attempt to contemplate the unknowable One that is the Good beyond being. To whatever extent this *Noûs* is "a" mind, it nonetheless lacks the key characteristic of the monotheist God, which makes that God a true "person" in the sense we've tried to delineate here: it does not create through an act of inscrutable Will and, concomitantly, it does not *exclude* other minds. On the contrary, all other minds, whenever they know anything rationally, are embodying the actual activity of this divine Intellect. For Plotinus, in fact, even at the level of Soul, which is a further level of emanation down, all individual souls, qua soul, are in fact really the one All-Soul, divided only insofar as they are combined with matter (which similarly emanates from and unsuccessfully emulates what remaining unity there is in Soul), but is in itself complete at every locus. Matter as such, on the other hand, is a structureless mush until imprinted with the unities derived from the emanations above it; claimed to have no unity, and thus no form and no being of its own—no determinacy of any kind—it is, strictly speaking, nothing at all.[39]

So while it is true that unity is privileged here at the expense of multiplicity, and the basic *Noûs* model continues to shackle the entire system to a single-aimed teleology, nevertheless we have not reached the absolute mutual externality of souls, bewailed by Bataille, that tends to follow the adaptation of this system into a more robustly monotheist framework and its absolutization of purposive personhood. Instead, whatever personalities there are, whatever is engaging in actively conscious experiences in real time, are on the one hand multiple and nonultimate, and on the other hand internal to the one Soul of the world. Similarly, all instances of experienced intellection—rational knowledge of the eternal Forms that constitute *Noûs*—that are experienced by all these "parts" of the one Soul (i.e., our individual souls) are internal to the eternal contemplation activity of the eternal Knowing-Known of *Noûs* itself. Our minds and the mental dimension of such a "God" overlap, rather than relating externally to one another as two consciousnesses in a personal relationship. So we do not have a single personality of the deity, which is by definition *other* to all other personalities, or the true God, who repudiates all other gods as idols. To the extent that there are any *personalities* belonging to *Noûs at all*, they are, by nature, multiple. All of them are excluded by the One that they attempt to contemplate and approximate, for this transcends Being entirely. But to the extent that there *is* any *Noûs* at all, it is present—indeed wholly present—as the rational thinking of all other minds rather than requiring the exclusion of all other minds. The same goes for the one Soul and each individual soul.[40]

I do not endorse Plotinus's doctrine of Soul and Intellect, which marks the point where he diverges most glaringly from atheist mysticism. *Noûs* is still the ultimate *Arché* of the world here, though here as in Aristotle, it undergoes no temporal processes of the kind associated with finite intellects and does not plan or design or intentionally interact; it has no forethought or opinions, it performs no judgments. Nevertheless, it is the locus of all determinate essences, the eternal Forms, and thus determinateness is still the ultimate ground of temporal existences, bestowing on each entity a single, definite essence toward which its existence is striving: purpose—single, predetermined purpose—is still grounding all real existence. It still amounts to granting ultimacy to determinateness and teleology as the real ground of all that exists. With the prioritization of definiteness over indefiniteness, form over formlessness, finitude over infinity, we are still on the wrong side of the Great Asymmetry: form excluding formlessness rather than formlessness that includes forms. And here we see how even Plotinus's One, in spite of being unknowable itself and beyond being, nevertheless is still construed as an *exclusive oneness* rather than an inclusive oneness, leading to what we regard as his crucial misstep: ignoring the Identity of Indiscernibles between matter and the One. The beyond-form unknowability of the One must be somehow different from the sludgy, formless unknowability of matter. Both are allegedly utterly inaccessible to any determinacy of their own, and yet they are somehow not one and the same thing. On the contrary, they are the opposite ends of the system, somehow supposed to be the most mutually exclusive of all, to have nothing at all in common: two different nothings. This is in sharp contrast to the case in the true atheist mysticisms, where the indeterminable concreteness of all material particulars is no different from the indeterminable universality of their unifying ground. For Plotinus, matter and the One are the two extremes, posited as opposites. Both are, in themselves, free of all predicates. But one of them, matter, is, as it were, *below* the Intelligible Realm of *Noûs* and all its Forms, and their temporal manifestation in the Soul; the other, the One or the Good, is *above* it. The One is not a Being. But matter is not really a Being either. This weird distinction between two kinds of nothing is precisely where the true atheist mystics differ from the Plotinian, and more generally, all the inheritors of Greek thinking, including the monotheist negative theologies. In Daoism (e.g., Laozi, *Daodejing* 14), the Identity of Indiscernibles straightforwardly applies to these two extremes: the two are identified, which really means the One in *Daodejing* is not like the Plotinian One, and matter—stuff, "the unhewn"—is also not like the Plotinian matter. For Plotinus, a distinction is made between these two Nothingnesses, in spite of the fact that both are strictly beyond any predication: the distinction between the two is in the level of dependence and self-sufficiency and productivity they are claimed to have, with matter being the last emanation, the one where the outer rings of fecundity finally peter out, which produces nothing beyond itself, which has no activity or actuality, which itself depends entirely on the prior existence of the Soul, itself depending on *Noûs*, itself depending on the One. Why these differing features of the two, without which they cannot be meaningfully distinguished at all, are not themselves considered determinations remains mysterious. It is at this point that the two systems diverge radically. Plotinus gives us a hierarchy of both being and value between the two: the overflowing Nonbeing of the One emanates down into the *Noûs*, which then emanates into Soul, which then emanates into matter, each coming from the prior state and striving in vain to be more like it, but through this teleological striving getting its life and its good and its actual form, its actual being. The Good, the One beyond Being, is on top, sharply distinguished from the worthlessness of matter, although our analysis suggests that there is actually no way to distinguish them independently of the presupposed hierarchical schema of dependence.

Here we have the knot at the heart of the contrast between the two models, between the omnipresence and omniabsence of indeterminacy on the one hand and those of determinacy on the other: in the latter, there are two different conceptions of alleged "nothing," one of which (the Plotinian and its inheritors) is not really nothing, since in that system it is claimed to be distinguishable from another "nothing," that of matter. That there is a criterion to distinguish them, that is, fecundity of emanation, proves that they are not really nothing, but just more somethings dressed up in the garb of nothingness. As definite somethings, they are still subject to the PSR, still conditional, still mutually determinative through their determinate contrast, whereas when seen properly, when the last vestiges of the *Noûs* as *Arché* model are put behind us, both matter (or the Worthless) and the superessential One (or the Good) are Dao, precisely in the interface that is their indistinguishability. The fact that they are, in reality, one and the same, however, changes the implication of both radically. In Plotinus, the alleged Nonbeing turns out to be a something after all—for otherwise it could not exclude something else. As a something, it remains conditioned as well as conditioning. Hence it is not only that it necessitates the PSR in all other things, in spite of being free of it itself, as already noted; here we see that it too remains only a specific being, distinguishable and determinable in spite of claims to the contrary—since it is differentiated from matter. It is in this smuggled-in exclusivity that we observe most directly the failure to entirely transcend mutual exclusivity, which is to say, to escape the clutches of the PSR. We have still fallen short of what is needed for that: the full convergence of conditioned and unconditioned, and of omnipresence and omniabsence, such as our atheist mystics alone will provide. The same will be true for the monotheist negative theologians who follow in Plotinus's footsteps—and in this respect, both may be regarded as valiant and impressive moves in the direction of atheist mysticism, huge breakthroughs, in fact, when put in the context of the prevailing philosophical trends of their cultures, but both of whom get blocked from taking the most crucial step by the same inherited premise.[41]

With the Determinacy-Omnipresence model, as it plays itself out not only in the thought of Plotinus but in that of his inheritors, we can indeed say that both God (*Noûs*, pure Form, Thought of Thought, Formal Cause of Formal Cause) and also what is beyond God (the One, the ineffable God-head) are, in an important sense, present in everything, even present *as* everything insofar as anything is any thing at all—that is, insofar as we can say it is real, actual, something rather than something else insofar as it is has form, insofar as it is a one, insofar as it is determinate. In that sense at least, we can say "everything is God"—for "being there" just means "being determinate" which for Plotinus means being a unity, a "one," a this versus a that, something that by including what it includes can concomitantly exclude what it is not. The beingness of any given finite thing is that thing's best approximation of the oneness of the One that exceeds it and exceeds all Being and knowability, but at the same time informs and makes real all that exists. So we can say not only that everything is God (that is, everything instantiates *Noûs*) but that everything is also beyond God (instantiating the One, the Good that is beyond all determination and being).[42] This remains the case also when full-fledged monotheism incorporates both the God as eternal willing mind and Godhead as beyond all conception and being into the conception of God as such. Everything we can genuinely *point out* and *cognize* as truly a "something" is good, is the ultimate reality, is truth. All things, qua things, are good. But some entities are not fully developed, haven't sharpened the articulations of their boundaries completely to form a perfectly distinct "thing"; they are vaguely or imperfectly or ambiguously what they are, what they claim to be, what we can with effort discern in them—they are not completely "good at" being that putative thing. They are *undermined* by the blurring leaking effect of matter, of potentiality, of unrealizedness, of infinity destabilizing their boundaries, making them bleed into what lies outside their determinate borders. Here, although matter is alleged not to really be any entity as such, to be nothing "actual," nothing determinate and actualized, it nevertheless provides us with a way to claim both that "all being is good" and "all being is God" and both that "every being, insofar as it is a being, is wholly good," but also, "every concrete thing is somewhat evil." This turns the Nonbeing of the One into the pure transcendence whereby "God must transcend and negate all material things." Even when, as often happens in the monotheisms, this has not been converted into a question of the corrupt or disobedient Will of fallen creatures, the problem is that something (matter, or creaturely will) is not being controlled completely enough by the Form, which is the vestige of *Noûs* and the One and the Good. It turns out that all things we experience are negated to some degree; we get a hierarchy of degrees of reality, which is also a hierarchy of degrees of goodness. Almost everything turns out to be extremely deficient because it is extremely far from being truly (i.e., *exclusively*) itself: it is not yet *sufficiently* a thing, in Bataille's sense of "thing." This picture of the world thus remains conceived in a way that is deeply committed to the mutual separation of things, emerging from the tool-using model of teleology, even as it tries to transcend it.

Hence we can say that even in Plotinus, even in the ineffability of the One beyond Being, we have not passed beyond the tyranny of Form and separation, beyond the tyranny of an ultimately purposive universe. Though he usually he speaks of emanation as an involuntary and inevitable process, we see Plotinus beginning to struggle with this point in *Enneads* 6:8 (in MacKenna's translation, "On Free Will and the Will of the One"),[43] where even the unknowable One at its pinnacle is painted, albeit in language that Plotinus is careful to insist is unavoidably inexact, not as atelic but merely as autotelic, which would make it still beholden to the general conception of teleology, and not finally beyond teleology altogether, as he suggests elsewhere. What seems to motivate this, as is very evident in Plotinus's rhetorical skittishness around this theme, is an urgency to deny any hint that the One has anything to do with *pure happenstance, chaos, chance—the old specter of apeiron*, which in this tradition of thinking inspires nothing but horror and contempt. It is here that we see most glaringly the profound effects of the "Great Asymmetry": by making *Noûs* ultimate, by prioritizing purpose, even what is beyond *Noûs* remains beholden to the *dichotomous relation between purpose and purposelessness, between chaos and order*, established by that ultimacy. In spite of quite clearly stated knowledge that the One's general ineffability and indivisibility make it impossible for this description to be literally true, Plotinus feels some need to present the One as something at least inexactly describable as being in control of itself. As such, he still cannot bear to divest it completely of Will; for him that would mean equating it with what this way of thinking sees as the only alternative to control, that is, with chaos, happenstance—with matter, in fact. This tiny rhetorical chink in the armor of his otherwise robust apophaticism proves to be a fateful opening for the monotheisms that use him as a conceptual resource: encouraged by their anthropomorphizing scriptural language, even when it is explained away as metaphorical, they will find here a foothold to retain Will and control in some inscrutable form as the last remaining characteristic attributed to an otherwise absolutely unknowable God, even to equate not freedom but free *will* with ineffability itself.

So the One, the Indeterminate, is, on this model, still omnipresent only in this rather restricted way: the One is what all Form (all unity, hence all being) is striving to approximate, and the omnipresence of the indeterminate One thus follows the contours of the hierarchy of partially expressed omnipresence endemic to the Determinacy-Omnipresence model. The omniabsence we get here is similarly compromised, retaining everywhere the shadow of a controlling presence. In contrast, the Indeterminacy-Omnipresence approach lends itself initially to a mereological (whole/part) model, which is generally found in materialist systems. This is what many also tend to imagine for pantheists like Spinoza, when they claim that the world itself is the Absolute: since we are "parts" of the world, we think, we must be "parts" of the Absolute. Naive presentations of Spinoza would have him telling us that we are all parts of God, that our bodies are "parts" of the body of God, and our minds are "parts" of the mind of God. As we will see in part II, this is a serious misreading of Spinoza: a closer analysis shows that for him "part and whole" apply only to the realm of separable things, modes considered in isolation from the Attributes of Substance, and not to Substance or those Attributes themselves, which have no parts. In the Determinacy-Omnipresence model the presence of the unconditioned is felt in each finite conditioned thing as the striving toward their own single definite telos (final cause), embedded in them as their determinate exclusive form (formal cause), and further toward the ultimate *exclusivity* of the ultimate Good. In the Indeterminacy-Omnipresence model the unconditioned would be felt in all conditioned beings rather differently: as the restless impulsion toward transcending any and every limitation, the intrinsic outreach toward every possible relationship and transformation, the thirst and thrust for self-transcendence and self-enlargement in all directions toward the whole. In the initial version of the Indeterminacy-Omnipresence model, however, where the whole/part disjunction remains in place, this impulsion must be balanced against the opposing desire to preserve oneself against dissolution into the external chaos, that is, not to die. We have seen a version of this problem in Bataille's account of the compromise-formations at the heart of religious forms, and we will soon see, in Spinoza, the way the full self-overcoming version of this model will resolve this tension between the finite and the infinite, the conditioned and the unconditioned. For we should note here that in this initial pre-Spinozistic form, the materialist version of the Indeterminacy-Omnipresence approach leaves us just as finite as before, if not more so: parts are parts and the whole alone is the whole. In this as yet uncompleted version of this model, we ourselves are merely parts of that absolute unconditioned totality, and must recognize ourselves as such. Both the omnipresence (everything is part of it) and the omniabsence (no thing is all of it) of the unconditioned remain quite weak here, as they do in the other model—yet for completely different reasons.

Both models come to be extended beyond the limitations of these naive original versions, delivering an unconditioned omnipresence that is, in some sense, also ineffable, but with quite different implications in the two cases. In the West, the two turning points are Plotinus and Spinoza. Aristotle had given us perhaps the purest version of the Determinacy-Omnipresence model, as yet unequipped with the Plotinian breakthrough of the indeterminate One at the top of the hierarchy. In doing so, while removing the crudest version of the world's universally unescapable teleology—the literal idea of a demiurge who forms the world purposefully—he further entrenches it: out of the frying pan, into the fire.[44] In fact, the deep structure of the Determinacy-Omnipresence model is revealed right off the bat by the role of God in Aristotle's system. We might imagine that a universal hylomorphism would ensure that *both* indeterminacy (matter) and determinacy (form) are omnipresent, giving them exactly equal status. But what we end up with instead is one glaring exception: God, pure Form, divulging the conceptual bias that was built into the edifice from the beginning. But at the same time, Aristotle's approach sets the stage for Plotinus to give us the self-overcoming of the naive Determinacy-Omnipresence model, the result of pushing the idea of the primacy of Determinacy (Form) to its utmost logical conclusion, which entails a certain reversal: the indeterminate is reintroduced, now not only as indeterminate matter but also as the indeterminable One—the pinnacle, the origin, the ground, indeed in some sense the inner essence, of all form and all determinacy. The original determinacy-indeterminacy dichotomy is here eliminated to the greatest extant the model will allow. In the West it is Spinoza, in contrast, who first gives us the *self-overcoming of the naive Indeterminacy-Omnipresence model*, pushing a model of immanence hitherto associated mainly with the idea of primacy of matter to its utmost logical point, and also entailing a certain reversal, as we will explore in chapter 5. The original whole/part dichotomy is there overcome to the degree allowable by that model. But the important point here is that the degree allowable by the Indeterminacy-Omnipresence model is much greater than that allowable by the Determinacy-Omnipresence model. For as we'll soon see in Spinoza, in taking the Indeterminacy-Omnipresence model to its logical conclusion, in fomenting its immanent self-overcoming, a similar immanent self-overcoming occurs concomitantly for the PSR itself: the hybrid cusp concepts of Necessity and Reason, already glimpsing the nondichotomy of oneness and multiplicity but expressed in a language still mired in their dichotomy, are overcome precisely through their radicalization, reversing into freedom and beatitude, and thus from Reason to Intuition. When the Determinacy-Omnipresence model reverses at its extreme, it goes beyond Determinacy and gives us at least some version of the omnipresence also of the indeterminate and unconditioned and does so systematically for the first time in Western thought. But it retains the marks of its origin, a hierarchical and teleological structure, which is teleologically hierarchizing even its two alternate forms of Nonbeing: the One and matter. In contrast, when the Indeterminacy-Omnipresence model overcomes itself and reverses at its extreme, it goes beyond the mutually external one/many distribution or one-way whole/part inclusion model typical of matter, and gives us a genuine immanence, approximating in some important ways the Daoist and Buddhist solutions and even interpretable as adjacent to the Tiantai solution: a full convergence of determinate and indeterminate, of conditional and unconditioned, in every instance and every aspect of every possible experience and reality. The first is compatible with a specifically theist form of omnipresence of the divine. The latter is not—instead, it points us toward atheist mysticism.

There are two different treatments of the idea of *infinity*, which are decisive in the tension between these two models, accompanied by two contrasted attitudes toward inclusion and exclusion. The whole/part structure of the incomplete materialist version of the Indeterminacy-Omnipresence model gestures outward beyond any definite thing to a larger whole, and thus, through its own immanent structure, easily produces a notion of *spatial* infinity: for any given whole, conceived in its ordinary, naive spatial sense, is inevitably also considered a part of a larger whole, and so on ad infinitum. Here we have quick access to the ideas of an all-inclusive infinity. On the other hand, the Determinacy-Omnipresence model, which equates being with definiteness, begins as a *pushback* against raw infinity as such, which is equally a pushback against inclusivity as such. For it is precisely the indeterminate that is the infinite, and this is the deadliest enemy of definiteness and thereby of all teleology, of all form, of all structure as end and goal. As we saw back in chapter 1, continuous, all-pervasive, all-inclusive infinity—extensive infinity, spatial infinity—is the alternative to teleology, all the way back to the ancient atomists. In a certain important sense, the retrospectively dominant Greek tradition associated with Plato and Aristotle is one long war against infinity and all-inclusiveness. Recall that although Anaxagoras says *Noûs* is "infinite" (*apeiron*), this is really an idiosyncratic way of highlighting its *separateness*. As we have seen, this simply means it is *transcendent*, in the sense of not being identical to any of the known physical elements; but here this is just another way of saying precisely that it is separate, for it must be in the position of controller that stands above and apart from the matter it *controls; it is omnipresent only in that it must be in control everywhere.* It is infinity as exclusion rather than infinity as inclusion.

And here we discover something important: the type of infinity that can properly be granted to *Noûs* is conceived in relation to temporality, but a particular kind of temporality, *even when this infinity is conceived as belonging only to an eternity stricto sensu; that is, as beyond time altogether.* The dispositive model is of time as experienced by a certain kind of subjectivity: one devoted to purposive activity through time, engaged in a process of establishing narrative continuity and accountability, of controlling choice and progressive exclusion of alternatives; even its retention of the past is subordinated to its narrative identity and its purposes. Its specific mode of interpenetration of both past and future is structured according to the requirements of purposive conscious willing. The infinity here is modeled on the temporal experience of a responsible agent invested in unilateral control of its own actions. Such an infinity, even when understood as timeless rather than of infinite duration, is structured in accordance with the contours of this model. It may be "formless," beyond any finite determination, but only and precisely as separate and separable from all transient particularities in that it is situated as their *controller.* Such temporal infinity is infinity as exclusion, *not* infinity in the sense of an endless expanse of disinterestedly encompassing spatiality that both pervades and includes an inexhaustible array of particular entities, which is, in principle, unclosable and unendable, space as the giving of room for whatever appears, an openness applied also to every moment of past and future time and further, as in Spinoza, as identical with all the active objects that occupy it, understood as modes of spatiality itself.[45] This basic limitation remains in place throughout the future application of the Determinacy-Omnipresence model, of the omnipresence of the divine: throughout history, monotheists, who emerge from this tradition, have consistently opted for a limited kind of infinity, which is still basically the infinity proposed by Anaxagoras—the controller who is "infinite" only in the sense of standing apart, above, all finite entities, but doing so perpetually and without cease. "Omnipresence" in these traditions comes to mean simply the presence everywhere of the controller—the controlling mind, the controlling purpose, the controlling form. For on this model, mind, though understood to be inclusive of and even identical with its thoughts and ideas, must stand beyond what it controls, even if located "inside" it as its distinct core or essence or forever in reach of its watchful presence. Such an infinity must, by nature, *exclude* something, because the controller must be distinct from what it controls, and because mind remains first and foremost *Noûs,* intelligence,[46] which always *chooses* the best, which is preference and exclusion in its very essence, even if this intelligence is itself atemporal and free of discursive planning through temporally distinct steps. God is this intrinsic contradiction: an infinity that excludes, a transcendent oneness that exists to effectuate division and duality, to exclude and transcend and control. God is the apotheosis of the infinity that excludes: an inescapable presence, to be sure, but a presence of a controller throughout all time, which is omnipresent in space only in the sense of laying claim to every locus of space without exception. The types of omnipresence attempted through this model thus always end up being in a certain sense blind alleys and false dawns: what is everywhere, if it is God or any other derivative of the Determinacy-Omnipresence model, is the controller, which must also be an *excluder,* by definition. What ends up being omnipresent and inescapable is—exclusivity itself.[47]

In itself, the idea of "omnipresence of exclusivity" actually points to an important truth. We will discover in part II that when the Indeterminacy-Omnipresence model does reverse itself beyond the limitation of its initial materialist form, in Spinoza and onward, this exclusivity too—limitation, finitude, the PSR—becomes omnipresent and inescapable, just as does the all-inclusivity of infinity. But there this exclusivity converges into perfect coextensivity with omnipresence as inclusivity. Conditionality—the PSR, finitude, exclusivity—is everywhere without exception; but precisely being finite, being conditioned, *just is* what it is to be all-pervasive, infinite, unconditioned: the two become Mobius-strip synonyms, always two and always one. Rather than omnipresent exclusion as omnipresent control, we will have there, quite literally, omnipresent exclusion as the inclusive omnipresence. We've already seen this expressed in its strongest possible form in the overview of the Tiantai Buddhist conception of omnipresent conditionality: both determinateness and indeterminateness, rather than just one or the other, are everywhere and nowhere—but not because these are two separate characteristics, both of which are everywhere, but because these are two mutually entailing descriptions of the same fact. For on the one hand, indeterminateness is here understood to be just another determination, and on the other, determination per se just as indeterminate: local coherence is global coherence, and it is this ambiguous (in)coherence that is everywhere and nowhere. In part II we will be exploring ways in which the Indeterminacy-Omnipresence model is radicalized by some of its inheritors, to such a point of reversal and self-overcoming that it reaches a similar conclusion. But the case is otherwise for the Determinacy-Omnipresence model and its inheritors. Indeed, this convergence of omnipresence as inclusivity and omnipresent exclusivity, their Mobius-strip oneness and difference, is just what the idea of God makes impossible, by making both absolute exclusivity (Form excluding matter, the Good excluding evil, God excluding creatures) and absolute inclusivity (all things are Form, all things are good, all things are God's) the property of one being (God) to the ex-clusion of others: it is the enforcement of the dichotomization of oneness and difference that we identified as the essence of control as opposed to necessity, and which is exacerbated all the more when these two remain both opposed and also under the control of a single exclusive being. Let us then modify our conclusion: what ends up being omnipresent and ines-capable in the Determinacy-Omnipresence model, even in its most radical developments, is not just exclusivity—it is the mutual exclusivity of exclu-sivity and inclusivity. God is the secondary external attempt to stitch the two back together—after they have been torn asunder by that selfsame God.

RECAP AND GAME PLAN

So there we have it: what we have in our sights here is not only the literalist idea of God, but also everything that is left over as its legacy: the God of the philosophers as universal *Noûs*, the Godhead beyond God and Being, the purpose and/or orderliness of the universe, the prophetic thirst for justice, the Sermon on the Mount's seemingly gentle lesson of love,[48] the ideals of freedom and life as opposed to servitude and death, being versus noth-ingness, the Will to remake the world according to an ideal, the allegedly obvious finitude of human life—all of these go together, and for the atheist mystic, all of it has to go. All the concomitant forms of love, justice, free-dom, life, being, accepting our finitude, improvement of the world—what do we find when these are all finally abandoned?

Our focus will be historical examples of atheist thinkers who not only make a claim to some kind of redemptive experience or doctrine in tan-dem with their repudiation of God—which would merely demonstrate the possible coexistence, the compossibility, of atheism and redemption—but rather for whom their atheism is *essential* to their redemptive claims, as their key catalyst, and who experience atheism as a life-transforming rev-elation that solves their central existential problem. It should be evident, then, that I am not here concerned with the mere possibility of coexistence between atheism and a sort of "spiritual life." Rather, like Hitchens when he claims to be not merely an atheist but an antitheist, in the sense that he not only disbelieves in God but thinks it would be horrible if anything like the monotheist God did exist, we want to address the sense in which precisely the absence of God is the "good news," the one thing needful, the essential salvific point, the realization of which is the central transformative hub of religious life and practice. To do this, we will interweave the threads of atheist mysticism in its many forms as borrowed from its exemplars who have lived so far.

The discussion to follow in part II will begin with Spinoza, whom we single out for our most extensive treatment, not only because of the intricacy and thoroughness of his philosophical system, but also because his work, breaking the back of monotheism *from within*, illustrates most directly the main themes of part I: how the key move of refuting the ontological ultimacy of personality and teleology pushes the cusp-dwelling conceptions of *necessity* and *whole/part immanence* over the edge of the impasse in which they are stuck when marginalized by the ultimacy of purposivity and conceived in terms of its dualistic entailments, allowing them instead to blossom into the coextensive coinstantiation of conditioned finitude and unconditioned infinity for every entity, which is the very kernel of full-fledged atheist mysticism. The more idiosyncratic versions of this vision developed by Nietzsche and Bataille depend on this breakthrough and, though treated in less fulsome detail, are of equal interest as pointing toward the still unfolding vistas of possibility opened up by the mystical overthrow of God.

Online appendix B takes a closer look at the non-European sources. We will take a tour of the Uberatheisms of the Indic Buddhist world: early Buddhism, Mahāyāna Emptiness and Two Truths thought, and ideas of infinite supernormal, polymorphous bodhisattvas and the "eternal Buddha" as presented in a text often cited for precisely the opposite purpose, that is, to show how cryptotheistic a religion Mahāyāna Buddhism has become: the *Lotus Sutra*. Here we can embark on further radical explorations of atheist possibilities for religious experience, conceived entirely outside the dominance of ideas of ultimate ontological teleology. We will also consider at length both mainstream and dissident traditions in China—perhaps the historical home-ground world of atheist religiosity: not only the Daoist and Tiantai ideas that have figured in part I, but also Confucianism and the Chan schools of Chinese Buddhism.

The criterion for inclusion in these explorations is inversely indexed in the characteristics of God pointed to earlier: conscious purpose, creation ex nihilo, omniscience, omnipotence, command, obedience, reward (not mere consequences) for good behavior and punishment for bad, as well as the concomitant ideas of autonomous free will, activist zeal, and natural law. A doctrine is identified as atheistic in the sense relevant to us here to the extent that it lacks these features. The mystical Emulative Atheist experiences the elimination of divine purpose and control, not merely as step toward the liberation *of* human purpose and control (which were previously off-limits as divine prerogatives), as in the case of their Compensatory Atheist brethren, or only liberation *from* the ultimacy of human purpose and control, as for the Compensatory Theist. The critique is rather pushed to the point of undermining the ultimacy of *all* purpose and control, the status of the very concepts of purpose and control, and all conceptions of meaningfulness dependent on them—*and this too is regarded as a good thing.*

A universe devoid of all these things may thus sound quite horrible even to those who believe themselves to be atheists: it will mean a vision of life where every purpose is always saturated with purposelessness, where any possibility of creating anything new is saturated with the past, where all freedom of the individual Will is saturated with necessity, where all order and all law (divine, natural, or human) is saturated with chaos, where all moral justice is saturated with randomness, where all reform of social conditions is saturated with the unbudgeable brute ineradicability of alternate desiderata—an existence whereby no one really gets exactly what he wants, and no one can do what he thinks he's doing, and no one knows what's going on, and no one and nothing is in control. My hope is that at the end of this exploration, the rare and exquisite charms of this prospect will have become somewhat harder to ignore.

PART TWO

Varieties of Atheist Beatitude

"The ghost is not your own, and yet you worship it—that is sycophancy."
非其鬼而祭之，諂也

—CONFUCIUS, *Analects* 2:24, translated by Brook Ziporyn

CHAPTER 5

Spinoza, or Intoxicating Sobriety

THE THEOLOGICAL PROOF OF GOD'S NONEXISTENCE

Nowadays atheists are generally content to leave the burden of proof to the believers. It is enough to show that the hypothesis of God's existence has no evidence in support of it, that it is no more or less likely, to borrow Bertrand Russell's famous zinger, than the existence of an undetectable teapot revolving around the sun between earth and Mars in an elliptical orbit, which (since it is stipulated to be undetectable) can't be disproved either. There is no reason to suppose that either God or the invisible teapot exists, and until anyone can come up with one, it would be lunacy to believe in anything so preposterous and improbable. Anyone proposing such a belief had better have good reasons for it, and also for why everything else in the world is set up to make it so exceptionally unobvious. But not to believe in the existence of God or the teapot, the default position, requires no special justification.

Yet if anyone ever came close to actually *proving* the impossibility of the existence of God, it was surely Baruch (Benedict) Spinoza. At least, we may say, he was fully convinced that he had constructed such a proof and that it was irrefutable. The supreme glory of this achievement, however, is that he did it by means of the very conceptual equipment that had always been used by theologians to prove the *existence* of God, and much more, he did it *in the form of* a proof of the existence of God!

Spinoza's equivocal relation to the God problem is legendary, and it is in the folds of these complexities that we see what makes him genuinely exemplary. Expelled from the Amsterdam Jewish community for heretical views and scorned as an atheist by Christians, he was also, according to the German Romantic poet Novalis, "the God-intoxicated man." For the God whose nonexistence Spinoza proved is God the supreme, transcendent, personal, intentional creator, the God who created, makes, and controls things for a specific *purpose* and who exists outside the things he creates.

He proves this nonexistence, however, by proving that there is an *inherent contradiction* in this notion of God—that it is an oxymoron, that if it is true it must be false, that the meaning of the word "God," as established by its most thoroughgoing theological defenders, implies that God cannot be a purpose-monger making things other than himself according to a preference or plan. He refutes God by taking seriously the meaning of the word "God," which turns out to lead to a change in its meaning. *God, taken literally, is non-God, is the opposite of God.*

Given all the concomitants of the idea of God, this has enormous consequences. Spinoza ends up seeming to be the most paradoxical of thinkers, not only on the God issue, but on every issue. He comes across as the ultimate rationalist, but also as the ultimate mystic. He is the ultimate advocate of determinism but also finds freedom in the very midst of determinism, as the full comprehension of precisely causal determinism. He fully embraces the traditional valorizing of activity as opposed to passivity, but he is also the man who dissolved the dichotomy between them, eliminating the concept of total passivity altogether. He is the most fanatical advocate of the absoluteness of the Principle of Sufficient Reason (PSR), but he is also the man who overcame it immanently by accepting the necessary connection between premise and conclusion so thoroughly that he collapses the distinction. He sees the Absolute as dissimilar to all finite things to the point where it not only cannot be said to be a body but also cannot be said to be any determinate Intellect or Will or being or One, like the most extreme negative theologians, but also that we innately have an adequate idea of the infinite essence of God, that it is not only knowable but already fully known by all minds, indeed that it is the one thing all of us cannot not know. He is the ultimate objectivist and stickler for absolute fact and absolute truth, but he also holds that all possible thoughts qua actual thoughts are true, which makes him the ultimate relativist. He utterly rejects the real existence of universals for any class of beings, recognizing the existence only of individual things, coming out as an extreme nominalist, and ridiculing the entire Realist tradition, but he also introduces something even more universal than universals, not limited to any subset of being and absolutely complete and the same in every part as in the whole of reality, which forms the basis of all true cognition ("Common Notions"). He calls our minds "part" of the mind of God but also claims that God can have no parts. He advocates absolute immanence of essence in existence but also asserts that a specific eternal essence precedes and grounds each finite existence. He accepts and even radicalizes Descartes' absolute dualism of mind and body, such that they have literally nothing in common and can have no causal interaction at all, and yet for that very reason he is able to conclude that mind and body are one and the same thing. And while he insists that the body and the mind are one and the same thing, he also believes that the mind exists eternally before and after the existence of the body. He is all about clear and distinct ideas but also sees them as a stepping stone toward the realization that no ideas can be divided from one another and that "Reason" is a stepping stone to a form of "Intuition" that collapses any substantial distinction between premise and conclusion, cause and effect. He is all about Reason, but he also declares that desire is the very essence of man and that all activity is motivated by the desire for pleasure, which is utterly wholesome. He is the ultimate advocate of oneness and also the overcomer of the oneness of God and the preacher of infinite diversification. He rejects the ultimacy of purpose and ridicules the idea of universal teleology but also enables the infinite proliferation of immanent striving as the very essence of beings, even for seemingly inanimate things. He regards being itself as perfection and all things as equally perfect and yet also finds each striving to increase its own perfection.

For seeing the absoluteness, not of God, but of non-God, everywhere— as necessary, as inescapable, as present in all events—results in a unique experience of joy in the infinite and eternal, with a joy that is itself infinite and eternal: in other words, beatitude. For the *absence* of God, the absence of any ultimate personal purposeful intention behind things, the absence of exclusive oneness, is the *omnipresence* through all my body and mind, through all my experiences, through all things in the world, of *necessity*, of *eternity*, of inclusive oneness, of infinity—indivisible, infinitely generative infinity.

SPINOZA IN TWELVE STEPS

Common sense regards the world as a collection of objects separated from one another in space. Some of these objects are sentient and others are not. The sentient ones have feelings and perceptions, and in some versions, some have free will while the insentient ones do not. The spatially separated objects come into existence due to prior causes, exist on their own power for awhile, and then pass out of existence. While they exist, they are independent in the sense that they are nouns rather than adjectives, subjects rather than predicates: they are things that have properties and undergoes changes of states rather than being properties or states of something else. The series of prior causes in some versions tracks back in time to a first cause like God or to the Big Bang, and in other versions it simply extends infinitely into the past. In the God version, God as cause of the world remains something distinct from the world. In the non-God version as well, the causes of things remain outside those things, so that one thing simply succeeds and replaces another in time. In both cases, causality is viewed as a matter of mutual exclusivity of effect and cause: after the cause does its job in producing the effect, the effect breaks free of the cause, either replacing it or separating from it. In the God version of this story, one entity is putatively infinite (God) but to the exclusion of all other entities, which are finite. The mutual exclusive model of causality continues to apply also to this infinite creator: creator must be distinct from creatures, and infinite from finite. In the non-God, secular, scientific version, it's finitude all the way down: like the God version but without the God, leaving the known world populated only by finite creatures, a world of only finite things, perhaps governed by infinite laws. These laws then transcend all finite things just as God had, or else are merely virtual or nominal entities rather than realities in their own right. Finite and infinite remain mutually exclusive in any of these versions. Spinoza's vision of the universe differs from all versions of the commonsensical vision of the world, the monotheist as much as the secular atheist, in many ways. We can perhaps make adjustments step by step to take in the full extent of this difference:

Step 1: Imagine the physical universe as a whole, one continuous loaf of being. There are no separate bodies and no empty spaces. So-called empty space is really a thin medium that connects all beings. Nature is one continuous field of matter, and you are a piece of this matter, one piece of this whole. There is nothing beyond this whole.

That is a step toward how Spinoza sees it. But it is still far from Spinoza's vision.

Step 2: Imagine the world is, not just one continuous, material whole, but one huge, living body. You are an organ in that body. The parts are all actively exchanging energy at all times and function together; they are interconnected and working together so closely that if any one were removed or changed, all the others would thereby be removed or changed.

That is closer but still not Spinoza's vision.

Step 3: Imagine that the world is one huge, living body of which you are one organ but that the organs are distinguished from one another only by their patterns of motion: they are all made of the same Substance, a kind of all-encompassing field of matter-energy, with individual organs constantly exchanging the materials of which they are made, each distinguishable only by virtue of its characteristic pattern of motion: like steady-state whirlpools in an ocean, the being of each singular entity is defined purely by the motion it maintains.

This is closer but still not Spinoza's vision.

Step 4: Imagine the model we reached in step 3, where you are one part of the body of the world that is an all-encompassing field of matter-energy and consider your body to be one of these patterns of swirling energy. Now consider this body of yours to be itself composed of smaller swirls, smaller bodies, which are composed of smaller swirls, and so on, down to every cell in your body. You are a swirling pattern of motion and rest that is part of the whole, but the parts of you are also structures of swirling energy, and these are nested in hundreds and thousands and millions of levels of complexity. The parts of each of these whirlpools—the smaller whirlpools—can be replaced, and each whirlpool may grow larger or smaller, encompassing more or fewer whirlpools, and may move in various directions; as long as the pattern, the precise ratio of motion to rest and the manner in which motion is communicated among the parts remains the same, it counts as identifiably the same body, the same whirlpool. The various alterations that can take place in its parts without changing its defining ratio, its defining pattern of motion, are the changes of state it is able to undergo while remaining the same individual whirlpool. A finite body can sustain various impacts and incorporations while remaining the same body, and these are that body's experiences. If some impact or incorporation is too much for it to accommodate, disrupting its characteristic pattern and ratio of motions beyond its capacity to adapt by altering *other* parts of its whirl, that body dies and dissolves. The same structure applies to the whole in which you and all the other swirls are embedded: though these parts are constantly changing, constantly arising and perishing, all their alterations balance and cancel each other out, so the whole remains unchanged. But since, unlike the finite parts, the infinite whole has nothing outside it, there is nothing that can disrupt it, so it can never die.

This is closer but still not Spinoza's vision.

Step 5: Imagine the model in step 4, where you are a nested swirl of swirls, but now every swirl is at once a particular pattern, *and an endeavor to continue that pattern*—a striving or tendency that pushes to maintain itself as that pattern. Motion and the tendency to continue that motion are one and the same thing, distinguished only in thought. Moreover, "existing" and "persisting" are the same thing, such that the more duration something has, the more of it exists. So "to maintain itself" and "to expand itself" are the same thing. To be "moving in this way in region X" means the same thing as to be "endeavoring to be moving in this same way in regions other than X." Every region is different and has different parameters, with new factors that can be incorporated and new conditions to be expressed in, which means that to survive into a new moment is expanding your pattern of motion into new ways of expression. Me surviving is me expanding my power to act. So to be doing X is to be trying to do X more, which is trying to do more than X as it's presently constituted. To maintain X is to expand X into new regions of time and/or space, new regions of experience. The swirl that is your body strives, not only not to die, but to have more power of activity, to experience more things and affect more things in the world, to be the cause of a greater number of effects — both as partial cause, which is usually called "passive" ways of *being* affected, like perception and experience, and also as complete cause, bringing about effects in self and other, which constitutes active thought and action. It does this either by incorporating elements into its characteristic pattern that increase its power of activity without destroying that pattern, by changing its size or environment, or by allying with other swirls to be part of a larger swirl that allows it to increase its own activity and also has other activities to which the original swirl's activity contributes.

This is closer but still not Spinoza's vision.

Step 6: Now imagine that the world is not one big body but rather one big mind, which is a totality composed of many ideas just as the big body is a totality composed of many organs. Every conscious entity, including you, is an *experience* of this mind. Just as your mind has many thoughts, many conceptions, many perceptions, the one big mind that is the universe has many experienced contents, each of which is what we call a conscious being. Just as conscious experiences are both conditioned by the presence of a consciousness and also parts of that consciousness, remaining contained in and inseparable from the totality of the mind that experiences them, each of these conscious beings is an *idea* that is caused by the one big mind and yet also remains contained in that mind. Moreover, each idea is an *activity* of the mind rather than merely an immanent but static part of the mind. An idea, in Spinoza's sense, is a conscious *act* — the acknowledgment, recognition, or affirmation that something is so. The most basic idea of a tree is, "There exists such a tree!" A more complete idea of a tree is, "There exists such a tree, right there and right now, and it is green and tall, and relates to other things like this, and was caused by this and that, and has done and undergo this and will do and undergo that." In this context, a still more complete idea of a tree would be, "The universal body has within it, and therefore causes and is inseparable from, a swirling whirlpool which is composed of many smaller swirls, an organ of that universal body, which is this tree, right there and right now, and . . ." Or better: "The universal mind is thinking an idea of an organ of the universal body, a whirlpool within this field of matter-energy, this tree, which . . ." My mind is the idea that my body exists, and is doing what it is doing, and perceives what it perceives, and is as it is, and is an organ in the big body. My mind is the idea that says, "This guy Brook right here and now exists, and . . . !" I can have an idea of this idea too, and also the idea that "This idea—my mind—is one of the ideas being thought by the universal mind." Just as each idea is part of a mind, as it acts in a particular circumstance, each consciousness is a part of the whole universal mind and remains contained in the universal mind.

This is closer but still not Spinoza's vision.

Step 7: Imagine the model we reached in step 6, but look around you and see all the colors and sounds and objects of your perception, not as spread out around you in other parts of the one mind that is the universe, but as internal to the one idea in the universal mind that is you. The world as you see it is how all the other ideas that are in the one mind impact on you, resulting in changes of state to the idea that is you by replacing or rearranging the parts that constitute you in such a way that the total swirl that you are remains unchanged—so that all of them exist in an internal version that differs from the idea as it exists in the one mind considered in general. That impact of other ideas on you is internal to you and is your perceived world. What you see is not them, but their impact on you. You are an idea, a patch of consciousness, that includes this particular set of impressions and perceptions and conceptions. You are the action of the mind that is an idea of precisely whatever you are experiencing right now: the universal mind thinking, "There is a body here perceiving this and this and this, and doing this and this and this."

This is closer but still not Spinoza's vision.

Step 8: Combine the models reached in steps 5 and 7, so that each internested, swirling pattern of material activity in the one universal body *is* one idea in the universal mind, one and the same thing seen from two different sides, described in two alternate ways. The one universal body is aware in all its swirling organs of energy; each one is lit up as a translucent field of sentience, consciousness, awareness. We can call it one big mind or one big body—one body that is conscious, or one consciousness that is embodied. These are just two alternate descriptions of one and the same thing. The same is true for each of the elements in each description. Each idea in the big mind is composed of internested smaller ideas just as each swirl of energy that is an organ in the universal body is composed of many internested smaller swirls. These organs-ideas in the one body-mind of the universe are its actions, not merely its static parts, and are caused by the action of the universal mind-body, inseparable from it like a field of space within space or a whirlpool within water, or like an idea within a mind that thinks it. Just as the swirl that is your body strives to maintain its existence and to increase its activity and effects and experience, the complex idea that is your mind, as composed of many smaller minds, strives to persist and expand. It does this through *understanding*, which is the "mind" equivalent of "activity." It strives first to understand its states, which are ideas of the states of the body-swirl: when that body-swirl that is me goes through a change of state (by encountering, perceiving, and incorporating new elements while nonetheless maintaining its same overall style of motion) that expands its overall power of activity, my mind experiences an affect: pleasure. When that body-swirl undergoes a change of state that decreases its overall power of activity, my mind experiences an affect: pain. When my mind understands something, one of the ideas that are its component parts is having an effect: something is following entirely from an idea I already have as part of my mind. That means that my mind is "active," and its power of activity increases with each act of understanding. Understanding is itself an increase of my power of activity, that is, pleasure, whether I am understanding something pleasant or painful, and thus all understanding is pleasurable, even when it also involves pain—indeed, it's the only thing I can be absolutely sure will be pleasurable and good for me.

This is closer but still not Spinoza's vision.

Step 9: Regard all the idea-organs of the universal mind-body as following *necessarily* from the nature of the universal mind-body itself, in the manner that the properties of a circle follow from the nature of a circle and remain inherent and inseparable from the circle, not just as a pool of water might have a whirlpool immanent in it, or as a mind might freely have a thought which remains immanent in it, but rather as a property is inherent in an essence, for example, as "having three angles that equal 180 degrees," inheres in the essence of "a triangle," and necessarily follows from it. Moreover, regard not just the existence of all those idea-organs as necessarily following from and remaining inherent in the one universal mind-body, but all their actions and interactions as following with the same absolute necessity, so that nothing at all that happens, from the smallest wisp of feeling to the explosion of planets, could possibly have happened otherwise. The universe must exist, and everything that happens in it, without exception, has to happen.

This is closer but still not Spinoza's vision.

Step 10: Instead of thinking of the mind-body as a finite whole made up of parts or of discrete actions, imagine that it is infinite. The idea-organs are not "parts" of it, not even active parts of it, for they do not preexist it and cannot exist independently of it, as parts from which a whole is built are thought to do. Rather these "parts" depend on the "whole" for their existence every moment, and there are an infinite number of these idea-organs. They are not parts of a whole but modes of a Substance — that is, states of the infinite, ways of expressing the infinite, predicates of the infinite — and this infinite is necessarily indivisible power of activity. As existent, they are finite and transitory, but as formal essences, they are eternal and infinite. Further, the one mind-body can no longer be thought of as a mind or body, because both "a mind" and "a body" are concepts that only make sense if they are finite. Infinite body is not *a* body, not a particular determinate body, for a body must have an outside. Infinite mind is not *a* mind, not a particular determinate mind, for a mind must have an outside (which is composed of the *objects* of awareness and intention). Infinite body is really infinite space necessarily endowed with the infinite powers of motion and rest. Infinite mind is really the infinite power of consciousness. Your individual body is merely one particular *part* of the larger body of motion and rest, but it is more than part of the infinite power of motion and rest: it is an *expression* of it, a way in which that infinite power is expressed. Your mind is one particular idea that is merely a constituent *part* of the infinite mind, the infinite Intellect, which is the unchanging totality of all these changing active ideas. But it is more than a part of the infinite power of thought: it is an expression of it, a determinate and finite way in which the infinite power of consciousness is expressed. For ideas presuppose power of thought (experiences presuppose ability to experience), just as motion and rest presupposes space. Neither active space nor the power of thought can be divided or limited, so all their expressions are not only caused by them and remain included in them as parts but are also the infinite power itself acting in a particular way, suited to a particular causal situation. Finitude is a mode, not a part, of infinity. Its infinite power, meanwhile, must produce all possible causal situations within which it can act.

This is closer but still not Spinoza's vision.

Step 11: Instead of thinking of this infinity as having only these two infinite aspects — infinite power of consciousness expressed as an unchanging totality of infinite numbers of changing ideas and experiences, and infinite active space expressed as an unchanging totality composed of infinite numbers of changing bodies—think of it as having an infinity of other kinds of infinity about which we can know nothing, all of which have exactly the same relations among them.

This is very close but still not Spinoza's vision.

Step 12: The infinite ideas that are also bodies (and an infinity of other unknown types of ways of expressing unknown types of infinity) or infinite bodies that which are also ideas (and an infinity of other ways of expressing of infinity) are not parts of the whole that is the universe. They are "fixed and determinate expressions" of Infinite Thought and Infinite Extension, which in Spinoza really mean infinite active awareness and infinite active space. Infinite awareness is itself both all possible experiences—not just thinking, but also perception, imagination, love, desire, emotion, and so on (E2a3)[1]—including whatever appear to be gaps between these experiences, which are themselves just more modes of experience. Infinite space is itself both all possible physical entities and whatever appear to be gaps between these entities, which are themselves just more modes of physicality (PCP2p2).[2]

Infinite means *"indeterminate."*[3] But indeterminacy, correctly understood, entails *infinite power to determine and be determined.* And since there is nothing outside this infinite, all determining and being determined done by indeterminacy are determinations and undeterminations and redeterminations of itself. Absolute infinity is absolutely indeterminate. Infinite awareness and space are each "infinite in its kind" (E1d6e), which also means *indeterminate in its kind*: they can be no particular limited mind or body or set of minds and bodies. They are infinite, indivisible, and constantly causative, expressing their infinity in an infinite number of alternate ways. Infinite awareness and infinite space are merely two of the infinite Attributes of Substance, each of which expresses its particular type of infiniteness in a different way and from each of which necessarily follow an infinite ways of expressing that particular form of infinity.

When a finite way of expressing infinity does not actually exist in any particular causal situation because the required prior other finite expressions that would allow its manifestation are lacking, its "formal essence" is still inherent in the very nature of infinity. This is the possibility of that mode emerging whenever a series of finite causes allows it to do so. For it follows from the nature of Substance in the same way that an infinity of undrawn, internally inscribed rectangles, all of equal area, necessarily inheres in the nature of a circle (E2p8). But the possibility is not really a different entity from its actuality. This essence of X is not something *about* X; it is what X itself is. When X does not exist in a particular temporal sequence, the thing is called "formal essence of X": it is the possibility of X, which is just its necessary entailment in the nature of Substance / Nature / God. When it does exist, it is called X itself. This formal essence of X, which is X itself when X exists, is determinate. Infinity, in which it eternally inheres, is indeterminate. This means each determinacy is nothing more than an expression of indeterminacy and all determinacies are inherent in indeterminacy— indeed, each determinacy is just as eternal and omnipresent as the infinite indeterminacy in which it inheres. The dichotomy between determinacy and indeterminacy is here overcome.

This same essence is present during the existence of the body of X as the *conatus*, as X's distinctive pattern of motion and rest that also *just is* the tendency and endeavor to continue precisely that pattern of motion and rest. There are infinite ways in which the sequence of temporal causes that allow this finite being, X, to come into existence can happen, infinite sequences by which this outcome can be reached. The infinite power of infinite Substance is such (arguably) that all these sequences must occur: it produces infinite things "in infinite ways."[4] Just as the "triangle" of formal essence can be formed by a three-car collision or from a chalk lines on a chalkboard or in innumerable other ways because it is inherent in the very nature of space, so can every formal essence be brought into actual existence through an infinite number of alternate possible chains of causes. The formal essence of any finite mode is itself an indispensable and eternal, and indeed infinite, fact about infinity itself (i.e., "a mediate infinite mode" [E1p22]). It is always and everywhere present as a necessary aspect of omnipresent infinity. But it must also, on this reading, reappear into concrete existence an infinite number of times. This eternal infinite *formal essence* of mine is present to me, while I exist, as my conatus, my will to continue existing (my *existing essence* as opposed to my *formal essence*, to use Spinoza's terms), which itself is constantly expressed in this or that specific and context-dependent manner, in and as all my actions, desires, pleasures, and pains, for these just comprise my endeavor to maintain and increase my power of activity and the changes of states I undergo while doing so. It is this essence, currently felt as my desire to keep existing and to act and interact in more and more ways, that is eternal and reborn infinitely, not my memories and perceptions as they occur after my birth.

Indeed, my present personality itself is an inadequate understanding of the essence of my body, an imaginary and highly one-sided concept of it, which is formed by this particular set of experiences and conditions in this one among infinite sequences that can bring into existence this particular bodily essence, and by my adaptations to them and endeavors to persist as impacted by them, That personality too is not reproduced. It occurs only this once. My personality is thus finite and mortal, and it partakes of the meaningfulness of that closed horizon; this is a unique occurrence and a unique struggle that will perish forever when I die. It is in this context that my conscious purposes have meaning. Nothing that happens on that imaginary level, the level of my self-recognition as a personality with memories and perceptions, living in this particular society at this particular time, has the slightest impact on my immortality, my eternity, my specific infinity.

But one type of experience after my birth, one sort of thing I can do while alive, does matter, not for my unchanging immortality itself but for my temporal experience of it, my participation in it while alive as this personality: adequate understanding of each thing as a necessary body and a necessary idea of that body, each as an eternal and infinite formal essence, an expression of infinite, indeterminate awareness and space. This can make my finite life on earth more rational and virtuous and happy, and it can facilitate more desirable forms of social and political life. But when pushed even farther, from "Reasoning" that grasps Necessity (as a relation between two putatively distinct essences) to the "Intuition" of Necessity (as the two necessarily related terms now seen to be collapsed into one richer essence, i.e., as both comprehended necessarily in the sole infinite essence, such that the oneness and multiplicity are simultaneously experienced as one fact), this is what produces the greatest form of activity, the ability to act in the greatest number of ways and experience the greatest joys. And since love is pleasure accompanied by the idea of its cause, it also produces the greatest love for the cause of all these joys, infinity, which increases the more I understand things as directly caused by infinity. Greater knowledge of things (if it is knowledge of what Spinoza calls the Second or, especially, the Third Kind, i.e., Reason and Intuition respectively) is greater knowledge of the essence of God / Nature / Substance / Infinity (E5p24). This, in turn, is a greater understanding of my own eternal and infinite formal essence, which is an inalienable property of that infinite essence (E2p8). This understanding is itself a part of the eternal, infinite self-understanding that this infinity necessarily has of itself, and this love is itself part of the eternal, infinite self-love infinity has for itself (E5p36). This also overcomes the fear of death for the individual personality, allowing him to perceive himself as a distorted, imaginary, finite readout of an eternal and infinite idea that is necessarily inherent in the nature of infinite reality. It is through understanding individual things, ultimate reality, and myself each as a "species of eternity," as determinacies inhering eternally and omnipresently in the very nature of necessarily existent infinite indeterminacy, that this is accomplished.

It is our Intellect, which is a part of the Intellect of God, that accomplishes this understanding. But in doing so, our Intellect (and therefore also God's Intellect) also understands that there is something that goes beyond the Intellect of God, and also beyond the Will of God (since for Spinoza, Intellect and Will are one and the same). Spinoza's language here is potentially confusing, as he gives the name "Thought" to one of the Attributes of God, expressing God's essence (i.e., expressing infinity). But the Intellect of God is not the Attribute of Thought. The Intellect of God—also called the mind of God or the idea of God—is not an Attribute, but only a *mode* of that Attribute, albeit an "immediate infinite" mode. Although it is therefore omnipresent, and thus coextensive with all of Nature, it belongs to what Spinoza calls Natura Naturata: all existence considered as passive, as effect, rather than as cause—as considered with respect to its divisibility and determinacy. Nature as cause, which he calls Natura Naturans, is infinite, indivisible, indeterminate, generative power. The Intellect of God, as Natura Naturata, is only a determinate expression of this indeterminate power; it is still a kind of infinity only in that it consists entirely of its determinate expressions, of which there are infinity many. It is infinite in its kind but not absolutely infinite, and not even infinite in its kind as is the Attribute of Thought: considered in itself, in isolation from that Attribute, it is a divisible infinity of determinate, finite expressions of infinity. It is the infinite totality of all *adequate* ideas, the objective essences of all determinate expressions of this power—that is, the ideas of all determinate things without exception. As such, being determinate all the way down, it can be divided into parts. My Intellect is a *part* of the Intellect of God. But the *Attribute* of Thought, infinitely active awareness, is Natura Naturans (the same contents but considered as cause, as active), which is the indeterminate, infinite power of thinking and experiencing the totality of itself expressed as these determinate, finite, adequate ideas. This is also omnipresent, but it has no parts, only various modes of expressing itself. Since it has no parts, each expression of this indeterminate power is an expressing of *all* of it. What are merely objective essences in the Intellect, considered in isolation and divisible from one another, and thus each eternal but not infinite in the sense of omnipresent, are formal essences in the Attribute of Thought, and each formal essence is not only eternal but also infinite in the sense of omnipresent. The infinity of the Attribute (Thought) and of the infinite mode (Intellect) are each infinite in their kind, and this is one of the ways in which these kinds of infinity differ. Absolute infinity (i.e., God, Substance, Nature), being infinite *in infinite ways*, includes both of these kinds of infinity. Moreover, this Attribute of Thought expresses itself, not only as all adequate ideas about all things, but also as all emotions and desires and inadequate ideas *about* these ideas, which exist in absolute infinity insofar as it is modified in some particular way, which it must be because it necessarily expresses itself in infinite ways, from the lowest to the highest (E1p29s, E1p31, E1 app., E2a3, E2p36d). The infinite Attribute of Thought, as opposed to the infinite Intellect, includes every possible state of awareness, every way of expressing it, including all these inadequate emotional responses to all ideas, all forms of awareness and experience without exception—including all possible desires, emotions, imaginings *about* all possible things, that is, all inadequate, partial and confused apprehensions of those adequate ideas. Each of these too expresses the *entirety* of the Attribute of Thought, Natura Naturans, as indeterminate, infinitely determinable, indivisible, infinite generative power.

One of the things the Intellect of God understands, because it understands all things rightly, is that it itself is not only dependent on, but is merely a mode of, expressing something more fundamental than itself. That something is this power of Thought itself, considered as infinite, indivisible, and active: indetermination that is also infinitely determinable and infinitely determining awareness. These *inadequate* ideas themselves are now understood *adequately*: they are understood to necessarily follow from the nature of God—from the nature of Thought, not Intellect, not *Noûs* (E2a3, E2p36, E5p3, E5p4). By understanding its own embeddedness, as mode (albeit infinite mode), in a broader infinite power of active and infinitely generative awareness (the Attribute of Thought), the Intellect understands itself, not merely as this one, determinate idea, but as the infinite (and thus indeterminate) power expressed in thinking this determinate idea—and all other ideas, both adequate and inadequate. It overcomes the dividedness of its own particular ideas, and all other ideas, experiencing their indivisibility and the identicalness of what they all express, at the same time overcoming the very dichotomy between determinate and indeterminate, between finite and infinite. All ideas are determinate expressions of the same thing: indeterminacy. All determinacies are different forms of the same content: indeterminacy. The Intellect understands itself as a necessarily determined expression of the indeterminate, infinite power of Thought. This is what I participate in when I have adequate ideas, when my ideas are parts of the Intellect of God: they see that the categories of "whole/part" and of "series of separate causes and effects" are not adequate, that the separation of premise and conclusion is invalid, that time and finitude are forms of division that do not apply to the infinite active causative power that is the essence of Natura Naturans—and that this applies as much to inadequate ideas as to adequate ones (E2p36, E5p3, E5p4). That means to understand the Intellect as expressing something beyond the Intellect: the power of Thought itself, that is, illimitability itself conceived as indeterminate awareness. The dichotomy of indeterminate and determinate, of infinite and finite, has thereby evaporated. This is Intuition, the Third Kind of Knowledge.

My formal essence is a *necessary and inalienable* expression of the *entirety* of absolutely infinite, indeterminable, indivisible generativity. It is felt in my temporal existence as my conatus, my endeavor to continue to exist, and is expressed in all my pleasures, pains, and desires. It is known as an objective essence in God's Intellect, as the idea of my body, and my mind is this idea and the ideas of this idea. To the extent that my Intellect has *adequate* ideas of this idea, it is knowing it as God's Intellect knows it, and as such it is a part of the Intellect of God. When I know the idea of that eternal, objective essence adequately as part of God's Intellect, I know that it is eternal though divisible from other ideas, but I also know that this same essence is also a formal essence that is eternal and infinite, indivisible from other essences. This formal essence pervades and is pervaded by all other formal essences, which, insofar as they too are necessary expressions of this same infinite, indeterminate power, are forms of expressing the same content—a content that includes each of these formal essences as a necessary and unexcludable form in which it must be expressed—and are thus themselves all necessary, eternal, infinite, and omnipresent. My temporal activity cannot increase or decrease this eternity. But the more my *temporal* acts of understanding encompass what is always there as this *eternal* aspect of my mind, the greater is the proportion of the (joyful, active) eternal to the (unsatisfying, passive) perishable in the totality of ideas that constitute my temporally experienced mind, and the less the unsatisfying and passive noneternal aspects (memory, perception, personality) will matter to me, thereby diminishing my fear of death.

This is, I think, Spinoza's vision.

Let's try to unpack how he gets there.

THE NONTHING, THE ONLY THING, EVERYWHERE, ETERNALLY

Perhaps no dryer style of exposition has yet been devised for the conveyance of metaphysical truths: Spinoza models himself on Euclid, laying down a few axioms that he expects to be self-evident to his readers and then purporting to show the precise manner in which everything else follows from them.

And what is it that follows? What does Spinoza claim he has proved? Leaving aside both the form and the technical, scholastic vocabulary in which it is expressed, Spinoza's main point can be stated rather simply:

There exists only *one entity*. That entity is *infinite*, is *indivisible*, is *indeterminate* (has no finite set of characteristics that would identify it in contrast to something else);[5] it is *causally unrelated to anything other than itself, cannot be acted on by anything other than itself, infinitely active, and infinitely generative*. Therefore, that entity is, in fact, not any specific "thing."

An entity, in this context, is what can genuinely exist independently of anything else; without depending on any external cause, it simply is what it is and is not merely a characteristic or aspect or part belonging to something else. Spinoza, using the technical philosophical jargon of his time, calls it "Substance." He tries to show that, by definition, no Substance could be causally related to another Substance. No Substance can make another Substance what it is or change the state of another Substance. All things that in any way interact, therefore, must somehow be characteristics or aspects or parts belonging to the same Substance; they must be included within the same Substance. Whatever seems to be outside any really existing entity, such that it circumscribes or otherwise determines or limits it, must therefore actually be *more of* that selfsame entity, that Substance. Otherwise this limiter would not be able to succeed in limiting, for to limit something is one kind of having an effect on something, of causally interacting. And so it goes, *ad infinitum*. Therefore, to be Substance is to be infinite.

Similarly, anything that succeeds in dividing two parts of any Substance can only succeed in having the effect of doing so if it also belongs to that Substance. Hence, the intervening bit of the same Substance does not really divide any two Substances but is simply more of the same Substance. Substance is therefore indivisible.

Again, whatever could act on or control or limit or affect a Substance must also be more of that Substance. Whatever affects it must, ipso facto, be more of itself. No other can do anything to it. Therefore that Substance must be active, never passively subject to determination by anything outside itself. Whatever determinations it assumes must be due to its own action, not the action of another.

If anything in the world did not interact with anything else, that would be tantamount to that thing not existing. Even to be impervious to all influence would be a way of interacting: it would be a way of determining all other things as not entering that thing, not interacting, not penetrating. It would be limiting and excluding other things. But to do that it would have to be of the same Substance with those other things. Therefore, all things — all possible things — are within the same Substance.

Whatever appears to be a separate entity, a determinate entity, a static entity, a finite entity, is really only a particular form of that one entity which is all that exists.

We might be tempted to say that all things are thus "parts" of the one infinite entity. But when speaking of Spinoza, "parts" is a misleading term, just as "entity" is a misleading term if it is taken to denote a "thing" — something with a finite set of definite properties and fixed limits.

Generally we think of "wholes" as things that are *assembled* from parts. The parts are prior and exist independently of the whole. Here, on the contrary, the so-called parts cannot be. or be conceived. without the whole. So really, the one entity that exists is not merely a "whole" in the ordinary sense (something made of divisible parts). And thus the parts are not merely parts in the ordinary sense. What are they, then?

Here we have again the problem of the infinite and the finite. The one Substance is infinite. The modes are finite. Are finitude and infinity mutually exclusive here, as monotheism and its secular descendants would lead us to expect?

Not exactly. I am finite — a particular something. To be something determinate is necessarily to be finite.

I am infinite — the one Substance that is shared by all possible finite forms. Actual being really pertains only to this one thing that *is*, so necessarily the answer to the question of what anything *is* has to be "the one infinite indivisible active Substance."

To be infinite is to express itself as infinite modes, to be infinite modes. To be a mode is to be the infinite, indivisible action in some state. The infinite is *what* it is. Any finite mode is *how* it is.

To be finite, it is necessary also to be infinite, and finitude expresses only infinity, which could not be infinity, could not be what it is, could not exist, if *even one* of its infinite finite expressions did not exist — if any *possible* finite expression did not exist.

So what kind of entity is the one entity?

It can only be described as in *all ways* infinite: expressing infinity in infinite ways. In his letters, Spinoza does not hesitate to make the startling assertion that infinity — or perfection, utter plenitude of being — is identical to *indeterminacy*. This may strike us as strange, but it is an unavoidable conclusion. The one thing is infinite — that is, it is perfect and indeterminate. For "determination is negation" (letter 50): to be determinate is to have a terminus — to terminate, to end somewhere. The one real being, Substance / Nature / God, has no terminus, and thus has no determinations. If God were some X — any X — this would mean an exclusion of Non-X, which would be an imperfection, a lack of being, a limitation of its infinitude. Thus, no specific determinations can be predicated of the one real thing. But this indetermination is not to be imagined as the exclusion of all determinations. That too would be a determination, that is, the definite characteristic of

blankness or inertness. Rather, it is no fixed or specific or limited determination. It cannot be limited to any finite set of characteristics. It must
always be more—whatever more there could possibly be. It is an infinitely
generative, infinitely active, infinitely productive, and thus infinitely *inclusive* unity—unity as inclusiveness, inclusiveness as unity. This is a way to
conceive of a unity that is sharply distinguished from the type of unity we
see in personality, in God, that is, the exclusive unity of accountability and
narrative continuity, of tool and work and purpose.

Yet we are able to understand this infinite Substance that exceeds all finite characteristics—indeed, according to Spinoza, in fact to understand it
completely or adequately. Indeed, we necessarily always have an adequate
idea of it (E2p47). How so? We are not asked to form any mental picture
of it, for to do so is impossible. Rather, to know God is simply to know the
fact that, necessarily, such infinitely active and indivisible indetermination
is the one thing capable of actually existing in itself, and thus that whatever may exist is precisely that. This can be turned around to yield more
clarity: just to know that any de/finite thing is not self-causing, is not self-
grounding, is not really and substantially existing in its own right, and that
no de/finite thing or de/finite set of things can be all that is, is to adequately
understand the one real entity.

Borrowing theological lingo, Spinoza says of this one real entity that
its essence involves its existence. This simply means that it cannot be conceived of other than as existing. To think of it is to already admit its existence. The "essence" of a thing is its defining characteristic. The essence
of gold, for example, is thought to be something like: a certain constant
molecular structure, from which the constant properties of shininess and
malleability are derived. The essence of the one actually existing thing,
however, is this: necessarily existing (and thus being infinite, indivisible
and actively generative).

What? Does anything we know fit this definition? Yes. In fact, there *seem*
to be *two* such things.

Spinoza follows his mentor Descartes in noting that there is one thing
that is immediately incapable of being doubted: thinking itself. To imagine
"imagining" and doubt its existence is already to demonstrate its existence.
To doubt the existence of "doubt" is already to admit doubt's existence.
To wonder if you are "wondering" is already to wonder. Thinking, doubt,
consciousness—these cannot be imagined without admitting that they
exist. It is crucial to understand here that "thinking" refers to all sentient
states, all conscious experiences as such, not merely to the discursive cog-
itations of which doubt and wondering are examples. Those examples are
singled out, on this reading, because they are the maximal possible *nega-*

tions of experience: they are instances in which experience endeavors to negate itself. But they turn out to be experiences as well, which is why they are what can prove the unnegatability of experience. Among all types of conscious experience, there are a handful that call the reality of experience into doubt, as Descartes had explored in the *Meditations*. One of these is doubt itself; a subcategory of thinking, it is able to negate all stipulated contents. What the indubitability of doubt reveals is that the one thing that can even raise the possibility of the nonexistence of experience is itself an experience, which thus undermines its own attempted undermining. This is the key, peculiar structure of the infinite: *it is instantiated in its own seeming negation.* You can try to negate it, to remove it, to eliminate it, as much as you like: but in so doing, you are only further demonstrating it.

But there is something else like this: space. Space (i.e., spatiality as such, including both "empty" and "filled" space) is something that cannot be removed without at the same time establishing itself all the more. If I imagine the evacuation of all space, what is left is space. If I now try to negate the space that is left over, I have space once again. Space is what is left over when anything is removed. When space is removed, I would just have the space in which that space had been. To think "space" is already to admit its necessary existence.

These two things—mind and space—are conceptions that necessarily involve their own existence. They are asserted even when they are negated. Merely to conceive of something with this structure is tantamount to knowing for certain that it exists. To have correctly conceived it is the same as knowing that it necessarily exists.

Mind and space thus open up to us dimensions that are infinite and indeterminable in Spinoza's sense, for any particular mental event and any particular disposition of self always occurs within a context of more of the same. There is greater space around every space. There are more thoughts, other experiences, around and beyond every thought and every other experience. Something in space may push out or destroy something else in space, but the space is not thereby destroyed—it is only further established by this destruction. One thought or experience may push out another, but experience itself is not thereby negated: it is further established by this destruction. Space and mind are infinite. Space is negated (excluded) only by other space, not by mind. Mind is negated by more mind, not by nonmind. An experience is negated only by another experience, not by nonexperience—and not by nothingness, space, or matter (at best it is only negated by the *thoughts* of nonexperience, of nothingness, of space, of matter, which are themselves experiences).

Thus far we would be inclined to think that there are two infinite things, space and mind, each of which meets Spinoza's definition of Substance: their conception involves their existence. But Spinoza thinks he has proved that, by definition, there can only be one Substance. Therefore, he concludes, what look like two distinct Substances must each be "Attributes" of the one Substance. An Attribute of Substance, in this sense, is "what Intellect perceives as constituting the essence of Substance" (E1d4). The essence of Substance, what makes something qualify as matching the definition of a Substance, is to be infinite, indivisible, nonpassive, indeterminate, perfect (i.e., lacking nothing), unrelatable to anything outside itself, and eternal. "Attributes" are what Intellect answers when asked, What is this Substance? What is it that is has the essence of being substantial in this way? What is it that is instantiated by its own negation, that can be conceived only as existing, that is infinite, indivisible, nonpassive, indeterminate, complete, unrelatable to anything outside itself, and eternal? Our Intellect can conceive two different answers that match those criteria: space and mind. Spinoza thus claims that, given the oneness of Substance, these are the same thing, the sole thing that exists, as viewed in two different ways.

Each of the Attributes models the infinity of Substance for us in its own way. Imagine space extended out in all directions forever. Since it is infinite, it is neither square nor round nor cubic nor triangular, for all of these are necessarily bounded figures within space, which would have to have more space outside them. Furthermore, it is not red or green, not black or white; it is not hot or cold, not alive or dead. For all of these likewise have to be bounded, contrasted to something outside themselves. Furthermore, it cannot itself be alive or dead; it must include all that is living and all that is dead. Finally, it cannot be either empty space or filled space: the apparent distinction between things on the one hand and the spaces between them on the other are both included in it and are inseparable. We should not imagine it as a filled or as an empty space, but as all spatiality, all ways of expressing spatiality, whether filled or empty. Spinoza, following Descartes, calls this aspect "Extension." All particular things or spaces between them are "modes" of Extension, that is, ways in which to be extended, manners of taking up space, styles of spatiality, types of space.

Extension must be infinite because by definition, however much Extension we may think of, there is more outside it. What is determined is limited. Whatever limits it must be something in space, something spatial, more spatiality. Whatever limits that limit, if it has a limit, also has to be something spatial. The one thing is, in this sense, infinite Extension, which can have no other particular characteristics as such but must include all possible ways of being extended.

But Spinoza thinks this is not the only way to think about what is infinite.

We have access to another way: there is something else of which we are aware that is not Extension at all. We call it mind, or awareness, or experience; Spinoza, again following Descartes, calls it "thought." Besides a triangle as a form of spatiality extended in space, we can entertain the idea of a triangle, or think about the definition of a triangle. This is a mental event rather than a physical event—a "thought." There is always more thought to be thought beyond any particular thought, just as there is always further room to extend beyond any Extension. Every particular determinate thought exists in a context of more thoughts. Most basically, a thought, to be a definite affirming of something, must be related to and exclusive of the negation of that thought, of that something. It is impossible to conceive an ultimate reach of thought or images or mental acts beyond which there is nothing further, for each of these only counts as a definite mental entity or event if it is contrasted to something that differs from it, and this necessary contrast can only succeed if both sides are mental. So the one thing that exists can also be described as infinite, indeterminable "thought," meaning infinite, indeterminable mental activity, and thus infinite experiencing.

What is the relation between the Extension and Thought? Spinoza says that they are merely two ways of apprehending the same thing. They appear to be two different things, two different "Substances." But Spinoza purports to prove that it is, by definition, impossible for more than one Substance to exist. Therefore the two apparent Substances are really aspects of or ways of viewing the same thing. We need not ask, then, how the two are connected. They are not connected—they are the same thing. They are two names for the same entity.

This applies also to each *way* of being extended and each *way* of being experienceable. It applies to a particular human body and the associated human mind as well. They are not connected—they are the same thing, but seen in two different ways. The mind is the idea of the body. The body is that of which the mind is an idea.

Texas is the Lone Star State. What is the relation between "Texas" and "the Lone Star State"? Do they border each other? Are they far away from each other? Is there a bridge between them? Is it difficult or easy to send letters between them? Who handles the flow of mail from one to the other? Are they at peace or at war? All these are meaningless questions: Texas is the Lone Star State. They are different ways of naming the same thing, the same Substance—different names used in different contexts, with attention to different concerns. One of them names that thing in relation to the official titles of American states; the other name names the same thing in relation to its state flag and motto as a holdover from a particular part of its history.

Similarly, there is no relation between mind and body, between Extension and Thought. Mind does not cause action in the body. Action in the body does not cause thoughts. Rather, thoughts are one way of naming what is, in other contexts, described as actions of the body, and vice versa. Neither is primary; neither is secondary. Neither is the Substance of which the other is an Attribute. Rather, body and mind are modes of the two known (to us) Attributes, Extension and Thought, each of which expresses in its own way the essence of the one indivisible indeterminate nonpassive infinity that exists, that is, each of which expresses the infinitude that is exemplified even by its own negation.

And it is this that Spinoza calls God, borrowing the formulation of the Ontological Proof of God's existence, which Descartes had revived after St. Anselm (though it had long been rejected by Catholic dogma via the work of St. Thomas Aquinas). The Ontological Proof for the existence of God, it turns out, is a knockdown weapon for proving the absurdity of monotheism. Perhaps, then, Aquinas was smart to deny it—and Descartes, who knew (as his epitaph says) that "to hide well is to live well," was smart to revive it. For Anselm, God was a being of which a greater could not be conceived, and existing was greater than not existing, so the conception of God included the proof that he existed.

Spinoza turns the terms around, saying, in effect, let's just start with the question of something that can be conceived only as existing, whatever it is, and then define *that* as what deserves the name "great," or "perfect." He says, therefore, that no one can actually doubt the existence of God. Let us pause here to note that this seemingly pious pronouncement has an enormous sting in the tail. He means that if you are asking about whether something exists, if you can argue about whether it exists, or take one position, or even find someone who is able to deny it or doubt it, then *ipso facto*, that thing cannot be God as properly understood. Let us pause to consider the atomic bomb of a weapon Spinoza has just given us atheists. He has given us the means to prove *in one second flat, and incontrovertibly*, that the God of the Bible or the Quran cannot be God, is a contradiction in terms, does not exist. How so? I will prove it right now. Ready? All I have to do is *doubt* that such a God exists. Can I imagine it? Can I worry about it? Can there be an either/or of faith about it? Then it's not God. Here I go—I am *doubting* it. I am *wondering* about this God. It is not something I know to be true as soon as I imagine it, like the proposition "this is this" or the statement, "I wonder whether there can be wonder." *Thereby* I have successfully proved that what I have been calling God, the biblical God, or any derivative idea of a purposeful God, cannot really be God. If it is meaningful at all to ask me *whether* I believe in God, then what you are referring to is not God. Monotheism, the personal God, the exclusive unity, the either/or demand—all thus stand *self-refuted*.

TRUTH AS ADEQUACY AS MORETOITIVITY

It is crucial here to see how centrally Spinoza's unique epistemology depends on his thoroughgoing denial of the personhood of God. It will be remembered that Spinoza's mentor Descartes sought an idea that he was literally unable to doubt and found one in the Cogito, due to its uniquely self-verifying structure: doubt about whether I am thinking verifies that I am thinking. Or at least, omitting the unnecessary and controversial "I" (it was abandoned by Spinoza, who admits no finite thinking Substance), doubt about whether thinking is happening instantiates that thinking is happening. My doubt about whether doubt is occurring verifies that doubt is occurring. Even when I try to disconfirm the certainty of doubt I end up confirming it, so it is impossible to doubt doubt. It is something of which the very thought ensures its existence—its essence involves existence. To doubt that "doubting is occurring" is simply not to understand what "doubting is occurring" means. But though this indubitability was thus completely clear and distinct to Descartes, he still believed that to convince himself of the indubitability of his own clear and distinct ideas, he had to find a way to assure himself that God, as the source of his sense of indubitable certainty, was not a deceiver—which he attempted through a highly questionable procedure sometimes critiqued as "Descartes' Circle." Spinoza inherits this notion of the value of literally indubitable ideas, whose self-evidence is clear and distinct—the conviction that true knowledge, which is proof against the vicious circles and infinite regresses of doubt, is only possible on the basis of a *self-verifying idea*: as he puts it, "truth needs no sign" (TEI36).[6] But Spinoza thinks this is already present there in the structure of the Cogito and that of the Dubito (leaving out the unnecessary "I" as the subject of the thinking or doubting): it is confirmed also by its own putative absence; it is conceivable only as existing and its essence involves existence. He doesn't think he need fear that his own literal inability to doubt, the literally self-contradictory nature of doubt about this, might be an error, that it might not be in accord with a truth that lies outside the limits of his own mind. This is because his God, the source and indeed the thinker of his thoughts, is not a person, has no goals, and is completely immanent to its own causal process, and thus his God cannot represent anything other than what is. For the same reason, the adequate ideas of the mind and what they represent are actually one and the same entity (i.e., the same mode of God, and i.e., of causally efficient reality) as seen in two different ways: under the

Attribute of Thought and under the Attribute of Extension. There is not an object at a distance that the ideas "refer to": they just *are* what they refer to, as seen in a specific way. "For certainty and objective essence are the same" (TEI35). If I can know that my ideas are "adequate," I can then know that they are "true." But what does "adequate" mean here?

An idea is "clear" only if thoroughly understood, and "distinct" only if it is cleanly divided from other ideas, that is, if the admixture of extraneous or superficially similar ideas is excised from it. A truly clear and distinct idea is an idea that is neither "fragmentary," a mere part of a whole idea so that something in it remains inexplicable, nor "confused," mixed with, overlapping with, or superimposed on other ideas. It is a *whole* idea standing alone. What makes an idea "whole"—or in Spinoza's language, "adequate"? Spinoza thinks the answer lies in correctly conceiving what an "idea" actually is. An idea is a *causal event,* an act of affirming or positing that something is so or not so, not a "dumb picture on a tablet" (E2p49cs). In other words, it is an act of affirming that something is the case. But simply knowing that something is the case without knowing anything about *why* it is the case is, for Spinoza, not a whole and adequate idea—it is a fragmentary idea, a fragment of an actual idea. And most of our experience and perception belong in this category: "Knowledge of the First Kind," that is, Imagination, including the image-centered, perceptual experience of empirically present objects. Actually, what we take to be knowledge of external things is just partial, confused, fragmentary apprehension of (the ideas of) causal events in our own body, the effect of an affirmation of something being the case without being able to affirm anything about the cause of its being the case. As such, it is an impotent fragment of a causal event rather than a whole causal event. A complete idea must include a full and adequate causal step. For Spinoza, a true causal step is a logical step, the apprehension of a logical necessity: the immanent causality between a premise and the conclusion that follows from it. In short, understanding what an idea is, that is, how a cognitive act actually produces new contents and how one idea necessarily produces another idea, requires a rethinking of the very notion of causation, the recognition of a truly immanent form of causation, such as we find in a conclusion "necessarily following" from a premise. A true idea is the understanding of an essence, knowledge of "what something is." To know the true definition of something is to have an adequate idea of it. In a true definition of the essence of a thing one can see its *generation,* from which all its properties can be deduced. As an example Spinoza gives the idea of a circle as "a figure drawn by rotating a line-segment with one end fixed and the other unfixed" (TEI72). Once I have that definition, I will know that all the points on the circumference are equidistant from the center, and from that I will be able to derive all the properties that follow from the nature of a circle. If I know the definition of a triangle, I will "be unable to doubt" that its three angles add up to 180 degrees. If I erroneously claim that the angles of a triangle add up to 140 degrees, it is because I am not actually thinking of a triangle (E2p47c). "Being literally unable to doubt" is what Spinoza, along with Descartes, means by "know with certainty."

But in the case of the triangle, given a certain definition, I may be unable to doubt what its properties are, but I can still doubt *whether or not* triangles, as defined, exist. To know that, I'd have to see triangles themselves as following from something in the same way that thing's properties follow from the definition of it. And I have something like that: space (or the Attribute of Extension), from the definition of which follow the properties of points, lines, and figures, including the triangle, in the same way that the idea of the triangle's angles adding up to 180 degrees follows from the idea of the definition of a triangle. Given what I think space is, it follows that I think there are triangles as defined (e.g., three-sided, bounded figures) and that their angles add up to 180 degrees. In other words, when I say it is true that the triangle as I define it has angles adding up to 180 degrees, I am simply *reporting* something about my ideas—about an actual event taking place in my mind.

But is "space" a given? Does "space" exist? This is where Spinoza repurposes the *structure* of Descartes' Cogito to great effect, against Descartes' own limited application of it. The existence of space cannot be doubted, not because of its dependence on or involvement by another idea, but by the nature of the idea of space (Extension) itself: space is what is left when anything is taken away, so it is what is left when space itself is taken away, so it is something that can be conceived only as existing. That is, *if* I do have this idea of space, which I correctly understand according to its definition, I cannot doubt that it exists. I am unable to doubt the triangle's properties if such figures exist, for I actually enact the necessary transition from the premise to the conclusion in my own mind: the idea of a triangle that is a component part of my mind has the property of also necessarily entailing just those properties. One "necessarily follows" from the other. "Necessarily following" means that when one is given, the other must also be given, and that if the consequent is not given, the premise is not what I thought it was. But I can still doubt whether there are any such figures like those I am imagining. Then I find that I am unable to doubt their existence on the condition that space exists, for they are similarly entailed in the thought of space, and the power of my own thinking experiences the necessity of this entailment: I cannot think one without thinking the other. Finally, I cannot doubt that space exists because of what the definition of space itself

is: I cannot think correctly about what "space" means without necessarily
affirming that it exists.

Now all this depends on my mind being such that its subjective sense
of necessity and certainty, its inability to doubt, is reliable. I am still just
reporting about the activities of my own mind—the affirmations entailed
in my own ideation. Could I be wrong about this? Perhaps my reportage
at a later time could be wrong about a previous mental activity, but while
engaged in it, the claim that "it is true" and the actual event are one and the
same: the claim is simply the affirmation intrinsic to the idea itself. Could
this be unreliable? Spinoza holds, following Descartes, that the only way
it could be unreliable is if my experiences were being *deliberately* manipulated so as to deceive me. That would require that the cause of my ideas be
capable of dissembling, of creating fictions—of having an intent to create
an impression of a causal series other than the one actually occurring in
the actual event of the generation of the ideas. But in fact, my adequate
ideas just *are* the causal events in question: the cause is immanent, being
contained in the event itself, as is the result that follows necessarily from it,
which is incapable of being altered by any other idea or intent. The source
and cause of any idea, any act of affirmation, is simply the prior idea that
logically entails it, the previous act of affirmation, which is an event I am
directly experiencing. To experience it is to see that the second idea follows
from the first idea purely through the nature of the first idea, necessarily,
without the help of any additional idea, such as a purpose of any kind, let
alone the specific intent to deceive. I am a witness to the very generation of
the idea, and to understand it adequately simply *is* the seeing of the absolute
necessity of its emergence from the prior idea alone, so I can be sure that
no additional motives belong to the source of my ideas. So I need have no
worries that my adequate ideas can be false.

Spinoza gives a single example, the relation of proportional numbers,
to illustrate the nature of the First, Second, and Third Kinds of Knowledge, that is, Imagination (including perception), Reason, and Intuition
(Ep40s2). I will here offer another example that I think more conclusively
conveys what I take to be his meaning. Imagine a circle with diameter AB.
If I ask you whether a line twice as long as the diameter is greater or lesser
in length than the circumference of this circle, you might try to draw the
figure, double the diameter, cut a piece of thread to match the length of
this line, and wrap it around the circumference to see which is longer, or
perhaps you might just try to eyeball it and make an assessment. This is
Imagination, the First Kind of Knowledge. You might apply the formula
for the circumference of a circle, learned by rote: $C = \pi d$. Since π is greater
than 2, you will conclude, correctly, that the circumference (C) is longer

than double the diameter (d). This is still mere Imagination since you are applying a formula by rote without understanding the steps of its derivation, even though your answer is infallible. If you go back to your Euclid and learn, step by step, how this formula was derived logically from the nature of the circle, realizing in this way that once you know what a circle is, it follows necessarily and is beyond the possibility of doubt that the circumference is longer than twice the diameter, this is Reason, an adequate idea that enacts the actual causal generation of the conclusion, the Second Kind of Knowledge. However, you can also notice that the semicircle of the half-circumference and the diameter are both ways of connecting the two points A and B. The diameter is the straight line that does so, while the half-circumference is a curved line that connects the same two points. Seeing this, you perceive all at once that a straight line is the shortest distance between two points and that this is inherent in the very definition of what "straight" means, what "points" mean—indeed what "space" means. No calculation is needed—no memorized formula, no numbers, no steps, no possibility of doubt. Straightness and shortness are not two different things; you need take no steps to connect them or derive one from the other; it is in the nature of space itself that shortness and straightness are one and the same. The relation of necessity between them collapses into a tautology rooted directly in the very nature of space—the Attribute of God that Spinoza calls Extension. Understanding what straightness is *just is* understanding what shortness is, and both of these are just understanding the nature of space per se. By applying this method, you can answer the same question for an oblong, football-shaped figure, however flattened, without needing any calculation and without discovering any formula for this mathematically tricky figure: the straight line will always be shorter than the curved line connecting the same two points. This is the Third Kind of Knowledge, Intuition. I can no more doubt this conclusion than I can doubt that I am conceiving the figure at all: the two are revealed to be tautological.

But, you may ask, Do my ideas have anything to do with anything outside my ideas? Do they correspond to facts in the physical world? Spinoza thinks, on the basis of his conception of what mind and body actually are, that one's ideas actually *are* those things. Seeing adequately *what bodies are and what ideas are*, on the basis of the necessary steps following from the self-verifying idea of a necessary (and nonpersonal), indivisible Substance with infinite Attributes given in *Ethics* parts 1 and 2, the truth of my adequate ideas is literally impossible to doubt, as is their correspondence with bodies. This is why, when asked in a letter how he knew his philosophy was the best possible one, Spinoza answered that he did *not* know it was the best philosophy but he did know it was true (and not that it was "the" true philosophy—Latin having no definite or indefinite articles), and that he knew it was true in exactly the same way that he knew the angles of a triangle add up to 180 degrees (letter 76).

Thus, "power of thinking," the immanent, productive, causal power of ideas, is the sole criterion of truth. That means that the value of rational thoughts is not in their order or accuracy in the sense of corresponding with external facts. For when understood correctly, an idea is already precisely identical with whatever it is the thought of; the idea of a body is just the same mode as that body but as seen in the Attribute of Thought as an idea instead of in the Attribute of Extension as a body; and the same applies to the relation between any two ideas within the Attribute of Thought itself. Every thought is, in this sense, "true" to the extent it has a positive referent at all, as opposed to a privation in comparison to another thought, which alone is what we refer to when we call it "false" (E2p33). Nor is rational thought valued because it accords with the intention of the creator of the corresponding facts, as a monotheist might claim, for there is no such intention, and the creator of the facts is an immanent source of both the thoughts and the facts.

Rather, literally, the point is that an idea that *produces more other ideas* is better than one that produces less, and particular forms of connections between ideas are valued because they are more productive. For God's essence is his power (E1p34)—his productivity—and every act of understanding is a participation in that productivity, that power of thinking, to a greater extent. Randomness is not opposed to order and is not rejected for its own sake: indeed, Spinoza tells us that there is no such thing as "order" in the universe: what we call order is just whatever configuration of things our particular type of mental apparatuses have a relatively easier time imagining or holding in mind (E1 app.). All possible configurations are equally just what they are, all equally necessary, and there is no *intention* to arrange them according to any plan or pattern. This is a deep atheist move, which reveals a key structure of atheist mysticism. A related atheist move is Spinoza's declaration, much invoked back in part I of this book, that "we do not desire something because it is good, but call it good because we desire it."[7] As we have seen, this is a key identifying marker of the atheist outlook. Similarly, the problem with irrational thought is not its failure to match a pattern of Logos or the order of the real world; its problem is that it is literally *less productive of other experiences* than rational thought.

On the ordinary notion of random thought, of what Spinoza calls "Imagination," it appears to be infinitely productive: I can randomly think of any item at Will, whereas Reason, considered monotheistically, is a limiter of Thought. Spinoza's doctrine claims the reverse. This may not be intuitive,

SPINOZA, OR INTOXICATING SOBRIETY   >   225

so we can try a Spinozistic experiment: make a list of random objects, for example, horse, wall, tennis ball, sky, elephantiasis of the thyroid, Mexican hat, Toledo . . . At first it seems as if we can go on forever. But we soon notice a certain fatigue setting in, a certain strain, a certain delay in coming up with the next item. We begin to be overpowered by the objects of our immediate surroundings. Spinoza would claim we have a limited power of thought and not free, random thought: in fact, all those items were what happened to be lingering near at hand in the waiting room of consciousness, and all of them were there for some specific, associative reason, either due to perception or ongoing chains of thought. The set is highly limited, and their production is really no more than a kind of housecleaning of left-over ideas. They do not generate new forms of awareness, new experiences, because they are disconnected and have no premise-conclusion or cause-effect structures. They are dead ends.

What the mind wants is not to think rationally per se, not to know truth per se, but *to experience more things*: literally, to have more experiences of more quiddities, which simply means that there is more mind, more awareness—a greater portion of the mind of the universe—being experienced. Adequate ideas are good and "true" because they enable more experience, period. They do this because they possess the full productive capacity of every idea qua idea; that is, every idea in God as an expression of God's essence, which is productive power per se. Above all, they lead to the thought of God as the infinite, necessary, indivisible power that necessarily expresses its infinity in infinite, mutually necessary ways. The more I can be aware of, the greater will be my beatitude. This means that even being aware of my own false (inadequate) ideas, which follow with the same necessity as adequate ideas (E2p36), is better than not being aware of them, and that even an awareness of chaos or evil is better than lacking that awareness, for the Good is just moreness, just expansiveness, just including more. More power means more being, which means "having a body that can move in more ways" and "having a mind that can think (perceive and conceive) many things," and that is all there is to "having a mind the greater part of which is eternal" (E5p39). Here we have one of the most delectable fruits of atheist mysticism.

THE BIG RETHINK: BODY, MIND, CAUSE, AND PURPOSE

All apparently separate objects in space are really *modes* of spatiality—its illimitable ways of being extended and expressing the infinitude of Extension, ways of taking shape that are just its infinite patterns of motion and rest. For individual bodies are not Substances and so they are not distinguished from one another by their Substances; what individuates bodies is simply the varying patterns of motion that follow from the nature of Extension itself. Bodies are like whirlpools in water: all are made of the water, but they can be picked out and distinguished as individual things (i.e., modes of water) by the way in which this water is moving here rather than there and by the relatively stable pattern in which the parts of this clump of motion communicate their motion to each other and endeavor to preserve this relation.

Likewise, all apparently separate minds and all apparently separate thoughts are really just *modes* of the conscious experience—the illimitable ways of being conscious and expressing the infinitude of consciousness in which it takes shape. Each individual mind is an idea in this conscious Substance, as is each individual thought and experience of each mind. These ideas *are* precisely the bodies of which they are the ideas, considered with respect to the Attribute of Thought (which includes all forms of consciousness) rather than the Attribute of Extension (which includes all forms of spatiality).

It is relatively easy to imagine what might be meant by saying that all physical objects are actually regions or fields of some particular character within one big thing, especially if the dichotomy between filled and empty space is dismissed, as it must be if we are considering space as Extension, as expressing the essence of Substance (i.e., indivisibility, infinity, activity, etc.). It might also be easy to imagine, if we have a spiritualist bent, what is meant by saying that each mind is the partial action of one Ubermind: a Universal mind that embraces all consciousnesses, as is found in, say, the Vedantic notion of Brahman. But it may be more difficult to understand these two ideas when they are combined with the assertion that the mind is the body, simply seen in an alternate way, that is, that there is no consciousness apart from bodies. This, however, is just what Spinoza asserts: consciousness is merely an alternate way of describing a particular body. This is one of the ways in which we can be clear that, although Spinoza still uses Descartes' term "thinking thing," the universal mind he describes does *not* "think" in the way that Anaxagoras's *Noûs* is a thinking thing, that is, an intelligence. It does not plan, it does not order, and it has no *goals*. It is emphatically nonteleological. We have seen already that the term *thought* is used to cover all experience, with the ordinary cogitative idea of thinking singled out precisely because it is the *least* all-encompassing and self-verifying instance of experience, and thus the locus of apparent negation. For that very reason it demonstrates the unnegatability of experience. But Spinoza views all specific experiences as ways of expressing the infinite, indivisible, nonpassive power of experiencing, which means, with respect to any finite experience, its indivisibility from other experiences and its inevitable transition from and to further experiences. As such, we can distinguish between more and less complete or inclusive experiences. The more an experience includes and expresses its relation to other experiences, the more complete it is. A thought is a casual agent insofar as it is an expression of the active indivisible power of infinity. The more it includes awareness of that active, indivisible power of infinity, the more adequate, that is, complete, it is. A "thought" here is just the adequate idea of a causal relation, where "cause" has been determined only as efficient causality, and efficient causality has been determined only as necessary consequences of premises. It is the *awareness version* of a causal event, nothing more and nothing less. For Spinoza, the only intelligible notion of causality, of how one state of affairs can bring about another, is what we know from the relation of logical premise to its necessary conclusion, where a full understanding of the premise entails the transition to the conclusion. The relation of necessary entailment is thus the inclusion of the thought of the infinite, active, indivisible, indeterminate power to produce. An idea or experience is thus called adequate to the extent that it involves an awareness of the necessary indivisibility of at least two differing experienced contents, of premise and conclusion. The mind of the universe "thinks" only in this radically redefined, nonteleological way: being adequately aware of the necessary oneness of a prior and a subsequent condition, comprehending events as necessary and unseparated from their immanent cause, which is active indivisible indeterminate infinity. It does this only as the particular modes that do this.

Strangely enough, although Spinoza makes consciousness an irreducible feature of all existence, and thus unexplained and unexplainable, he also gives a template for the only possible explanation for what it is. Given that we are thinking about whether consciousness exists, consciousness exists. Spinoza can thus simply assume that consciousness exists and can even offhandedly posit a panpsychism: all things are "alive" and all are modes, simultaneously, of both Thought and Extension. All things are conscious. But by allowing that a simple body like my coffee cup is also, in some way, conscious, Spinoza just means that the difference in complexity and richness and "perfection" (i.e., completeness) of the cup's "mind" and my mind is the same as the difference in complexity and richness and perfection of the cup's body and my body. My consciousness is more elaborate, just as my body is more elaborate. The difference between me and the cup is not the adding on of some mysterious extra property, *consciousness*, to one of the bodies—mine—and not the other. Rather, it is intrinsic to all bodies to have the rudimentary form of what, when it becomes very complex as my body is complex, we call consciousness—a conception that Don Garrett has aptly named Spinoza's "incremental naturalism."

It is the complexity, not the Substance or the addition of some extra thing, that makes my consciousness different from the very simple consciousness of the cup. What is the cup's consciousness? I think Spinoza means that it is "causal efficacy" itself, to borrow Whitehead's phrase (which I think derives from this idea of Spinoza's). All things are "alive." Spinoza tells us in an early work what "alive" means for him: in means able to maintain its existence, to persist in being what it is (PCP app. 2.6).[8] The cup has a certain rigidity and can withstand certain external shocks without losing its identity as a cup, its general shape and function as a cup that qualify it as a cup. Also, if "left alone," it keeps on existing for quite a while. It may do this to a greater or lesser extent, and to what extent it is doing so may be judged differently by different observers. But to whatever extent it is doing this, to that extent it is alive. And to whatever extent it is judged to be doing this, to that extent it is being judged to be alive.

But "being left alone" is really, for Spinoza, being exposed to a myriad of influences, the constant onslaught of Infinite Substance's inexhaustible generativity, which this cup, given its structure and material (which is also just a kind of structure) withstands. We call this withstanding of influences "the passing of time." The cup is a structure. It maintains that structure for a certain amount of time. That means that *this cup can be causally affected*.

Note well: it can only be causally affected by interactions because it is not *destroyed* by interactions. Rather, it can incorporate a certain (rather narrow) range of shocks into itself. What is "itself"? The particular set of relations between its parts, "a certain ratio of motion and rest," as Spinoza schematically says (in the case of bodies, i.e., the modes of Extension).

The cup retains this cup shape—handle, cylinder—even when I pour tea into it, even when I set it on a table, even when the wind blows. When I move the handle, the cylinder moves along with it, maintaining the previous relation of motion and rest. That ability to remain attached in spite of the force that moves the handle is the cup's adaptation to an external influence, its endeavor to maintain itself. That is its life. That shape, and the properties of its material to hold water and remain a solid at a certain temperature, is its "self." When it undergoes these interactions and maintains that self, it is alive. The concomitant idea of its taking of these causes into itself, subduing or integrating them however it can while retaining that shape and function, is its "consciousness." It is very rudimentary, and it probably resembles our own experience of consciousness as little as—well, as little as the structure of our brains resembles the structure of the cup.

To be engaged in causal interactions is to be, in a sense, *two things at once*. To be a cup affected by, say, the wind—for there to be any "impact of wind on cup" rather than simply "wind replacing cup here"—is to be cup and wind at once. Consciousness is to be both "this" and "that" *at the same time.* I can see this bottle here. There is something that is both "bottle" and "me" at once: my consciousness of the bottle. The "bottleness" does not replace my self, my mind, my being, my characteristic form in this locus; rather, somehow, seemingly miraculously, I continue to be me, but in addition there is added this determination, "this bottle," at the same time. The two coexist, overlapping at this locus that is my consciousness of the bottle. If I were less complicated, if my structure were less intricate, it could be destroyed by the imposition of this bottleness.

To the very small extent that the cup is affected by the wind while remaining a cup, it is conscious. The wind does not replace it—it *bends* it slightly, let's say, or *stretches* it in some way. Yet the characteristic of cupness—its ratio of motion and rest, the way its parts communicate motion to each other—remains present at the same locus. This is consciousness in its most rudimentary form. Obviously, this means we have an almost infinitely finely grained scale of different levels of so-called consciousness. Spinoza speaks of these as "relations" or "ratios." This is what gives him an actually comprehensible model, one that we confidently use all the time, for what it might mean to be "two things at once."

The more ways in which something can be affected and yet maintain its "characteristic ratio," the more it can perceive, the more active it is, the more it persists in its being, the more of beatitude it has, the greater the swath of Infinite Substance it is. A human brain is more complex than a horse brain. That means the human is capable of more adequate ideas—he is more active and less passive than the horse, his body can affect and be affected by the world in more ways, and this is also to say that his mind can form a greater number of conceptions. What this actually means is that he can be affected by a more varied array of causes without thereby ceasing to be what he is, as defined by a certain characteristic ratio of motion and rest among his parts. The more complex this structure of parts is, the more variables it can accommodate without altering this characteristic ratio.

Spinoza conceives of this model by means of a mathematical analogy, as is his wont. Our essence is a ratio: in the case of the body, it is a specific relation of systems and subsystems of motion and rest. A ratio can be maintained even if its constituent terms are changed. One-third equals 2/6 equals 3/9 equals 4/12 and so on. For the ratio "one-third" to continue its being is for it to increase its ability to manifest, to express itself, in the greatest available variety of ways: not just as 1/3, but also as 2/6, as 3/9, as 4/12. "One-third" can also participate in and experience "fourness" as long as it has the power to adjust its denominator accordingly to a 12. So if my essence is 1/3, I will strive to remain this precise ratio but in more and more complex ways, to grow into 2/6 or, if I can find a way, into 257/771, 700,113/2,100,339, and so on. This is how to grow more powerful and yet remain the same being. The larger the numbers involved, the more powerful these selfsame essences are. To continue the metaphor, if I am "one-third" only as 1/3 and a 9 hits me from the environment, forcing itself into my nominator, I will only be able to maintain myself if I can somehow procure from my environment and incorporate, in the correct position, a 27, or reposition this new 9-ness, which outweighs my entire prior being, partially into my nominator and partially into my denominator. If I can't, I will be overwhelmed, and the "one-thirdness" that I am will perish. If I am the same essence, one-thirdness, in the more powerful form of 257/771, on the other hand, and an external event forces a 9 into my nominator, I will have more inner resources to simply shift around; all I need to do is find within myself some 6 in my original 257, any 6, to shift down into my denominator. This means I can perceive all these numbers and be affected by them and yet remain myself without being destroyed. I can affect and be affected by the world in a wide variety of ways—I can perceive and conceive a vast number of different things and yet maintain myself in the face of their "otherness." Similarly, the more complex a structure any body possesses, the more changes it can accommodate while maintaining itself, which means the more it can conceive adequately and the more it can be active. For to perceive is to take something into myself, making it a component of my mind, while remaining who I am. That is what it means to be more powerful, to be able to remain the same in many more ways, perceiving many more things—both affecting and being affected by more things. We are always striving to be more powerful, which is to say, to have our ratio be operative in more moments and places, intersecting with more othernesses; to express our specific ratio in more and more particular ways; to "affect and be affected" in a greater number of ways; to do more things and experience more things while yet remaining who we are. Even existing for one additional moment means our ratio coexists undestroyed in and through, not only the previous moments, but also in and through this one additional moment.

Naturally this means that even when I am destroyed by some modification that exceeds my power to incorporate it, something else is maintaining itself in that interaction: for Spinoza, God, Infinite Substance, as well as the "infinite modes" of Substance, namely, "motion and rest," "infinite thought," and "the face of the entire universe," which also retain their self-same identity even though their component parts are constantly changing, just like all other modes. If they lose this one-thirdness that I am, these infinite modes maintain themselves by adjusting in such a way that they may continue the same ratio of motion and rest they had when I was there. In their case, however, since there is nothing external to them by which they could be destroyed, this maintenance is eternal.

What anything "does" is just what follows from its nature, in the same way that what a triangle "does" is to have angles equaling 180 degrees. Every action is an expression, in more and more ways as circumstances demand, of the causal power of the essence and nature of that thing, taking in new materials and changing its parameters so as to preserve its characteristic ratio of motion and rest. What the cup does when its handle is moved is "move the cylinder at the same pace." That is why it can experience "being grasped by the handle and moved" rather than being destroyed, as it would if its handle were shot off by a bullet or if it were made of soap bubbles: that force would be too much for the rest of the cup to keep up with, it would fail to maintain its characteristic ratio, and that would be the death of that cup. That is why that cup cannot perceive a bullet to the handle. But when any force within its range of adaptations at any given time affects it, it perceives that as a change in state of itself, as a perception of an outside object and as a concomitant endeavor to "do something" to maintain the inertia of its characteristic form of motion, its ratio of motion and rest, its particular shape. It experiences this, we may say, as a strong desire to move its cylinder.

But imagine a more complex structure—perhaps a gyroscope-type contraption of wheels within wheels, spheres within spheres, some filled with oil, some filled with ball bearings, some filled with sandy water, some filled with other spheres, all rotating at their own rate in order to maintain the constant rate of the ball rolling over the concrete and capable of taking in or letting out ballast from and to the environment and growing or shrinking as a result. Spinoza tells us that the life of the ball as a whole is only that of the summed motion—10 mph with 1 rotation per second, let's say—and a constant way in which its internal parts communicate their own motion to each other. It will endeavor to adjust the internal motions so as to maintain its total motion as a whole. It can do this and remain itself in several ways, we are told: first, it can change the *materials of which it is composed*—it can eat or excrete, learn or forget, as long as whatever it takes in to rebuild itself from can maintain its original motion and internal relations as a whole; second, it can change its *scale* as long as the *ratio* of relations remains the same.[9] It will automatically do whichever of these it can do, given the resources available in the new situation, to keep from losing as much of the power to continue what it was previously doing, when considered as a whole.

A human being is an exponentially more complex version of the same sort of contraption. If someone pushes my arm, to maintain my ratio of motion and rest I don't need to do as the cup did and simply move the rest of my body along with it in the same configuration. No, I have billions of ways of adjusting other parts of my motion so as to compensate for this new impact. I can easily absorb it and neutralize its effect by assuming a new state, one that sustains my characteristic pattern of motion in the whole. As I continue into every new situation, I am faced with new challenges, and I endeavor to continue this ratio of mine using these new elements in new ways. I am striving to continue manifesting the same ratio in new moments, in new environments, in new contexts, in new manners, which means I am striving to be *capable* of assuming more states, of moving the body and the mind in a greater *number* of ways, *and yet* remaining the same entity: the more changes you can go through without being destroyed, without ceasing to be yourself, the more powerful you are, the more life you are having. A body whose essence is X and can roll around on the floor without ceasing to be X is having more of the X-life than a body whose essence is X and cannot roll around on the floor without ceasing to be X. The greater number of ways in which your essence can be expressed means there are greater numbers of modes that are compatible with being what you are. It is not just maximal change, nor maximal stability. It is finding the maximal ways of change that maintain one's stability. Water remains water when it is choppy, frothy, wavy, still, muddy. That is water being able to have more of the being of water than if it failed to be capable of remaining itself in all these different states. It cannot be water and flame at the same time, though, which means water has no desire to be flame; being flame would simply be its destruction. But when it encounters conditions that force it to become choppy or frothy or wavy in order to maintain its essential ratio, it joyfully embraces them: it is able to have these new ways of moving and being without ceasing to be itself. Hence, "We are always striving to be more powerful" means exactly the same thing as, "We are always striving to continue to exist."

That is what all the desires of finite beings are and what all our motivations ultimately come down to. And other than the motivations and purposes of finite beings, there are no other motivations and purposes. This is what we learn from Spinoza's doctrine of *conatus*, a term that means, "endeavor, striving." It means a striving to *continue*. And this, Spinoza says, is the really existent essence of any individual mode, that is, of any particular thing. The real essence of any X, as present in the actual sequence of causal existence, is the endeavor to continue to be X. This is the source of all its more local and restricted purposes, as Spinoza goes on to show in detail in *Ethics* 3 and 4. The experienced desires and motivations and actions of any being are entirely reducible to its conatus, its desire to continue to exist in more and more times, situations, contexts, and the vicissitudes of its power to do so, either increasing (experienced as pleasure) or decreasing (experienced as pain). Desire, pleasure, and pain account for all purposes, and all of these are derived from the career of a conatus, an essence striving to continue to exist.

What does "continue to exist" really imply? Spinoza's analogy from an early work connects the idea to the idea of *momentum* in physics, a trope he picks up from Descartes. A body in motion has a tendency to continue moving in just that way unless it is subjected to an external interference. If it is going in a straight line at forty-nine miles per second, it will continue in that direction and at that velocity until something else affects it, sways it, stops it. In the same way, an object at rest continues to be at rest unless something external puts it in motion. Spinoza says that the seeming distinction between "the motion" and "the tendency to continue just that motion" is merely a convenience of thought; in reality, the motion *is* the tendency to continue moving—the tendency to continuing moving is precisely the motion. That is the case with us too, with all finite modes, all things: our "existing" and our endeavor to "keep existing" are just two names for the same activity—to be alive is to be striving to stay alive.

But to be continuing to exist means to exist in more ways, to express precisely this essence in whatever ways are possible in the newly encountered swath of space through which the object passes—and if an object continues to move through space, that means that it is continually encountering new contexts, new causal situations, which call for new adaptations to express the same essence. For Spinoza, after all, as for Descartes, there is no causally neutral empty space; to keep going is to go into new causal situations. Thus to continue is never accomplishable merely by remaining the same. To continue necessarily requires constant change, constant adaptation. What we will desire in any situation will be determined by the particular interface between our conatus, trying to continue to be itself—that is, to continue to affect things and survive being affected by things—and the particular causal parameters it is now newly encountering, otherwise known as its situation. And this is the source of all the purposes in the universe: they come from what we are as it interfaces with what we are encountering, not from an ideal commanded from without. Indeed, all purpose is an endeavor to continue becoming what we already are. And the best way to do that, it must be added, is (as we learn finally in part 5 of the *Ethics*) to learn to see everything that happens in and around us as coming from this kind of *necessity*, which has no purpose outside itself, rather than from the original *inadequate* conception found in the idea of "extrinsic purpose."

And this is what all purpose is, what all desire is. It is a way of staying the same: my only purpose is to keep being myself. But since I am finite and always surrounded by and overpowered by external forces (that is, because God / Nature / Substance is infinite and thus productive of infinite situations, of always more than whatever I have before me), this means constantly coming up with new ways, new schemes, new ideas for expressing myself—for "expressing myself" means only finding a new way to be what I've always been, to make that essence of mine applicable (that is, causally efficacious, capable of having an actual impact and to survive being actually impacted) in a new environment. What I want, whenever I want anything, is really just for *more and different* things to be mutually compatible with me and non–mutually exclusive with me-ness, things that are expressive of me-ness.

Thus we have the breakthrough: the universal mind is not *Noûs* controlling or creating the world. The crucial change made here is not only the obvious one, that this universal mind *is* the universe itself, is immanent, and that all of our minds are thus aspects or parts or expressions comprising it rather than confronting it from outside as an other-mind, a mind with which we must interact socially in terms of accountability and purpose and personality. Our minds are thoughts in the mind of God, not new minds created by the mind of God in order to interact with, obey, praise, love, be companions to, and be judged by God. But just as importantly, when Spinoza tells us that the universe is in one sense everywhere alive and conscious, is in one sense a single enormous universal mind, he means the world is in one sense an indivisible, active infinity of an aware, qualitative causality, of qualities leading to other qualities, of self-maintaining systems of qualities that can at the same time incorporate new qualities without losing their characteristic relation. It is also an indivisible, active, infinity of moving-and-resting *quantitative* causality, of quantifiable states leading to other quantifiable states, of bodies that can maintain their characteristic ratio while incorporating new causal influences, that is, the material universe. The entire universe as Thought, considered as a whole, is one such ball of self-preserving awareness, this ability to be two things at once—a kind of pun not of meanings but of identities, being itself by simultaneously being all this otherness that comprises it, going through various states but remaining itself. That is the mind of God, the mind of the Universe. Its unity is not the unity of personal self-consciousness, which is peculiar to one type of animal body, but the unity of necessity, indivisibility, indeterminate activity, which views itself in as many different ways as there are modes of Thought, each of which is indivisibly and necessarily connected to all the other ways of viewing. The same entire universe, considered as Extension, is also one such ball of self-preserving identity-pun activity, another way of being both thus and otherwise at once, going through various states by maintaining itself nonetheless: motion and rest, which is all bodies and all spaces, as Body of God, moving and resting in as many ways as there are modes of body, each indivisibly and necessarily connected to all other ways of moving. They are two ways of viewing the same thing. Neither plans the other. Neither controls the other. No one, in fact, controls either, or anything, and no real being can possibly be ontologically external to another real being.

What is at stake here is the notion of a rational plan, and that brings us to the real heart of Spinoza's atheism as a truly redemptive system. The key question is, of course, the idea of *purpose* in general. Spinoza famously skewers the traditional theological notion of teleology in divine providence in the appendix to part I of the *Ethics*, as quoted in part I of this book. Modern readers will perhaps find this easily palatable, though it was wildly provocative in the mid-seventeenth century, when it was composed. Spinoza tells us flatly that God—nature, the universe—does nothing for a purpose. The whole concept of "purpose" is an inadequate idea that grievously misrepresents God (or Nature, or the Universe). There is no purpose for the world; there is only *cause—power*—which is God's own nature and what necessarily follows from it.

Nothing, then, has a purpose. There is no purpose to life, to existence. However, we soon learn, in *Ethics* 3, that this really means not that there is no purpose in the world but rather (1) purpose is an inadequate misnomer for something very real, namely conatus, the only purpose of which is itself. Yet it will not do to translate this into the Aristotelian stopgap concept of the autotelic, which is a disastrous confusion of the true nature of conatus, since the conceptual apparatus of purposivity is entirely founded on the structure of *extrinsic* purpose; making it internal to any being simply replicates and further entrenches this structure. Instead we must rethink purpose from the ground up, which is what Spinoza does in this part of the *Ethics*. And (2) to the extent that we can speak of purpose at all, far from lacking purpose, the universe is a burgeoning explosion of purposes. Substance has no purpose at all. The immediate modes of Substance, which are themselves infinite (motion and rest for Extension, Infinite Intellect for Thought) have no extrinsic purpose: their one purpose is to continue being themselves, which they eternally succeed in doing in spite of the constant change of all their parts: they maintain their ratios even when all their parts are replaced. This one purpose of the universe, to keep being the universe, is coextensive with the infinity of purposes that constitute it, the infinitely diverse and constantly changing component conati of this one collective conatus. The only purpose of each of these as well is simply to continue being what it is. Since what they are is infinitely diverse, the purposes that make up the one purpose of no-external-purpose are equally infinitely diverse. These infinite endeavors of each being to continue to be what it is manifests as myriads of specific desires as these beings confront the challenges of ever new contexts, as they necessarily must every moment precisely because they are finite beings situated in a literal infinity of external situations. The universe is not devoid of purpose, but infinitely productive of *purposes*, plural. The universe has no single purpose, just as God has no single personality. But the universe—God—has many purposes, many personalities. You the reader are one of them. I the author am another.

What is the purpose of life? Life. What is the purpose of any particular life? The continuation of that life: more of that particular life. What is the purpose of my life? My life. And *more* of my life.

Spinoza is often described as an arch-rationalist, asserting that all that happens is rational. But this is extremely misleading if we carelessly assume that "rational" means what it meant for the *Noûs as Arché* crowd: rationally arranging means to attain ends, intelligently ordering the universe, planning and arranging things in the best way possible, for the Good. For Spinoza, the "rationality" of God lies solely in necessity, in intelligibility—not in teleology, planning, arranging, controlling, ordering, or aligning means to attain ends. Intelligibility lies only in seeing the indivisibility between premise and conclusion, between one finite mode and another; its lies in the inherent generativity of the essence of any finitude, the way any finitude is beyond its own finitude and exists only as a way of expressing infinite, indeterminate, indivisible generativity. Spinoza does *not* think that everything in the universe is perfectly "ordered," if by "ordered" we mean arranged according to a rational *plan*. For Spinoza, order just means "whatever sequence of events occurs, occurs necessarily." But the world is not "orderly" or "harmonious" in any other sense: those concepts are purely relative to our senses and Intellect. When we say things are orderly, all we mean is that "they are relatively easily imagined by us."[10] In fact, the orderly and the disorderly are equally rational: that is, equally necessary, equally indivisible, and equally modes of expression of the indeterminate infinity.

NOT MERELY PARTS OF THE WHOLE: HOW THE TEMPORARY FINITE MODE I AM IS *ALSO* ETERNAL AND INFINITE

We are already closing in on a problem that has bedeviled interpreters of Spinoza at least since Jacobi: how to conceive the transition from the infinite to the finite. How can an indeterminate infinity possibly produce definite determinations, since according to Spinoza all determinacy depends on prior determinacy? The answer is that there is no transition at all: the finite is the infinite and the infinite is the finite. This is, in fact, the defining formula of atheist mysticism. There is no finite thing apart from the infinite, and at the same time, if the ability to manifest as finitude is in any sense something that would be *more* than lacking that ability, then infinity qua infinity must turn out to produce and include every possible finite thing. Infinity would not be absolute infinity if it did not cause an infinite number of finite things, that is, if it expressed itself in less than an infinity of finite ways. If finitude is possible, infinity must do it and not lack it. What makes it possible? Just the fact that infinity is indeterminate: to *exclude* finitude would make it more determinate than infinity, would turn infinity into something determinate—for determination is negation (exclusion).

This answer may seem simplistic, vacuous, even trivial. It can be viewed as another example of Spinoza's typical practice of adopting a traditional theological motif and then turning it on its head by thinking it through much more literally and thoroughly than monotheist theologians allowed themselves to do. This answer is a twist on the post-Plotinian privation theory, which regards being itself, insofar as it is being, as good. God, as a perfect being endowed with maximal goodness, therefore is the maximal possible being. But now this is understood to mean that God's perfection requires the production and inclusion of all possible entities, of every possible type and mode. As Spinoza puts it, God "lacked not material for creating all things from the highest to the lowest degree of perfection; or, to speak more accurately, the laws of his nature were so comprehensive as to suffice for the production of everything that can be conceived by an infinite intellect" (E1 app.). Spinoza thinks he has already proved that God is an *absolute* infinity from which infinite things follow in infinite ways. Hence it is intrinsic to the definition of infinity that there be infinitely many finite modes. Without producing whatever could be produced, God would not qualify as absolutely infinite.

But this claim that "the finite is the infinite and the infinite is the finite" can be understood in several senses.

The least significant of these pertains only to the relation between the infinite modes and their component finite modes, which, because we are speaking only of *modes* here, is a straightforward whole/part relation. The whole universe at any given time is an infinite thing, a whole of which we and all finite things are parts. The universe considered in this way is not Substance, but an eternal and infinite mode of Substance. Spinoza speaks of this whole, this infinite and eternal mode, which he calls "the face of the entire universe," as an *unchanging* whole. But the parts of this whole can change without changing the whole. Even here, he provides a way to transcend the one/many, same/different, and infinite/finite dichotomies that puzzle metaphysicians: the one is the whole and the many are the parts; they have never been otherwise and there is no other kind of oneness, no other kind of manyness. We come and go, we finite modes, but the infinite mode of which we are a part, the universe as a whole, remains constant. The universe as a whole remains the same, somewhat as the total matter and energy in the universe are unchanged by the particular configurations they assume may come and go. Spinoza has stated it plainly:

> For since each one of its parts is composed of several bodies, each single part can therefore (preceding Lemma), without any change in its nature, move with varying degrees of speed and consequently communicate its own motion to other parts with varying degrees of speed. Now if we go on to conceive a third kind of individual things composed of this second kind, we shall find that it can be affected in many other ways without any change in its form. If we thus continue to infinity, we shall readily conceive the whole of Nature as one individual whose parts—that is, all the constituent bodies vary in infinite ways without any change in the individual as a whole. (E2p13L7s)

The parts change but the whole does not change. Because it is infinite, the whole can and must change in infinite ways, generating infinite changes in itself without changing at all what it is and has always been and will always be. It has always been there, unchanged yet changing. The infinite series of finite states is simply the infinitely many *rearrangements* of the finite modes, including their arising and perishing, that constitute the eternal, *unchanging* infinite mode. This infinite mode is composed of an infinite number of finite modes; it is simply their constant ratio of motion and rest. This is the weakest sense in which we can say, "The infinite is precisely the finite and the finite is precisely the infinite; the one itself is many and the many themselves are one."

But there are further implications of this trivial definition that get us closer to the heart of the matter. So far we have only been considering the relation between two types of mode, not the relation between modes and Substance per se. In this relation between finite and infinite modes, we are parts and it is whole. We are transient and it is eternal. We are finite and it is infinite. We are conditioned and it is unconditioned. This is the traditional assumption about the relation between ourselves, poor finite things that we are, and the whole universe, which in this way at least is just like the creator God of monotheism: something infinitely greater than us, and which we must never ever have the hubris of claiming to be equal to.

But Substance is this same eternal mode, the whole infinite universe, as understood *adequately*: not merely as the unchanging face of the universe considered in isolation but along with an understanding of that which it is dependent on, that of which it is a mode, that which it expresses, which is self-caused in the sense that its essence involves its existence: Substance. Both the infinite mode that is the universe as a whole and the Substance it expresses are "Nature." Substance, with all its Attributes, is what Spinoza calls *Natura Naturans* ("Nature as productive"). The universe as a whole is what he calls *Natura Naturata* ("Nature as produced"), which includes all *modes*, both finite and infinite. The former is the *immanent* cause of the latter, which means the productive and the produced can never be separate. An adequate idea of God must involve both.

The universe as a whole, qua infinite mode, has parts. But infinite Substance has no parts. All the so-called finite entities belonging to this infinite Substance thus are inseparable. Truly inseparable parts are, ultimately, not merely "parts"; rather, they are "modes." For Spinoza, it is not enough to see that "we are all parts of the one eternal whole which is God, Nature, Substance, the Universe, the One Mind," or what have you. "Parts" is a misleading term here, just as "thing" or "whole" or "one" or "mind" or "God" or "Nature" are misleading terms here. We have seen that this is not a whole in the way in which wholes are usually imagined: something assembled from separable parts, where the parts are prior to, and can exist independently of, the whole. That's not the kind of whole this is, and thus it's not the kind of parts these are. So really, the one thing that exists is not merely a whole and not merely a thing. And the parts are not merely parts. The whole in question is indivisible, active, and infinite. Since it is indivisible, it cannot be broken down into separate parts. Since it is active and causative, it is not a passive result of the activity or arrangement of the parts as in the usual whole/part relationship. Those two points are enough to show that these cannot really be parts at all in the usual sense. But finally it is also *infinite*, and this too ensures that this cannot be a whole/part relation of the kind that we know from finite wholes and their independent parts.

From here, we can delve somewhat deeper into the problem of the finite and the infinite. Recall here that for Spinoza, infinite means *indeterminate* as well as indivisible, necessarily existent, actively causative, and endlessly generative. A finite whole has an essence that differs from the essences of its parts. For example, a triangle is made of lines. The triangle is the whole and the lines of its three sides are the parts. A triangle has certain properties, which can be denoted by different equations; lines have certain completely different properties, which are expressed by different equations. The essence of the whole and the essence of the parts are qualitatively different.

They are, as we say, two different things. In the case of absolute infinity, however, this cannot be the case. It is impossible to definitely *differ* from something indeterminate, full stop. Since the nature of infinity is to be inclusively indeterminate and necessarily expressed in infinite ways, whatever nature the "part" has must be nondifferent from it. On the other hand, for any definite thing to be *nondifferent* from something infinite and indeterminate is just as impossible as being different from it. One is infinite and the other is finite; one is indeterminate, the other determinate. Clearly, the essence of a definite thing can neither be different from nor identical to the infinite. Modes can neither be identical to nor different from Substance. How can we conceive this?

Spinoza's answer to this conundrum is concealed in a curious definition plunked down on the first page of the *Ethics*: "By eternity I mean existence itself insofar as it is conceived as necessarily following solely from the definition of an eternal thing" (E1d8). To exist is to be eternal, *insofar* as that existence is conceived as necessarily following solely from the nature of Substance. *Mutatis mutandis*, we must say the same of infinity: to exist is to be infinite, insofar as that existence is conceived as necessarily following solely from the nature of an infinite thing. And to be infinite is to be omnipresent: to exist is to be omnipresent, insofar as that existence is conceived as necessarily following solely from the nature of an omnipresent thing.

Must not each thing then be omnipresent? And yet to be a determinate existence at all, each thing must be finite. How is this possible? To what extent and in what exact way is the finite mode also infinite, also eternal, also somehow present in and involved in everything that happens? To what extent is the infinite also, necessarily, expressed as each of an infinity of finitudes? To what extent do these finite existences have the divine essence, for Spinoza, in spite of his clear declaration that "God does not pertain to their essence" (E2p10s)? That is, to what extent is God, the unconditioned, the eternal, the infinite, the omnipresent, something that is in my nature? Do I have an eternal, infinite, omnipresent essence? Is it in God's essence to be Brook? Is it Brook's essence to be God? In what sense is the infinite the finite and the finite the infinite?

Martial Gueroult, one of the most incisive of all twentieth-century interpreters of Spinoza, takes on this problem directly:

This Substance, with regard to its nature, is complete in each mode. Moreover, this conclusion is evident in the very concept of indivisibility, for *what is indivisible by nature can only be complete where it is*, that is, "equally in the part and in the whole" (E2p37, E2p38, E2p46). Substance is thus, with regard to its nature, equally, that is, entirely, in the totality of its modes as it is in each of them, in each of them as it is in each of their parts, and in each of their parts as in each of the parts of these parts, etc., to infinity. . . . Hence every mode, whether small or large, envelops within itself the indivisibility of infinite Substance, which is completely bestowed upon it, while by virtue of its definition as a finite being, it must admit divisibility. This divisibility is infinite, however, since division will never be able to *really separate it*, either from other modes or from the indivisible Substance immanent in it. Thus, in each part (or mode), however small it may be, we rediscover in its integrity the indivisible infinite which allows it an infinite divisibility in act. In addition, this infinite divisibility along with the indivisible infinite which underlies it being *circumscribed in the sphere of each of the modes*, there are as many different infinitely divisible infinites as there are different modes.[11]

Note that we have a full flowering of *both* finitude and infinity in each mode. The manner in which the infinite is present in its indivisible wholeness is precisely as *divisibility*, but *infinite divisibility*, an infinite variety of alternate divisibilities. That is, indivisible infinite manifests in each mode as its own dividedness, its own division from the rest of the world, and also, concomitantly, the copresence of an infinite variety of alternate ways of dividing up itself and the world. If divisibility were ultimate, there would be one and only one correct way to divide up the self from the world: "at its joints," where one Substance was truly separated from another. Indivisibility of Substance implies the infinite divisibility of modes, which means there is no smallest unit of matter or of mind, of Extension, or of Thought, and any and all possible ways of grouping and dividing are equally authorized. We see the upshot of this often in Spinoza's use of his characteristic expression "in so far," or "in that respect," most notably in the blanket definition of individuality as such at E2d7: "By individual things I mean things that are finite and have a determinate existence. If several individual things concur in one act in such a way as to be all together the simultaneous cause of one effect, I consider them, in that respect, one individual." What counts as a single individual is not a simple fact of the matter: something may be one individual in one respect but several individuals in another respect.[12] What indivisibility excludes is not division; what it excludes is the existence of any one single univocal system of divisions. The impossibility of real division means, not that there can be no divisions, but that there must be infinite alternate divisions, infinite alternate versions of the world as defined by individual, one-sided, partial perspectives. The infinity of indivisibility is the infinity of ways of dividing—the infinite varieties of finitude.

At the same time, the infinite is wholly present in each infinite mode purely by virtue of the indivisibility of the infinite. To be infinite is literally to be indivisible, and both of these are literally to be *active*. That is why the infinity that is present in each finite mode is present, not only as its own infinite divisibility, but also specifically as its *cause*, the infinite, immanent cause that it feels as its innermost self; this is its actually existing essence (E3p7), which is what we are feeling when "we feel and experience that we are eternal" (E5p23s). Gueroult is very astute on this point as well:

> If each instant encloses in itself the infinite, as Leibniz will intend, it is in a different sense, for [in Spinoza] it encloses only the infinite of the cause which sustains it and not, at the same time, the infinity of all the predicates, past and future, of my existence. Indeed, the infinity of these predicates and my existence itself do not depend solely on God insofar as he causes my essence absolutely and sustains my existence from within, but also on the determination of this divine cause by an infinite chain of finite causes transcending my essence and its sufficient cause. My essence then includes only the reason of what defines it, *sub species aeternitatis*, that is, as understanding . . . and not the reason of the predicates of its existence, that is, of what imagination perceives. . . . The reason for all its predicates is not in itself, but in that infinite chain of causes external to it which God must necessarily produce in order to make it exist. Hence, every instant of my duration envelops, not the infinity of past and future moments of this existence, that is, the infinity of its predicates, but only the identity of the indivisible duration of my existence, directly expressing the infinity of its cause, whose eternity, although having no common measure with the succeeding instant, is nevertheless immanent to them.[13]

The infinite is present in its undivided essence, whole and complete, in my finitude as mode as my *immanent cause*. In actual temporal existence, I experience this as my conatus, my desire to continue to exist as myself. And this innermost sense of myself is an infinite mode of God. I contain the infinity, but I also confront the infinity, which overwhelms and dwarfs me. I sense myself as an infinity confronting an external infinity. God is expressed as both these infinities, and both these infinities are expressions of the same infinity.

This interpretation is strongly bolstered by Don Garrett's recent argument concerning the distinction between "formal essence" and "existing (or actual, active) essence" in Spinoza. Garrett has persuasively argued that the "formal essence" of a *finite* mode, such as my body, is itself an *infinite* mode of God (Garrett takes these to be among the referents of E1p21–23, the so-called infinite modes that follow from the absolute nature of any

Attribute—and I agree). That formal essence of a temporary and finite mode is eternal and infinite, that is, *omnipresent*, in the manner Spinoza struggles to describe in E2p8cs: like one of the infinite number of rectangles of exactly equal area that can be drawn taking any two intersecting lines drawn within a circle. It is a property of a circle that these rectangles are infinite in number and that all of them are equal in area. To exist, to come into being concretely in a particular time and place, in this analogy, is likened to one of these rectangles being actually drawn. But before and after being drawn, it remains true of the essence of a circle that these exact, infinite rectangles, including their property of being equal to one another, follow necessarily from that essence. These rectangles do not exist, but their formal essences continue to exist insofar as they follow eternally from the essence of the circle. Hence, these essences are eternal. But with Garrett, we claim that they are not only eternal but also *infinite*, as anything that follows directly from the nature of God is said by Spinoza to be not only eternal but also infinite (E1p21–23). As Garrett puts it, the formal essence of, say, my impermanent and finite body is "the omnipresent (i.e., pervasive and permanent) modification of the Attribute of Extension that consists of its general capacity to accommodate and sustain—through the general laws of [that Attribute] expressible as the laws of physics—the actual existence of a singular thing possessing a specific structure or nature whenever and wherever the series of actual finite causes mandates it. The formal essence of the human body thus *grounds* the actual existence of the finite human body, but it *necessitates* that existence only in concert with the infinite series of actual finite modes."[14] In the example of E2p8cs, the essence of each of these undrawn rectangles is wherever and whenever the circle is, is everywhere in the circle, for it follows necessarily from the essence of a circle. Wherever there is circularity, this characteristic of "this particular rectangularity along with infinite different rectangularities to which it is equal" is there too. The circle here stands for "God," that is, infinite, indivisible, active Substance. Wherever there is the infinite, there also is the formal essence of any finite thing, for example, of me. The infinite formal essence is instantiated as the "actually existing" essence when the lines are drawn. That infinity is then constrained to the finitude of an existing finite mode, and this actually existing essence is what we call the *conatus* of the finite entity: its endeavor to continue indefinitely (E3p7). My own infinity is present in my finite existence as my *desire* to be, to act, to do, to continue, to cause effects. Our *finite actual* essence, our conatus, appears when the entire series of finite determinate causes allows our *infinite formal* essence to actually exist as a spatiotemporal event.

These are not two essences but rather one essence seen in two ways.

Both the infinite essence and the finite existence follow necessarily from the nature of Substance; that is, they are *caused* by the essence of Substance. That cause is an immanent cause, not a transitive one (E1p18): it is always part of what its effects are, always part of what we are. This causation is Substance's activity, and that activity is indivisible.

Externally we see this same indivisible totality of Substance's activity as "the whole of nature as one individual whose parts—that is, all the constituent bodies—vary in infinite ways without any change in the individual as a whole" (E2L7s). This infinite whole is unchanging though its finite parts are always changing in infinite ways, just as all bodies maintain a fixed essence even though their constituent parts are constantly changing: it is the physical universe as a single body, with its own character as a universe. This is an infinite mode, and we can properly be said to be "parts" of this infinite "whole" if (and only if) it is regarded in abstraction from the Attribute of which it is a mode (i.e., Extension, in the case of bodies). We are located in only one tiny place in the matrix of causes and are born, change, and die, whereas it—the whole of Nature—is everywhere the same and never changes.

But *internally*, this selfsame infinite and indivisible activity is the immanent cause of our own specific activity, our characteristic essence, which we feel bodily as our particular ratio of motion and rest among the parts of our bodies and feel within ourselves as our own, causative, active essence: our conatus. It is what we feel to be ourselves most intimately when we confront the world and actively endeavor to live in it. Our own essence, which necessarily follows solely from the infinite essence of God, is present in us as our conatus, which is the cause of our being, our action, our endeavor to continue to be. Just to exist, as finite and determinate, is to be infinite and indeterminate as long as we do not abstract our existence from its cause. As cause, as conatus understood as following from the nature of God, which is undivided action, we are, and feel, eternal and infinite; we are the activity of God himself, of the Absolute, of the infinite; as effect, constrained and modified by and tangling with other effects and considered in isolation from our true cause (the indivisible infinity of Substance), we are finite and transitory beings.

It is as our obscure impulse to exist and keep existing, our unconscious *drive*, we might say, that we are eternal, infinite, undivided, indeterminate. But this drive is not "Will" in the sense understood by teleology, by the *Noûs* as *Arché* tradition: it is not Will that sees the Good and then wills it, but Will that is identical to my being, which posits and dismisses goods according to the nature of that being. It is purposeless Will, adopting and dismissing infinite purposes. It is atheist Will. It is Will that does not proceed from an isolated being who is me, that is, not my Will as opposed to the Will of the universe or the Will of God, but rather my own Will as coming from the creative power that produces all Wills. It is Will as another name for indeterminacy and infinity of existence itself, for the restlessness this imparts to any finitude, for the overflowing of any finitude, for the impossibility of static being or static goods. But it is not only that we feel the infinite indeterminacy and generative power, the universal purposeless Will in ourselves: we feel it specifically as the Will *for the finite, determinate being each of us are.* Being me is finite; willing to be me (rather than willing to be anything at all, or willing in general) is infinite. My existence specifically as me is finite. My purposeless unjustifiable desire to exist *specifically as finite me* is myself as God, myself as infinite.

It is in this way, in that to be finite qua mode of infinity is to be more than finite, that we are both finite and infinite. As effect, one link in the chain of existing transitive causes among determinate beings that constitute the totality of Nature, we are our finite selves. As immanent cause of that effect, felt as our nonnegotiable drive to continue to exist, we are infinite.

I concur with Ulysses Pinheiro in interpreting these formal essences pointed out by Garrett as specifically the "mediate infinite modes" mysteriously posited in E1p22 and in viewing them as infinite in number.[15] Each of these is infinite, but they are also mediated by and distinguished from the *immediate* infinite modes of E1p21, which are usually taken to be "motion and rest" (which for Spinoza would include all matter and all space, plus, in some interpretations, the laws governing that motion and rest) for Extension and "Infinite Understanding" (i.e., the totality of the Ideas of all modes) for Thought. Sometimes the "mediate infinite mode" of Extension that derives from these in E1p22 is instead interpreted to mean only the "the whole of Nature as a single individual." This, as we said, stays the same in spite of the alterations of its parts (E2L7s), and is described as "the face of the whole universe." Garrett argues that, *in addition,* the formal essence of *each* finite mode is *also* itself an infinite mode. He regards the formal essence of X as the possibility of the existence of X whenever the proximate causes for X in the sequence of Nature are in place, by which he means "unchanging forms that can be instantiated or exemplified by existing things, and without which those things would not even be so much as possible."[16] Garrett makes a strong argument defending the compatibility of this notion of "possibility" with the general exclusion of unactualized possibles in Spinoza's necessitarianism. He says that the formal essence of a finite singular thing is:

the omnipresent modification or aspect of an attribute of God that consists in the attribute's general capacity to accommodate—through the general laws of its nature as an attribute—the actual existence of a singular thing of the given specific structure whenever and wherever the series of actual finite causes should actually determine it to occur. Although the singular thing itself can exist only for limited duration, this general modification of the attribute constituting the thing's formal essence is permanent and pervasive and follows universally, via the general laws of nature, from the "absolute" or unqualified nature of the attribute itself— just as we would expect of an infinite mode. Although the formal essence of a singular thing is not identical to the singular thing, it is nevertheless the essence "of" that singular thing, in the sense that the instantiation of that essence produces the singular thing itself.[17]

The formal essence of a finite thing is "*omnipresent*" and "*pervasive*." That means it is everywhere throughout infinite Extension and everywhere throughout infinite Thought. In note 22 of the same essay, Garrett takes up the key question of squaring this with E2p37, which stipulates that what is common to all things (i.e., the "common notions") cannot constitute the essence of any singular thing. If the formal essences are omnipresent and pervasive, they would have to be common to all things, and this would seem to exclude the idea that they could be essences of singular things. Garrett's answer is that being omnipresent and pervasive does not imply being common to all things "in the sense employed in Spinoza's account of the second kind of knowledge," that is, in the sense of the common notions. I am not sure about this: we might rather go on to say that the formal essence of each individual thing *is*, in fact, a common notion, which is present equally in all things. What is at issue is whether an adequate knowledge of any singular thing X would require or in any sense even be derivable from, the formal essence of singular thing Y, as it would require or be derivable from the common notions. After all, in E5p39 it is stipulated that the more we know of individual things, then the more we know of God, which seems to imply the truly "omincentric" idea that knowing the formal essences of things would count as adequate ideas of the absolute nature of God, that is, that they function just as common notions do, in that by knowing them we are able to know all other things more adequately. A simple solution might be to invoke the language of E2p8 again and interpret E2p37 accordingly, thus: "What is the essence of any singular thing cannot be common to all things, *except insofar as it is comprehended in the Attributes of God*." That would be equivalent to saying, in accordance with Garrett's distinctions, "What is the *actually existing essence* of any singular thing cannot be common to all things, but *its formal essence* necessarily is common to all things."

Let us try to unpack this. "Modes" means at once both "modifications" and "ways." The first meaning normally implies an addition of something (a modifier or modification) that is not Substance itself per se, something that could cause it to change its state even if it could not create or destroy the Substance itself. But an external modifier is, *stricto sensu*, impossible in a thoroughgoing monism such as Spinoza's. If they are modifications of Substance, it is Substance itself that is doing the modifying: being infinite, it cannot be acted on by anything outside it as it alone is active, so they are rather self-modifications, self-alterations of state. We might call these "manifestations" or "expressions."

The second meaning, "ways," gets us to the same place: it implies that the same content in its entirety is present and presented, unchanged and undiminished, in a variety of forms, a variety of "ways." All that varies from case to case is "modal." Modes are the infinite various ways the *selfsame content* (in this case, active indivisible infinity) is expressed. The "what" is the same. The difference is only in the "how."

Substance is present in all its Attributes, Substance is all its Attributes, and Substance is the interidentity of all its Attributes. Each Attribute expresses the entire essence of Substance, albeit in its own particular way. But in an important sense the same is true for the *modes* of the Attributes as well: Substance is in all its modes, Substance is all of its modes—and Substance is the interidentity of all its modes. Each mode is its own limited way of expressing *the entirety* of its Attribute, which expresses in its own way the *entirety* of Substance. And the entirety of Substance *must* be expressed in an infinity of such finite ways.

There is indeed a difference between a mode and an Attribute, between finite and infinite, indeed an unbridgeable difference, and something does have to alter to get from Attribute *simpliciter* to any particular mode as such. But this is only a change of mode, of the manner of expression. It is the entire infinity of the Attribute that is expressed finitely as each finite mode and infinitely as each infinite mode, the latter being an infinite number of differently infinite expressions of each Attribute's infinity. "Expression" is a modal change, not a substantive change, for according to Spinoza, there *are* no substantive changes.

This leads us to the following conclusion: the *entirety* of infinite Substance is the content expressed by my "formal essence," which is an infinite, eternal, omnipresent way (mode) of expressing this infinite content (i.e., a content that is just "infinity" itself). And the infinite, eternal, omnipresent mode that is my "formal essence" is expressed in the modality of temporal, finite, existence as my conatus—my "actually existing essence," my endeavor to continue to exist—which is present to me as all my desires. Though one is infinite and the other is finite, it is the selfsame entity expressed in two different ways.

How to understand this? We will start with an example. Our first description of modes was to consider them as *states*. An unchanging thing is always in some changing state. A face may be wearing a happy or a sad expression, but is always a face, and is always *the same* face, with its own characteristic look. Think of the *skin* of Elvis Presley's face as *Substance*. Think of that skin-over-skull seen specifically as a "face" as an *Attribute* of that Substance: skin as face. Think of the very same skin-over-skull structure seen as "cannibal's pancake" or "tissue sample for biopsy," or "cluster of molecules" or what have you (any true but nonface way of regarding the face as a whole, seeing it as something other than "a face"); these are *other* Attributes of that Substance.[18] Think of the necessary entailments of a face qua a face, of what it is to be a face, as the *immediate infinite mode* of this Attribute: for example, for a face to be a face it must always have some expression (including a "blank" one at times), it must have at least some sense organs in it, it must have facial features that are seen as interrelated, and so on. Think of Elvis Presley always looking identifiably like Elvis, having that "Elvisy" look, as the first of the *mediate infinite modes* of that face, pervading the entire face. Think of the mouth, or any other specific feature, as a "finite mode" which is constantly changing in such a way as to maintain the ratio of relations that allow the "Elvisiness" of the face, the "infinite mode," to remain constant. And think of the Elvisiness of Elvis's mouth as the *formal essence* of that mouth. This Elvisiness, expressed by the mouth in a mouthy way, *unchangingly pervades* the entire face. Elvis's face is always and everywhere Elvisy, always and everywhere has the characteristics intrinsic to faces, always and everywhere is a face, and always and everywhere is skin-over-skull. Particular facial expressions, with any particular disposition of mouth, eyes and brow, come and go without changing any of the above. But also unchanged in the coming and going of these various dispositions of the mouth is the Elvisiness expressed in the mouth. It is just the same Elvisness that is the content expressed in another form (mode) in Elvis's eyes, nose, and chin.

What does it mean to say that the formal essence, the Elvisiness expressed in a mouthy way by Elvis's mouth, is not only unchanging but expresses the entire Elvisiness of the face, which is present undivided wherever the face is present? How can we conceive of the Elvisy mouthiness always and forever expressing also the Elvisiness of Elvis's eyes, nose, and chin? In the case of a finite thing like a face we *might* be able to imagine the

parts as separate because we can transpose them in our imagination to another locus, but this is impossible with infinite Substance. We see a mouth
as a *part* of a face; similarly, we might imagine that a finite mode is a *part*
of the infinite mode. Spinoza does speak this way sometimes, for example,
when he calls our minds "part of" the infinite Intellect of God (E2p11c)—
and again, it is important to note here that the infinite *Intellect* of God is *not*
the *Attribute* Thought itself, but merely an infinite mode thereof, as stated
in E1p31—a decisive break with the *Noûs* as *Arché* tradition. We see this
"part/whole" language again in the famous metaphor of the worm in the
blood in letter 32. But in that letter itself, he first clarifies that whole and
parts are only manners of speaking, intellectual constructs.[19] Spinoza still
clearly holds to the view expressed directly in the *Short Treatise*, that in
reality there are no such things as "wholes and parts" in Nature. In letter 32,
after the worm in the blood example, he thus goes on to say,

> Hence it follows that every body, insofar as it exists as modified in a defi-
> nite way, must be considered as a part of the whole universe. . . . Now
> since the nature of the universe, unlike the nature of the blood, is not lim-
> ited, but is absolutely infinite, its parts are controlled by the nature of this
> infinite potency in infinite ways, and are compelled to undergo infinite
> variations. *However, I conceive that in respect to Substance each individual
> part has a more intimate union with its whole. For . . . since it is of the nature
> of Substance to be infinite, it follows that each part pertains to the nature of
> corporeal Substance, and can neither be nor be conceived without it.*[20]

What is this "more intimate union"? When we think of a mouth *as mouth*
rather than as a collection of cells or tissue, we are thinking of it as inseparable from "face," the Attribute. If we are thinking of skin-on-skull as cannibal's pancake rather than as a face, the mouth will also not be mouth but
rather a clump of meat. Even for a finite thing, it is not simply that a face
is whole, mouth is a "part" of that whole. We mustn't think that the smile
qua smile is the modification, not of a face as a whole, but simply of a part
of that whole, called "a mouth" or "the lips." For the mouth *as mouth* or
lips *as lips* are inseparable from the face as face. The part/whole relation as
ordinarily conceived thus breaks down even when we start talking about
any finite Substance and its modes, as correctly conceived. For Spinoza, of
course, there simply *are* no finite Substances: there is only Substance. And
this breakdown of the whole/part relation is even more glaringly the case
with Substance, which is a necessarily active and indivisible infinity. So we
must be careful not to think of Spinoza's finite modes as if they were changing, finite modes of what we imagine to be unchanging, passive, *finite* Sub-

stances, inadequately conceiving them as divisible. In the case of a mouth on a face, we are thinking "inadequately" when we think of it as a part that "can be or be conceived without" the whole, the face: we imagine that the mouth could, in some sense, exist outside of a face—perhaps Cheshire Cat style, floating in space, or perhaps on a vivisectionist's table: "mouth" could refer to the material elements composing the lips, and the "smile" would be a particular mode in which those elements could be disposed. In that sense, the smile would seem to be temporary mode of its own immediate local substrate, a finite Substance, the physical lips. But this would not be a smile as smile; we are confused by the imagination of a smile that could exist without being "in" a face (and in fact, when we look at the smile as smile in the case of a picture of the Cheshire Cat, we are imaginatively providing the face context that allows us to read it as "smile"). This translocation is, of course, impossible in the case of infinite Substance: if we remove the mouth to a different locale, it is still a mode of the same Substance—of Extension, of space—for it still has *some* locale. There is no outside to which it can be moved. Any other place is also a "place"—and "being in a place" is to "the Attribute of Extension" what "being in a face" is to "the Attribute of face." So we must imagine a smile that literally vanishes if it is removed from a face. A smile cannot be or be conceived without a mouth, which cannot be or be conceived without a face. The mouth is not merely a part of the "face" (Attribute) and its characteristic look (an eternal mode of the face, present whenever and wherever there is face, and conceived adequately only when known as a mode of face rather than an independent entity in its own right): it is a way in which the face and its look are expressed. In the same way, finite modes are more than mere parts of Substance, and as long as we are considering the infinite mode *adequately*, as a formal essence following solely from the nature of Substance, as a mode *of Substance*, a way of expressing the entire content of Substance, caused by Substance and inseparable from that cause, finite modes are more than mere parts of the infinite mode. They are Substance itself, expressed in this or that way, just as the Elvisy mouth is not merely a "part "of the Elvisy face or a mere part of Elvisiness; it is one of the many ways of expressing that total Elvisiness present everywhere in the face. The smile on the mouth in this sense is to be understood not as a "part" of the total facial expression of happy Elvis, but as an expression of the totality of it. A finite mode is, in this sense, the infinite itself. To speak of one mode as different from another mode must be understood only in this sense: as a different *way* of expressing the same content.

Spinoza is claiming that if we consider the face as a face, or the man's look as a look, or the expression as the expression of a face characterized by its look, it has no separable parts. Insofar as it is an expression, it is an expression of a face—of this face. Only if we consider the nose and mouth and chin in isolation from their condition of being expressions of the state of a face, just as a set of factual material components, they can be considered separable, mere parts. This would be like seeing modes not as modes *of* Substance, but simply as separate individual things, as finite Substances. Only then are they considered separable things, which can be then assembled into "parts of which a whole is composed."

In the case of skin-over-skull, there are a finite number of Attributes (face, cluster of cell tissue, cannibal's pancake, etc.) which can truly be said to constitute its essence, and for each of these finite essential Attributes there is only a finite number of ways in which this essence (such as faciality and its eternal immediate mode, e.g., having an expression, and its eternal mediate mode, Elvisishness) can be expressed (happy Elvis expression, angry Elvis expression, etc.). But in the case of Substance, there are an infinite number of Attributes, each of which can be expressed in infinite ways. "Motion and rest" (and the laws thereof) and "the face of the entire universe" are not the only infinite modes of the Attribute of Extension: the formal essence of each *finite* body, "the general capacity to accommodate and sustain the actual existence of a singular thing possessing a specific structure or nature whenever and wherever the series of actual finite causes mandates it," is equally an *infinite* (omnipresent, eternal) mode of Extension.

The same applies, *mutatis mutandis*, for every other Attribute. The formal essence of my finite mind, which is the idea of my body, is an infinite, omnipresent, eternal mode of the Attribute of Thought. I feel these two infinite formal essences as my conatus: the momentum of the particular ratio of motion and rest of bodies that make up my body—that motion as the Will to keep moving this way—and the idea or consciousness of that momentum.

Any finite thing is thus, in one sense, a part of a particular, divisible, infinite state of the infinite, thingless, indivisible action, but just in being so it is, in another sense—in its formal essence, actualized as its conatus—one *expression* of the infinite, thingless, indivisible action, not a mere *part* of it. A mouth is part of an expression, but the essence of that mouth, the omnipresent capacity to accommodate and sustain that mouth, is more than just a *part* of "the way you look," or "your face." Your whole face, your recognizable look, is in the look of your mouth, correctly understood as a striving to continue to be that mouth, which is an actualization of the capacity for it to be accommodated and sustained in such a face, coterminous with the entire face in both space and time.

Any finite thing is one expression of the entirety of the infinite. Your mouth is one expression of your entire face.

Any finite thing is one expression of the essence of the infinite. The essence of the infinite is *infinite, indivisible, active, causative power*.

Any finite thing is one expression of the infinite indivisible action of the infinite.

Any finite thing is one among infinite ways of expressing the infinite indivisible action of the infinite—each one expressing the entire infinite action, not "part" of the infinite action.

The universe as a whole is expressed in its own "way" in and as each mode. This is certainly the lesson Leibniz took to be hidden in Spinoza and offered as his own doctrine, with some monotheist modifications. It is also what the early Schelling understood to be going on in Spinoza, such that each mode (and *not* each Attribute) is, by his lights, "infinite in its kind."[21] The entirety of omnipresent eternal infinity is present not just with, not just to, not just causing, not just sustaining, not just within, but *as* every localized temporary finite being. But there is more, as we will see: each finite being is what is omnipresently and eternally expressing itself *as* every other finite being.

FINITUDE AS THE INTERSECTION OF TWO INFINITIES

We are now in a position to explain not only the (non)transition from infinite mode to finite modes—there is none, as they are merely two ways of viewing the same thing—but also why there are modes at all, whether finite or infinite.

God's essence and existence are the same, and both are eternal and unchanging. In God there are not two different entities, not two tiers of reality. There is only this necessary essence-existence, God. Considered only as a bare existent, in isolation from the essence as if it were, only the result of a causal process rather than as a way in which the infinite causal power itself appears, it is the unchanging infinite mode, the face of the entire universe. Considered in this way, it can be divided into parts, whereas when considered as a mode of Substance, undivided from its immanent cause, it cannot: those "parts" are really indivisible modes of Substance. But we have established that *all* these modes are infinite qua formal essences, whereas finitude comes into the picture only because there is also existence: an infinite "formal essence" becomes finite only when "actually" existent. But why is there, among all these infinite modes, also the mode of *existent* "face of the universe," which is divisible into finite parts? Why is there *existence* as opposed to simply *essence?*

This is where the seemingly trivial point about God's *"absolute infinity," from which infinite things must follow in infinite ways*, again comes to our aid.

If absolute infinity were expressed in less than infinite ways, it would not be absolute infinity. If the infinity of the selfsame thing that is both God's essence and his existence were expressed only as the infinite series of infinite essences and not also as the infinite series of finite existences, which is another way in which that selfsame thing can be expressed, then its expressions would not be infinite—and thus it would not be *absolute* infinity. It turns out that God's essence can also be understood as his existence; and his existence can also be understood as his essence. If only one of these aspects had infinite, necessary consequences, then the absolute infinity, its literal nonexclusion of whatever can be, would be compromised.

So why can it be understood in these two different ways at all? Why is there an essence/existence split at all, since these are, in God considered absolutely, one and the same? Again, it is simply because infinite things follow from that one and the same thing in infinite ways. Among them there must therefore be existence as well as essence. If God's essence did not also involve his existence, if essence were limited only to being essence and existence only to existence and if either of these lacked the ability to be equally justifiably expressed as the other, God would not be God.

So there must be existence. And because there must be existence, there must be finitude. Existence is one of the ways of being infinite: namely, it is the kind of infinity that can be divided into parts. These parts are the finite, existent modes. Finite modes are finite only because, for them, existence and essence *cannot* coincide. Since there must be finitude, there must be a division between essence and existence, for this is the definition of finitude. Lacking these finite modes, absolute infinity would not be absolute infinity. Comprehending what God is involves comprehending *both* what he is and what follows from him, which therefore includes finite modes and their ideas—their minds—which *necessarily* require the split between essence and existence. In just this sense, this split is also *necessarily* included in the idea of God.

To understand the implications of this conclusion, we must remember that there are thus *two* infinite chains of causality in Spinoza's thought, going all the way back to his early unfinished *Treatise on the Emendation of the Intellect*.[22]

The first is the chain of necessary *essences*, each of which is an eternal truth. Strictly speaking, there is thus no "sequence" here: they are simultaneous. But there is a logical order to them, as some ideas presuppose other thoughts and are formed from them. The second is the chain of necessary *existences*, that is, existent determinate modes determining other existent determinate modes ad infinitum.

Now the two infinite series, the infinite series of infinite essences, on the one hand, and the infinite series of finite existences composing the infinite existence Spinoza calls the face of the universe, on the other, are both equally necessary in God. God's essence is his existence, and both the essence and the existence of each thing are immanently caused by God. God's essence coincides exactly with his existence: they are one and the same thing. Are the two series, which follow necessarily from his essence and existence respectively, therefore also one and the same thing? Not exactly.

The finite essences, when thought of in isolation from their necessary cause, the essence of God, do not involve existence. For example, to think about what *triangle* means, what the essence of a triangle is and all that follows from that essence, is not to be thinking of what "Extension" means, of the essence of Extension—as long as I am isolating the thought of triangle from the thought of its immanent cause, which is, in fact, Extension. *Extension* means necessary existence, infinity, inexhaustible productive power, which is the immanent cause of the essence of triangularity. To understand the essence of Extension is to understand that Extension necessarily exists. Thinking about the triangle in isolation from this cause, in contrast, does not yet tell me whether any triangle exists here and now or at any other particular time I might imagine.

But as following necessarily and eternally from the nature of God, all formal essences are also eternal and omnipresent, whether or not they "exist"; that is, whether or not they are present at any particular portion of the second series. God would not be God without them—in fact all *formal* essences pertain to the essence of God. My mind, the idea of my body, is a formal essence in God, which follows necessarily from the nature of God as the nature of a triangle follows necessarily and eternally from the nature of space / extension. Even before and after the duration of my life, this formal essence is in God (E2p8).

To "exist" would have to mean being an essence that is in relation not only to its immediate premise and conclusion as adequate ideas, that is, as eternal formal essences (in the first "sequence"), but it would also have to mean being in the second sequence, that is, of determinate existences— which is the same essence but as existing. This means it causally participates also in effects of which it is *not* the sole and adequate cause, and thus is not only active but also "passive" in Spinoza's sense—*this* is the definition of "existence" according to Spinoza. The sunlight coming into the window "exists" in the room, but its essence, what it is to be this sunlight, is not created by the opening of the shutter.[23] The essence of "sunlight" interacts in collaboration with other factors; that is, it operates in an "inadequate" way: it acts in concert with the window and floor to appear just here and just now and in just this way. When it does, though, it has the properties of sunlight that derive from its place in the eternal order of essences. Three cars may get into a collision and come to a halt in the shape of a triangle. The cars and all the other factors leading to their collision are the proximate causes of that triangle in the sequence of existences. But the Euclidean derivation of a triangle from the nature of space, points, and lines is the cause of the essence of triangularity that is instantiated there and then, and the properties it displays are those of the triangle so conceived—for example, certain angles of motion of a passenger that goes flying through the window and bounces off the other cars. To whatever extent the triangularity is the sole cause of this trajectory, the triangle is the one that is "active" here, and we can understand the trajectory adequately by understanding the triangle. To the extent that other factors have an effect on the outcome (for example, a strong wind that bends the trajectory, the shape of the passenger's body, the pavement's coefficient of friction, and so on), merely considering the triangle would not yield an adequate idea of its effects and its causal power alone would be inadequate to produce that effect; to that extent it would be "passive."

Genuine causality is the relation of premise to conclusion, and the occurrence of the effect is really only the more adequate understanding of the cause. Real causality happens only through the essence sequence. It occurs in the existence sequence only with respect to the *whole* of existence: the whole state of the infinite Substance (an infinite mode, the states of "the face of the entire universe") logically entails the next whole state, and one changing "state" of the whole unchanging "face" is the real cause (premise) from which the next "state" (conclusion) necessarily follows. Among the parts in existence, however, there is no real one-to-one causality. Apparent efficient causality among single things is an entity of the Imagination; it is the result of inadequate ideas.

These inadequate ideas themselves, however, are a *necessary* concomitant of all finite modes, including all human minds. In Substance there is no inadequate causality except in the thoughts of finite minds, that is, insofar as it is modified by some finite mode. That is, inadequate causality is a function of inadequate *ideas*, and inadequate ideas pertain only to the finite minds of finite modes. *These* however, are real, and they are really and necessarily in Substance—and thus, "inadequate ideas follow with the same necessity as adequate ideas" (E2p36). That means that the distinction between essence and existence is an *ens imaginationis*, existing only in the minds of finite beings, but the essences of those finite beings, and hence of that *ens imaginationis* as *ens imaginationis*, are really eternally in God. There is existence as opposed to essence *because*, even considering the essence series alone, finite modes follow from the nature of God. And yet, contrastingly, in this nature of God considered as such—that is, not insofar as it is modified in some determinate way—existence is not different from essence. Existence in duration pertains to me only because I'm finite, but I'm finite because I am one of the infinite series of infinite formal essences that inhere in the infinity of God—which, as such, are also eternal and infinite.

Thus there is a split between essence and existence only because of inadequate ideas, but inadequate ideas themselves are a necessary aspect of the essence of God. These adequate and inadequate ideas are not really two different things—for there are no two different things. The relation between inadequate ideas and adequate ideas is illustrated by Spinoza with the relationship between "seeing the sun to be 200 feet away" and "seeing the sun to be 200 feet away but also understanding that why it appears that way, and thus knowing it at the same time not to be 200 feet away" (E2p35s). The experience does not go away or change in any way: indeed, this illusion too is an eternal fact necessarily entailed in God. It is just also *supplemented* by additional information, additional ideas, which allows me to see it differently, to see it as *necessary*. The inadequate idea is a *part* of an adequate idea. But Reason, the Second Kind of Knowledge, means understanding the relations of the parts of this adequate idea as *necessary*. This amounts to seeing the cause as immanent and not transient to the effect, which means that both are *modes*, not parts, of this adequate idea: aspects of it, alternate ways of expressing it in its entirety. If I see a sequence of cause and effect in isolation from Substance, the causality between them is transitive. But in advancing through and beyond necessity and Reason, these same two events, understood as modes of Substance are further seen by Intuition as tautological. As such, even the causality between individual modes, qua modes, is immanent: since each is the whole of infinity and the whole of infinity is the cause of each, the cause remains in the effect: the formal essence of each finite mode is omnipresent, infinite, and eternal, and hence immanent to both the existence and the essence of all other modes.

In me as "actually existing," brought to birth (necessarily) through the second series in a particular time and place, this infinite essence is present as my finite actual essence, which is not present as my knowledge of myself but as my conatus. This is (in Thought) the (unknown to me) adequate and active idea of what is (in Extension) the specific ratio of motion and rest that is my body. It is—I am—not a Substance, after all, but distinguished from other modes of body only by my characteristic motion; my body is a certain specific type of highly complex interesting of motions within motions of Substance (like one of the infinite different velocities of matter in motion flowing between the two nonconcentric circles that Spinoza invokes in the "Letter on Infinity").[24] My mind is the complex idea of that motion and its interactions.

Now this ratio, this specific type of motion that I am, has to be what I would be doing unceasingly if all my actions were limited only by virtue of my own nature, and not because they were curtailed by the blockage of other things. I move my right foot forward while walking. But I do not continue this forward motion forever: its nature "moving forward" is limited by a quantitative restriction; I move it forward this much but no more. I am not endeavoring to engage in an infinite moving forward of my leg: it must be curtailed, and I will and desire it to be curtailed. That is how I know "moving my foot forward" is not an adequate idea of my conatus, that my essence does not involve moving-foot-forward per se. My conatus is that motion that I'm always involved in, that I'm involved in infinitely, with no *intrinsic* negation at all. For this reason it's the criterion of all my other actions, the ultimate goal of all my other, instrumental motions. For *this* type of motion, again, "to persevere" and "to expand" are exactly the same, just as the motion of a projectile and its endeavor to continue and extend that motion are one and the same thing.[25] To be moving a certain way is to be trying to continue to move that way. For it is infinite motion of this particular type without any negation. Indeed, it is the "self-creation" (*causa sui*) of Substance in a finite and determinate mode: in each moment God re-creates me, said Descartes, which Spinoza now reinterprets to mean: I *am* Substance's power to re-create me at every moment. My continuing to be me, my own conatus, is God's command that I exist and continue to exist: my desire to live into more and more moments and more and more situations *is* God's continual re-creation of me in each moment. There is nothing intrinsic to this motion that would limit it; in its essence it is this motion and the tendency to continue this motion forever, to overcome whatever external thing (in the existence series) gets in the way.

As an existent being, I am involved in all kinds of actions. However, most of them seem to be terminated by me even before they are cut off by external forces—they have "privations" in the sense of something considered to belong to my own nature that I nonetheless negate. This is because they are merely instrumental to my real desire, my conatus—they are the way my real conatus is expressed in a particular, externally determined situation. My conatus is the one action I'm involved in that involves no intrinsic negation at all—that's precisely why it is an essence (i.e., part of the first series). Its negations all come from its inadequate relations, that is, its place in the second series ("existence"). Imperfection is a matter only of existence, not of essence: all essences are perfect and eternal. In letter 36, to Hudde, Spinoza says:

[Imperfection] means that a thing lacks something which nevertheless belongs to its nature. For instance, [any instance of] Extension can
only be said to be imperfect in respect of duration, position or quantity,
namely, because it does not last longer, or does not retain its position, or
is not greater. But it can never be said to be imperfect because it does not
think, since nothing of this kind is required by its nature, which consists
only in Extension, that is, in a certain kind of being, in respect of which
alone it can be said to be limited or unlimited, [or what are synonymous:]
imperfect or perfect.[26]

In one sense, this imperfection is just an *ens imaginationis*. Strictly
speaking, everything is perfect in being what it is (i.e., in its whatness, its essence), for everything coincides exactly with its own individual nature and
is absolutely necessary. In fact, "nature," "essence," "form," and the like are
all just words for the Idea of a thing, which is none other than that thing itself considered through the Attribute of Thought. But the term "its nature"
is an "aid to the Imagination" that merely allows us to designate that with
respect to which something can be limited, or exceeded, by something else
(as in E1d2). All modes of any Attribute can be exceeded by other modes in
that Attribute. Extension is less perfect (more limited) if it is less extended,
less of those things that pertain to extendedness qua extendedness—less
firmly positional, lesser in size, and less enduring.

But this goes also for specific essences, like my conatus: I can be perfect
or imperfect only with respect to my specific conatus. A horse qua horse
would not be made more perfect by become a human; it would merely be
destroyed. And likewise, 1/3 doesn't want to become 2/3; it wants to become 1,000,000/3,000,000 or the like. Nor do we humans want to simply
become "one with God." That would mean our destruction. What we want
is not to be God (for that would just mean God being God, and God is already being God just fine), but for *myself* (not my conscious recognition of
myself, but my conatus) to be God. My conatus is really seeking to express
itself more fully, with less restriction. I am my conatus to a greater or lesser
extent. How so?

What is the conatus of my body? It is a specific ratio of motion and rest
that is identical to its own tendency or endeavor to extend that motion to
infinity. It is only prevented from doing this, being this one way of expressing infinity, because as existent, it is hemmed in on all sides by other existences, which restrict its tendency to keep doing what it's doing forever and
in all places. Its restrictions, however, can only be in terms of limitation in
extent (in space, in duration, or in position). That means that the *range* of
application of this ratio is limited. It is itself the endeavor to extend further

in space and duration and to cover a greater range of ideas. If my ratio is 1/3, say, it is limited in that 1/3 extends only over this small range of space (my body): only the elements of my body are in the 1/3 arrangement. To extend, it would be to have more physical power, extent, duration, and position. The same applies to my mind, which is just the same mode as understood through the Attribute of Thought. In this case, this expansion would mean a greater number of ideas that can coexist with the 1/3 arrangement—that is, "I" am able to become aware of a greater number of things. For in being aware of some idea, I am placing that idea in some kind of 1/3 arrangement with other ideas. Two stones and three stones, plus two trees and three trees, plus two cats and three cats, seven million pizzas and twenty-one million pizzas, and the ideas of all these . . . This is the picture painted by the Lemmas in E2: I can retain my nature in spite of changes in (1) size (range, extent) and (2) elements composing my ratio. The ratio remains constant but the items arranged in that ratio are greater or fewer in number, including more or fewer types of materials, covering a greater or lesser range of Extension. In Thought, I (i.e., the ratio) think (i.e., incorporate and arrange in this ratio, without being destroyed) a greater or lesser variety of ideas (ideas of differing materials extending over a greater or lesser range).

What I want is, not to be God, but to be Brook's-conatus-as-God! Not for all things to be, but for all things to be included in Brook's conatus. Not for all things to be known, but for Brook's mind's conatus, his own peculiar ratio, a particular *rhythm and style* of understanding, to know all things. It is not enough for me to be joined to "the" infinite; the real infinite is infinite *in infinite ways*, and my essence is one of those ways of being infinite. My conatus is this essence plunked into the existence-series, endeavoring to express its own infinity, to become infinite in its own way also in the existence-series, to contain infinite things, not as they are in God per se, but as they are in God insofar as he is modified, expressed as Brook's essence, and felt as his conatus. I do this not by becoming God, but just by (1) understanding more things adequately, which enables me to experience more ideas and move my body in more ways—to affect more things as adequate cause and be affected by more things as the power to sustain their incorporation without perishing; (2) behaving rationally in social cohesion with other rational agents, so that we collectively have greater causally efficacy than we would in isolation; and (3) expanding my love for my own body/mind into love for God, as the Substance of which my body/mind is a mode, and thus conceiving my own body/mind more adequately (i.e., as a necessity or even tautology in God) and expanding the range of my mind to include "more of" what is eternal—understanding each thing through the Third Kind of Knowledge as another expression of God's essence, as another infinite and eternal expression of infinity, each of which is likewise a style of being subsuming all other things into the eternal style of its mind, including myself. Thus does the "selfishness" of my conatus, my Will to expand my very specific selfhood to swallow up everything in the world, impressing it with my very specific style of being, become also a Will to an infinity of alternate ways of being, to alternate infinities: the full convergence of finitude and infinity, going beyond itself as a way of being more of itself, and vice versa. And we will see this key convergence in all our atheist mystics in one form or another.

The entire existence series as a whole is caused by God as considered absolutely — this is the first mediate infinite mode, "the face of the entire universe." But each particular existing finite mode is caused in two ways: (1) by the infinite sequence of existences that precede it — the occasioning prior determinate mode or modes, and (2) by the essence (the light coming through the window) directly from God. The "power of existing" of both derives necessarily from God, but the concatenation within inadequate causes is true only of the existence series. That there is X at all — that is, that there is X in the essence series — is directly due to God's activity: it is his infinite activity expressed in a specific manner. Following Garrett, we take this formal essence of X to be one of the mediate infinite modes, and as such it is eternal and omnipresent. But that this X is occurring right here and now in the existence series is only indirectly due to God as considered absolutely. Its proximate cause is rather the previous determinate mode or modes, which are God too, but they are "God insofar as he is modified in a particular way." Spinoza's conception of my finitude and my infinity, their convergence and their divergence, requires us to understand both of these at once as well as their relationship to one another.

For Y to be the essence of X, Spinoza says, it is not enough that X cannot be conceived as existing without Y. It is also necessary that Y cannot be conceived as existing without X (E2p10cs). On this ground, he denies that God is man's essence: God can be conceived as existing without man, or without this man, or without Brook (E2p10). If the being of Substance pertained to the essence of a person, then Substance being given, this person would necessarily be given. But this is not the case. Brook does not necessarily exist. That is, there are times and places in which Brook does not exist, which is not the case with God, with a necessary and unconditioned being. There are states of being that do not involve Brook.

But in E1p33s2, Spinoza states what seems a contradiction of this: God cannot be conceived of as existing without his decree that any particular thing exist. He is not prior to his decrees but coeternal with them, and indeed they constitute his own essence: he cannot be conceived without them any more than they can be conceived without him. No thing could be other than it is without God being other than God is. This is the final straw of necessitarianism: nothing could ever be any different from the way it is because God's nature could not possibly be any different from it is, and *God's nature is nothing other than his decrees themselves*—his *causing* each thing to be exactly as it is. If God did not make me exist, he would not be God. In this sense, God depends on me in order to be God, it would seem—and this would seem to make God pertain to my essence by Spinoza's own definition: I cannot be conceived without God, and God cannot be conceived without me.

But this is not exactly the case. Is it the case that he cannot exist without me, without my *actual* essence, my conatus *as felt in a particular place and time*? No. Rather, God cannot be conceived without the ratio of motion and rest that this felt conatus is endeavoring to maintain; that felt conatus is this ratio itself insofar as it exists at a particular time, when the chain of finite causes opens the shutter to let its sunshine in. This ratio itself is my formal essence, and it is this that is the decree that I exist, as necessarily entailed in the nature of God. God cannot exist without the "decree" that I exist and that I exist exactly as I do and do exactly what I do. That decree is not my existence. That decree is the *demand* that I exist. That is what is eternal. That is what is present to me *as*, in the form of, my actually existing essence (E3p7). The latter is my conatus: my own *desire* to exist, to continue to exist, and all other desires I have are manifestations of that desire when facing some particular externally encountered situation.

My desire to exist is God's *command* that I exist. Put a bit less anthropomorphically, my desire to exist is the universe's *need* or *necessity* for my existence. This need, which I feel as my own-most self and life force, is eternal and omnipresent. This is something that follows from the definition of an infinite thing, God. And therefore it is itself eternal, by Spinoza's definition: "By eternity I mean existence itself insofar as it is conceived to follow necessarily from the definition alone of the eternal thing" (E1d8).

So what perishes? My existence. What is eternal? My essence. What is my essence? My formal essence is present to me as my actually existing essence, as its manifestation in a particular time and place, which is my conatus—my desire to exist. This is what is eternal and omnipresent: my desire to exist, which is my experience of the eternal demand that I in particular exist; it is God's eternal decree, inseparable from his own essence, with is none other than his own existence, that demands that I must exist, and it is this which actually causes me to exist.

My duration of existence is just another name for my existence. As he explains in chapter 4 of part 1 of *Metaphysical Thoughts*, "From this it clearly

follows that duration is distinguished only by reason from the total existence of a thing. For as much as you take away from the duration of thing, so
much you necessarily take away from its existence."[27] My existence is a certain patch of the total existence of things that are in God. There are expanses
beyond its reach. As much time as I occupy is as much of me as there is.

There are expanses of God that are not me. Hence, it is possible for something to be God and not to be me: this is what Spinoza means by saying my
essence is not the divine essence. But there are no expanses of God that are
conceivable without the desire for me to exist and to exist in the amount of
God in which I do, in fact, exist. God can exist without me existing in 1485,
but God cannot exist without me existing in 1966. At all times and places,
for all eternity, there will be built into the world the desire, the demand,
the absolute command that I exist for at least fifty-nine years, beginning in
1964. There can be no world, no existence, no God, without this decree. I
feel this decree directly and precisely right now as my desire to go get some
breakfast. That desire, which is really just a mutation in form of the basic
desire that my body should exist, is eternal and omnipresent.

And to understand just is to understand *necessity*.[28] To understand necessity is to understand the necessity of all that happens to me and all that
I do, in the nature of a necessarily existent being. Our purpose, in this purposeless, infinitely purposed, everywhere autopurposed universe, is just to
understand our purposes as a function of our preexistent essence, which
itself is a necessary entailment of the absolutely necessary being. The next
step is to see necessity as tautology: the Intuition that my essence, felt as
my conatus, is not just a necessary entailment of the infinite, as if these were
simply two distinct things, but is itself the infinite, as expressed in this particular way, a way that is itself necessary and infinite and omnipresent. But
I must also see the infinite series of determinate events that affect me externally, and therefore my endless stream of inadequate ideas, as the equally
necessary existence series, which itself is a necessary inadequate idea that
comes with my equally necessary finitude.

It must be stressed, then, that Spinoza has finally given us a way to understand ourselves here as necessarily both *infinite and finite*, as constantly
confronted with infinite externalities and constantly all-encompassing—in
an exact description of the human condition, the precise phenomenological description of life, I submit, when cleared of monotheist prejudices and
their aftermath. The desire to exist I feel as my innermost self, my conatus,
my general Will to continue to be me, is the full infinity of God—eternal,
all-encompassing, indivisible, omnipresent, as space is encompassing of
all possible form and expressed in the laws of all movements of all bodies, indivisible and whole in each: that is what I'm feeling at the bottom

of myself as myself when I desire, move, act, love, or hate. I feel and know myself, not only as eternal, but also as infinite, as a manner in which the indivisible nature of God expresses itself, that is, as conatus, as the desire to exist and produce, to express myself in all possible ways, in all possible modes, to be infinite in infinite ways: in short, the very essence of God qua God, but expressed in this particular, determinate way. But this infinity that is my essence confronts an infinity outside itself, beyond itself, other than itself, as the temporal infinity stretching out beyond my grasp in perception (i.e., grasped only inadequately via "Imagination" in Spinoza's terms), undermining me, blocking me, overwhelming me; it is infinite precisely as infinitely other. That infinity is also God—the very God that is the infinite desire to exist and infinitely express myself that I feel as my innermost self.

Though I may not know the exact character of the decree of God that is my specific essence among all the essences that God necessarily wills, I experience the necessity itself of that willing in and as my own Will. My desire to exist—purely qua desire, purely qua necessary, causal efficacy—is the entire nature of God itself. This is the same internality, necessity, adequacy— the same tautology (completeness, nonseparation of cause and effect) I see when I view *any* event adequately, that is, in terms of necessity, and finally in terms of tautology with my own conatus. If I view these adequately but via the Second Kind of Knowledge—the Understanding, or Reason—I see these as separate but necessarily related expressions of the global necessity that is God, as I might understand, of an equilateral triangle, that it necessarily has the property of being equiangular and also necessarily has the property of having a surface area equaling $\sqrt{3}/4 \times (\text{side})^2$. I can see these as two separate facts, each of which is necessarily and inseparably related to the nature of the triangle as equilateral. But in the Third Kind of Knowledge, Intuition, this division of steps vanishes. The link of necessity collapses into tautology: I grasp the nature of the triangle as a whole, all at once, and I understand any particular property I see as directly and inseparably an expression of that totality, which is accomplished by the triangle itself. That is what it means to experience myself, and the world, "from within," that is, to experience it from the standpoint of withinness itself, of necessity, of tautology, of nonseparation. Experiencing my desire to exist is like being an angle of this triangle, like experiencing my own specific angularity. Coming to see my angularity as necessarily entailed in the triangle is like coming to understand the equiangularity of this equilateral triangle and also understanding that my own specific angularity is a necessary entailment of it. This is a metaphor for understanding my conatus to be an eternal, necessary, omnipresent mode of God, following from his nature. Now once I have done this, looking at something else in the universe—that chair over there, for example—is like seeing some other aspect of the triangle in which I have my being, for example its surface area. Understanding *its* necessary entailment in God is like grasping that the area of the equilateral triangle is $\sqrt{3}/4 \times (\text{side})^2$, and as such has a necessary relation to the angularity that is me through the medium of our shared necessary entailment in the nature of the triangle itself. Both the equilateral triangle's equiangularity and the formula for its surface area exist as long as the triangle does, and they are omnipresent throughout the triangle. Understanding the surface area as likewise necessarily following from the nature of the triangle means to see both it and me as simultaneous necessary effects of the totality of the productive power of the triangle as a whole, of what necessarily follows from its nature. The very productivity—the following, the necessity, the inseparability—is the infinite whole, which expresses itself in all these ways. The necessity felt in each case is the whole *as* that case: it is the whole nature of the triangle as this essence, pervading the entire triangle forever.

The universe is, of course, infinitely more complex than a triangle, and it has infinitely more properties, infinitely more things that necessarily follow from it. To see myself as separate and finite—to see all things around me as separate finite things, to see causality without seeing necessity—is to see each angle as a brute fact and to see the fact that the three angles are equal as a coincidence. I experience my relation to other things initially via the Imagination, as nonnecessary. When I discover my equality to them, this reveals to me something necessary about my own nature and my relation to infinity. When I discover that the area of the triangle follows necessarily from the nature of the triangle, I also discover something about my own nature, which also necessarily follows from it. When the area of the triangle interacts with the angle I am in such a way as to produce effects that do not follow from my nature qua this angle considered in isolation, I know that they follow from my nature qua equiangularity considered as a necessary and inseparable aspect of the nature of the triangle. I experience the transition from one moment to the next as the same triangle considered in another way, something else that follows necessarily from it. I experience the world both finitely (imaginatively, contingently) on the one hand, and infinitely (necessarily, adequately, rationally) on the other. In the former, I feel awe at the infinity of otherness that is God qua eternal; the sublime overpowers me as if I were a very small speck in the ocean of being. In the latter, I am that otherness, and all transition to otherness is the further unfolding of my nature, the necessary and inseparable expression of what I am, It is what I feel myself to be as my own conatus, my own desire, that is that ocean, that productive power, that necessity itself as a whole. And I must always experience both: even my finitude is necessary, my inadequate ideas are necessary, my Imagination is necessary too. My externality is also internal, and my finitude qua finitude is also the infinite.

I am infinity (God), facing infinity (God), as the limitation that makes me finite. To be is to be a mode of God, which is to be finite-infinite, infinite-finite. I am at the mercy of this external infinity, which dissolves me like a minute grain of salt in an ocean, drowns me, overpowers me, erases me. But that ocean is also me. The oceanic meets the personal here; the definite meets the indefinite: infinite is beyond any determination and yet every determination follows from and expresses its infinite (indeterminate) nature. To be indeterminate and formless necessarily entails expressing as modes, as determinate, finite ways of being, just as the infinity of space can only exist by being infinite spaces. I am eternal precisely as myself, but to be myself correctly understood, *sub species aeternitatis,* is not to be merely me, not merely confined to my boundaries, but to be the infinitely productive force that I feel as my own essence, which expresses itself equally and completely as every other possible mode. Spinoza is exploding precisely the either/or between finite and infinite—that is, the monotheist God. The explosion of that dichotomy is beatitude.

BEATIFIC VISION, SPINOZA STYLE

I am making tea. Shaking the leaves into the pot, I see that they tumble and twist through the air, bounce against the walls and bottom of the pot, and scatter there in all directions, ending up spread unevenly on the bottom. Then I light a flame under a pot of water, which soon starts to boil. I pour the water over the leaves and watch the leaves dance and flutter through it. A dark cloud of flavor-bearing molecules gradually diffuses around them into the water.

There is a knock on my door, startling me. As I turn toward it, my elbow hits the teapot and knocks it off the cabinet. It crashes onto the floor, sending boiling tea and shards of porcelain flying in all directions. My reflex step away crashes a foot down on a shard in a puddle of boiling hot tea, giving me a slight cut and a slight burn simultaneously. Cursing, I hobble to the door. It's my neighbor, a divorced dad who, in trying to find an activity for his eight-year-old daughter on his custody Sundays, has repeatedly brought her and their recent baking project door to door: "Would you like a cupcake?" she asks. I absolutely do not want a cupcake, but to be polite I take one, immediately dumping it in the trash once the door is closed. Then I go to put antiseptic and a bandage on my foot, angry at the pain and the mess that I will have to find a way to clean up in spite of my injury.

If I am a Spinozist, though, this is how I am experiencing this event: as the beatific "intellectual love of God," which is God's love for God—or to put it plainly, the universe itself taking joy in the eternity and infinity of the universe, infinitely and eternally, in the form of my own experience. Watching the tea leaves flutter through the air, I am aware that each one is twisting through the air exactly as it does, and necessarily has to do, according to the laws of physics, as determined by the properties of space itself and derived necessarily in Euclidean geometry. Given the force of gravity and the precise angle of the packet of tea leaves over the pot, and given the velocity and amplitude of the shake communicated through my arm muscles due to impulses in my nerves coming from my brain, each leaf flies and twists and impacts and bounces in a precise trajectory. It could not be even minutely different from what it is, given those initial conditions. But those initial conditions could not have been different from what they were for exactly the same reasons: my desire for tea and decision to make it are exactly as necessary and exactly as precise. They could not have been different without the universe being different, *and the universe could not have been different* for the exact same reason. *That* there is *any universe at all*, and that there is precisely *this* universe, are both necessary down to the last detail in exactly the same way. The question, "Why is there something rather than nothing?" is a nonquestion, a category mistake: even putative nothing—an infinity of silent, empty space, for example—would have been something, and whatever there was would have been there necessarily, even if it were nothing. But actually, "nothing" is a contradiction in terms: the *least* possible assumption forces me to assume an infinite plenitude of being that are infinitely producing infinite things. I don't need to import a special intervention into nothingness to produce this; rather, I just need to see that my assumption that a special intervention into nothingness was needed was itself a faulty idea based on self-contradictory assumptions. The most "nothingy" of nothingnesses is actually the most robust and inexhaustible plenitude of infinite being.

The leaf is an expression of infinity. My body is also an expression of the same infinity, and my mind is just my body viewed in a different way. Each of my experiences is something happening to my body, to my mind, or something that is necessarily generated by the nature of my body, of my mind, as a conclusion is necessarily generated by a premise. This, Spinoza says, is the only intelligible way to understand what is meant by causality, by an effect being caused by a cause. It is one of the things that follows necessarily from that necessarily existing infinity, which is indivisible and infinitely generative of necessary consequences. Among the ways in which my body is affected is by seeing the tea leaf. That is a fragment of an experience that can be supplemented to become a thought about the necessity of the tea leaf and its motion as it flutters, down to the last detail. When I supplement this perception with other ideas, ideas of its necessary premises, so that it is seen as part of a larger idea involving necessity, the quality of the experience is radically altered: it is changed from something that happens to me into something I am doing. In seeing the tea leaf in this way, in terms of necessity, I am experiencing an increase in my power to understand, which Spinoza tells me is the same as my power to act. For "action" as opposed to passivity means that what I do follows from what I am, as a conclusion follows from a premise, rather than as inflicted on me by something external. My mind is thus "active" to the extent that I understand necessity, for necessity is some part of my mind, that is, an idea, which brings about a consequence purely and solely by virtue of what it is itself. So by understanding this event as necessary, what I am, what I'm able to do, is now shown to be more than I previously thought it was. For the idea of necessity, of infinity, is also part of my mind since nothing can exist or be conceived apart from the idea of infinity. Actually, the idea of infinity is always actively involved in every thought and experience I have, for it is a premise without which they are unintelligible, just as I cannot understand what "motion" is unless I already understand what "space" is. I cannot understand what a finite being is unless I already understand, albeit tacitly, what infinity is. For a finite being in space always presupposes more space around it, and thus an infinity of indivisible space. All determinate beings are determinate because they are finite. So to have any characteristics at all, to experience anything at all, is to engage some finitude, and all finitude involves boundariedness, which involves what is beyond the boundary, and so ad infinitum: hence, infinity. When I make the connection between that innate and inescapable thought — "infinity" — and whatever is happening now, when my power of thought is able to draw out from that premise the necessary further thought that "necessarily infinite things follow in infinite ways," then this idea of infinity in me and what follows from it, considered purely in itself, is experienced as actively producing whatever happens to me. Since that thought of infinity is revealed to be innately a part of my mind, my mind is now revealed to also include this experience that this-tea-leaf-fluttering-left-13° is also a necessary consequence of my existence, of my mind, and thus *is* my own mind's activity.

I am aware of something in particular because I am something in particular, a specific determinate body, the awareness of which is my mind. That I am or perceive anything discernible is *necessarily* because I am finite: determination is negation. So I see that I am a finite body, and thus my essence does not involve existence, and not everything that I experience can be derived merely from myself (E2p10; E2p16). *Necessarily*, then, some of the experiences I have come from a conjunction of my body and causes external to me. *Necessarily*, I know those experiences inadequately, being only partially the cause from which they arise. That includes my perception of the tea leaves and teapot, and all other perceptions. I know these things imperfectly and incompletely, but *necessarily* so. What I can know perfectly is the necessary laws of motion as derived necessarily from the nature of space and matter, for I have an innate and complete understanding of what space and matter are by virtue of my experience of myself as finite and dependent. This is because the idea of finitude presupposes and involves an idea of infinity and the idea of a finite body presupposes and involves an idea of there being something beyond that finite body, and thus beyond any finite body; it is involved in simply knowing what a body is, knowing what finitude is—which I know by virtue of the very fact that I am not the sole initiator of all my experiences, that they come partially from outside. So "having perceptual experiences," or "being affected by causes beyond my control, which thus appear to me as contingent" are both *necessary*, and if I experience that necessity, I also increase my own power, one power of my mind that does, in contrast, derive entirely from my mind's own nature as a finite thing which, precisely as such, always involves the adequate idea of infinity (E2p47). As I can understand the necessity of trajectories and angles and bounces of matter, I can also understand the necessity of my own emotions and desires. So I know that I like and desire this tea because I have had previous experiences of drinking tea that affected my body in such a way as to increase my ability to act and thus the range of my being, and that those experiences have left impressions in my body, and also in my mind, that have been linked to other things labeled with the word "tea." Moreover, because I am finite and necessarily too weak in my power of imagining to know each in all particulars, I unjustifiably consider these other things to be individual instances of the universal tea, which allows me to (unjustifiably) expect that the new tea experience will also increase my power and therefore give me pleasure, and which I therefore *necessarily* desire. When certain conditions converged, I necessarily endeavored to make myself a pot of tea. My plan going awry was just as necessary; and so also necessary was my response to the plan going awry: I know that when something that causes me pleasure is obstructed or kept away from me, I necessarily feel pain. I know that when an external thing causes me pleasure (increases my power to act) I love that thing, so I love the tea, but when an external thing causes me pain (diminishes my power to act), I hate that thing, so I hate that I broke the pot and don't get my tea. I also know that when something helps the activity of something that causes me pain, and that I therefore hate, I will also hate that thing, so I hate my neighbor for startling and interrupting me and I hate his daughter for causing him to do that. But I also know that I can love and hate the same thing, since any single thing is associated with many other things and acts on us in many ways, including the default way of experiencing their pleasure as my own pleasure to the extent that I imagine us to be similar (E3p27), and as linked to various memories and associations of my own, so I also experience some pleasure and hence love for the neighbor and his daughter: I'm ambivalent toward them. Experiencing the necessity of all this in as much detail as possible, I thereby experience, in addition to my suffering, the pleasure of understanding, which is the pleasure of expanding the ability to act of my mind, which is also the expansion of ability to act of my body, and the revelation that more follows from what I currently am than had previously seemed to be the case, and since necessarily what follows from X is really more of X, that I am more now than before. But in experiencing this increased compatibility between the conatus of my own mind and some further singular event or thing and in understanding that this experience is one of the infinite necessary effects of my conatus itself, through understanding both to be necessarily entailed in God, I experience an increase in the power to act of my conatus. That means I experience pleasure. Because this pleasure is also associated with an external cause insofar as I am (merely) a part in the modal existence series and thus the infinite temporal series of events (including the external event and the dawning of this new adequate idea, this new understanding, in my mind), though also entailed in God, this pleasure is external to me. Thus, I experience this as love (which is "the feeling of pleasure associated with an external cause" [E3p13s])—of God, of the event, and of this newly added component idea of my own mind, which is also God's love of me, of the event, and of God—and is also the event's love of me, of God, and of the event itself. This is beatitude.

This is just the beginning, but let's pause here for a moment. The precision of each event as determined by the absolute source may appear to have some similarity to the monotheist idea that "every hair is numbered." But it differs in several ways, and these are crucial—for it is here, in Spinoza, that we will find *the ancient antithesis between design and infinity resuscitated and brought to its fullest expression*. First, Spinoza has broken the back of the *Noûs* as *Arché* tradition once and for all. The physical universe is not created for a purpose, nor indeed is it even created as something necessarily following from the nature of a nonpurposive, infinite mind. The material universe is produced necessarily from the nature of Extension itself—that of physical infinity, space, matter. All ideas, all conscious experience, on the other hand, *are* indeed the results of an infinite intellect: mind produces mind, matter produces matter, and these are, as we have seen, just alternate ways of designating the one infinite Substance, which is itself exclusively neither matter nor mind. Causality, however, does not flow from one to the other, and thus the old model of a planning, intelligent, designing mind disposing matter has been taken permanently off the table. The infinite intelligence in Spinoza is an infinite and eternal mode of Thought, to be sure; but (1) it is devoid of purpose, (2) it is devoid of free will (and thus plans, designs, etc.), and (3) it is the larger whole of which our own minds are parts. Free will and purpose are functions of the finitude, not the mindedness. For Spinoza, "Intellect of God" is a name for the infinity of ideas, which is itself just another name for the infinity of modes of Substance when considered in terms of the Attribute of Thought, which are at once the very same modes that are called bodies when considered in terms of the Attribute of Extension (or any other of the infinite unknown Attributes), with causal priority granted to neither one nor the other. Everything is thus causally necessary, down to the last detail; but Spinoza is careful to specify that this is by no means to be construed to mean that the universe is "orderly" as opposed to chaotic, that is, that it accords with some mental plan. Instead, "order" itself is just an inadequate idea that boils down to saying some arrangements of items is relatively easier to picture and imagine than others for our particular minds. There is no such thing as absolute order, and "Intellect" is not used to mean something that causes or guarantees or even *knows* the order of the universe: for there is none. The monotheist version of this idea meant there was an accountant keeping track of these details, which were underwritten by that accountant's purposive Will in creating them and ordered according to a plan. Here there is no accountant and no purposive Will. That is also why it is no longer a matter of being controlled by someone *else*, but rather an expansion of oneself: for necessity, as the antithesis of purpose, is the revelation that what seemed other is really self. My power of action is the infinite anti-God's infinite power of action as expressed in the finite, fixed, and determinate way that is me. This is therefore an inclusive rather than an exclusive oneness, which is manifest in the precise unfolding of each event, and thus it does not mean there is any relation of control, which requires an extraneous controller. The second point is directly related to the first, for the range of what is precisely unfolding is not all-inclusive. In the monotheist version, the precision is linked to God's care for "every sparrow that falls," which meant his concern that things turn out one way rather than another, with at least some *possible* outcomes being excluded and protected against. Here, however, both what goes according to any specific plan and what does not are equally necessary. The monotheist might be able to say, "Making the tea was your plan, but breaking the pot was the Will of God, the plan of God." But this is, of course, our main point about Compensatory

Theism as contrasted with Emulative Atheism: here, it is not one type of control replaced by another type of control, but rather that the *only* plans are finite plans, and thus what contravenes any finite plan is not due to the infinite plan but rather to the infinite planlessness that is infinite *necessity*. The infinite's determination of all events is not "control" because the infinite is not other to those events: this is what *immanent necessity* means. They are itself. We may note also that, even if we were to include the breaking of the pot in God's plan, most monotheists would probably have to exclude our own first-order anger at this event and our emotional lack of charitable feeling toward our neighbor as things for which we, rather than God, were responsible, for these are matters of Will. Or, if we were monotheist deniers of human free will (of which there are many), we would have to somehow conclude that, even if God willed us to be evil, there is something wrong with being evil that is *deserving* of punishment or destruction. For the real question is not whether *we* have free will, but whether *God* has free will. A monotheist may claim that either we do or we don't, but a monotheist must claim that God does. This is just what Spinoza denies for God, as he does for man: both function by necessity, which is the seeing of oneness in the disparate, and this is Spinoza's model of Emulative Atheism. Hence there can be no question of reward or punishment in any case, even if there are consequences that some finite beings do not desire. For Spinoza, the adequate as well as the inadequate ideas and experiences are equally determined, down to the last detail, by God. Beatitude depends precisely on accepting all of them, without exception, as completely manifesting that necessity and being known as such. If this is not done, they will, of course, suffer destruction. But this is not because of "deserving" it—a concept that drops out as soon as purposive creation does. There is no reward or punishment, though seeing all things as God does redeem them (as long as God is precisely the opposite of "God") and secure their eternity. Rather, as Spinoza says, virtue is its own reward: the reward is the increase in power and activity constituted by knowing them to be determined necessarily in God and by knowing thereby that the knowing of them, and they themselves, are eternal.

It's not just that I will feel the increase of my power, and thus joy, in contemplating the necessity of all these events. I am thereby to see them "sub species aeternitatis"—"as types of eternity." Recall again Spinoza's stunning circular definition of "eternity": "By 'eternity' I mean existence itself, insofar as it is conceived as following solely from the definition of something eternal," says Spinoza (E1d8). To exist is to be eternal. He explains: "For such existence, for example the essence of any thing, is conceived as an eternal truth, and thus cannot be explicated through duration or time, even if that duration is conceived as beginningless and endless" (E1d8). Eternity does not mean infinite continuation through time but rather timelessness: lifting entirely out of the PSR, to causality and sequence and arising and perishing, as it pertains to individual things in time. Spinoza's unique approach to this beatitude is a self-transcendence of the PSR through the radicalization of the PSR itself. The essence of anything is eternal, though its existence is not. Every whatness is eternal. For there is no difference between the possibility and the actuality when it comes to the essence: the essence is just the possibility itself. Thus, that there can be tea leaves in the universe follows solely from the definition of the eternal thing. Tea-leaf-iosity is therefore eternal. That means it is fully present even when there are no tea leaves in existence (though those temporary periods of time when they do exist *also* follow necessarily from the eternal thing, through the existence series in conjunction with the essence series). Tea can exist in the universe in the same way triangles can exist in space, while square circles cannot. Due to the nature of space, and that of triangles, squares, and circles, *there is* the essence of a triangle as an eternal possible mode of expressing space. Inasmuch as this mode of expression is present in other things, it exists: the triangle as aspect of a pyramid, for example. But *what* is expressed is, in all cases, the eternal nature of space itself, along with all that necessarily follows from that nature—and that always exists. As such, the formal essence of a triangle always exists as well. The existing form of this essence of a finite thing, again, is its conatus, its endeavor to keep existing—which is expressed derivatively in all its desires, expressed in turn in all its emotions and all its actions. What is expressed in all of these is the nature of the eternal thing, which is the only thing; it is no particular thing and all particular things. It is in seeing the necessity of our essence, of our own desires and actions—including our contemplation of the necessity of the teapot's breaking and our own reaction to it—and the failure to understand the necessity of other things that we see our eternity, and that we see that our seeing of our eternity is the eternal's seeing of the eternal's eternity.

For what is the greatest obstacle to this beatitude? "God." That is, the non-Spinozistic God, the God of the Imagination, the personal, omniscient, providential, creator-and-judge God, who makes things for a purpose external to their own activity. Atheism, the realization that such a God is literally and strictly impossible, is redemption. Our purpose is to keep becoming what we are. Becoming what you are means, in all the infinitely varied forms of endeavoring to express causally what you are in maximally numerous situations, to understand that what you are is this very endeavor, which is its own purpose and which is inextricable from the universe. God is the claim that you exist contingently, as the consequence of an act of Will that is not your own, and for a purpose that is not willed by yourself, that is, to please someone *else*—to please God.

This is our claim: it is *not* just that Spinoza arrives at a mystical beatitude in spite of his rejection of God, but rather that he arrives at it precisely due to his rejection of God. If God exists, no true spiritual life is possible. Fortunately, Spinoza thinks, he can prove that God does not exist—using precisely the premises of the proof of God's existence put forward by the most radical theologians. By simply thinking through their premises to the end, we can dispel the imaginary picture of a God who demands something of us beyond being what we are in as many ways as possible, which is what we are necessarily always doing anyway. We need to learn to do that very same thing *better*: that means to *understand* it, which means to understand it *as necessary*. This is the very opposite of questioning it or subordinating it to an external purpose. It is the very opposite of subordinating it to the purposes of God if these are in any way contrary to its own Will. Rather than Jesus's "Not my Will, but thine, be done," Spinoza gives us, "My Will is one among an infinitely diverse array of activities which are your Will, and it always has been, and necessarily must be; and my Will is best fulfilled by understanding precisely that my Will to be me is your Will for me to be me as much as I can, and to will what I will as much as I can." This means, first, to understand that whatever you are doing and whatever you have ever done is nothing but a necessary expression of your essence, which is the endeavor to continue to maintain your activity, your expression of your essence in causal effects, in as many ways and as many situations as possible. Then, second, it means to understand that this understanding itself happens necessarily, and then, third, it means to understand this necessity as a tautology, grasping both the oneness and the difference in a single apprehension, which is the most active, effective way of continuing that very activity. This is beatitude, and it is only possible when God is gone, exploded by his own proofs.

SPINOZA AND SCHOPENHAUER ON THE UNIVERSAL WILL AS UNREASON, REASON, AND BOTH

In a certain sense, the true inheritors of Spinoza's breakthroughs in rethinking God, Reason, and teleology to the point of their self-overcoming are the early Schelling and Hegel, who were turbocharged by the new tools provided by the Kantian revolution—above all in discerning and developing the conception of Beauty in the full convergence of purpose and purposelessness, as informed by Kant's "purposiveness without purpose," and the door this opens toward Spinoza's elimination of the theistic conception of a

planned universe. Since, according to Kant, purpose simply *is* the causal efficacy of a concept and concepts simply *are* ways to unify particulars, being
limited to no finite set of particulars, the infinite productivity of Spinoza's
unintentional, infinite, unity of infinities itself does the job that purpose
would do, but precisely as purposelessness, instantiated in an infinite plenum of purposes whose oneness resides only in their irreducibility to any
particular one.[29] Yet both Schelling and Hegel end up veering away from
this trajectory in their mature work.[30]

The post-Kantian inheritor of Spinoza who remains committed throughout his career to something closer to Spinoza's rejection of traditional theism is, rather, Schopenhauer. In the terms we've developed in our reading
of Spinoza here, we can easily see that what Spinoza calls God is simply
what Schopenhauer calls the universal Will: the indeterminate purposeless generative power that stands as the ultimate ground spitting forth all
existence, the *entirety* of which, not a mere part of which, each of us feels
as his own inmost self, as our own Will—for, being prior to the PSR and
all the categories of Understanding, it cannot be either one or many and
admits of no division into parts. For Spinoza, our specific conatus is an
eternal truth that necessarily follows from the nature of Substance, sharing
its eternity and infinity; for Schopenhauer, it is rather a "specific grade of
objectification of the Will," which forms our "intelligible character." Hence,
for Schopenhauer its specificity is a function of its objectification, not its
nature, and thus it can only obscurely feel itself as the entirety of the Will
that is present in everything and everyone (which is the basis of the feeling
of empathy at the basis of ethics), while for Spinoza its specificity is necessarily and eternally built into the absolute Substance as such, which can
be known through the Third Kind of Knowledge and also recognized in
the absolute necessity of all other things. Nevertheless, the blind drive that
is present to us as our own conatus, purposeless yet purpose-providing,
is what is omnipresent throughout Nature and is the true metaphysical
nature of the world. Schopenhauer himself acknowledged this connection to Spinoza, objecting only that there was no good reason to call this
universal Will by the name "God" except to praise and worship it—and
that, moreover, it was unworthy of such praise and worship since it was
a horror show of conflict, carnage, and suffering. Schopenhauer accused
Spinoza of, in effect, using the term *God* as an unexamined holdover from
raw monotheism—the assumption that the ultimate reality must be God
and that it must be Good—whereas he himself had broken away from this
blindness and called a spade a spade: the universal source of all reality is
a shitstorm of violence and frustration and pointlessness and is in no way

good or worthy of praise or worship; if anything, he says, it should be called the devil, ruler of this world.

But in reality, we may say it is rather Schopenhauer who is blinded by raw monotheist prejudices, and as Nietzsche keenly pointed out. In effect, Schopenhauer notices that this universal Will is certainly *nothing like Noûs* in any way, shape, or form: it does not intend the Good, it is not intelligent, it does not unify means under the umbrella of working toward a goal, and it does not priorly design things to make them good according to some notion of what the Good is. It is not teleological in the sense of progressing toward a single goal. But Schopenhauer is still under the thrall of the *Noûs as Arché* tradition insofar as he continues to cling to this as the only possible idea of what "good" might even mean. Spinoza, on the other hand, has genuinely moved away from this tradition: he sees all goodness as nothing more or less than a word for whatever is wanted by *anyone*, on the basis of the various desires and endeavors inherent to being a *conatus*, that is, to being a finite being at all. Being is simply necessary, and it is in no way a product of any prior conception or idea of goodness. In this his atheism actually runs deeper than Schopenhauer's, for as we have seen, this attitude toward the relation between goodness and being is a key identifier of deep structural atheism. Schopenhauer has an independent notion of what goodness should be. Since the universal Will does not accord with it, he declares the universal Will evil. Spinoza sees this universal, goalless Will as simply the nature of necessary being. Whatever it wants, however many things it wants, is by definition good, in the completely different sense that "good" just means "what someone wants." Good is just what is *called* good, and the various aimless manifestations of universal Will all call something good—that is, themselves, their own *conatus*. It is true that we are more good the more we resemble Substance, that is, the less dependent and more active we become, the more ways we can express the essence that we are. But that is precisely because goodness is a function of being, and specifically being what each of us is in particular, our conatus, our own, specific, actual essence, not the other way around: it is only the relation to what we ourselves are that counts in making something good, and the more of *that* goodness we get to be and experience, the "more" being we inhabit as ourselves, the better off we are—which really comes down to a tautology.

But this sense of goodness has a deeper significance if we again consider the problem of the PSR. For we have seen that Schopenhauer, precisely because he sees the world as evil and worthless through and through, conceives goodness as its precise antithesis. But Schopenhauer, with the help of newfangled Kantian conceptions of the transcendental *a priori* unavailable to Spinoza, conceives this antithesis as linked to the transcendence of the PSR in all its forms, thus seeing through the veil of phenomenal filters like cause-and-effect, premise-and-conclusion, time-and-place, purpose-and-motivation. When this happens, the Will stops its torturous, self-lacerating, onward trudge and we experience a moment of relief and clarity—in art, in music. Next, from that clarity, we can see objectively what the Will is—and then we turn against it, in compassionate morality, in asceticism, in denial of the world. Those are the only possible goods.

Spinoza is unarmed with the Kantian distinction between phenomena and things-in-themselves, so he has no quick exit from the PSR. On the contrary, he seems to absolutize it to an extent beyond anything ever before attempted, subjecting even God, and even nonexistence, to the stringent demands of the PSR: for God to exist, there must be a reason for him to exist (it turns out to be his own essence: he is self-caused); for anything even *not* to exist, some reason must account for its nonexistence. There would seem to be no escape at all from the PSR, and it is perhaps for this reason too that Spinoza is sometimes considered the supreme rationalist of all time. But as we've already begun to see, this is not at all the whole story. In fact, Spinoza's Third Kind of Knowledge is a return of all causality to God, to immanent self-causality—that is, to the peculiar form of necessity that requires nothing *outside itself* to be so: necessity is really seeing that what had seemed to be two different items are, in fact, tautologically one item, such as God's existence and God's essence. Spinoza absolutizes only one form of the PSR: premise-conclusion entailment. He completely repudiates the other three (motivation-and-purpose, temporal-and-spatial position, and efficient causality—the last of which is considered real but completely subsumed into premise-conclusion entailment) as having anything to do with reality as correctly understood: they are nothing more than aids to the Imagination at best. To see necessity is to see that the conclusion is entailed already in the premise, that it follows from that alone. But this means that the conclusion is really not anything new, not anything added: it is just an aspect of the premise that was there all along. The premise and the conclusion are one and the same thing, just variously viewed. We might say, in Kantian terms, that all true propositions are, in the end, analytic propositions, but a more precise account would be that Spinoza's view of all causality as immanent infinite productivity annuls the distinction between analytic and synthetic propositions. The necessary conclusion (effect) is not something added to the premise (cause) because the premise (cause) was never a simple, finite entity to begin with; it was a way of expressing infinity, and a true understanding of it must therefore reveal its necessary implication of every other thing that exists. The many are one only because each one is already many. And it is this Third Kind of Knowledge, where everything is folded back into the necessary kind of unity and infinite variety that pertain to God, where blessedness, beatitude, is found. This unity is the end of the PSR as normally understood, that is, where one thing depends in some way or other on something *else*. There is no more "something else" for Spinoza. And that means that his deification of the PSR is, at the same time, a transcending of the PSR: it is precisely by pushing it all the way to its extreme, by admitting nothing except logical entailment as the principle of all being, that he transcends the conditionality of the PSR in all its forms. This lifting of the PSR to contemplate things *sub species aeternitatis*, is, as in Schopenhauer's aesthetic experiences, the experience of beatitude. Although it is true that all things are locked into the matrix of causes all the way back to God, this is now seen, as we explored in the previous sections, to be the transcendence of the other-dependence that is normally conceived as endemic to finitude. Moreover, because this is beatitude itself and because Spinoza carries over no *Noûs as Arché*, monotheistic prejudices in his conception of what goodness means, he is able to declare as the highest good the contemplation of this eternity, this unconditionality, this infinity, this all-inclusive necessity and unity—which is experienced indeed as good in the same way anything is experienced as good, as the increase in the scope of our participation in being, of our range of the indivisible necessary power of activity itself. Spinoza does not condemn this purposeless, unordered, trillion-purposed, power-driven, and overpowering universal Will for its stupidity, its violence, its lack of planning, or its aimlessness and pointlessness, as Schopenhauer does in his nostalgia for another kind of good—the *Noûs* kind of good, which he clearly sees is not there. For this reason, Spinoza does not need to move beyond the aesthetic experience of the lifting of the PSR—in his case, through radicalization of the PSR—to the *denial* of the pointless, violent, self-conflicted, universal Will, now finally seen in all its horror, as Schopenhauer does. The PSR-free vision *sub species aeternitatis* of the universal Will in all its pointless, violent, self-conflicted, necessity is itself the beatific vision. Pointlessness and violence and self-conflict are themselves, when seen *sub species aeternitatis*, beauty, beatitude—the Good. In both the early Schelling and Hegel and later in Nietzsche and in Bataille, each in their own way, we see the continuation of Spinoza's approach and a departure from the ascetic world denial of Schopenhauer.[31] These must be counted as victories for atheism, for the *Noûs as Arché* standard is here falling away in favor of an immanent conception of the Good, as the full realization of self-affirmation of Being itself raised to the level of vision of the unconditioned. To put it paradoxically (and echoing a key Tiantai motif), evil seen as unconditioned is, ipso facto, good, for the goodness resides in the unconditionality, not in the content that is considered unconditioned. Or as Emerson said, "Money, which represents the prose of life, and which is hardly spoken of in parlors without an apology, is, in its effects and laws, as beautiful as roses."[32] It may be beautiful in its effect and laws—in its PSR, but only when that is absolutized and pushed, as in Spinoza, to the point of its self-overcoming. It is just this implication that comes to the fore in the work of Schopenhauer's great successor and overthrower, Friedrich Nietzsche.

CHAPTER 6

Nietzsche, or the Divinely Vicious Circle

In the bulk of his writings, Nietzsche presents himself as a classic Compensatory Atheist, and it is under this rubric that some his most characteristic doctrines must be classified: man must give himself a goal, his own goal, in the absence of a goal for the universe. Purpose is all-important, the highest value; willing liberates, and willing requires "a yes, a no, a straight line, a goal."[1] The goal Nietzsche proposes is the overcoming of man and the creation of the Overman.

But on closer inspection, it is not the goal itself that Nietzsche values, but rather the creative Will itself. The fact that this creative Will always needs to set up a purpose for itself is just an inconvenient detour. "Man would rather will nothing than not will."[2] Any goal is better than no goal: any port in a storm. What particular goal we end up pursuing is largely a question of what happens to be randomly available to pursue, and is not what really matters. "You say it is the good cause that hallows even war? I say to you: It is the good war that hallows every cause."[3]

This is, of course, the classic atheist inversion of Emulative Theism: we do not will what is good, but rather we call good whatever it is that we will. It is the creative Will itself, the value-giver, that genuinely has value. But that is a complicated sort of value.

Nietzsche's idea of the Will to Power is a uniquely compelling notion because in a certain way it is both a tautology and a self-contradiction. That alone would be a good recommendation for its inescapability, its claim to stand at a unique summit or limit of thought. For normally, what is tautological cannot contradict itself and what contradicts itself cannot be tautological. But the Will to Power does both. And this, as we have seen, is precisely the structure of thinking that conveys the convergence of finitude and infinity, of the conditioned and the unconditioned, found also in Zhuangzi, in Tiantai, in Spinoza, in Hegel: the negation as necessarily the affirmation, the affirmation as necessarily the negation.

It is a tautology in that "Will to Power" is really just a fancy way of saying

"Will" as such—all Will, qua Will, is Will to Power. For to will is simply to want it to be the case that what occurs is what you want to have occur, as a result of you wanting it. To will is to be willing that the Will has efficacy in bringing about what it is willing—that is simply the definition of willing. To want your wanting to make what you want to happen happen—that is Will; that is Will to Power. But this is also a self-contradiction in that, therefore, what Will really wants when it wants any object or state (call it X) to occur is not really X but the power to bring about X. In fact, the mere facticity of X is a limit to its power. Facticity itself, the "it was" as much as the "it is," is offensive to the Will as long as there is no way for the Will to affect it, no way for it to be the result of one's own willing, no way to experience it as one's own doing. Whatever is willed, once accomplished, thus also becomes a hated obstacle to the Will. All aims, all purposes, have this double status, being loved as the aspiration and inciter of the full creative Will but then hated as the limitation to further willing. No purpose can be ultimate, then; Will to Power is. Will to Power means that whatever X is willed, we must also (perhaps at some later time) will the opposite, the destruction of X or the overcoming or transcending of it. *This applies to "power" too*. That is, if "power" is thought of as any particular state, condition, or entity, it cannot be what Will to Power wants—Will to Power wants that *and more*. It wants to be *able* to do both any X and the corresponding Non-X, to transcend any limitations at all to its ability to move and bring about effects. We begin to see that Will to Power can well be regarded as simply a transcription of Spinoza's *conatus,* thought through in greater detail. But that means if I could only be powerful and not weak, that would be a limitation to my Will to Power, which would necessarily seek to overcome that boundary and attain what had previously escaped its abilities: the power to be weak and powerless. This is not merely a matter of the affirmation of infinite striving, the Compensatory Atheist attitude of valorizing control and purpose such that we strive to control as much as we can and affirm the joy of the infinite task of controlling more and more, even though we know there will always be more to do. Instead, the very univocity of purpose itself has been altered; control itself now has to be treated ambivalently. Dionysian loss of control must always stand behind and within Apollonian control. We may take seriously Nietzsche's early declaration that art is the true metaphysical activity of man, but only if we understand art as itself Will to Power in this way, as something other than merely an attempt to control. Yes, our own selves, like all living organisms, are art; they are Will to Power in the sense of dominating, subordinating, shaping, and controlling the multiple centers of power—the multitude of contending drives that compose us in an unstable combination. But this sort of creative art is the type of creativity

Schelling had singled out as the missed Spinozistic implication of Kant's *Critique of Judgment*: an art that is both conscious and unconscious, both purposive and unpurposive, and never quite in control of itself or completely aware of what it is doing, which is feeling its way through its material, improvising according to a vague instinct rather than trying to form things according to a preknown purpose. We are not created by God as conscious *Noûs*, as purpose fashioner—but equally we are not created by *ourselves* as conscious Apollonian *Noûs*; we do not deliberately form and dominate our constituent drives in accordance with a plan that is known in advance. In the year 1800, Schelling had floated the idea of a half-conscious God who creates the world as a genius creates, not as an artisan creates, that is, not from a fixed utilitarian idea in his head in advance of the work. This God of Schelling's doesn't know the purpose in advance. A novelist creates some characters and a situation: he *sort of* knows what he's doing, in some vague way, and you cannot say he is acting entirely without purpose—but he does not himself clearly know what his purpose is. This is just what, in ancient times, Plato had Socrates complain was wrong with poets: they cannot themselves explain what they did or what they were trying to say. Schelling's reappropriation of Kant's alteration of the idea of teleology gave him this idea of a world-spirit that creates all things *sort of* with a purpose but without being able to see in advance where it's all headed. Whether or not he *ever* has to see clearly what it's all about is perhaps the point that divides Schelling and Hegel: Hegel retains this notion of teleology at the base of his mature concept of the world-spirit realizing itself in history, but he feels the need to put full transparent self-awareness at the end of the process, the philosopher who knows all this is the world-spirit finally having made clear to itself what its purpose was all along, even if that purpose was just to have created the world and its history in precisely this groping, half-conscious, semipurposive way and then come to realize that this is what it has done. The early Schelling, the originator of this idea of developmental, world-spirit artist, puts the human *genius*, who remains equally conscious and unconscious of what he's doing, at the end of the process: thus, the world-spirit need *never* find out what its own obscure purpose was in unilaterally clear, conscious terms.

Now Nietzsche, of course, would reject the overall world-spirit as a unified agent with any unified project of any kind, whether to end in full consciousness of itself, as in Hegel, or in genius-like semiconsciousness of its own goals, as in early Schelling. But the point to be grasped about the Will to Power as it applies in irreducible multiplicity, as the process of temporary unities occurring severally at all points in the cosmos with neither a prior nor a resultant overall unity, is that it must be modeled on the (early)

Schellingian conception rather than the Hegelian, much less the Platonic or classical theist notion of creation via control and conscious purpose. That is, we are artists of ourselves as Schelling's world-spirit was an artist, not like Hegel's world-spirit, Plato's demiurge, or Christianity's God. Intelligent design, whether of the cosmos as a finished whole or of our individual lives, is not art. We form ourselves, not purposelessly, but also without any clear idea of a purpose, without trying to control the elements to fit into a particular purpose or plan. We do not have a purpose, but we are also not unpurposive: we are purposivity without purpose. We are, therefore, beauty, and beauty is the ultimate metaphysical category. Aesthetics is the true metaphysical activity of man. We are neither in control nor out of control of ourselves. Our controlling also feels like an obeying—not, needless to say, of a superior controller, but of its own imperative to undermine itself, to lose control. As Nietzsche has Zarathustra declare, the Will to Power must always walk crooked paths, always turning against itself, proceeding only in a zigzag. This is why, contrary to initial appearances, Will to Power is not the same thing as Will to Control—and indeed, it is an excellent antidote thereto.

This zigzagging and self-overcoming are well exemplified in Zarathustra's parable of "The Three Transformations of the Spirit," that is, the transformation from Camel to Lion to Child. And if we may be permitted to adopt this rubric as applying to, and helping us make sense of, the wildly contradictory strains that coexist in Nietzsche's writings, we can understand this precisely as a transformation from Theist to Compensatory Atheist to Emulative Atheist. That is, though the numerical bulk of Nietzsche's writings occupy the position of Compensatory Atheist, the Lion (including his critical works, his genealogical work, his psychological breakdowns and take-downs, his Enlightenment bona fides and Voltairean inheritances and continuances, his posturings of heroism and strident orders of rank, his creation of values and endorsing of purposes, his cultural evaluations and prescriptions), these are not his ultimate goals. His goals lie instead in the vision of Emulative Atheism of the Child, embodied in Nietzsche's notion of the Eternal Recurrence. The atelic and omnitelic, atheist mystical potentials that had lain hidden in plain sight in the autotelic circle, first posited by Aristotle and then revived by Hegel, are finally given their fullest expression.

The idea is almost disappointingly simple. Nietzsche himself seemed to realize that, even with all the fanfare he attached to it, there was no way to state it directly without making it sound flat, feeble, flaccid. So he decked it out in riddles, embellishing it with prophetic fireworks, with dwarves and snakes and poetry. But the bottom line is simply this:

All things, including us, are random combinations of forces—not exactly atoms, but centers of Will. These combine willy-nilly, with each exerting its force over whatever it can exert its force over, thus drawing its last consequence at every moment. There is no free will. The process follows with strict necessity at all times. The number of these combinations is finite, but time is infinite. Therefore, every combination has to recur an infinite number of times. Something similar to me—let's say something that is 98 percent the same—may happen to come together. But that will still not be me. It may do 98 percent of what I do, its life may be that close to mine, and the world it knows may be almost identical to mine and situated in an almost identical world history. But that still isn't me. The only combination that counts as me is this exact one: these exact particles, coming together in this exact form. Near misses are much more likely. But since time is infinite, that is irrelevant. Eventually the exact match will recur. It is just as unlikely to appear twice as to appear once, given infinite time, and just as likely. It is just as likely to occur an infinite number of times.

To me, the time in which I do not exist is nothing. Nietzsche thus gets to hold to his beloved Epicurean view. Death is nothing to us. My body is ultimately real and time is ultimately real. When I die, my consciousness disappears, but it returns when this body reconvenes. Only then will this consciousness recur. I will not be aware of the guy who is 98 percent like me. The only thing I'm aware of is this finite lifespan of mine. But it repeats an infinite number of times.

WHY NIETZSCHE THOUGHT SO HIGHLY
OF THIS WACKO IDEA

Never mind that the science no longer works for this idea. Never mind the failures of the nineteenth-century mechanistic physics, new ideas of infinity, new ideas of the structure of space-time, the Big Bang, entropy, quantum mechanics—all of which topple the obviousness and elegance of Nietzsche's assumptions. Never mind that he stole it from the ancient Greeks. Never mind that it may strike us, even, as a failure of nerve—the grandiloquence involved, the flimsiness of it all, the cartoon bluster, the sheer silliness. Why did he think it was so important?

Perhaps it was because it reconciled a number of opposites. Nietzsche thought it solved some philosophical problems by suggesting a convergence of several opposed notions, as we will see: eternal recurrence is equally mechanism and finalism, being and becoming, truth and fantasy, permanence and flux. It affirmed the materiality of the soul and the realness of death, but it also affirmed eternal life. It was the only kind of eternal life that he could reconcile with his materialism, his biologism. It is a singularity, a perfect coinciding, of finitude and infinity. It affirms our irreducible individuality without having to posit an immaterial soul. It even eternalizes our individuality. It does not subordinate this individuality to any higher being, nor to an immaterial doppelganger.

It motivates us, he thinks, to do things to beautify life rather than slandering it: we have to live life infinite times so we had better make it good. It is an eternity that affirms selfishness and self-beautification. It is a perfect coinciding of the fleetingness of the moment and the eternity of the moment: of the lightness and heaviness of being. It joined the Heraclitean and the Parmenidean concepts of becoming and being.

Each moment is fleeting, random, contingent, impermanent. But each moment stands firm in the structure of the universe eternally, as unchangeable as a Platonic Form. Every moment goes on forever—but it still goes. It is a still a passing, a transition. And this is important. A moment that does not go is not a moment. To provide the content of what happens, happening has to happen. It must go, and go away. It is creative, it creates beyond itself, and in so doing it destroys itself. But in destroying itself, it also asserts itself, establishing itself forever. Eternal return is a convergence of purpose and purposelessness.

Eternal return is also a convergence of "sameness" and "difference." But, as Gilles Deleuze suggests, it reverses the usual attempts to bring these two together. All previous systems bring difference under the umbrella of sameness. Difference is ultimately "the same" as sameness. In contrast, Deleuze says, "The eternal return does not bring back 'the same,' but returning constitutes the only Same of that which becomes. Returning is the becoming-identical of becoming itself. Returning is thus the only identity. But identity as a secondary power; the identity of difference, the identical which belongs to the different, or turns around the different. Such an identity, produced by difference, is determined as 'repetition.' Repetition in the eternal return, therefore, consists in conceiving the same on the basis of the different."[4]

To be in time is to always fail to really be what one seems to be—to fail to be what one is attempting to be, what one identifies oneself as. One is always a work in progress. One is always slipping away from oneself and can never really be what one is. If time is radically real, identity can never fully exist. You cannot step into the same river twice. Sameness is an illusion, and things have no "identity," no self-coinciding as between an essence and its manifestation, between reality and appearance, or between the concept and its actualization, until they return. Here difference is primary and identity is secondary, says Deleuze.

But perhaps we can simply say instead: here identity and difference are finally on equal footing. Or we can say that here there is no identity but difference, no difference but identity. Hegel tried this and failed, on this view, being encumbered by his Greek inheritances. In the end difference was subordinated to sameness.[5] What both want, though, is this: time is ultimately real and eternity is ultimately real. Time itself is eternity. *Time* and *eternity* are synonyms.

PROOF IN THE PUDDING

Nietzsche's Eternal Recurrence, though, is supposed to have practical implications. These show what he thinks is so good about it and how it differs from all previous attempts to get sameness and difference together and call them "time." It allows no escape from this life, from the earth, from being exactly who you are and living precisely the life you have lived. It means there is nothing at all for you beyond your own finitude. It means that if you want anything, you'd better do it now—there is no other life. Your Will is to be directed toward beautifying this little patch of time that alone is yours forever. It gives a standard for willing. Indeed, it redeems the Will. It makes Will free in the only way in which Will can be free.

In the Eternal Return, each moment is a necessary cause of every other moment. Each moment is also a necessary result of every other moment. To desire even one joy is thus to desire all things. What, then, should I will? I should will to create joy so intense that it will allow me to will everything else as the cause and effect of this moment of joy. The Eternal Return beautifies the world: it motivates the creation of joy as the sole good. What we should be doing all the time is trying to create the most intense joys. A true joy, a joy deeper than the sorrows beneath the superficial joys, will redeem and justify all the moments that lead to and away from it. If I can experience something so joyful as to want it with all my Will, I will desire all of existence. This is the redemption of all existence. Where I will with all my Will, there is beauty. And beauty is where I must will with all my Will.

The Will is tortured by its inability to change the past. That is the source of its resentment. Redemption would mean learning how to will backward: to say of each "it was" that "I wanted it so." The only solution is *willing backward*. Will is trapped by the irreversibility of time. It resents, it wants revenge, because it can only will forward. It is tortured by the unchangeability of the past. Eternal Return means that to will the present is also to will the past. Every past mischance must become the precondition of this present, this future, this act of willing itself in its self-affirmation. To require the past mischance as a necessary condition of a future victory is to will backward—that is redemption. Time moves both ways in this act of willing.

Nietzsche thought the eternal recurrence of the same would be horrifying to most people. It meant for him that there would be the nothing—meaninglessness—forever; meaninglessness multiplied indefinitely. Some might say that Nietzsche must have grown up with a stronger sense of meaning than the rest of us, and thus the loss was more traumatic. Meaninglessness—the lack of any unity, any goal—meant worthlessness for him. But meaninglessness extended forever is precisely meaning. Meaninglessness is conditionality, and conditionality forever—all-pervading, unescapable—is unconditioned, is being, is bliss; it is more meaningful even than *a* meaning. Nietzsche too glimpsed this: the eternal recurrence of the same is the convergence of the two extremes, Being and Becoming. And this too: the problem is not, is never, meaninglessness; it is the superabundance of meanings. Meanings are unavoidable. The problem is what to do with so many of them—how they relate to one another.

If zero is multiplied by infinity, is it infinity or is it zero? Or perhaps a piece of information about the relationship between zero and infinity? What if zero and infinity were alternate names for one another?

THE SAME LIFE AGAIN MAKES NO DIFFERENCE IF TRULY THE SAME

Here's why the Eternal Recurrence is meaningless, and therefore why it is truly profound and important: a moment of experience is closed off to being any other way than it is. For this reason, it cannot check against itself or against any other moment to see if it has repeated.

A moment of experience is what it is due to its context, its pace, its rhythm, its rise and fall, and its placement in the entire sequence of experiences. Sustaining a moment would make it cease to be the same moment. The extending of a state—of an experience or a moment—would not make it eternal. On the contrary, it would destroy the possibility of that moment being that moment. The only kind of eternity there could be for an experienced moment—for any state, for any experience—would be repetition. For this moment to repeat, the entire sequence of moments of which it is a part must repeat. The repetition would have to be exact; it could not include the slightest change. This means that, assuming it did not include the knowledge that it was repeating, its repetitions also could not include this knowledge. Even a moment in which the thought of eternal recurrence occurs could not *know* that it has recurred and will recur.[6] So the only way any experience could be eternal would be for it to repeat without knowing that it is repeating. It would have to experience itself as not repeating—that is, as fleeting, as noneternal. The only way a moment of experience could be experienced as eternal would be by experiencing itself as noneternal. The experience of eternity and of noneternity are indistinguishable. What would it be like to experience eternity? Just like this.

Not existing after death is something that will never *happen*. It will never be confirmed. No one will ever experience it. The eternal recurrence—its happening or not happening will never happen. It will never be confirmed, and it is impossible to experience. It thus has the structure necessary for all absolute truths: its opposite is indistinguishable from itself. In a round-about way, it fulfils the conditions of Spinoza's definition of Substance: it cannot be conceived as not existing. But why is that the case?

It is precisely because of the strict stipulation that *nothing*, not even the most minute molecule of experience, would be different. This means that "living this moment only this one time" and "living this moment over and over an infinite number of times" are *literally* indistinguishable. The fleetingness would be the same fleetingness. The nondisclosure of eternal recurrence would be the same nondisclosure of eternal recurrence. The sense that it is only happening this one time would be the same sense that is only happening this one time. The sense of imminent, irretrievable goneness of it would be the same sense of imminent, irretrievable goneness of it. There can never be any experience that could ever confirm or disconfirm it.

This is the very definition of meaninglessness, of course. But it is important to note that it is not just that no *empirical* experience could confirm or disconfirm it. It is that no *conceivable* experience could confirm or disconfirm it. Experience per se is defined in such a way that does not allow distinguishing whether it is true or false.

This does not tell us something about the idea of eternal recurrence—namely, that it is meaningless. Rather, it tells us something crucial about *what experience is*. It tells us something about the *necessary nature of experience*. It tells us something about *time*. What it tells us is this: a moment that is fleeting, that occurs only once and then vanishes forever, is *no different from* a moment that recurs forever, that is cumulatively going on *infinitely*! By the very nature of experience, an experience that goes on forever is identical to a moment that flashes forth just once and then disappears forever, never to occur again. This means that the nature of a moment of experience is such that it is equally valid to describe it as occurring once and as going on forever. The nature of experience, the nature of *time*, is such that it is ambiguous with respect to fleetingness and eternity.

A "moment of experience" can even be defined this way: it is that which can be/could be/is just as eternal as it is fleeting and just as fleeting as it is eternal. A moment of experience is the kind of thing that would be no different whether it was eternal or fleeting. It is what is indifferent as to fleetingness and eternity. It is what is neither fleeting nor eternal, what is both fleeting and eternal. This is because it has a start and a stop but cannot perceive beyond itself. This is because it is finite. Because it is finite, it is neither finite nor infinite, both finite and infinite. Because in the moment after I cease to exist, I do not know I have ceased to exist. Because I will never have confirmed my fear of ceasing to exist. Because there is no overlap of moments. Because each moment is all the moments that exist. Time is Tiantai.

In finding a convergence of purpose and purposelessness, Nietzsche was perhaps inadvertently restoring the deep atheist meaning to Kant's aesthetics, which had been briefly stumbled on by Hegel and Schelling. He has found that the world is justifiable and life is worth living only as an aesthetic phenomenon, only as beauty, but as tragic beauty, as beauty defined in a very specific and surprisingly Kantian way: as purposiveness without purpose. That is what the Eternal Recurrence unexpectedly delivered. Eternal Recurrence is an alternate version of the convergence of purpose and purposelessness. All existence is Will to Power—"and nothing besides!"[7] Insofar as there is nothing but Will, nothing happens without being willed—without *some* purpose. But like the infinite diverse conati of Spinoza, these purposeful events do not add up to a unity of purpose, a single purpose. They are, in fact, in deep conflict with one another, with each vying to overcome and master the others. Will wills, which means that it wills forward. But Will wills backward as well, to its own preconditions. In subordinating absolutely everything, past, present, and future, to its purpose, Will has identified with the purposelessness: "God as vicious circle," as Nietzsche put it with tongue in cheek—or perhaps not so tongue in cheek.[8] The universe has no endpoint, no final purpose: if it did, it would already have been reached long ago, to Nietzsche's way of thinking. That's almost the *only* thing we can know for certain. And yet the universe is a totality of purposes—all of them futile and fleeting and doomed—but also eternal and destined to achieve themselves again and again, infinitely and eternally.

For Spinoza, to be is to desire and to desire is always just an indirect way of desiring more of oneself, the continuation and the expansion of oneself. We desire because of what we are, and what we desire is what we are. For Nietzsche, my desire for power over other things—my war against other things as embedded in my specific being and my specific purpose—is also a desire for myself again: for more of myself; for an eternity of my finite self. It springs from me, it is me, it posits what it wants as good, and ultimately that is one form or another of it wanting itself again. It also seems to want to go under, to destroy itself, to go beyond itself. These two desires finally converge in the Eternal Recurrence. By going beyond itself, it reaches itself.

By going under, it returns. By submitting to otherness, by failing, it sets the conditions for its own rebirth. But by ultimately reaching a joy in self deep enough to justify every condition as a condition for what it wills, its own arbitrary, pointless purpose takes on the purposelessness of the whole and affirms it as part of *its own* purpose—its own pointless, contingent, random, finite purpose. It is here that we have the tragic beauty of doomed Will as the real metaphysical depth of man.

Nietzsche was responding to and turning against the Schopenhauerian doctrine of the denial of the Will. Deeply apprehending and internalizing the justification, profundity, and necessity of this doctrine, he also read it, along with his own readiness to internalize it, as symptomatic of a larger nihilistic trend swallowing up almost all existing spiritual culture. The response against the total repudiation of willing and desiring (which are not exactly equivalent, as Nietzsche himself had shown, yet importantly similar),[9] borrows heavily in both cases on the precise formulations of the targets of their critique: Nietzsche's affirmation of the Will relies on a radical twist on the Schopenhauerian doctrine of Will, but one that is unintelligible without that premise.

In "On Redemption," close to the end of part II of *Thus Spoke Zarathustra*, Zarathustra redescribes the old Schopenhauerian problem of Will and suffering in strikingly novel terms:

> To redeem that which has passed away and re-create all "It was" into "Thus I willed it!"—that alone should I call redemption!
>
> Will—that is the liberator and joy-bringer: that is what I taught you, my friends! And now learn this as well: the will itself is still a prisoner.
>
> Willing liberates: but what is it called that puts even the liberator in fetters?
>
> "It was": that is the will's gnashing of teeth and loneliest sorrow. Powerless with respect to what has been done—it is an angry spectator of all that is past.
>
> Backwards the will is unable to will; it cannot break time and time's desire—that is the will's loneliest sorrow.
>
> Willing liberates: what does willing itself devise, that it might be free of its sorrow and mock at its dungeon?
>
> Alas, every prisoner becomes a fool! Foolish too the way the imprisoned will redeems itself.
>
> That time does not run backwards, this arouses the will's fury; "That which was"—that is the stone which it cannot roll away.
>
> And so it rolls stones in fury and ill-humour, and takes revenge on whatever does not, like itself, feel fury and ill-humour.

Thus did the will, the liberator, take to hurting: and upon all that can suffer it takes revenge for its inability to go backwards.

This, yes this alone, is what *revenge* itself is: the will's ill-will toward time and its "It was."[10]

This is a radical rethinking of the Schopenhauerian problem of willing. The problem here is no longer the blindness and insatiability of the Will as such, conceived by Schopenhauer in post-Kantian terms as beholden eternally to its unchangeable essence of restless dissatisfaction. This was because its metaphysical status as thing-in-itself put it beyond the sway of the phenomenal Principle of Sufficient Reason, hence beyond the principle of individuation in time and space, and therefore beyond the possibility of ending as a result of (i.e., being satisfied by) any particular temporal action. Rather, Zarathustra gives us, not a conflict between the Will as atemporal thing-in-itself and futile phenomenal temporal attempts to satisfy it, but rather declares that the Will's usual self-defeat lies in its own temporal structure. We are told that the *impossibility of willing backward* is the source of the Will's self-conflict and suffering, which are what produce the need for the slanderous claim that all existence *deserves* its suffering, which marks the end of the innocence of becoming and thus the source of the drive for retributive remorse and revenge. Will wills in only one direction: toward the future. It is impotent with regard to the past. Hence it is always structurally doomed to less than total satisfaction, to banging its head against an unmovable wall. Will to Power really wants nothing except *more power*; whatever finite goals it may posit are always just temporary proxies for its real goal, which is, not to attain X, whatever it is, but to *be able* to attain X and whatever is beyond X. Once X is attained, and proved attainable, X is necessarily no longer of interest and Will to Power must expand to find some other object—it must demonstrate ever increasing numbers of diverse capabilities. In this way it can never rest finally at any finite attainment. It cannot really be satisfied unless *all that exists* is willed by its own Will, is brought to being by its willing it to be so, in a demonstration of the limitlessness of its own power. For Will only affirms what it can see as "thus-I-willed-it," and unless Will to Power can affirm universally, or at least affirm itself—its entire life—exceptionlessly, it can never be satisfied: Will to Power always wants *more*. It craves expansion, the overcoming of resistances, the overstepping of limits. But every moment of willing simply arrives too late for it, the Will, to have been in charge of forming its entire world and its entire life according to its own image; it is premised on a prior givenness. Will to Power is thus always, to some degree, suffering, always frustrated—as Will in general is always, according to Schopenhauer, in need of redemption. Even the most powerful being, the most idealized satisfaction of Will to Power, would be powerless here, being unable to change the past. If this is the case, and all is Will to Power, then all is suffering. It is not just that there is always an indivisible remainder of being, however small, that the Will can, in principle, never touch, though this single exception to its power would already be enough to drive it to crazy paroxysms of folly and vengefulness. It is that even an omnipotent Will that has always experienced only what it has itself willed, if constrained to the structure of time that is inseparable from the future orientation endemic to willing as willing, will be faced with its own past deeds as no longer its own action but rather as a limit on its action. It is trapped, then, in a prison of its own making, constantly willing, since that is its nature, but with no possibility of attaining anything that would really be worth anything, by its own standards: what it really wants is never some specific thing but rather its own increase of power in attaining that thing, yet its power is intrinsically self-limiting and self-conflicted; its very successes form the walls of its own prison. Whatever it attains through its actions limits its ability for action all the more. Thus willing inexorably wills, but there is nothing really commensurate with its desire for the total power of affirmation: it is doomed to posit goal on goal, investing each one with value only to be frustrated each time with the horrific realization that since each becomes a past after being attained, and thus a limit to what the Will can do, there is nothing worth wanting and nothing worth doing.

For Nietzsche, this vengefulness toward all being—this impulse to *blame*—is based on a misapprehension about the Will itself. As he puts it in *Twilight of the Idols*:

> In the past, alteration, change, any becoming at all, were taken as proof of mere appearance, as an indication that there must be something which led us astray. Today, in contrast, precisely insofar as the prejudice of reason forces us to posit unity, identity, permanence, Substance, cause, thinghood, being, we see ourselves somehow caught in error, compelled into error—so certain are we, on the basis of rigorous examination, that this is where the error lies.
>
> It is no different in this case than with the movement of the sun: there our eye is the constant advocate of error, here it is our language. In its origin language belongs to the age of the most rudimentary psychology. We enter a realm of crude fetishism when we summon before consciousness the basic presuppositions of the metaphysics of language—in plain talk, the presuppositions of reason. Everywhere reason sees a doer and doing; it believes in will as the cause; it believes in the ego, in the ego as being,

in the ego as Substance, and it projects this faith in the ego-Substance upon all things—only thereby does it first create the concept of "thing." Everywhere "being" is projected by thought, pushed underneath, as the cause; the concept of being follows, and is a derivative of, the concept of ego. In the beginning there is that great calamity of an error that the will is something which is effective, that will is a capacity. Today we know that it is only a word.

Very much later, in a world which was in a thousand ways more enlightened, philosophers, to their great surprise, became aware of the sureness, the subjective certainty, in our handling of the categories of reason: they concluded that these categories could not be derived from anything empirical—for everything empirical plainly contradicted them. Whence, then, were they derived?

And in India, as in Greece, the same mistake was made: "We must once have been at home in a higher world (instead of a very much lower one, which would have been the truth); we must have been divine, because we have reason!" Indeed, nothing has yet possessed a more naive power of persuasion than the error concerning being, as it has been formulated by the Eleatics, for example. After all, every word and every sentence we say speak in its favor. Even the opponents of the Eleatics still succumbed to the seduction of their concept of being: Democritus, among others, when he invented his atom. "Reason" in language—oh, what an old deceptive female she is! I am afraid we are not rid of God because we still have faith in grammar.[11]

Being, atoms, souls, matter, atoms, God, things, rationality: *all* of these are, for Nietzsche, mistaken hypostatizations of becoming, erroneous delineations into fixed, separate, repeatable entities of an originally wild flux of particular effusions of force. Nietzsche here blames it on Indo-European *grammar*. The same list would be explained by Bataille as the results of *tool-making*. Both men see what lies beyond this reification process, whatever its source, as a thingless, broiling mass of the becoming and destruction of individual forms, the formless, fluid Dionysian world of Will to Power or Intimacy, respectively, where everything invades and usurps and mixes into everything else. There are crucial differences in what is left over when the offending thought-forms are removed. But what is crucial here is that Nietzsche's Will to Power, like Bataille's Intimate realm of sovereignty, has nothing to do with what we normally call "*Will*"—for as we see here, Will itself is another item that belongs to this list of false reifications. The idea of the efficacy of the Will, of the self in control of events, is just one more erroneous by-product of grammar: language itself, after all, is a tool, and here we find the convergence of Bataille and Nietzsche. The source idea of monotheism—*Noûs* as *Arché*, the *controlling self* and its Will as the real basis of all things, as the locus of genuine efficacy—is rooted in this primal error, emerging from thought-forms that are almost unavoidable in language-using beings, which is to say, tool-using beings, though this would seem to pertain especially to those using highly grammatically inflected languages requiring subject-predicate structures, such as Indo-European languages. (When we turn, in online appendix B, to a more sustained consideration of classical China, we will have an interesting possible test case on our hands, insofar as China has tool-using and empire but not Indo-European grammar. And indeed, broadly speaking, classical Chinese thought is the one great culture that predominantly eschews the monotheist turn in all periods of its history.)

Even the resistance to this idea in Western thought, in Democritus's idea of atoms and the void, was but another example of this same grammatically inevitable mistake: there are no atoms just as there are no selves and no Will. Here Nietzsche has returned to a Spinozistic vision, but one that also eschews Reason, which Spinoza considered the crucial first step as the Second Kind of Knowledge, which views all things in terms of necessity. Actually, this ideal is very much present in Nietzsche in the broadest sense, in *amor fati*, the love of necessity: he is at pains to distinguish this from any "logical spider" of a God and to insist that necessity is not to be confused with "Law," whereby one separate thing actually constrains another separate thing. But however much his style differs from Spinoza's, there is no escaping the similarity of their stance on this issue. Reason, the apprehension of necessity, is for Spinoza simply the insight that two apparently separate things are really one and the same, two aspects or phases of a single, inseparable whole. Spinoza passes beyond Reason to the Third Kind of Knowledge, which eliminates the sense of separate steps implicit in the use of syllogism altogether, seeing the premise and conclusion as one in a single tautological flash and linking both all the way back to an absolute necessity, an Attribute of Substance, something that can be conceived only as existing. In Nietzsche's case, having seen beyond the language-produced misperception of separability that is the key premise for the sense of the Will's responsibility, one regains a sense of one's own actions as inseparable from "the whole." Which whole is this? Is it Spinoza's? Aristotle's? Hegel's? It is the whole of past-present-and-future, which was conceived by Nietzsche in terms of the Eternal Recurrence as a finite single indivisible sequence of events recurring infinite times. This is what restores the innocence of becoming:

Let us finally consider how naive it is altogether to say: "Man ought to be such and such!" Reality shows us an enchanting wealth of types, the abundance of a lavish play and change of forms—and some wretched loafer of a moralist comments: "No! Man ought to be different." He even knows what man should be like, this wretched bigot and prig: he paints himself on the wall and comments, "Ecce homo!" But even when the moralist addresses himself only to the single human being and says to him, "You ought to be such and such!" he does not cease to make himself ridiculous. The single human being is a piece of fatum from the front and from the rear, one law more, one necessity more for all that is yet to come and to be. To say to him, "Change yourself!" is to demand that everything be changed, even retroactively. And indeed there have been consistent moralists who wanted man to be different, that is, virtuous—they wanted him remade in their own image, as a prig: to that end, they negated the world! No small madness! No modest kind of immodesty!

Whenever responsibility is assigned, it is usually so that judgment and punishment may follow. Becoming has been deprived of its innocence when any acting-the-way-you-did is traced back to will, to motives, to responsible choices: the doctrine of the will has been invented essentially to justify punishment through the pretext of assigning guilt. All primitive psychology, the psychology of will, arises from the fact that its interpreters, the priests at the head of ancient communities, wanted to create for themselves the right to punish—or wanted to create this right for their God. Men were considered "free" only so that they might be considered guilty—could be judged and punished: consequently, every act had to be considered as willed, and the origin of every act had to be considered as lying within the consciousness (and thus the most fundamental psychological deception was made the principle of psychology itself).

Today, we immoralists have embarked on a counter movement and are trying with all our strength to take the concepts of guilt and punishment out of the world—to cleanse psychology, history, nature, and social institutions and sanctions of these ideas. And there is in our eyes no more radical opposition than that of the theologians, who continue to infect the innocence of becoming by means of the concepts of a "moral world-order," "guilt," and "punishment." Christianity is religion for the executioner.

What alone can be our doctrine? That no one gives a man his qualities—neither God, nor society, nor his parents and ancestors, nor *he himself*. (The nonsense of the last idea was taught as "intelligible freedom" by Kant—and perhaps by Plato.) No one is responsible for a man's being here at all, for his being such-and-such, or for his being in these circumstances or in this environment. The fatality of his existence is not to be disentangled from the fatality of all that has been and will be. Human beings are not the effect of some special purpose, or will, or end; nor are they a medium through which society can realize an "ideal of humanity" or an "ideal of happiness" or an "ideal of morality." It is absurd to wish to devolve one's essence on some end or other. *We* have invented the concept of "end": in reality there is no end.

A man is necessary, a man is a piece of fatefulness, a man belongs to the whole, a man is in the whole; there is nothing that could judge, measure, compare, or sentence his being, for that would mean judging, measuring, comparing, or sentencing the whole. But there is nothing besides the whole. That nobody is held responsible any longer, that the mode of being may not be traced back to a primary cause, that the world does not form a unity either as a sensorium or as "spirit"—that alone is the great liberation. With that idea alone we absolve our becoming of any guilt. The concept of "God" was until now the greatest objection to existence. We deny God, we deny the responsibility that originates from God: and thereby we redeem the world.[12]

There we have it: it is absurd to hand a person's being over to some *purpose* or other. This is the most incisive of Nietzsche's many-pronged attacks on the idea of God. To deny any one thing is to deny the whole. The elimination of the purpose of the world is the reaffirmation of the dignity and ultimacy, the autotelic/atelic/omnitelic necessity, of each and every particular event, each and every becoming, as an end in itself. No one, and nothing, is responsible for anything being what it is—not even itself. "Responsibility"—accountability—itself is the centerpiece of the error of separate things, projections of individual selves, controlling their own actions in isolation from the total concatenation of events that form the world. The world is without purpose, without aim, without meaning. But this really means that is without any *single* purpose, aim, or meaning, and this is the solution to its own problem. Nietzsche has up his sleeve an idea for the establishment of the autotelos and intertelos of every single event: the Eternal Recurrence. And this is indeed the atheist mystical vision that alone would redeem the world. As Nietzsche says in his posthumously published notes:

That this "in vain" constitutes the character of present-day nihilism remains to be shown. The mistrust of our previous valuations grows until it becomes the question: "Are not all 'values' lures that draw out the comedy without bringing it closer to a solution?" Duration "in vain," without

end or aim, is the most paralyzing idea, particularly when one understands that one is being fooled and yet lacks the power not to be fooled.

Let us think this thought in its most terrible form: existence as it is,
without meaning or aim, yet recurring inevitably without any finale of
nothingness: "the eternal recurrence." This is the most extreme form of
nihilism: the nothing (the "meaningless"), eternally!

The European form of Buddhism: the energy of knowledge and
strength compels this belief. It is the most scientific of all possible hypotheses. We deny end goals: if existence had one it would have to have
been reached.

So one understands that an antithesis to pantheism is attempted here:
for "everything perfect, divine, eternal" also compels a faith in the "eternal recurrence." Question: does morality make impossible this pantheis-
tic affirmation of all things, too? At bottom, it is only the moral god that
has been overcome. Does it make sense to conceive a god "beyond good
and evil"? Would a pantheism in this sense be possible? Can we remove
the idea of a goal from the process and then affirm the process in spite of
this?—This would be the case if something were attained at every moment within this process—and always the same. Spinoza reached such
an affirmative position in so far as every moment has a logical necessity,
and with his basic instinct, which was logical, he felt a sense of triumph
that the world should be constituted that way.

But his case is only a single case. Every basic character trait that is
encountered at the bottom of every event, that finds expression in every
event, would have to lead every individual who experienced it as his own
basic character trait to welcome every moment of universal existence
with a sense of triumph. The crucial point would be that one experienced
this basic character trait in oneself as good, valuable—with pleasure.[13]

This is the antithesis of pantheism and at the same time the final consummation of pantheism pushed to its ultimate conclusion: a universe with no
aim or purpose, which must have no purpose because, inasmuch as infinite
time has always already elapsed, any possible final state would already have
been reached. Such a universe has no beginning and no goal; it simply repeats its senseless course of necessity endlessly. And yet it is thus a system
that can equally well be viewed as reaching its end at every second, as exemplifying every single being's fundamental desire in each moment. For
Spinoza, it was a delight in necessity, and this produced his delight in seeing
the universe exemplifying this at every moment. But for someone else, the
dominant passion may be not for necessity but for caprice—and this person, according to Nietzsche, should also be able to see his own most desired

trait manifested in every moment of existence, and thus experience it with an equally intense sense of joy and triumph. Every creature embodies a goal, a passion, and the universe is such that each and every one of these goals is what is satisfied at every moment. In having no telos, it satisfies every telos. This is the point; this is the atheist mystic vision. How can we unpack it?

THE ABSOLUTE AFFIRMATION OF ANYTHING IS THE AFFIRMATION OF ABSOLUTELY EVERYTHING

Schopenhauer proposed the possibility of suspending all willing as the only liberation, the achievement of a state of pure contemplation without Will that would be able to disinterestedly perceive the worthlessness of things — the inability of finite things to satisfy a constitutively infinite and self-contradictory Will — and thus renounce desire for them. He provided a bit of a loophole, though, in his aesthetic theory, as detailed in part III of *The World as Will and Representation* and elsewhere. For Schopenhauer, beauty is a foretaste of redemption: a temporary state of will-lessness brought on by the contemplation of a pure Platonic form, temporarily lifted out of the time-space-causality matrix of the principle of individuation and the Principle of Sufficient Reason and thereby revealing a "pure gradation of the objectification of the Will."[14] By perceiving the world without Will, one perceives only timeless beauty. In this way the perceiver simultaneously becomes a "pure, timeless will-less subject of knowing,"[15] no longer a particular individual limited to a certain time or space, and no longer driven by the "miserable pressure of the Will."[16] This is liberation from the tyranny of time and Will (but, paradoxically, it is only temporary). This "transparent eyeball" (as Emerson would later describe an analogous transformation of the experiencer of redemptive beauty) perceives the world aesthetically, and thus, for Schopenhauer, it does so without Will. And this, in an odd way, opens the door to a kind of world affirmation in the very heart of the world denial doctrine. For the *content* of this will-less knowledge is nothing but the Will itself, having been objectified and expressed with maximal distinctness and vividness of detail and without the phenomenal forms of time, space, and causality. To disinterestedly see in total clarity the full range of objectifications of the Will, fully absorbed in the perception (not conceptualization) of these Ideas that express the Will most fully, most timelessly, eternally, and universally, is, it turns out, simultaneously *liberation* from the Will: pure will-less knowing. The fullest presence of the Will, as object, as Idea, is pure knowing, and therefore liberation from the Will. To fully experience the Will in its greatest distinctness and completeness, but only if this experience is specifically in the mode of pure will-less know-ing, is beauty. Here Schopenhauer offers an alternate path back to Kant's key insight about beauty: it is purposiveness per se (the Will itself made fully and vividly present to awareness) without purpose (seen to have no specific goal and to suspend the viewer's own personal goals).

Zarathustra, however, spoofs and repudiates this view in the chapter, "On Immaculate Perception":

"This would be for me the highest thing"—thus your lying spirit talks to itself—"To look upon life without desire and not like a dog with its tongue hanging out:

"To be happy in looking, with a will that has died, without the grasp-ing or greed or selfishness—the whole body cold and ashen, but with drunken moon-eyes!

"This would be for me the dearest thing"—thus the seduced one se-duces himself—"To love the earth as the moon loves her, and to touch her beauty with the eyes alone.

"And let this be for me the *immaculate* perception of all things: that I want nothing from things, except that I may lie there before them like a mirror with a hundred eyes"—

Oh, you sentimental hypocrites, you lechers! You lack innocence in your desire, so now you slander desiring itself!

Verily, not as creators, procreators, or enjoyers of becoming do you love the earth!

Where is there innocence? Where there is the will to procreate. And whoever wants to create beyond himself, he has for me the purest will.

Where is there beauty? Wherever I *must will* with all my will, where I want to love and go under, that an image might not remain mere image.[17]

While admitting, in the same section, that it once tempted him deeply ("Even Zarathustra was at one time fooled by your godlike skins; he never guessed that they were crammed with coils of snakes"), he now sees this moonlit, desireless apprehension of the world as a pale parody of true world-affirmation and real beauty. Beauty is instead just the opposite: "where one must will with all one's Will." Beauty is not the denial of willing, but the experience of its intensification, exacerbation, totalization, excep-tionlessness, inescapability. But this move is itself a fuller expression of the strange paradox already incipiently present in Schopenhauer's version: in some sense, full immersion in and hyperpresence of the Will is liberation from the Will as a full embrace of purposivity per se is freed of the vicissi-tudes that normally come with any partial purpose.

This is of a piece with Zarathustra's stunning revaluation of the predicament of the Will in "On Redemption" (as quoted previously): the proposition that willing, far from being merely a prisoner in need of liberation, is also itself the great liberator. The creative Will liberates. It is to make this proposition possible that the doctrine of Eternal Recurrence appears. All things are causally interlocked. By accepting the past's unchangeability all the more radically, such that it applies deterministically to the future as well, we see a kind of turnaround where the Will's time problem is solved, where the exceptionless relevance of the Will and its liberation are made possible, and where all is now in the desired sense "changeable," that is, susceptible to the Will's quest for self-affirming power. This is because, even though it remains undeniable that the past is the cause of the future and willing is always, by definition, willing toward the future, yet according to the Eternal Recurrence doctrine, the future is also the past's past, and thus the future also causes the past. Thus, *to will the future is also to will the past.* To will any one thing is to will that all the past and present be such as to cause that thing to come about; but all the past and present are also an effect of the thing that is willed. All things—past, present, and future—are causally inextricable, with each serving as cause and as effect of each of the others. Thus, to will any one thing is to will all things. But to really be able to will any single thing, to thus will the entirety of often terrible premises and consequences that are entailed in willing any one thing, I have to will that one thing *intensely*—with all my Will.

To authentically motivate such a Will, we need at least one transformative experience of joy and beauty deep enough to incite so strong and irresistible a desire. We see this state exemplified, after many twists and turns, in the "Drunken Song," just about four pages from the end of *Thus Spoke Zarathustra*:

All joy wants the eternity of all things, wants honey, wants lees, wants drunken midnight, wants graves, wants graves'-tears consolation, wants gilded evening-glow—

—*what* does joy not want? She is thirstier, heartier, hungrier, more terrible, more secret than all woe, she wants *herself*, she bites into *herself*, the ring's will wrestles in her—

—she wants love, she wants hate, she is overrich, bestows, throws away, begs for someone to take her, thanks the taker, she would gladly be hated—

—so right is joy that she thirsts for woe, for Hell, for hate, for disgrace, for the cripple, for *world*—this world now, you know it well!

You superior humans, it is for you that she yearns, this joy, intractable, blissful—for your woe, you that have failed! For failures does all eternal joy yearn.

For *all* joy wants herself, thus she wants misery too! Oh happiness, oh pain! Oh break, heart! You superior humans, do learn this: Joy wants eternity,

—Joy wants all things' eternity, *wants deepest, deep Eternity!*[18]

Joy wants eternity—not just its own eternity, and not just all things as ineradicable causes of its eternity, but the eternity of all things: it wants, we are told, the eternity (Eternal Recurrence) also of honey, of lees, of graves, of graves' tears' consolation, of love, of hate, of being taken, of being hated, of woe, of hell, of disgrace, of cripples, of the world, of failures, and of pity for and disgust with the world. Such is its joy and its desire for itself, for its own eternity: it wants the eternity also of all that is not it, all that seems to contravene and undermine it. Zarathustra's joy in that moment, in willing the future of his work there with the Superior Human Beings, is deep enough to will without reserve, and thus to will all things—to will the past, to liberate the Will from its disgust with the unwilled brute facts of the small man and the failure of the great man, from its enslavement in unwillable pasts, and yet also to liberate it from the will-lessness of immaculate perception. It wills both its own going-under and its own eternity, finally seeing these as one and the same.

But this liberation from will-lessness must also be a second-order affirmation of even will-lessness. As Zarathustra says in the chapter "Before the Sunrise," once again invoking the cat and moon images for immaculate perception:

For I would sooner have even noise and thunder and weather-curses than this suspicious, dubious cat-like stillness; and also among human beings I hate the most all pussyfooters and half-and-halfers and doubting, hesitating, drifting clouds.

And "whoever cannot bless shall *learn* to curse!"—this bright clear teaching fell to me from a bright clear Heaven, this star still stands even on black nights in my Heaven.

But I am a blesser and a Yea-sayer, if only you are around me, so pure! so bright! you light-abyss!—in all abysses I carry my blessing Yea-saying.

A blesser I have become and a Yea-sayer: and for that I struggled long and was a wrestler, that I might one day wrest my hands free for blessing.

But this is my blessing: to stand over each and every thing as its own Heaven, as its round roof, its azure bell and eternal security: and blessed is he who blesses thus!

For all things are baptized at the fount of eternity and beyond good and evil; but good and evil are themselves mere intervening shadows and dampening sorrows and drifting clouds.

Verily, a blessing it is and no blasphemy when I teach: "Over all things stands the Heaven Accident, the Heaven Innocence, the Heaven Contingency, the Heaven Exuberance."

"Lord Contingency":—that is the oldest nobility in the world, which I restored to all things when I redeemed them from their bondage under Purpose.

This freedom and Heaven-serenity I placed like an azure bell over all things, when I taught that over them and through them no "eternal will"—wills.

This exuberance and this folly I put in place of that will, when I taught: "In all things is one thing impossible—rationality!"

A *little* reason, to be sure, a seed of wisdom scattered from star to star—this pinch of leaven is mixed into all things: for the sake of folly is wisdom mixed into all things!

A little wisdom is no doubt possible; but this blessed certainty I found in all things: that they would rather—*dance* on the feet of chance.

O Heaven above me, so pure! so high! That is what your pureness means to me, that there is no eternal reason-spider and–spider-web:—

—that for me you are a dance-floor for Godlike accidents, that for me you are a Gods' table for Godlike dice and dice-throwers!—[19]

We should notice the two-step back-and-forth here: first to curse *but then* to bless. Cursing is seen as a predecessor to blessing, as its precondition, as the only way to enable eventual blessing: world denial is seen as a means to world affirmation and rationality as a means to folly—wrestling is seen as a means of wresting the hands free for blessing and nay-saying as a means of freeing oneself for yea-saying. This, of course, recapitulates the last of the three transformations of the spirit in Zarathustra's very first sermon, "On the Three Transformations of the Spirit," from the lion, which denies and destroys, which tears down ideals, denying them along with the value of the world, to the child: "But say, my brothers, what can the child yet do that even the lion could not do? Why must the predatory lion yet become a child? Innocence the child is and forgetting, a beginning anew, a play, a self-propelling-wheel, a first movement, a sacred Yea-saying. Yes, for the play of creating, my brothers, a sacred Yea-saying is needed: the spirit now wills *its own* Will, the one who had lost the world attains *its own* world."[20]

Here we see the resolution of a tension that may seem to have existed between Zarathustra's various claims about the eternal Will. On the one hand, redemption and beauty lie in willing, in the creative Will that must will with all its Will: "will liberates" and "joy wills eternity," and this willing of eternity is, because it is also eternally returning, also itself eternal, and hence an eternal Will. And yet we are also told that redemption lies precisely in freeing the world from the tyranny of believing "that an eternal Will wills through it and in it." But the contradiction is only apparent, pointing us to the deeper implication here. Play, chance, contingency, Will, creation, redemption: it is not *a* Will, a single universal Will, God's Will, that wills eternally through all things; it is *my* Will that wills eternally through all things. Redemption lies, not in Jesus's words, "Not my Will but thine be done," but in something like: "There is no eternal Will in things except the Will generated eternally in and for all things, past and future, good and evil, superior and inferior, by my specific momentary experience of this precise joy." In this sense, the eternal Will is thus *my* eternal Will; the eternal world is *my* eternal world. Thus "chance"—the freedom from eternal willed rationality—is equated here with "exuberance": the joy that wills all things and wills the eternity of all things.

Joy wills this moment's Will deeply enough to affirm the world—every little piece of the world from the best to the worst, from the smallest to the greatest—including not only those moments of world that lead one to *deny* it, but even the world-denying minds within it, thus affirming even those "inferior" human states that bring with them hatred and denial of the world. This means even the affirmation of what Zarathustra himself had repudiated earlier in the book: the affirmation of *revenge* and *immaculate perception* and all the other markers of world denial that Zarathustra has been busy denying.

What is crucial to notice here, however, is that the turnaround from negation to affirmation entails also a totalization that brings with it a parallel turnaround: from willing to will-lessness itself. Ironically enough, Zarathustra achieves the equivalent of the original Schopenhauerian goal of nonwilling, not by renouncing Will but rather by *willing more intensely*. The key point here is that "not-willing" and "willing everything equally" are *exactly synonymous*. For "to will" is to *prefer* one thing over another, one state of affairs over another, one outcome over another. To will everything equally is thus no different from not willing anything in particular above anything else. To will all is to will none. Yet through the premise of the Eternal Recurrence, Zarathustra has found a way to achieve this goal of nonwilling, *not* by negating his Will for the particular small things that he loves and wills, initially at the expense of everything else, but rather as entailing in that very Will also the Will for everything else. For, given the impossibility of *not* willing some particular thing over another, the only way to achieve the ending of Will is to will that thing more deeply, more unreservedly, more thoroughly, such that to will that one thing is equally to will everything else. The Will thus wills the original desideratum but no longer in the problematic sense in which it was doomed to limit its own power with every past achievement. Willing no longer limits and frustrates itself, no longer finds itself constrained by and resentful of a past facticity that it cannot embrace as part of its own Will, once the *strict equivalence* of willing X and willing everything-other-than-X is established—through the doctrine of the Eternal Recurrence. The two paradoxical horns of "purposivity" and "without purpose" here converge without remainder: "purposivity" is not the mere form of purposivity as such or in general, but my own, specific purpose willed with all my Will; and insofar as this full willing of one thing entails willing all things and this omnipurpose is equivalent to no purpose, precisely this thoroughgoing embrace of my own purpose is "without purpose." When freed of the ultimacy of any single purpose, every purpose finds itself fulfilled in every other purpose; my willing of whatever I fully love is equally the love of all things, all wills, all loves. We love life, Nietzsche tells us, not because we are used to living, but because we are used to loving—because when it comes to loving, we simply can't help it. We just can't stop loving, desiring and cherishing something or other, willing, wanting. Indeed, since all things are nothing but Will, no thing can. It is through this senseless unjustifiable arbitrary unstoppable love for whatever random thing we find ourselves loving that we discover that *all things are in love with one another*. Such is the consummation of atheist beatitude.

CHAPTER 7

Bataille, or Fuckin' Chaos

GODLESSNESS AS LIBERATION FROM BOTH SPIRIT AND MATTER AND SEVERAL VERSIONS OF WHAT REMAINS

We have taken some time exploring how Spinoza and Nietzsche character-ize the mystical dimension that concerns them and what each one thinks is made possible once monotheism and all its entailments have been dis-pelled. In Spinoza's case, this is expressed through motifs like adequate ideas, necessity, intellectual love of Substance, and increase in power and in the ability to move mind and body in a greater number of ways. In Nietz-sche's case, we have *amor fati* and yea-saying to all existence via one's own Will to Power willing even a single moment of joy in the Eternal Recur-rence. In the case of Georges Bataille, we are confronted with a set of riffs that at first blush seem outrageously incommensurate with all that: orgi-astic sovereignty freed from concern for the future, expulsion of excess, joy in the vicarious contemplation of and participation in explosive torture and death expressed as religion, as sacrifice, as sex, as poetry, as luxury, as waste. Yet we are now perhaps in a position to see how these seemingly wildly different visions intertwine around a common center of gravity even as they splinter off from a common breakthrough.

As we saw in part I, Bataille offers a theory of religion that is closely re-lated to the present topic, as he is the only of the authors under discussion who explicitly identifies himself as "intensely religious" but also insists that the idea of God, the monotheistic God, is for him an obstruction to his religious life, a spiritual catastrophe, and the negation of true religion. We might read this between the lines in Spinoza: God as generally conceived is precisely what prevents true apprehension of the real God, which is to say, true religious beatitude. Nietzsche sometimes says something close, for example, in the quotation at the start of part I and also, as if to gloss that ringing pronouncement even more explicitly, "God, as created by Paul, is a negation of God."[1] But this is still a rather narrower critique, and Nietzsche doesn't self-identify as religious but rather sees the religious impulse as itself something to critique, in all its manifestations. Nevertheless, he does offer up the Dionysian religion of art as "the true metaphysical activity of man" in *Birth of Tragedy* and, after critiquing the addiction to the metaphysical need of man as something that can be overcome, gives us a further intensified form of the same experience in Zarathustra's presentation of the Eternal Recurrence as the highest formula for an antimetaphysical contemplation, one that many people would readily call religious.[2]

All these cases have something in common: they see the basic character of the idea of God as having to do with *external purpose*, and all of them see this is as a problematic obstruction to the real essence of religion. Spinoza rejects teleology and thus rediscovers immanence; Nietzsche gropes for the highest formula of self-affirmation in the Eternal Recurrence, which collapses ends-and-means, past-and-future—the very metaphysical underpinning of external purpose. But none of them declares frankly, as Bataille does, that God has *ruined* real religion and that real religion is what man wants, as we saw in the overview of his *Theory of Religion* in chapter 4. For Bataille, almost alone among thinkers, understands that religion is either a *scandal* or it is nothing; that the whole point of spiritual life is the upheaval of social order, or as Laozi says, "reversal, opposition, is the motion of Dao," and "true words are as if perverse"[3]—and he further understands that monotheism is a bait-and-switch of scandal, a peculiarly disastrous simulacrum that advertises itself as a "scandal" (the word is St. Paul's) but is really exploiting the need for scandal and transgression, the need for "Intimacy," in the interests of its opposite, to all the more fully seal the deal for the social order, for work, for fragmentary individuation, for purpose. Monotheism is like a bad-boy figure in a corporate boy band garbed in torn denim and tattoos and piercings and doing a public service announcement for abstinence: "Abstinence is what's *really* cool, girls! That's what I dig in a gal pal!" Grounding social morality in subservience to God ends up being a tragic example of frying-pan-to-fire naivete. The whole point of religion, of the spiritual life, is to burst through, not only morality, as even a slavishly God-hungry fellow like Kierkegaard knew, but purpose as such, ends-means structures as such, personality as such, univocal meaning as such.

But the really crucial points of resonance run still deeper. Nietzsche's view of natural causality, as we have seen, sees the projection of the unhealthy categories of conscious control perniciously projected into the natural world, not only in our explicitly teleological conceptions of Nature, like those of Aristotle, but even in the opposite, the allegedly atheistic atomism and mechanism that posits wholly separate "things" as the "atoms" of the world. Indeed, we may add a suggestive etymological fact that Nietzsche could well have invoked in this connection, though as far as I know he did not. The word Aristotle chooses to delineate his four "causes"—the material cause, the formal cause, the efficient cause, and the final cause—is *aitia* (αἰτία). The prephilosophical use of this term, in Homer for example, has the core meaning of responsibility, indebtedness, or culpability.[4] The idea of efficient causality itself, and thus perhaps the modern notion of push-and-pull mechanical causality that descends from it after the Aristotelian baggage of final, material, and formal "causes" is thrown off, can thus be viewed as rooted in core intuitions about personal responsibility, which we have seen as itself grounded in the prioritization of purposivity: both the opposed views of mechanism and teleology would then be by-products of teleology, as we have been suggesting. For Nietzsche more specifically, the very idea of separate independent things, which is the cornerstone of mechanistic thinking, is itself an erroneous projection of the erroneous idea of the self—the ego, the conscious personality—as a self-contained and self-sufficient unit. Causality as such, in its mechanistic sense of one thing causing another, and even purposeless causality, is thus an error, he tells us: there is no such thing as a "cause" in the strict sense. Sometimes he replaces "causality" with the notion of "necessity" and "thing" with "event," but in the final analysis even these are misleading, stopgap terms posited by consciousness as an extrapolation of its own unhealthy sense of itself as agent and thus rooted in the conscious self as cause, which in turn is rooted in purposefulness. The full implication of this is that the "necessary event is a tautology"—it is just another way of saying "event" *simpliciter*.[5] Here we see the entire conception of causal groundedness of one thing in another, the Principle of Sufficient Reason, collapse into the immanence of each event. What lies beyond both teleology *and* mechanism, beyond causality and necessity in the vulgar sense, and in which they are *still* contaminated by the notion of purpose, then, is what Nietzsche strives to articulate and to live in through his atheistic mysticism, which was developed around the Eternal Recurrence. Each event there is both cause and effect, both part and whole, both necessary and free.

Spinoza too roots his rejection of a creator God and his overall beatific vision of Godless raw infinity on the rejection of the very idea of separable entities, which he strives to prove is literally incoherent. Purpose and atomism fall with the same stroke here as well, and we should remember this when considering Spinoza's account of real causality in the world lest we confuse it with a form of mechanism, as has often been done. Mechanistic causality, after all, is a conception derived from an analogy to the relation of separately manufactured parts, which are manufactured *for a purpose*: the parts of a machine. When Nature is thought of in terms of billiard-ball, efficient causality between stable, discrete parts, it is being implicitly modeled on a purposefully made machine, a contraption that combines preexisting elements in a particular way in order to attain some particular purpose. Teleology and mechanism go together; they are the flip sides of each other.

We may thus think of atheist mysticism in general as the transcendence of *both* teleology and mechanism in the discovery of an alternative way of thinking about natural process and about ourselves. For Spinoza, this means thinking about the indivisible and infinite entirety of existence as the sole *immanent* cause of every event, as manifested as an infinite chain of particular causes, each of which is really a *mode of expression* of that whole and is joined, not by mechanical causality, but by logical necessity, which simply means their mutual entailment—the inconceivability of their existence in isolation from one another. Necessity, again, means that what appeared to be two distinct, isolated things are really just two inseparable aspects of one. What overcomes the idea of isolated objects conceived by the "Imagination" is, first of all, Reason, which begins to see genuinely necessary relations between what initially appeared to be genuinely distinct entities. Spinoza seems at first to view Reason much more favorably than Nietzsche does, but in fact, both men view Reason, when seen as a conscious, step-by-step, deliberative process, as a stepping stone to something beyond it, a potentially self-sublating ladder to something that supersedes it, a training in incorporating connections toward the reestablishment of a reliable form of Intuition.[6] Reason is a training similar to learning a musical instrument: the plodding, difficult, deliberative dimension is necessary, but only as a means to reach a state in which it is no longer necessary. It is not the goal, and while it may be the beginning for our activities, it is so only in the exceptional case of a few functions that need some fine-tuning, the human perfection of the skills of living in a wildly complex environment. Most of the universe gets along perfectly well without being determined by a conscious cause or purpose of any kind. Its Necessity is indivisibility itself, and it has no use for disjunctive reasoning from one step to another since actual efficacy is just another name for freedom from the disjunctions that produce ends-means consciousness in the first place. As we have seen, here too each moment of existence, each causally necessary event, is really a *mode* of the Absolute rather than a *part* of the Absolute, and, in a significant sense, is itself infinite and eternal: an action of the whole, and in an important sense more than just a single action of the whole; without ceasing to be the specific active mode that it is, it also *is* the whole. The experience of one's own action at any moment as this necessity beyond mechanical and final cause is precisely the beatitude of one's own eternity and infinity.

And for Bataille as well, and perhaps even more emphatically, teleology and mechanical causality are two parts of the same story and in some way correlative to one another—and *both* are closely related to the emergence of the monotheist conception of God. Bataille sometimes makes an effort to distinguish his notion of matter from the vulgar conception of matter in just this way. Our usual notion of matter, he will claim, is too reified, is too much a "thing" in his sense, and as such is really a kind of theological holdover. As he says in his essay, "Materialism":

> Most materialists, even though they may have wanted to do away with all spiritual entities, ended up positing an order of things whose hierarchical relations mark it as specifically idealist. They situated dead matter at the summit of a conventional hierarchy of diverse facts, without perceiving that in this way they gave in to an obsession with the *ideal* form of mat-ter, with a form that was closer than any other to what matter *should be*. Dead matter, the pure *idea*, and God in fact answer a question in the same way (in other words perfectly, and as flatly as the docile student in a classroom)—a question that can only be posed by philosophers, the question of the essence of things, precisely of the idea by which things become intelligible. Classical materialists did not really even substitute causation for the *must be* (the *quare* for the *quamobrem*, or, in other words determinism for destiny, the past for the future). Their need for external authority in fact placed the must be of all appearance in the functional role they unconsciously assigned the idea of science. If the principle of things they defined is precisely the stable element that permitted science to constitute an apparently unshakeable position, a veritable divine eter-nity, this choice cannot be attributed to chance. The conformity of dead matter to the idea of science is, among most materialists, substituted for the religious relations earlier established between divinity and his crea-tures, the one being the idea of the other.[7]

And more clearly spelling out the direct correlative relation between God and matter, he notes, in "Base Materialism and Gnosticism":

> If one thinks of a particular object, it is easy to distinguish matter from form, and an analogous distinction can be made with regard to organic beings, with form taking on the value of the unity of being and of its in-dividual existence. But if things as a whole are taken into account, trans-posed distinctions of this kind become arbitrary and even unintelligible. Two verbal entities are thus formed, explicable only through their con-structive value in the social order: an abstract God (or simply the idea),

and abstract matter; the chief guard and the prison walls. The variants of this metaphysical scaffolding are of no more interest than are the different styles of architecture. People become excited trying to know if the prison came from the guard or if the guard came from the prison.[8]

Bataille has glimpsed that our usual idea of matter, of the world of things whose form is distinguished from their matter, is a category mistake rooted in transposing a conception adequate to the parts onto the whole, for which it is not adequate and, as such, is a prison, from which human beings inevitably and rightly wish to escape. Indeed, it is just as bad as the idea of God, which is actually perfectly correlative with it: matter is the walls of the prison and God is the chief guard. To posit God is to posit the world as a world of things, as a prison, and to posit the world of things is to posit God. Both are derived from the fundamental form-matter split, which is also (as in Aristotle) the ends-means split, leading inevitably to the positing of a pure form separated from a pure matter for the totality of the world, choosing one as the ultimate ground of the other. Bataille's point is that it matters little which of the two we choose as ultimate; both are by-products of the rigid ends-means split of purposive tool-being, which makes sense for limited things but not for the whole of reality, and both exacerbate and entrench that very split. They go together, and pushing past the idea of God pushes us past the idea of matter. This should mean also that it pushes us past the kind of causality that pertains to things, the one-after-another, mutual externality of dead matter. The atheist mysticism of sovereignty that Bataille envisions, then, must be the overcoming of subordination, not only of subordination to purpose but, as entailed in that vision, the overcoming of conditionality in any form. By *conditionality* I mean simply any way in which any determinate thing finds its condition of possibility in something *other than itself*: but as we have seen in chapter 3, this determination by something truly ontologically *other* is exactly what I mean by *control*. Only where there are mutually external entities, "things," there can be conditionality, and thus control. Where there are no such "things," there is no conditionality, and thus no control. If the theistic absolute is the apotheosis of control, the Thing of Things, the atheist absolute is the exact opposite: the overcoming of control itself. But lest this lack of control become a "thing" in its own right, this purposeless absolute cannot exclude the emergence of pockets of control, including the human realm of purposes, as sketched in the section on "The Great Asymmetry" in chapter 2. And as noted in chapter 4, it is the coextensivity—the full convergence, of finitude and infinity, of conditioned and unconditioned, of purpose and purposelessness—that alone can deliver this, and that atheist mysticism alone can deliver. What other possible ways, besides Spinoza's rationally intuitive beatitude and Nietzsche's willful love of fate, are available for experiencing the boundlessness and unconditionality that is the opposite of control and purpose, that nevertheless not only includes them but is inexorably beholden to them as long as one is a finite being, that is, any particular being at all? In his answers to these questions, Bataille has his own, very distinctive contributions to make to the explication of atheist mysticism.

BEYOND WILL TO POWER AS WILL TO CONTROL: SQUANDERING THROUGH THE GORDIAN KNOT OF PURPOSE

Bataille's importance for us is nowhere more keen than in the crucial interpretative constraint he provides for understanding Nietzsche's central concept of Will to Power. Whether or not this is accurate of Nietzsche himself, Bataille makes it clear that for him, Will to Power is not ultimate insofar as power is thought of as in any sense confined to *control*. Rather, Will to Power, including whatever subset of that Will that may be construed as Will to Control, is a special case of something more fundamental, which appears as Will to Power under certain conditions (here Nietzsche is still too teleological, too much under the Schopenhauerian spell, from Bataille's point of view). Nietzsche gives us a stunning list of the ways in which Will to Power is *essential* to life: it means appropriation, dominance, exploitation, repurposing, gaining ground, growth, usurpation, invasion, and so on. These, he says, are not a special case or something malfunctioning: these are the essence of *life* per se![9] He has in mind things like *digestion* and *breathing*: we take over an alien thing from the outside world, we break it down, we undermine its original form and purpose, and we dominate and destroy it and use it for our own purposes. We exploit it. We steal its energy. We expand into its territory.

But Bataille gives us an extensive analysis of all these aspects of the life process as aspects of growth and expansion, which, he says, necessarily radically slow down when an organism reaches maturity: we grow for a few years and then, under the conditions of external pressure and lack of space, we stop growing and *have sex instead*.[10] What we need to do in both cases is simply *expend excess energy*. Growth itself is just *one way of doing this*. The other ways include waste, luxury, nonsense—all *nonteleological* forms of doing the same thing. This is an immense breakthrough. Dominance, control, usurpation, invasion, incorporation, growth: it turns out all of these comprise a special case of the need to *excrete*, to *expend*, to *unload*. These are all answers to the questions, What shall I do with all this excess energy? Where can I find some goal into which to expend it? Growth and gaining ground are a way of *overflowing*. Power-lust is just a temporary local form of *exuberance*. One wants to build monuments and dominate others just so as *to have something to do*. What all great works really want is not work, but play—they want to tire oneself out, to be able to forget about purpose. That is, as we've discussed, precisely to *break free* of the means-ends pipeline of the PSR. Purpose is only a narrow special case of purposelessness.

Let us consider the antecedents of this idea. Spinoza's modes want to continue to exist. This involves a desire to increase their perfection, that is, to extend and expand their power, the amount of alternate moments and modes they can internalize while nevertheless continuing to be the same ratio as before. What they do not want, in any way, is to perish. Spinoza stipulates explicitly that destruction always only happens from outside—indeed, that is literally his definition of what counts as "outside." A thing is only ever destroyed by something other than itself, something outside itself, for a thing is its own desire to continue; whatever is not working as part of its own activity to do so, whether seemingly "inside" or "outside" of it, is really, ipso facto, outside it, other to it.

Nietzsche's Zarathustra wants to go under, to go beyond himself; he wants, not man, but the Superman—and yet he also wants himself back infinitely, wanting "deep deep eternity." He finds both his eternity and his going-under in the Eternal Recurrence, which is the perfect convergence of permanence and impermanence, of eternity and the flashing transiency of an instant. And it is here that he finds the convergence point of being and becoming, of mechanism and teleology, of Will and Will-lessness, of perspectivism and *amor fati*, of purpose and purposelessness, of finitude and infinity.

Bataille seems to want several things, including eroticism and torture and waste and sovereign expenditure. And he wants them all for the same reason: they are the "affirmation of life to the point of death."[11] He wants both—the life and the death—and the ecstatic agonizing point where they intersect in experience. This too is a manner of trying to grasp the infinite and the finite as inseparable, to experience the point of convergence between purpose and purposelessness.

Bataille reads Nietzsche as primarily a thinker of the exuberance of "Chance," of chaos, the Nietzsche who declares, "You must have chaos in you to give birth to a dancing star."[12] But he also has important insights about Will to Power, although he does not often use the term. I contend that Bataille has correctly gleaned the difference between Will to Power and the concept of Will to Control, with which it is often confused—sometimes even by Nietzsche himself. In this sense, his thinking is an actual advance on Nietzsche's. Along with the Will to Power as Will to Control, he seems to have no use for other Nietzschean curiosities like Eternal Recurrence and

Superman. He likes the "chaos" version of Nietzsche—and he attempts to save Nietzsche from himself, from his need for "something to do" and his embarrassing interest in a "task" and "the future." Bataille insists on the moment that has ceased to care about future, not as a form of disintegration of the instincts, as Nietzsche would have it, but as the highest sovereignty, the fullest affirmation of the Will to Power properly understood. He's right in a way—and the side of Nietzsche he puts in the center of his thinking is, for me as well, the better Nietzsche. But Eternal Recurrence is a way to bring the two opposed parts together: future orientation as a way *back* to the present, to the sovereignty of the present. This is Nietzsche's Tiantai move, we might say: while most of the time Bataille stays in a "Zen" zone of the paradoxical quest for the questless, the self-laceration of the impossible quest to attain the unmediated, as if that were present only in some specific state or moment or experience rather than being an aspect of every possible experience. All too often Bataille's writings are no more than drooling yearnings for those moments when he can forget time and future and prudence—sexual abandon above all, but also squandering, gambling, intoxication, expending, luxury, pain, torture, pullulation, and death.

This attitude is part of Bataille's general picture of the relation between prudential work and toolmaking (as sketched earlier in this book), on the one hand, and luxurious squandering and potlatch destruction, on the other. And of course, this is closely related to Bataille's unique view of sex and eroticism. He begins his discussion with what seems a nonsensical analogy: "the sexual act is in time what the tiger is in space." But then he explains the basic conceptions of sex, food, death, growth, energy, squandering, destruction, exuberance, and luxury that form the cornerstone of his worldview:

> The eating of one species by another is the simplest form of luxury. The populations that were trapped by the German army acquired, thanks to the food shortage, a vulgarized knowledge of this burdensome character of the indirect development of living matter. If one cultivates potatoes or wheat, the land's yield in consumable calories is much greater than that of livestock in milk and meat for an equivalent acreage of pasture. The least burdensome form of life is that of a green micro-organism (absorbing the sun's energy through the action of chlorophyll), but generally vegetation is less burdensome than animal life. Vegetation quickly occupies the available space. Animals make it a field of slaughter and extend its possibilities in this way; they themselves develop more slowly. In this respect, the wild beast is at the summit: Its continual depredations of depredators represent an immense squandering of energy. William Blake asked the tiger: "In what distant deeps or skies burned the fire of thine

eyes?" What struck him in this way was the cruel pressure, at the limits of possibility, the tiger's immense power of consumption of life. In the general effervescence of life, the tiger is a point of extreme incandescence. And this incandescence did in fact burn first in the remote depths of the sky, in the sun's consumption.

Eating brings death, but in an accidental form. *Of all conceivable luxuries, death, in its fatal and inexorable form, is undoubtedly the most costly.* The fragility, the complexity, of the animal body already exhibits its luxurious quality, but this fragility and luxury culminate in death. Just as in space the trunks and branches of the tree raise the superimposed stages of the foliage to the light, death distributes the passage of the generations over time. It constantly leaves the necessary room for the coming of the newborn, and we are wrong to curse *the one without whom we would not exist.*

In reality, when we curse death we only fear ourselves: The severity of *our will* is what makes us tremble. We lie to ourselves when we dream of escaping the movement of luxurious exuberance of which we are only the most intense form. Or perhaps we only lie to ourselves in the beginning the better to experience the severity of this will afterward, carrying it to the rigorous extreme of consciousness.

In this respect, the luxury of death is regarded by us in the same way as that of sexuality, first as a negation of ourselves, then—in a sudden reversal—as the profound truth of that movement of which life is the manifestation.

Under the present conditions, independently of our consciousness, sexual reproduction is, together with eating and death, one of the great luxurious detours that ensure the intense consumption of energy. To begin with, it accentuates that which scissiparity announced: the division by which the individual being foregoes growth for himself and, through the multiplication of individuals, transfers it to the impersonality of life. This is because, from the first, sexuality differs from miserly growth: If, with regard to the species, sexuality appears as a growth, in principle it is nevertheless the luxury of individuals. This characteristic is more accentuated in sexual reproduction, where the individuals engendered are clearly separate from those that engender them and *give* them life as one *gives to others.* But without renouncing a subsequent return to the principle of growth for the period of nutrition, the reproduction of the higher animals has not ceased to deepen the fault that separates it from the simple tendency to eat in order to increase volume and power. For these animals sexual reproduction is the occasion of a sudden and frantic squandering of energy resources, carried in a moment to the limit of possibility (in time what the tiger is in space). This squandering goes far beyond what would be sufficient for the growth of the species. It appears to be the most that an individual has the strength to accomplish in a given moment. It leads to the wholesale destruction of property—in spirit, the destruction of bodies as well—and ultimately connects up with the senseless luxury and excess of death.[13]

Here we see what Bataille means by full affirmation of our own Will and how this entails the wholesale affirmation of all existence, but does so in a way that does not require the Nietzschean detour of the myth of the Eternal Recurrence. We ourselves are the most intense form of wasteful luxury; our lives are supported on a mountain of corpses and our pleasure all the more so. When we affirm ourselves, we affirm this. But this is equally our own death, the exuberance of our own fornicating-dying-squandering existence. The affirmation and the destruction of the prudential self come together in one kind of experience quite directly and unmistakably, Bataille thinks: orgasm. But this provides the key to our whole relation to eating, to death, to space, to growth, to excess and scarcity—above all, for our interests here, to purpose as such. By assenting to the virulence of our own Will, we are affirming our own death in our affirmation of life. Bataille dwells on the threshold phenomena, the places where our coherence as individuals begins to fray in a manner that we ardently seek, where the interface of selfness and otherness becomes a direct experience: not, as in early Schelling, in beauty; not, as in Nietzsche, in the moment as eternal; not, as in Spinoza, in my innermost conatus as the most inexorable, eternal, omnipresent necessity; but rather, in sex, intoxication, luxury, and laughter, and equally in the strange attractions of death and pain, both our own and those of others.

Bataille sometimes speaks of his project as a way of extending mystical negative theology "all the way." He calls it *atheology*, which would not be a bad term for the project of this book as well. Bataille wants to take seriously the claim made by the best negative theologians that God is not even an entity, does not even "exist"—to take their claims more seriously than they themselves take them. Pure incommensurability and alterity are proposed here, but not as an "other," because that makes it a thing and thus a purpose to be pursued. In principle, Bataille is thus against "salvation" and "serving God" as *purposes*. What is wanted is that the autotelos should veer into the atelos of each moment: chance, play, dance, laughter, "sovereignty"—but not as control of one thing "over" anything else but rather just as the nonsubmission of each moment, nonsubordination of each moment, of action per se.[14] But then he often ends up with the same kind of problem we find in those types of Zen that fetishize "enlightenment" as an experience to be had in certain moments and not others: the absolutely incommensurable experience as pure immediacy, as unmediatedness, as absolute immanence, as absolute purposelessness—but paradoxically posited as a purpose. In Bataille we have a similar problem, a similar slipperiness in acknowledging the impossibility but also knowingly embracing it. "Impossibility" becomes a new word for the highest—but the highest what? The highest goal.

THE PRACTICE OF JOY BEFORE DEATH

However, just as in Zen or Guo Xiang, this paradox itself is sometimes taken up deliberately and skillfully deployed as a method. Bataille sometimes manages to propose a way out of both the impasse of the making a goal of goallessness and the overly crude disjunction between form and form-lessness.[15] We might even say that in those places, he has found his own unique way to reach a self-overcoming of purposivity itself that parallels what we've seen in Nietzsche's self-overcoming of Will to Power and Spinoza's self-overcoming of the PSR (and in both cases, thereby overcoming also self-interest)—and in each case, doing so through the most thorough possible embrace of what must be overcome by bringing it to its extreme of exceptionlessness. In each case we have an analogue of the old Daoist principle of reversal through extremity (*wujibifan* 物極必反), a principle operative in its own way in both Tiantai and Zen, which is deployed here to profound effect. In his "mystical" exercises, he proposes a way of literally becoming the destructive force of chaos, to actually embody Nietzsche's Dionysian vision, but he also sees that this is not merely the destruction of all form but also the emerging of infinite forms—though indeed he does not stress this cheery aspect much! His short text, "The Practice of Joy in the Face of Death" ("La pratique de la joie devant la mort"), is perhaps the clearest presentation of this atheist religious vision. It begins with an epigraph from Nietzsche: "All that I am, and want to be: simultaneously dove, snake and pig." This is the many-headed chaos, the Yes to all things as one's own identity, that we will also find reached in another way in *Zhuangzi*. Here, characteristically, it is violence and death and chance that define the milieu: "He alone is happy who, having experienced vertigo to the point of trembling in his bones, and being no longer able to measure the extent of his fall, suddenly discovers the unexpected ability to transform his agony into a joy capable of freezing and transfiguring those who encounter it. However the only ambition which can take hold of a man who, in cold blood, sees his life fulfilled in rending agony, cannot aspire to a grandeur that only extreme chance has at its disposal."[16]

Bataille here begins to address and fold in the tension in his paradoxical aspiration for a state that transcends all aspiration, all future, all work, and

all gain by turning it into formal meditation, embracing the paradox somewhat as the Buddhist practice constructs itself as a raft to get beyond rafts,
engaging in calm, systematic work to reach the goal of transcending the
very idea of work, achievement and goals. In both cases, we have a deliberate redirection of the inescapable lust for purpose, indeed, a repurposing of
purpose itself, into a procedure designed to make it explode itself. It is here
that he gives us perhaps one of the most striking and forthright descriptions
of self-aware atheist mysticism available to us:

> While it is appropriate to use the word mysticism while speaking of "joy
> in the face of death" and its practice, it implies no more than an affective
> resemblance between this practice and those of the religions of Asia or
> Europe. There is no reason to link any presuppositions concerning an al-
> leged deeper reality with a joy which has no object other than immediate
> life. "Joy in the face of death" belongs only to the person for whom there
> is no beyond; it is the only intellectually honest route that one can follow
> in the search for ecstasy.
>
> Besides, how could a beyond, a God or anything similar to God, still
> be acceptable? No words are clear enough to express the happy disdain
> of the one who "dances with the time which kills him" for those who
> take refuge in the expectation of eternal bliss. This kind of timorous
> saintliness—which first had to be sheltered from erotic excess—has now
> lost all its power: one can only laugh at a sacred drunkenness which is
> allied to a "holy" horror of debauchery. Prudishness may be beneficial to
> those who are undeveloped: however anyone who is afraid of naked girls
> or whisky would have little to do with "joy in the face of death."
>
> Only a shameless, indecent saintliness can lead to a sufficiently happy
> loss of self. "Joy in the face of death" means that life can be glorified from
> root to summit. It robs of meaning everything that is an intellectual or
> moral beyond, Substance, God, immutable order or salvation. It is an
> apotheosis of that which is perishable, apotheosis of flesh and alcohol as
> well as of the trances of mysticism. The religious forms that it rediscov-
> ers are the naive forms that precede the intrusion of a servile morality:
> it renews the kind of tragic jubilation that man "is" as soon as he stops
> behaving like a cripple: glorifying necessary work and letting himself be
> emasculated by the fear of tomorrow.[17]

A mysticism without God, without a beyond, or more pointedly, a mysticism that consists precisely in the collapse of the beyond, of God, of the
fear of tomorrow, of necessary work, of means and ends, of purpose. This
is for Bataille a rediscovery of the real religiosity which has been usurped

and distorted by its later overlay with "servile morality." It is the real core of mysticism, from which later religious mysticism secretly derives its real resonance.

Bataille's method uses visualization and a kind of self-hypnotic mantra practice to imagine "the frozen moment" of one's own death, the unveiling of the chaos and violence that are oneself and all things, to the point of being able to laughingly declare, "I myself am the dark unknown," "I myself am joy in the face of death," and finally, in the concluding "Heraclitean Meditation," "I myself am war!":

I abandon myself to peace, to the point of annihilation.

The sounds of struggle dissolve into death, like rivers into the sea, like the sparkle of stars into the night.
    The strength of combat is fulfilled in the silence of all action.
    I enter peace as into a dark unknown.
    I sink into this dark unknown.
    I myself become this dark unknown.

I am joy in the face of death.

Joy in the face of death transports me.
    Joy in the face of death hurls me down.
    Joy in the face of death annihilates me.

I remain in this annihilation and, from there, I imagine nature as an interplay of forces expressed in multiplied and incessant agony.

I slowly lose myself in an unintelligible and bottomless space.
    I reach the depths of worlds
    I am devoured by death
    I am devoured by fever
    I am absorbed in somber space
    I am annihilated in joy in the face of death.

I am joy in the face of death.
    The depth of the sky, lost space is joy in the face of death: everything is cracked open.
    I imagine the earth turning dizzyingly in the sky.
    I imagine the sky itself slipping, turning, and disappearing.
    The sun, comparable to alcohol, turning and bursting breathlessly.

The depth of the sky like an orgy of frozen light fading.

All that exists destroying itself, consuming itself and dying, each instant only arising in the annihilation of the preceding one, and itself existing only as mortally wounded.

Continuously destroying and consuming myself within myself in a great festival of blood.

I imagine the frozen instant of my own death.

I focus on a point in front of me and I imagine this point as the geometrical locus of all existence and all unity, of all separation and all dread, of all unsatisfied desire and all possible death.

I cling to this point and a deep love of what I find there burns me, until I refuse to be alive for any reason other than for what is here, for this point which, being both the life and death of the loved one, has the roar of a cataract.

And at the same time, it is necessary to strip away all external representations from what is there, until it is nothing but a pure violence, an interiority, a pure inner fall into an endless abyss: this point endlessly absorbing from the cataract all its nothingness, in other words, all that has disappeared, is "past," and in the same movement endlessly prostituting a sudden apparition to the love that vainly wants to grasp that which will one day cease to be.

The impossibility of satisfaction in love is a guide toward the fulfilling leap at the same time that it is the nullification of all possible illusion.

If I imagine in a vision and in a halo that transfigures the ecstatic, exhausted face of a dying being, what radiates from this face illuminates out of necessity the clouds in the sky, whose grey glow then becomes more penetrating than the light of the sun itself. In this vision, death appears to be of the same nature as the light which illuminates, to the extent that light fades once it leaves its source: it appears that no less a loss than death is needed for the flash of life to traverse and transfigure dull existence, for it is only its free uprooting that becomes in me the power of life and time. In this way I stop being anything other than the mirror of death, just as the universe is only the mirror of light.

HERACLITEAN MEDITATION

I myself am war.

I imagine a human movement and excitation, of which the possibilities are endless: this movement and excitation can only be appeased by war.

I imagine the gift of an infinite suffering, of blood and open bodies, in the image of an ejaculation, felling the person it jolts and abandoning him to an exhaustion full of nausea.

I imagine the Earth hurled into space, like a woman screaming, her head in flames.

Before the terrestrial world whose summer and winter order the agony of all living things, before the universe composed of innumerable spinning stars, losing and consuming themselves without restraint, I only perceive a succession of cruel splendours the very movement of which demands that I die; this death is only the exploding consumption of all that was, joy of existence of all that comes into the world; even my own life demands that everything that exists, everywhere, continually give itself and be annihilated.

I imagine myself covered with blood, broken but transfigured and in agreement with the world, both as prey and as a jaw of time which ceaselessly kills and is ceaselessly killed.

There are explosives everywhere which perhaps will soon blind me. I laugh when I think that my eyes persist in demanding objects that do not destroy them.[18]

This is a method by which to remind myself and intensify my experience of "assenting to life to the point of death," as Bataille puts it memorably in the opening sentence of *Erotism*.[19] This is the convergence of Nietzsche's "will to go under" and his Will to the "deep deep eternity" of oneself and indeed all things, real Will to Power as opposed to the Will to Control. Our desire to eat, to fuck, to kill, to explode, to indulge, to squander—the virulence of that Will is exactly what we face and what we fear when we fear chaos or when we fear death: it is the virulence of our own Will. Bataille is here devising a way to "own" that Will of which we are terrified, to recognize ourselves in it and become explicitly one with it. Thus is our terror affirmed, exacerbated, and also overcome: we are no longer threatened by war when we realize that war is ourselves—that the very pleasures we were afraid of losing to the chaos of war were themselves just war pointed in the other direction. Our desire to live is the desire to destroy ruthlessly—so ruthlessly that we too are not safe. That desire is we ourselves. As the Chan/ Zen Buddhist motif derived from Dongshan Liangjie would have it, the only way to escape the heat is to let the fire burn you up, to become the fire—for fire does not burn itself. By deliberately and brazenly taking this step, constructing a practice whereby the futureless chaos and violence and sex, the impossibility of love and harmony, the impossibility that Bataille thinks is our own innermost core, are deliberately visualized, concentrated into a point of space on which to focus, or in imagining this violent future-less chaos as the agonizing moment of my own death, I bring that future moment into the present by bringing my purposive, deliberate conscious-ness into convergence with the purposeless chaos which is at its own core. Here, rather than in the tail-chasing attempts to invoke the purposeless as beyond all method, we see an entryway into the realized convergence of the finite and the infinite, the formed and the unformed, the structured oneness of purpose and the infinite chaos of purposelessness.

What is it that stops this from being just another appropriation or usur-pation of the purposeless by purpose, a dominating sublation of other-ness into the self? The difference, I think, lies in the thoroughgoingness and vividness of the violence imagined and the fact that what is proposed here is an ongoing practice rather than a theoretical representation. It is something to do, not something to know. It is the practice of the memento mori, the imminence and immanence of death, not as a means to remind me of the far greater importance of the world to come, as in Emulative and Compensatory Theist Christian versions, nor as a way of motivating me to make haste to make something of my short life, as in the Compensatory Atheist version. Nor is its purpose to undermine the attachment to life on the grounds that attachment per se is suffering and a cause of further suf-fering, as is often taken to be the purpose of the Buddhist meditations on one's own death and visualizations of one's own swollen, decaying corpse swarming with worms and maggots. But though, oddly enough, this Bud-dhist meditation is prescribed as a way of bringing calmness and detach-ment, we must note that it retains a great resonance with Bataille's more exuberant and debauched vision, for in both cases the crucial point is to incorporate and embody the breakdown of priorly assumed meaning and coherence—not, for the thousandth time, in order to be replaced by some other meaning (God), but to undermine the erroneous sense of security and coherent selfhood that regards itself as separate from, and mutually exclusive with, the meaningless. It was this ambiguity in the construction of Buddhist notions of calmness and detachment that seems to have haunted the tradition and issues in the various gesturings at wholesale reversal that occur throughout Mahāyāna literature: again and again some intimation is thrust forward asserting that Nirvana itself is greed, anger, and delusion themselves, that there can be no difference between samsara and Nirvana, that delusion is itself wisdom, and so on. Institutional Buddhism struggles, usually successfully, to find a way to hedge and contain these wild-sounding claims, domesticating them through familiar qualifications: *in their inner-most essence* these things are quiescent, and therefore nirvanic, and so on. But in some cases these claims are explained in a way that ends up closer to

Bataille's vision: and in the case of the great Tiantai thinker Siming Zhili, at least, we know that he also devoted himself to a highly deliberate "practice of joy in the face of death": a three-year ritual procedure in preparation for his planned self-immolation.[20]

That said, it cannot be denied that Bataille is far more forthright and extreme in his embrace of the profligate affirmations of such a practice, while at the same time lacking a good deal of the Buddhist theoretical subtlety, which causes him to continue to struggle at times with unresolved dualisms between continuity and discontinuity, between purpose and purposelessness. But in this text he seems to have briefly found a way beyond these dualisms. The point for both Bataille and the Buddhists (even the pre-Mahāyāna Buddhists) is to experience meaninglessness, purposelessness, chaos itself, and to experience as well one's own temporary, nonultimate meanings as emergent from, but always only one random slippage away from, that meaninglessness. The point here is to discover the convergence of self and nonself, of meaning and meaninglessness, of method and chaos. In Buddhist terms, it is to experience the self as always already dead, as always already nonself. Though Bataille's emphasis is usually, and characteristically, on dissolution, destruction, and chaos, in the present text he lets out the Dionysian subtext: "I remain in this annihilation and, from there, I imagine nature as an interplay of forces expressed in multiplied and incessant agony."[21] It is agony, yes, for all forms experience agony in their death throes. But this agony is also the birth pains of the infinite multiplicity of production of forms that one embodies in embodying the interface of one's life and one's death, whereby the frozen moment of one's own future death is experienced in the present as possible at any moment, bearing within it the dizzying cacophony of all possible future moments. To live with this moment constantly at the center of our being is the essence of Bataille's atheist mysticism.

Meaningfulness Revisited

Styles of Suffering, Sublimity, and Beatific Vision,
Theistic and Atheistic

This book has been, among other things, a polemic against the very idea of ultimate "meaningfulness," a wholesale rejection of the idea of the world as a whole having any specific meaning. This negative judgment on meaningfulness was rooted in the suggestion that "meaning" is fundamentally a synonym for "purpose," the ultimacy of which was the real target of the attack. But at this point we may perhaps take advantage of the space cleared by this scorched earth approach by suggesting another possible way to understand the meaning of "meaning," one that is not only distinguished from purpose but in some sense is its most extreme opposite.

This alternative has considerable support, not only in the thinkers we have visited in this book, but even in everyday linguistic usage. For when we ask about something, "What does it mean?" we might be asking simply what can be inferred from its presence, what is betokened by the existence of this thing, of what state of affairs is the appearance of this entity a sign or clue or guarantee. When freed of concerns about purpose, this amounts to asking *what else*, what *other* than "this," is entailed in the presence of "this." If the "this" in question is something required by our commitment to purpose—if it is something we want, either as a means or an end—then the "other than this" will have to be either a means to what we want or something we don't want, something either in line with our purpose or opposed to it. But once our apprehension of the "this" and the "other than this" is freed from their beholdenness to any ultimate purpose, the always simultaneous presencing of "this" and "what is other than this," the highlighting of which forms the key insight at the heart of the *Zhuangzi*—what is that except a way of affirming at once both the finitude of this and the transcending of that finitude, the inextricable copresence of each "this" and its own "beyond-this," the finite "this" and the infinitude of whatever is "not-this"? Purpose-free "meaning," then, means simply that the "this" also betokens the copresence of the "not-this"—and that is precisely what we have identified as the essence of atheist beatitude: the overcoming of the (purpose-based) dichotomy between finitude and infinitude. Insofar as we deny, not purpose, but only the ultimacy of purpose, this beatitude means the copresence of our purposes (and their satisfactions) and whatever we may have wished to exclude from them, whatever might contravene them. And thus this sort of infinite meaning, this sort of beatitude, will also be found to have another, somewhat surprising, name: inescapable pain.

But precisely inasmuch as, for the atheist mystic, finite purpose is operative and yet not ultimate, there will be something more than pain brought by this pain: an opening into all otherness, a disclosure of infinitude, a copresence of worlds of pain and nonpain and other pains—for, by the very same token, pain itself will always bring with it nonpain, the more-than-pain that is its nonpurposive "meaning": its copresencing of all there is beyond it, of everything *else*. In traditional Buddhist or specifically Tiantai language, we might say that, since all conditionality is suffering and all conditionality is also an inescapable opening into all otherness, it is the inescapability and therefore unconditionality of suffering, of conditionality itself, that is the end of suffering: samsara is Nirvana, suffering (苦 *ku, dukkha*) is the omnipresent and eternal body of the Buddha (法身 *fashen*, Dharmakāya). We also have an old philosophical word for this joy in what contravenes our own purposes: the sublime. But unlike the Kantian sublime—a Compensatory Theist sublime haunted by its support in the necessary positing of a deferred but unknowable purpose—here we have the sublime unbound, the wild sublime, an Emulative Atheist sublime released from the ultimacy of purpose, and therefore, from the dichotomy between purpose and purposelessness.

Looking back over the many positions we have canvassed in this book with this idea in mind, we can now perhaps revisit the varieties of mystical experience that pertain to the monotheist and the atheist, expanding on the fourfold characterization of the Emulative and Compensatory Monotheist and Atheist sketched out in part I. Part of the interest of the imagined Venn diagram of these types is that they scramble the team affiliations: the monotheists divide into mystics and rationalist/moralists, and the atheists do as well, though for opposite reasons. In the crudest sense, both Compensatory Monotheists and Emulative Atheists would be the expected sources of mysticism, while both Emulative Monotheism and Compensatory Atheists would be the rationalists and moralists. Here I'd like to sum up the varieties made possible within a certain dimension of the mysticism shared by Compensatory Monotheism and, contrastingly, also by Emulative Atheism. The Compensatory Monotheist is privy to a very beautiful type of mystical experience that gives us a simulacrum of this alternate relationship to purpose: the experience of *Gelassenheit* that comes with deep faith in the goodness of God and the goodness of his creation. At its purest mystical extreme, it can be a sort of beatific vision in which the world is seen as perfect and all things as good, through which one can ecstatically trust oneself to the purposes of God, thus renouncing the usual obsessive commitment to one's own purposes—in a deeply liberating restructuring of subjectivity, or perhaps even a surpassing of subjectivity in its usual sense, insofar as that usual sense is so tightly bound to purposive agency. It allows us to see what is obstructive to our own purposes, what is bad to us, including our own struggles and our own pain, also as good. St. Paul's theology of the cross might be a good example. To give some idea of what we have in mind here, it may be worthwhile to offer a thumbnail sketch of a few of the other most influential of the theistically inflected versions of this beatific grace that allows an experience of all things without exception as "good":

PLATO: All things are as good as the purposive mind of the divine
demiurge, "the God," could make them, modeled on eternal
forms that are intrinsically good; anything bad comes from the
obstructions to the full realization of these purposes involved in
transferring these intentions into spatiotemporal realities in the
matter-like indeterminate "receptacle," which wouldn't allow the
full form of intended goodness to come through (*Timaeus*). But
look for the form in any thing! You will find that, in tracing it back
to the Will of the creative demiurge or the eternal form which is
its intended model, it is good. Even worldly things are what they
are solely through their form, and thus even whatever unstable
intermittent beauty is found in them is a clue to be traced back to
the true beauty of the form that alone gives them their real being
(*Symposium*). Indeed, even without the demiurge and his active
Will, the true source of all goodness, the Idea of the Good, can be
found reflected in all that exists (*Republic*).

ARISTOTLE: Same as above but now definitely excluding a temporal
creation or a fashioning demiurge. God is now just a Form of
perfect self-sufficiency and unified self-sustaining active actuality
that all of us are drawn toward, giving us the direction of growth
that forms us. God is the Good itself, which moves all things
without moving. The Good, and indeed *Noûs*, thought thinking
thought, pure Form as the Form of Formness per se, is still what
which gives real being to things. The Form of any given thing is
all that thing really "is," and this Form is some manifestation of
goodness itself, but usually matter, which isn't really anything at
all, gets in the way of the full manifestation of that goodness. As

form, the Good is precisely limitation, finitude. But fortunately, actual infinity, which would be evil chaos itself, does not and cannot exist: the Good is all that is actual.

PLOTINUS: Being is goodness (and thus unity) itself, but some things have more goodness (and thus more unity) than others. Evil is a privation of good—it simply means less good than something else.

AUGUSTINE: As in Plotinus to some extent, but he argues that evil is not merely a privation, but a *corruption* of the Good. Above all, corruption occurs when a rational being with free will loves what he's not supposed to, loves something lesser than God, which means anything other than God, more than he loves God. The free will itself is a good, but its misuse when directed to a lesser good is its corruption. The human soul is the highest created good, but disobedience leads to corruption of its goodness and the resulting privation is the deepest evil, which is deserves the harshest imaginable excoriation, quarantine, and punishment. Given original sin, everyone deserves eternal punishment, but God in his mercy spares a small number of souls from this deserved damnation.

MONOTHEISM GENERALLY: Some combination of the previous versions. Whatever God creates is, ipso facto, good, but for some or all of the previous reasons, not all that exists should be equally affirmed and loved and praised. Still, the presence of painful or nonideal things in the world also serves the Good of God's plan, since they serve as testing grounds that give the best thing of all, the human being created in God's image, an opportunity to correct them or resist them, and thus to become more good. Even God sending most human beings to eternal hell could be a good because God created it, it is necessary for justice, it fills out the plenitude of God's creation, and so on.

Human experience would be immeasurably impoverished if history had not produced these profound alternate ways of viewing reality and experiencing even our experience of what is painful to us as something good. But our point here is that this renunciation of specific finite purposes is blocked from its full expression as long as it is accomplished only through the expedient of the *displacement* of purpose to another locus—God—which retains the very dualistic structure of purposive existence that made it so problematic, and indeed, by absolutizing it, unifying all of it into a single locus, bestowing it ultimate value and ultimate status as the origin of all being, and removing it from negotiability and personal fungibility, severely exacerbates it. Purposive existence also has its rewards, of course, and in the same move this decentering of our small-scale purposivity also intensifies these rewards: the excitement and meaningfulness of our wee endeavors is now elevated to the level of cosmic drama, an action film pitting good against evil on a universal scale in which we play a part—which is one possible way to make life richer and more interesting. When we talk about atheist mysticism, we are talking about a *more complete* version of this same move of the decentering of our finite purposes, from a Compensatory Theist to an Emulative Atheist position, for here it is the ultimacy of purpose itself that is removed. But this does not merely leave us with a neutral world: it too produces its own versions of the beatific vision, whereby all things, even the painful, are experienced as good, as perfect, and where the rewards of purposivity itself are actually no less intensified, though in a less spiritually expensive way. These too can be roughly encapsulated as follows:

SPINOZA: All things in themselves are perfect, that is, complete, and indeed, completely whatever they are. Evil is only privation: by definition, no thing lacks whatever belongs to its own essence; it only lacks something possessed by something else. So we get the idea of privation only by comparing one thing with another: evil is merely a mental construct. Even the fact that we, as finite modes, must have these mental constructs of good and evil is necessarily entailed in God and therefore perfect. Each thing is exactly as Nature made it, with as much being and power as it has; having that power is identical to striving to increase that power, and succeeding in doing so is what each finite being will consider good, experienced as pleasure. Each thing is necessarily inherent in Nature as Substance, which is itself necessary and thinkable only as existing; as such, each thing's formal essence is also necessary and infinite and eternal and omnipresent. And knowing things in this latter way is an enhancement of our own power of thinking, which is itself a pleasure, which makes us love whatever caused that pleasure—in this case Nature itself, and more specifically whatever necessary event of Nature has enabled us to think this thought about it in each case. So we love whatever happens, love our own existence and essence, love the infinite Substance, and love our own love, and all of these loves run in both directions, and are ultimately one and the same love. Whatever happens is thus good in the only meaningful sense of good.

NIETZSCHE: All things are inseparable from one another, in love with one another. If I can love one thing enough to want it infinitely, I am, ipso facto, wanting and affirming all things, and wanting them infinitely.

BATAILLE: The practice of joy before death is available throughout life: I am the war that will destroy me—a war that kills everything except war. Such is my peace and joy.

In online appendix B, we will also hear from voices from other parts of the world, which I will only briskly summarize here (a fuller explanation can be found in that appendix itself). These include several stances derived from primary Daoist sources:

DAODEJING: What we call good is what we want, identified as definite things by this wanting and encoded in the way things are named in our language. But all of it is really an outgrowth of what we don't name, don't see—don't want—which always continues to saturate it and orient its activity. So it's actually in the fuzzy unwanted stuff that the real source of value lies. By reorienting toward the ambiguous and devalued states that lurk in the fringes of this world of values and objects we access real sustainable value, embedded in the oscillations between what we value and what we don't. The bad, in the broadest sense, is the privileged site of access to the real value of both the bad and the Good.

ZHUANGZI 1: Whatever is happening entails a transition from a prior situation which was different; every definite thing comes from not-that-thing, as in *Daodejing*. The already-formed-thing cannot access the exclusion of itself that preceded it; we cannot know the source that produced and determined us, if anything. We find ourselves being this and not that, and the mere being of this is an affirmation of this as opposed to not-this, entailing its own perspective on itself, in what it finds itself inexplicably being and doing and wanting and liking. This implicitly affirms a standard, in some form or other taking its own inexplicable inclinations as the measure of what is right or good. But this entails also a corresponding negation of all it is and does and wants as wrong and bad, posited in another perspective that is a necessary concomitant of the first. So there is necessarily something to affirm as right and good in every situation, but one that entails its own transition to alternate goods, embodied in its own negation and pain—and we can maximize our experience of rightness by enhancing our own flexibility and adaptability and openness to the infinite alternate goodnesses embodied by these infinite situations and perspectives.

ZHUANGZI 2: Or let's assume I have a prior fixed idea of what is good—perhaps the conventional one, that is, where being alive is better than being dead, being rich is better than being poor and so on. Well, something bad happens to me, a new "this" has thrust itself upon me: if I have taken in the total inaccessibility to the this of the not-this that must be its source and standard, I must be a thorough agnostic, how do I know it is really bad? What arrogance! Epistemological humility tells me to suspend judgment about whether anything is really bad just because it seems bad to me. In that way, the pure question, "How do I know?" does all the work necessary for an optimistic acceptance and affirmation of all that happens as potentially good, a "faith" in the possible goodness of whatever one is experiencing. As the old man says in the famous story of the lost horse, which then brings home a wild horse, which then cripples his son, who then survives because he was exempted from military service (not in the *Zhuangzi* but in the *Huainanzi*, but well expressing this aspect of the former), given that everything is prone to total reversal in an inevitably coming alternate perspective, how do I know that any particular thing is not good, even in terms of some specific fixed conception of the Good? Hence, nothing definitively bad ever happens to me.

ZHUANGZI 3: All things are so interconnected and inseparable that if I love one thing—like my life—I am also loving all the others, as in Nietzsche. "What makes my life good also makes my death good."

ZHUANGZI 4: I remain unbiased to life or to death, in death unbiased to being eaten above ground or below ground—for that unbiased and all-pervasive transformation is what has produced me to begin with. I throw myself into life completely, into death completely, into eating completely, into being eaten completely. I transform and I forget, I forget and I transform. Some resonance to Bataille can be found here.

GUO XIANG: "Good" is synonymous with "becoming-and-being-thus-and-so," for to be thus and so is all there is to affirming the value of thus and so, given that we exist in a thoroughly valueless atheistic cosmos. Whatever else we affirm as right is derivative of this primal self-affirmation. It is not the Good that makes us so or makes things so; rather it is being so that makes us affirm the value of things (cf. Spinoza on conatus and desire). The trouble is the carryover of some notion of the Good from one becoming to another, making us desire something extrinsic to whatever is going on already, whatever is involved in the event of our constant self-becoming. All things are so of themselves, and right to themselves, not motivated by any teleology: they do not become what they are by positing it as a goal, but simply by spontaneously becoming. After the fact of finding themselves to be something, they necessarily affirm the value of that something. So all things are good, because all are good to themselves. We can affirm that same goodness in everything simply by eliminating our own conscious goals, not imposing any blanket notion of good on other moments, and merging into the unconscious becoming and self-affirming of each event.[1]

We also have a few dips into this kind of territory from a different angle in Confucianism:

Philosophies rooted in the *Book of Changes*: Goodness, as what mankind finds desirable, is a continuation of what is beyond good and bad: the balanced interaction and alternation of yin and yang, of negative and positive, of dark and light, which is the only real source of life, growth, being, and everything mankind finds good. The conscious pursuit of goodness is necessary as a way to redress temporary obstructions and imbalances and limitations to this balanced alternation. Conscious pursuit of goodness is a way to get beyond conscious pursuit of goodness, in the restoration, completion and extension of this obliviousness to the Good, which is what lies at both the basis and the pinnacle of human activity and enjoyment, in the unplanned timely transformations of the seasons, the indeterminate middle point of equilibrium between determinate emotional extremes that enables both their arising and their smooth alternations into one another at the appropriate time, the spontaneous responses of the heart to the stimulations of unbalanced temporal situations in the world to restore balance, the self-forgetting of ritual virtuosity, and the effortless actions of the sage and the spontaneous ordering effect this has on the rest of the world. The Good is found everywhere, even in the bad, not only because the bad is a necessary component of the balance that constitutes the real source of goodness lying beyond good and bad, but also because even the human dislike of the bad, the failure to find goodness everywhere itself, the finding of the bad to be bad and our deliberate interventions to adjust it, is exactly as much a necessary component of that very balance, for the human is part of a trinity with heaven and earth, with the role of completing its balanced procession and production of ever fresh states of existence, season after season carrying out the life-giving work of the springtime, of birth and growth and harvest and preservation. Even the balance between finding some things bad and not finding anything bad, or that between trying to be good and not trying to be good, is a continuation of the source of the goodness that lies beyond good and bad.

We also find several quite different approaches to this problem in various forms of Mahāyāna Buddhism:

BUDDHISM (EMPTINESS SCHOOL): All things are empty of any self-nature, and hence free of any of the obstructiveness we experience as attachment to any particular thing, or any view of things being one way or another, including one outcome being good and another outcome being not-good. None are actually anything at all that we could attach to. That end of attachment is exactly what we experience as the end of suffering, Nirvana, as the most good of all. So all events are in their own nature liberated, nirvanic—all are good.

BUDDHISM (HUAYAN): All things are empty of self-nature, so what they really are is the interpenetration of each with all, the openness of each to all, the identity of each with all. It is that interchange itself which is the ultimate reality. Hence, all are free of any of the obstructiveness we experience as attachment to finite things or finite views of things being one way or another, including one outcome being good and another outcome being not-good. None are actually any one specific thing at all that we could attach to. That end of attachment is exactly what we experience as the end of suffering, as Buddhahood, and as the most good of all. So all events are good.

BUDDHISM (EARLY ZEN): All things are manifestations of the One Mind of pure unattached awareness, sheer openness, the allowing space enabling all appearances—and this awareness is all they really are, unconfined to any particular finite appearance. That freedom from attachment is exactly what we experience as the end of suffering, Buddhahood, the most good of all. This mind is what the Buddha experienced in enlightenment, and thus we can call it the Buddha-Nature. So all events are manifestations of the Buddha-Nature. So all events are good.

BUDDHISM (LATER ZEN): But calling it that makes it something to attach to, something finite and determinate, something attachable to, which makes it *not* good. So everything is good, as long as we don't make the mistake of regarding it as good (here we converge with the approach of Emptiness Buddhism brought together with that of *Daodejing*-style Daoism).

BUDDHISM (PURE LAND): We are powerless, corrupt, idiotic, deluded to the point that any judgment we make about true and false, good and bad, right and wrong, useful or useless is hopelessly corrupted by our conditionality, our benighting karma; fortunately, someone somewhere has claimed that there was someone else just like us who once vowed to make all of us useless fools capable of getting free of our complete delusion, which we are not capable of ourselves, simply by turning our attention to him; and then, reportedly, after making this preposterous claim, in some unknown way this being who was initially just like us spent trillions of eons somehow making it so. This is utterly improbable to us, but what do we know? We're total idiots. In any case we have no other possible path to salvation, so we might as well believe this one, recommended only because of its maximally nondemanding character—for anything that demanded anything at all from the likes of us would be a closed door for such weaklings and fools as we are. That very hypothetical vow itself leaps to our lips when we say "Namu Amida Butsu," thereby making it real. But this reckless and unjustifiable exclamation is an expression of hopeless gratitude rather than the merit of our own power: the agent of this gratitude to Amida is Dharmakara, the onetime fool who became Amida, and Amida, the Buddha produced by that fool: our words are the compassion that stipulated that he would not become Amida unless such words made us also into Buddhas. So even though the world and we ourselves are fully corrupt, we are too corrupt to even judge the world or ourselves or each others; all the world is neither good nor bad, but all of it is unobjectionable, judged by neither ourselves, who are too ignorant to judge, nor Amida, who views all with equal compassion and has no interest in judging—and our very despair is the realization of our unlikely salvation.

BUDDHISM (LOTUS SUTRA / TIANTAI): All things are empty of self-nature, which means all are ontologically ambiguous: any can be legitimately "read" as anything at all, when recontextualized ingeniously enough. Hence, as in Zhuangzi 1, we can go

ahead and see them in any possible way, and there will always be
something right about it: our seeing as this or that is all that is required to really disambiguate it into being this or that, not merely
as a projection onto a blank screen, but as a genuine bringing
out of something that is really there. It will, with its own inner
resources, be able to fully corroborate and contribute to this attributed identity. The best thing anything can be for us is a Bodhisattva (of the *Lotus Sutra* and *Nirvana Sutra* kind, that is, as the
eternal active aspect of eternal Buddhahood, not merely a means
to the end of eventually ending its activity in Buddhahood), who
loves us unconditionally as one loves and adores one's only child,
and who is constantly changing into whatever form will best liberate us from the sufferings brought by our attachments. We can
thus look at all persons and all things as loving us unconditionally
and constantly presenting something specifically for our own
benefit, tailored to our specific partial obsessions, false beliefs,
attachments, and sufferings. The bad stuff that happens is a bitter
medicine for something or other that we can surely discover there
if we look at ourselves in a certain way—for we too are constitutively ambiguous, and whatever problems there are are our own
problems, as much as their solutions are. Anything that happens
to us is good and makes us good. By the same token, there will
never be any experience, even supreme Buddhahood, that is not
also ambiguously pain, readable as pain, inescapably susceptible
to being experienced as pain. Indeed, not only as pain in general,
but as my specific pain at this precise moment of my tawdry finite
experience, as well as my delusion, and my stupid, self-defeating,
evil attempt to escape my pain predicated on that delusion. This,
however, means that this pain and stupidity and evil of mine
going on right here and now are equally present and absent—that
is, ambiguously present and ambiguously absent—right here and
now and everywhere else. In this form they are omnipresent and
omniabsent—and these two end up being two words for the same
fact about them. My pain's omnipresence shows me that it cannot
be escaped, for all things can appear as it, and it can appear as all
things. But this is my pain's omniabsence as well, for it can appear
as all things, and all things can appear as it. Because it cannot be
escaped, my second-order desire to change it, which entails the
interpretative focal setting that had insisted on reading it *only* as
pain, vanishes—I know that anywhere else I will be no better off
than I am here, but also no worse off—or rather, does *not* vanish,

but is also seen to be ambiguous, and is thus itself recontextualized, revealed to (also) be a compassionate *upāya* (skillful
means), and also a direct eternal expression of Buddhahood.
Precisely in seeing the inescapability of pain and the concomitant
desire to change it, I am free of both, while fully dwelling in both.
Anything that happens to me is the absolute unconditioned,
Mahāparinirvāna itself, Buddhahood itself, the best possible
state, omnipresent and eternal, manifesting in an infinity of alternate forms in response to the dispositions of sentient beings, each
form of which is readable equally as compassion and as delusion,
and as my own or anyone and everyone else's.[2]

    This last point gives us purchase on a remarkable datum pertaining to
the phenomenology of religion. We are speaking here of what ends up being a religion of universal love for and from all beings to and from all beings.
But this rests specifically on atheist premises, which help understand why a
religion of love based on the idea of *God's* love is so often bound to violently
undermine itself. Only feeling oneself loved unconditionally by all beings
allows one to love unconditionally all beings. When we see them as loving
us in this way, we in turn are able to see ourselves as loving them and doing the same for them, and thus constantly transforming in ways that will
liberate them. The Tiantai explanation for this interesting effect involves
the mutual inclusion of the lover in the loved and the loved in the lover,
without eliminating the difference that allows for the love. Each is both
sufferer and reliever of sufferer, for, being ambiguous, to be either of these
two is to be both of these two and neither of these two, to the maximal degree that anything can be or not be anything. It goes without saying, of
course, that this is also a religion of universal hatred, entailing hatred of all
beings for all beings just as much as love of all beings for all beings—for the
hatred and the love are themselves ambiguous, all hatred being readable as
love and all love as hatred. But far from being an objection, this is precisely
what clinches the case. For it is not only that this clears the way for a love
great enough to endure even within hatred, operative and discernible at all
times in and as that hatred, if and when one is focused on the love side of
the equation, as one may do when explicitly committed to the particular
religious practices enjoined. More important still is the love that obtains
between the love and the hatred themselves, if we may put it that way—that
is, precisely their ambiguity, their fungibility into one another, their recognition of themselves in one another, their irresistible draw toward and into
one another, their need for both the otherness of the other in contrast to
themselves and the overturning of that otherness in the recognition of that

other as a self-expandingly and self-revealingly alienated, alternate version of themselves, a bodhisattva transformation of themselves. The great love that is also hatred is also the great hatred that is also love. What is essential is to overcome both the "small love" and the "small hatred" in which we usually live our lives—the love and hatred that are simply mutually exclusive of one another—and these can only be "overcome" by loving them as well, helping them to be even more of what they already are, to expand their own range and power, to be more fully themselves. The trouble with both ordinary hatred *and ordinary love* is the ontological dualisms on which they are built and which they exacerbate. Hence it is clear that this effect will thus be made impossible if one of the lovers is God, whose nature we definitively cannot share, that is, as long as the ontological divide between creator and creature is maintained as on any level unambiguous (even if, perchance, they happen to be joined in indivisible hypostatic union within some single being, or for that matter in every being). If, however, Human Nature and Divine Nature are not defined as mutually exclusive, if there is no way to ensure that the one cannot be equally validly read *as* the other, we must eliminate the strict dichotomy between creator and created, or between infinite and finite—and in the final analysis, even between any two instances of putatively unilateral finitude. The denial of this dichotomy is the foundation stone of atheist mysticism.

But with this denial, we also deny the *ultimacy* of purpose and control, which is concomitant with this dichotomy: unless the controller is completely distinct from the controlled, control is not ultimate, not complete, not absolute. An absolute controller must stand above whatever he controls. We are thus left with only partial control, always saturated with and threatened by the uncontrolled—indeed, since the control is never complete, never the sole ultimate source, we can only view the entire complex of purpose and control as themselves dependent on something controlled by no one: purposes grow out of, and are forever dependent on and expressive of, the purposeless. But this is where our suffering begins—in the lack of total control.

We have already seen many ways in which atheist mysticism can valorize and "redeem" the parts of experience that violate our own conscious Will and purposes, yet without invoking an alternate Will or purpose. One solution, Bataille's, is to find a compromise formation allowing us to vicariously experience this torture, to be experiencing our death while also surviving it—either in the historical forms of sacrifice and its many religious vicissitudes, or the preferred form of deliberate contemplation of the violence and imminent dissolution at all times, but in the form of our own willing embrace of this thought, which translates into its own kind of ecstasy. That is one way to go about it—and a good case can be made for some form of communal self-torture as a core element in religious experience, which can further clarify for us the extraordinary religious value of some form of *pain* more generally. Among all the authors taken up in this book, Bataille seems at first glance to stand alone in the seemingly outsized place he gives to the ritual use of pain and death in his conception of the human condition, as well as in what he considers the only adequate response to that condition. But one of the great advantages provided by pausing to focus on the outrageously disproportionate treatment he gives these unpleasant matters is his thematization of the role of pain, which, in truth, resonates in subtler (and perhaps more judicious) forms in all our authors, allowing us to see its crucial role in the beatific vision of any mysticism, theistic or atheistic. Beatific vision is thought to be a kind of bliss, and that it certainly must be. But it is the bliss that issues from an embrace of the infinite, the unconditioned, and that means it cannot exclude any form of possible experience whatever. Whatever bliss there may be in beatitude must be a bliss that can coexist with or even be coextensive with agony, blissful in spite of or even because of its agony, and thus fearing no possible turn of events, for only then can it remain unshakable under all conditions, proof against any possible turn of temporal events.

This is worth considering in more detail. For it is certainly true, and initially quite surprising, that rituals built around pain are popular wherever there are human beings. The voluntary embrace of pain is seen in firewalking, self-crucifixion, self-flagellation, self-starvation, moral self-suppression and self-monitoring, and all sorts of other gross and subtle renunciations. We can understand this as a way of feeling the joy of retroflected aggression, or of the power shown in being able to endure these pains, or like all rituals, a way of giving oneself a sense of magical control, however spurious, over unpredictable natural situations and cognitive dissonances by artificially enacting and inflating them, thereby allowing us to genuinely experience them as valuable and satisfying, perhaps not without an influx of endorphins.

What is more puzzling is that these rituals of voluntary pain, especially the vicarious experience of pain by onlookers, build social cohesion, promote prosocial behavior and solidarity. Why do they have this effect? We can again invoke the vicarious structure put forth in Spinoza's *Ethics* (see E3p27),[3] somewhat corroborated by modern "mirror neuron" research. The observers of intense pain also experience this intense pain, in a fainter, peripheral, and above all, surpassable form. Then they snap away from it, realize they are someone other than the person suffering, and experience relief. They thus experience both the forms of power enjoyed by the self-torturer, listed in the previous paragraph, and one further power in addition, the power of going beyond this pain instantly. As Bataille says of animal sacrifice, they get to vicariously experience their own death and then live again, live to tell the tale, to recall the strife and pain in the tranquility of its "otherness" in time, place, and recipient. This is the first reason why pain is the most effective for building social cohesion: although it is true that the same effect can be seen in vicarious experiences of extreme pleasure (e.g., sex shows, rock concerts), the supplement in that case will be the letdown of not being the enjoyers, rather than the exhilaration of not being the sufferer.

We may add that the ritual form of externalization is also a concretization of the initially diffuse and omnipresent discomfort of everyday existence (for which each of the thinkers we've examined has provided an etiology), giving it a form as an object that is observable and hence at least minimally distanced, localizing it in a particular place, which makes it seem manageable in a new way, and there is some relief from this reduction in extent and this added sense of controllability. When all the pain is concentrated so vividly over there and I vicariously share in this pain, I have one less pain, that is, the pain of trying to locate the real source and locus of my own pain.

But pain is especially important for self-transcending social cohesion because to begin with pain is at once two different things at opposite ends of the spectrum with respect to the separateness of the self:

1. Pain is what is definitionally present precisely as the locus where my sense of self ends. Assuming that my sense of self is ultimately grounded in my sense of control—that I define "me" as the part of the universe I can control and "not-me" as the part that I cannot control—pain is where I lose control, where I begin to disintegrate. By definition it is what I would eliminate if I could. Pain is what goes against my Will in whole or in part; to be pain means that it is violating at least something that some part of me wants (my body, a particular organ of my body, some partial identification, my self-image, my health, etc.). Insofar as it is pain, it is an influx of not-me. (Voluntary pain, which is primary and unavoidable in all selves, is the pitting of one desire against another, above all the global desire to have or be more or other self; in undertaking a pain voluntarily I am effectively establishing another, broader self for myself—assuming that "voluntary" equals "self.")

2. And yet it is also what is most urgently and unavoidably related to me, something I feel in my inmost, least communicable, least sharable, least *escapable* kernel, concerning me and me specifically with the utmost urgentness. It is what I cannot escape (for by definition, again, it is precisely

what I would escape if I could). In this sense, it is my own-most self, what is most like an "essence" in the strict sense: that which I cannot eliminate from myself without ceasing to be, what I have always with me as long as I am me.

Pain is thus the overlap or convergence of self and nonself, of deepest self and deepest nonself. This crucial point was memorably evoked by Hegel with the phrase "the privilege of pain":[4] only very complex, self-maintaining, integrative organisms, negatively self-relating entities, beings that can somehow include their own Other, that persist and subsist even in their own negation can experience pain. A lesser being is simply annihilated when something that contradicts its present state of being impinges on it. The new thing simply pushes it away, replacing it at that locus. Pain is what demonstrates to us that we are not merely finite beings, that we are paradoxically always both limited and beyond that limit—not the abstract infinity that excludes finitude, but the true infinity that is the nonduality of finitude and infinity, the identity of identity and difference.

To some extent this is true not only of pain but of ecstatic pleasure as well—in sex, in music—but less so in that the self, although by definition losing and forgetting itself in these states, nevertheless wants them, attempts to incorporate them, and embraces them at least in retrospect. They can be smoothly accepted into a prospective *ideal* self, something I would have if I had total control, and thus can be extended into a future prospect with relative continuity.

It is thus that when I vicariously experience the pain of, say, the firewalker, that pain is at once both me and not me: the inaccessibility of the pain to the self makes all pain something not belonging to any one self: pain cannot belong to selves, and yet belongs inalienably to all selves that experience it at all. It is a cipher that is as much mine as his, as little his as mine. So the Crucifixion makes all Christians the one body of Christ (according to St. Paul), sharing in its pain and its glory. The ritual observers of a firewalk are bound into a community that will sacrifice for one another, overcoming the usual social boundaries between selves. The ascetics and rave-partiers become one through their extreme experiences.

Buddhism is, here as everywhere, a bit of an outlier. Suffering is the one thing all sentient beings share. I am to contemplate the suffering of all creatures as I suffer, to see it as truly universal. Here, instead of the ritual concretion into a specific locus, the original diffuseness of suffering is exacerbated, accepted fully, rather than fled from. It is no longer restricted to a single ritual enactment, but rather diffused into a universal principle. I am to deliberately contemplate this in myself and in others, as pervading the world in all directions—there is suffering everywhere. The Buddhist story of the mustard seed illustrates this well. An infant had died and his mother grieved. Unable to accept her infant's death, she carried the little corpse all around, begging everyone to help her bring him back to life. that a certain magical wise man, this guy called the Buddha, was nearby and might be able to do the job, she goes to him. He tells her that yes, certainly, it is very easy to solve this problem, he will make the potion right away, but he needs one small thing—the recipe requires a tiny mustard seed, but it must be from a household where no one has ever died. Overjoyed, the mother sets out to find this key ingredient, knocking on door after door. And of course at each stop she learns that in every place without exception a loved one has been lost. She gets the message, becomes a nun, and attains Nirvana, the only end of suffering.[5] This then *counts* as the fulfillment of the Buddha's promise to end her pain: it lies in seeing that the pain is universal, that is, inescapable—that is, if I may in typical Tiantai manner apply a Tiantai exegesis to this classic pre-Tiantai Buddhist tale, it is ended by seeing that *it can never be ended.* The pain is what brings her together with all other sentient beings, precisely in the realization that there is no place to escape it, and simply this is the ending of her suffering. Suffering is literally everywhere, even down to the smallest mustard seed's worth of space in the universe—as we are told in some scriptures that there is not a speck of space even as large as a mustard seed anywhere in the universe where the bodhisattva has not (over countless eons) sacrificed his life, been torn to shreds in agony and compassion for sentient beings. For equally omnipresent is my own compassionate desire to remove suffering—in essence, just my own default desire to stop suffering myself but experienced from within, where pain is neither self nor nonself, or both self and nonself. I experience my own pain as the pain of all sentient beings; I experience the pain of all sentient beings as my pain. I attempt to remove both at once and am constantly failing to do so—and the *constancy* of my failure is my success; it is the ending of suffering.

In Tiantai, we may note, this idea is extended to its ultimate conclusion, for there it is said that suffering itself is precisely the Dharmakāya, the universal and eternal body of the Buddha—it is both the pain and the attempt to eradicate it (which alone makes it pain), everywhere, always, eternally, ineradicably. Here we have the properly atheist religious experience of pain: the most direct and vivid possible experience of the coextensivity and copresence of self and nonself. This is the Tiantai doctrine: evil and suffering are ineradicably inherent in the Buddha-nature. Here as in all Buddhist systems, suffering and evil are both direct concomitants of finitude, conditionality, impermanence. The Tiantai move is to see precisely this finitude and this pain as literally omnipresent and infinite, and therefore inescapable. When I stub my toe, for example, it is a consequence of an encounter between my toe and the world, at the boundary that marks my finitude, impinging on my conditional existence and threatening its preservation. The moment I see this precise finite moment of toe pain as literally omnipresent, pervading the universe, present in all the oceans and rivers, moving the sun and moon and galaxies, exploding through the Big Bang, and persisting inescapably at every locus and every moment throughout the cosmos, my pain will be both hugely expanded and instantly transformed: my pain, I now learn, not only suffers on this side of my skin but also inflicts the suffering from the other side; it not only feels and gives pain but also plants and sows, grows and decays, walks and talks and flies and swims, loves and nurtures, hates and kills. My pain is present *as* all that happens. In Tiantai we do not need to say all the world is really God, or God's Will, or the pure Buddha-nature, or Nirvana, or Brahman, or Love, or Goodness, or Neutral Matter, or Sublime Indifferent Nature. Instead, any and every possible finite determination may be taken up, each as it occurs, as the source, the Substance, the omnipresent and eternal nature of all that exists. It is thus transcended as a datum *simpliciter*, in its raw finitude, for it now is revealed to have the power to appear *as* anything and everything else, even its most direct opposite. It has no determinate attributes because it now has nothing that contrasts to it; its "eternity and omnipresence" exclude no possible alternate attributes. As such it is, as a definite entity, unobtainable: it is nothing in particular. Yet it does not vanish; like everything else, the unobtainable still appears, only now it appears *as* and *in* all its opposites, all that it seemed to exclude. It is inescapable, it is unobtainable. Its inescapability is its unobtainability. The world is eternal/noneternal, finite/infinite, self/other, bliss/agony: that is, it is the Tiantai Three Truths, the Dharmakāya pervading all times and places, which is nothing other than this particular pain going on right here and now. Though it is not the only one, pain is one direct manifestation of our paradoxical nature and for us the most relevant one, since it is the locus of our suffering as finite conditional beings. Finitude is pain. In trying to escape this pain we had been sustaining it, for pain is rooted in the nature of the putatively finite, the putatively escapable. In realizing that we cannot escape it, we have escaped it. Here our pain reveals quite directly the paradoxical nature of all existence: the convergence of infinity and finitude, the infinitude of finitude and the finitude of the infinite—leaving behind neither one. And that convergence is the heart and soul of atheist mysticism in all its forms.

So it is comprehensible that we want pain in a sense, and for several reasons: first, pain is a unique way of being both self and beyond self at the same time. Second, pain is a way of breaking out of especially recalcitrant habitual forms of being, of forcing us into new ones when we have stagnated into an overstable, pent-up form of being—but one that, by nature, cannot be remedied by our Will and courage, which are themselves conditioned by the narrowed condition of our habituation structure. We secretly desire to be busted out, but by definition it is not something we can ourselves bust out of, since it is our own inability to bust out that we want to be busted out of. So we need a violent imposition of something from outside. This is the violence that we see Bataille romanticizing: what will transgress against our habitual self-recognitions, our usual boundaries, and free us from the realm of utility, of tooldom, of single-purpose, of thinghood. But even for Bataille, this violence only attains its mystical form if we can somehow experience this will to break us as the very same Will that we are, the heedless virulence of our own oceanic appetites to break the world apart for our own fleeting, wasteful delectation, our own ruthlessly unconditionally squandering love for ourselves. The mystical vision here is of an inhabiting of the violence that annihilates us as identical with the hunger in ourselves that unblinkingly consumes and discards carcass after carcass. In a certain sense this romanticized violence, in its mystical form, has to be willed and loved by the same Will and love that wills and loves our own being—by something who, in some sense, loves us. What wants to hurt us must also be what wants to cherish us. For otherwise it is not the more and the beyond of thinghood that we are promised by this violence, but merely the less—a lesser thinghood rather than the transcendence of thinghood altogether as realized in the convergence of the predator and the prey in the core of our experience. A violence that is not at the same time a loving Intimacy is simply trying to diminish or destroy us. Only in the identity of the love and the violence can a form of good-beyond-good be thus discerned in us not getting what we want, and this is the sine qua non of mystical ecstasy: there is finally nothing to fear and everything to celebrate when even what we most fear and detest—not only undesired events but even our own second-order pain in response to those undesired events—begins to be experienced as occasioning utmost joy.

We can begin to discern how a certain additional dimension is added when suffering is being imposed on us precisely by someone who loves us—which seems to provide much of the further hypererotic thrill seen in the great mystical experiences within the theistic sphere. For if we were to compile a list of what we, as outsiders, would guess might motivate people to want to believe in a personal creator God who oversees the world, we might list things like the comforting presence of an all-powerful caregiver or ally, a guarantor of impartial justice and a happy ending for history, a foundation for the coherence of the world and of our knowledge, a basis for hope of personal immortality, a feeling of being unconditionally loved, a bestowal of purpose, an assurance for an explanation for apparently sense-less events, and so on. We believe that without much trouble, on the basis of what has already been discussed, we can now see both how the idea of God as personal, as purposive, actually fails to do these jobs, instead under-mining precisely these desiderata, and also how a full-throated, mystical Godlessness might better provide some of these boons (if boons they are). But one thing the idea of a personal God provides that might seem espe-cially hard for Godlessness to provide has come into view in the more psy-chologically convoluted territory touched on here: what we might describe as *the need for erotic surrender to a loving torturer*. For there is undeniably a strain of this seemingly strange but unmistakable need being spectacularly satisfied in some of the most notorious exemplars of theistic mysticism, and it may not be at all obvious how a nontheistic mysticism could fit the bill.

Can such an end still be attained without an actual all-powerful and per-sonal torturer, God? Yes. Let us start with what might seem an unlikely candidate, Spinoza. The key is found in what we will see Spinoza calling "the Intellectual Love of God." Recall E5p18cs: "It may be objected that in understanding God to be the cause of all things, we thereby consider God to be the cause of pain [and therefore we *should* hate him, just as we always necessarily hate whatever is the cause of our pain, according to E3p13cs]. To this I reply that in so far as we understand the causes of pain, it ceases to be a passive emotion (E5p3);[6] that is (E3p59),[7] to that extent it ceases to be pain. So in so far as we understand God to be the cause of pain, to that extent we feel pleasure." Why do we love? Because something has made us able to do and be more than we had been before—"pleasure associated with an external cause"—we therefore love that something. Why do we want to be loved? Because whatever loves us wants us to do and be more than before, since its love for us is due to its perception that our presence makes it able to do and be more than it had been doing and being before, causing it pleasure associated with ourselves as the cause. That is its love for us, and it necessarily entails that in wanting external causes around that can do more to make itself do more of what it does, it wants to make us able to do more of what we do. Why, then, would we love what hurts us, as long as we see that it is ultimately Spinoza's Godless God? It is because what hurts us is also what makes us able to do and be more. And why is that the case? Because what is hurting us is necessity itself, and necessity itself is omni-presence, what is equally present in the part and in the whole, what can-not not exist, and what is therefore the omnipresence and eternity of our own necessity, our own ability to be and do. Even when it is, in one sense, thwarting or diminishing us, it is, in another sense, the enabling of our own moreness to the precise extent that we understand it is necessary—enabling what Hegel calls our "privilege of pain," the ability to be both what we are and also beyond what we are at once. For "to understand as necessary" is the endeavor and activity of our own minds, and whenever we understand one more thing as necessary, this endeavor has succeeded to a greater extent by just that much: our mind's power has increased, which is pleasure. Since this disastrous thing has served as the external cause of that pleasure, we necessarily love it. That is, when we understand the disastrous event as necessary, as nonnegotiably built into the structure of being, as actually inseparable from the built-in necessity of our own being, as part of the same Substance, that understanding itself is an addition to our ability to think, and thus to act and to be. That understanding is itself a complete convergence of maximized experience of the pain as inextricable and unavoidable and the direct enjoyment of that very fact. In understanding the necessity of pain, we are actively taking pleasure in our own pain; the indifferent torturer is actively present as the immanent cause of our understanding, internal to our own conatus to understand, the power of which is expanded by this additional act of understanding and which thus feels it as pleasure.

But this understanding of necessity passes beyond the Second Kind of Knowledge to the Third Kind of Knowledge: seeing this individual disaster as a mode that not only necessarily follows from but tautologically expresses the Attributes of God. The understanding of this necessity means understanding it as precisely a modality of the one Substance of which our endeavoring mind is itself a mode. The necessity experienced by our understanding in its striving and its pleasure and its love, when it understands the disaster as necessarily entailed in God and thereby loves it, is literally the same Substance as the necessity it understands in the occurrence of the disaster. Feeling pleasure, it loves the cause of the pleasure: therefore loving the necessity, loving itself, being loved by the necessity, and being loved by itself. Understanding our own pain as necessary and eternal is thus the full realization of the urge to enjoy God's torture with masochistic glee. As Spinoza says, this intellectual love of God—precisely, love for God's Godlessness, God's indifference, God's impersonality and necessity—is the convergence of our love for God and God's love for us: it is just because our love is such that we cannot possibly want God to love us in return (EVp19) that our love of God *is* God's love for us: "the mind's intellectual love of God is part of the infinite love wherewith God loves himself" (E5p36). Thus do love and torture, bliss and pain, finally fully converge: beatitude is the love of the radiance of God beyond God, God as Godless infinite space and all possible experience, necessary and indivisible and infinitely active, undergirding as much as undermining all personality and all purpose, including our own, and experienced as the infinite indifference of love and the infinite love of indifference. The experience of *amor fati,* to borrow Nietzsche's phrase, is the experience of a love that doesn't belong to me or to any other self and is not aimed only in any one direction, not gratified by any one purpose alone: it is necessary love that finds itself in love with necessity, with all necessity, where the love is the necessity and the necessity is the love, as we saw in another form in Zarathustra's affirmation of the eternity of all things. Again, this can only be accomplished fully in the most thoroughgoing atheism. If, on the contrary, we regard the event as merely contingent, or as caused by a personality with free will and thus not caused necessarily, and regard ourselves also as a nonnecessary being with free will, then we have simply a clash of wills, or a clash of one Will (our own) with a will-less world. This understanding itself is no addition to our power: it is itself painful, an experience of increased limitation, and in light of this understanding, the disaster is no fun at all.

In Nietzsche, this dimension is accomplished by a joy in the creative Will that is so great that it wills all its own preconditions, a Will therefore strong enough to desire and need all its own sufferings and pains, all that contradicts any specific form it may have assumed as a goad that pushed it to create further beyond itself, making it sufficient to say yes to all things, to all pains; the loving torturer of oneself turns out to be one's own Will. The creation of meaning is the means to get beyond meaning; purpose, the creative Will, is what transcends purpose and merges with fully affirmed purposelessness. In Bataille, the forward-pushing dimension of Will drops out of this picture: we are left with a direct Thou-Art-That experience of literally being the chaos and war of pre-tool-driven life/death itself. This is directly to embody not only the suffering but also meaninglessness, and to revel in this torture of one's other purposes. Purpose is deployed only to be redirected to union with the chaos that is one's own destruction. But this too is joy: the joy of erotic surrender to the torturer, which is oneself and beyond oneself, the self-nonself from which your self and all selves emerge and that just as exuberantly destroys them all. One is destroyed and undestroyed in entering into the destroyer of oneself, when one becomes, not a warrior but war, as the fire does not burn itself up but is the burning up of itself. We may here recall Bataille's blunt verdict: "In reality, when we curse death we only fear ourselves: The severity of *our will* is what makes us tremble. We lie to ourselves when we dream of escaping the movement of luxurious exuberance of which we are only the most intense form."[8] If it is the virulence of our own will that we fear when we fear this pitiless sublimity, it is equally the severity of our own love that we love, that loves and is loved, when we love it. Here in this paradoxical convergence of our finitude and our infinity, in the true infinity immediately experienced as the convergence of our breaking and our completion, in the awed and awful embrace extending in all directions as this fear and this love come to coincide, is the atheist's serene beatitude, the peace that passes understanding. We have landed back in the open wilds of the *Zhuangzi*:

> After three days he was able to expel the entire world from himself. Another seven days and he could expel all definite things. Nine more days and he was able to expel his own life. With life thrown aside, the dawn came crashing through. Crashed through by the daybreak, singularity lay in plain sight everywhere. Beholding only singularity, both past and present vanished. Free of past and present, he entered the undying and unborn.
>
> Killing all that lives, birthing all that lives: that is the undying, that is the unborn. There is nothing it doesn't send off, nothing it doesn't take in, nothing it doesn't destroy—and nothing it does not form, shape, complete, become.
>
> Such is this something; we name it the Tranquil Turmoil. For therein alone lies the consummation of its tumultuous tranquility: in the throes of the turmoil forming each and all.[9]

Acknowledgments

To paraphrase what a much greater writer once put at the beginning of a much more beautiful work: I'd hate to tell you how much this lousy little book has cost me in terms of time and worry and aggravation. But in this case, I was not the only one who was getting battered by the thing: it was also battering the hapless students and friends and research assistants whom I kept importuning with it. Back when it was a lot longer and a lot more unruly, back when it was called *Otherwise Than God*, and then *Towards the Opposite of God*, and then *Monotheism and Its Discontents*, and then *Epiphanies of Godlessness*, and then *Godless Beatitude*, and then *Ecstasies of the Aimless Cosmos*, and then *Raw Infinity and the Wild Sublime* . . . Back then, I had even gone ahead and made it the subject matter and primary reading of not one but two or maybe even three courses at the Divinity School of the University of Chicago, where I work. The book was not only a lot rougher and more sprawling in those days; it was also more unfiltered and aggressive, almost compulsively peppered with irreverent jokes and provocations, as well as the occasional embarrassingly personal cri de coeur. I got quite a few salutary surprises working through that mass of material with those students over the course of several years. Some were delighted where I thought they might be delighted, and some a bit offended where I thought there might be some possibility of offense; but in many other cases both the affective reactions and the intellectual points made either in support or opposition caught me completely off guard. In the process, I not only learned a lot about where there were shared intuitions that needed no belaboring and where, on the contrary, immense detailed exposition was required, I also learned a huge amount about where my assumptions were woefully misguided and where the holes in my knowledge were in urgent need of repair. For whatever extent I subsequently succeeded in plugging the holes and trimming the fat, those students are thus the first on the long list of the many to whom my gratitude is thus now owed.

But I didn't stop there in forcing this book on people. Over those years

I also hired a succession of student assistants to read, review, discuss, and help edit the manuscript; to help me track down citations I had vaguely conjured up from memory; to check my alleged facts — one after another as wildly different drafts emerged. These selfless laborers were the real front-line stalwarts in getting this thing into shape: taking great care on page after page, overcoming their own hesitation to be frank with me, in both extensive annotations and face-to-face discussions, about what made sense to them and what didn't, what went too far and what not far enough, where I was losing the thread and where overegging the pudding; not to mention tracking down, correcting, and standardizing my sometimes wayward citations, attributions, and summaries. All of these students have either gone on to make their own intellectual careers or are well on the way to doing so. But even this was not enough: I also buttonholed many respected friends and colleagues, people I knew to have a rare depth of learning in a variety of fields and who were endowed with mercilessly brilliant minds, sharp red pens, and refined philosophical and religious sensibilities, and imposed on them the task, in the name of friendship and collegiality, of slogging through whatever version of the monster I may have had available — hunting for errors, blind spots, and excesses or insufficiencies of fact, argument, or tone. Again and again these generous souls came through for me in flying colors, with keen observations, urgent interventions, eye-opening commentaries, and indispensable suggestions for rewriting, rearranging, or rethinking. I cannot thank them enough for the labor, the time, the attention, the generosity, the opposition — for the sharpening and clarifying that their superb brains contributed to making this book possible. The length of the list of their names gives such mortifying testimony to the promiscuity of my search for help that I find myself worrying that it might discomfit them. Nevertheless, gratitude is owed to Eun-Young Hwang, to Stephen Walker, to Jinhao Pan, to David Nirenberg, to Ryan Coyne, to Fabian Heubel, to Franklin Perkins, to Rebekah Rosenfeld, to Paul Napier, to Anthony Casadonte, to Alexander Douglas, to Alan Levinovitz, to Adam Safron, to Hans-Georg Moeller, to Evan Ziporyn, to Paul D'Ambrosio. And special thanks go to Kyle Wagner, acquisitions editor for the University of Chicago Press, who not only did the thing I was most hoping he might do — that is, *liking* the book — but also, crucially, rescued it from the limbo into which its unwieldy size and unruly structure had consigned it, finding a way to highlight the throughline and structure the divisions, hammering out a happy medium of linear printed presentation and unbuttoned online digression that finally gave it the kind of resonance and rhyme it needed to count as a coherent single edifice. Much much gratitude goes to all these kind and kindred souls, and any others I may have forgotten, for their open-handed help and their great-hearted goodwill. And in the case of a book like this one, there is perhaps room, here at the back of the line just among us Z-listers, to express another kind of gratitude: to whatever "obscure and again obscure" concatenation of causes and conditions it was that in the desert of the real brought into being, and brought me one fine day to stumble into, the oasis of the big LZ (not to mention ZZ and ZY and ZR and ZL)—for starting so much, for sustaining so much, for making so much possible.

Selected excerpts from Georges Bataille, *Accursed Share, Volume 1*, translated by Robert Hurley (New York: Zone Books, 1991), pp. 33–35. © 1989 by Urzone, Inc. Used with permission.

Friedrich Nietzsche, *The Anti-Christ, Ecce Homo, Twilight of the Idols, and Other Writings*, edited by Aaron Ridley and Judith Norman, translated by Judith Norman. © Cambridge University Press 2005. Reproduced with permission of The Licensor through PLSClear.

Baruch Spinoza, *The Ethics and Selected Letters*, translated by Samuel Shirley, edited with introduction by Seymour Feldman. © 1982 by Hackett Publishing Company, Inc. Reprinted by permission of Hackett Publishing Company, Inc. All rights reserved.

Georges Bataille, *Visions of Excess: Selected Writings, 1927–1939*, translated by Allan Stoekl, with Carl R. Lovitt and Donald M. Leslie, Jr. (University of Minnesota Press, 1985). English translation copyright © 1985 by the University of Minnesota.

This book is dedicated to the memory of my mother, Charlotte Weinberg Ziporyn (1931–2023).

Appendixes

For access to the online appendixes, see https://press.uchicago.edu/sites/ziporyn/index.html.

Notes

1. I had to laugh anew at this many years later when I stumbled on the reference: "Why did I like women's breasts so much? I mean, I knew why I liked them, thanks, but why did I like them *so much?*" Kingsley Amis, *That Uncertain Feeling* (New York: Harcourt, Brace, 1956), 56; italics in the original.

2. In exploring the doctrines of Tiantai Buddhism especially, I found some idea of how to think about what it would mean for something to be entirely unchanged while at the same time registering as utterly different, and to qualify as something utterly different while nevertheless remaining exactly the same—only because the general condition for the identity of any entity as such is structured via a thorough intersubsumption of sameness and difference; that is, because nothing is actually monolithically the same as itself to begin with.

3. There are, of course, Chinese schools that regard *wuwei* itself as subordinate to *youwei* (有為), that is, (the appearance of) purposelessness as a very useful tool in the hands of ultimate purpose—in this case, rulership. This is evident in Hanfeizi's interpretation of the *Daodejing*, where *wuwei* is read as nonaction as a tactic to conceal the ruler's intent, thereby the better to suss out the character and agendas of his ministers and servants. Here too the universe is probably believed to be *wuwei*, but we have a double structure: *wuwei* is the basis on which *youwei* comes to exist, but emulations of *wuwei* are then useful for the particular *youwei* of rulership. We would regard this as a special example of a kind of Compensatory Atheism.

4. Jan Assmann, *Of God and Gods: Egypt, Israel, and the Rise of Monotheism* (Milwaukee: University of Wisconsin Press, 2008), 110.

INTRODUCTION

1. What I mean by "mystical" will be explained in detail later, but for now I offer a maximally succinct placeholder: I mean something like the experience of copresence or even complete coextensivity or, ultimately, interidentity of finitude and infinity— that is, of unmeasured extra depth, of "moretoitivity," of an untotalizable infinity in and as each finite experience, and indeed in and as finitude as such. I realize that this, as stated, will not make much sense to many readers, but for now let's leave it at that.

2. Friedrich Nietzsche, *Twilight of the Idols: or, How to Philosophize with a Hammer*, trans. Duncan Large (Oxford: Oxford University Press, 1998), 19.

3. See Sigmund Freud, *The Origins of Religion: and Taboo, Moses and Monotheism, and Other Works* (London: Penguin, 1985), 142–146.

4. Jacques Lacan, *The Four Fundamental Concepts of Psychoanalysis*, in *The Seminar of Jacques Lacan, Book XI*, ed. Jacques-Alain Miller, trans. Alan Sheridan (New York: Norton, 1973), 59.

5. *Digha Nikaya*, DN 1. 2.3. [Wrong view 5]: "But sooner or later, bhikkhus, after the lapse of a long period, there comes a time when this world begins to expand once again. While the world is expanding, an empty palace of Brahmā appears. Then a certain being, due to the exhaustion of his life-span or the exhaustion of his merit, passes away from the Ābhassara plane and re-arises in the empty palace of Brahmā. There he dwells, mind made, feeding on rapture, self-luminous, moving through the air, abiding in glory. And he continues thus for a long, long period of time.

"Then, as a result of dwelling there all alone for so long a time, there arises in him dissatisfaction and agitation, (and he yearns): 'Oh, that other beings might come to this place!' Just at that moment, due to the exhaustion of their life-span or the exhaustion of their merit, certain other beings pass away from the Ābhassara plane and re-arise in the palace of Brahmā, in companionship with him. There they dwell, mind-made, feeding on rapture, self-luminous, moving through the air, abiding in glory. And they continue thus for a long, long period of time.

"Thereupon the being who re-arose there first thinks to himself: 'I am Brahmā, the Great Brahmā, the Vanquisher, the Unvanquished, the Universal Seer, the Wielder of Power, the Lord, the Maker and Creator, the Supreme Being, the Ordainer, the Almighty, the Father of all that are and are to be. And these beings have been created by me. What is the reason? Because first I made the wish: "Oh, that other beings might come to this place!" And after I made this resolution, now these beings have come.'

"And the beings who re-arose there after him also think: 'This must be Brahmā, the Great Brahmā, the Vanquisher, the Unvanquished, the Universal Seer, the Wielder of Power, the Lord, the Maker and Creator, the Supreme Being, the Ordainer, the Almighty, the Father of all that are and are to be. And we have been created by him. What is the reason? Because we see that he was here first, and we appeared here after him.'

"Herein, bhikkhus, the being who re-arose there first possesses longer life, greater beauty, and greater authority than the beings who re-arose there after him.

"Now, bhikkhus, this comes to pass, that a certain being, after passing away from that plane, takes rebirth in this world. Having come to this world, he goes forth from home to homelessness. When he has gone forth, by means of ardour, endeavour, application, diligence, and right reflection, he attains to such a degree of mental concentration that with his mind thus concentrated he recollects his immediately preceding life, but none previous to that. He speaks thus: 'We were created by him, by Brahmā, the Great Brahmā, the Vanquisher, the Unvanquished, the Universal Seer, the Wielder of Power, the Lord, the Maker and Creator, the Supreme Being, the Ordainer, the Almighty, the Father of all that are and are to be. He is permanent, stable, eternal, not subject to change, and he will remain the same just like eternity itself. But we, who have been created by him and have come to this world, are impermanent, unstable, short-lived, doomed to perish.'" Translation from *Long Discourses*, Brahamajāla Sutta, "1. The All-Embracing Net of Views, I. Talk on Wanderers (Paribbājakakathā)," trans. Bhante Sujato, accessed Dec. 7, 2023, https://legacy.suttacentral.net/en/dn1.

6. Harris has put his position on these matters most directly and completely in his

Waking Up, where he writes like a fine exemplar of the scientifically minded Buddhist-sympathizer, wanting to toss aside the superstitious dross of Buddhism and strip-mine it for its technology of mental and spiritual development. More power to him, I say; I like and approve of this project and hope it succeeds. But such is not my project here. Sam Harris, *Waking Up: A Guide to Spirituality without Religion* (New York: Simon & Schuster Paperbacks, 2014).

7. As is well known, this phrase comes from his work "On The Flesh of Christ" in the context of his defense of incarnation against Docetism. "The Son of God was crucified: there is no shame, because it is shameful. And the Son of God died: it is by all means to be believed, because it is absurd. And, buried, He rose again: it is certain, because impossible." Tertullian, "On the Flesh of Christ," in *The Writings of Tertullian*, vol. 2, trans. Peter Homes, in vol. 15 of *Ante-Nicene Christian Library: Translations of the Writings of the Fathers down to a.d. 325*, ed. Alexander Roberts and James Donaldson (Edinburgh: T. & T. Clarks, 1870), 173–174. Tertullian himself, though, is also the best example of how little this ingenious and profound method of unsettling conclusions avails in *settling* the matter. Tertullian later left "orthodox" Christianity, accepting instead the Sybilline revelations and becoming a Montanist. Apparently he had found something even *more* absurd.

8. See online appendix A, supplement 1: "A Classic Example of a Misfiring Atheist Argument from the Film *Inherit the Wind*."

9. On Kant's idea of transcendental unity in comparison with the Tiantai case, see Brook Ziporyn, *Being and Ambiguity: Philosophical Experiments with Tiantai Buddhism* (Chicago: Open Court, 2004), 103–125.

10. Jean-Luc Nancy, Gabriel Malenfant, and Michael B. Smith, *Dis-Enclosure: The Deconstruction of Christianity*, trans. Bettina Bergo (New York: Fordham University Press, 2008), 14.

11. Nancy, Malenfant, and Smith, *Dis-enclosure*, 21.

12. Nancy, Malenfant, and Smith, *Dis-enclosure*, 30.

13. Nancy, Malenfant, and Smith, *Dis-enclosure*, 21.

14. Nancy, Malenfant, and Smith, *Dis-enclosure*, 15.

15. Nancy, Malenfant, and Smith, *Dis-enclosure*, 16.

16. Nancy, Malenfant, and Smith, *Dis-enclosure*, 10.

17. See, for example, Nancy's discussion of Anselm's ontological argument. Nancy, Malenfant, and Smith, *Dis-enclosure*, 11–12.

18. Jean-Luc Nancy, *Adoration: The Deconstruction of Christianity II* (New York: Fordham University Press, 2012), 31.

19. Martin Heidegger, "On the Essence of Truth," *Heidegger: Basic Writings*, trans. David Krell (San Francisco: Harper, 1993), 118.

20. Here I roughly follow the view advanced by Spinoza in *Ethics* (pt. 1, app.) concerning the origins of belief in purposive deities in control of what happens in the world, which will be quoted and discussed at greater length in part I. Baruch de Spinoza, *The Ethics: Treatise on the Emendation of the Intellect*, trans. Samuel Shirley (Indianapolis, IN: Hackett Publishing, 1992).

21. "The fusion of soul and body in the act, the sublimation of biological into personal existence, and of the natural into the cultural world is made both possible and precarious by the temporal structure of our experience. Every present grasps . . . the totality of possible time; thus does it overcome the dispersal of instants, and manage to

endow our past itself with its definitive meaning. . . . But this power naturally belongs to all presents, the old no less than the new. Even if we claim to have a better understanding of our past than it had of itself, it can always reject our present judgment and shut itself up in its own autonomous self-evidence. It necessarily does so in so far as I conceive it as a former present. Each present may claim to solidify our life, and indeed that is what distinguishes it as the present. . . . What enables us to centre our existence is also what prevents us from centring it completely, and the anonymity of our body is inseparably both freedom and servitude. Thus, to sum up, the ambiguity of being-in-the-world is translated by that of the body, and this is understood through that of time." Maurice Merleau-Ponty, *Phenomenology of Perception*, trans. Colin Smith (London: Routledge, 1989), 84–85.

22. See "Non-X Is More Like X, Only More So," in Brook Ziporyn, *Being and Ambiguity: Philosophical Experiments with Tiantai Buddhism* (Chicago: Open Court, 2004), 168–179. Ultimately, however, I would trace this line of thought back to chapter 2 of the *Zhuangzi*.

23. "If anyone were inclined to put forward the paradoxical proposition that the normal man is not only far more immoral than he believes but also far more moral than he knows, psycho-analysis, on whose findings the first half of the assertion rests, would have no objection to raise against the second half." Sigmund Freud, "The Dependent Relations of the Ego," sec. 5 of *The Ego and the Id*, in *The Ego and the Id and Other Works*, vol. 19 (1923–1925) of *The Standard Edition of the Complete Psychological Works of Sigmund Freud*, trans. James Strachey (New York: Norton, 1976).

24. Again, see Ziporyn, *Being and Ambiguity*. Recent philosophy includes many attempts to restore primacy to some sort of backdrop of agreements, certainty, unity in the fact of the obvious pragmatic fluidity of things like belief—Santayana's "animal faith," Davidson's "principle of charity" (and necessary "massive agreement"), Wittgenstein's Forms of Life. I would claim that the attempt to find somewhere, in some meta level at least, a primacy of certainty and definite faith is yet another monotheistic holdover. In fact, the backdrop of unity is self-undermining, just as are the fluid individual propositions always being evaluated in terms of it. Ziporyn, *Being and Ambiguity*, 103–124.

25. Ludwig Feuerbach, "Preliminary Theses on the Reform of Philosophy," in *The Fiery Brook: Selected Writings of Ludwig Feuerbach*, trans. and intro. Zawar Hanfi (New York: Doubleday, 1972), 153; italics in the original.

26. See chapter 1 for the full excavation of the *Noûs* as *Arché* idea and its entailments. On negative theology, see online appendix A, supplement 8: "Monotheist Negative Theology, and Why It Doesn't Help Much." Another, somewhat different, example of a backfiring attempt to transcend the *Noûs* as *Arché* premise, which is, perhaps, even more consequential in its pervasive aftereffects, is found in Aristotle. See chapter 4, and also online appendix A, supplement 5: "Aristotle's Halfway House: Out of the Frying Pan and into the Fire."

27. See online appendix A, supplement 3: "What's in It for Them: The Backfiring Structure from the Consumer's Side."

28. Arthur Schopenhauer, *The World as Will and Representation*, vol. 2, trans. E. F. J. Payne (New York: Dover, 1966), 162.

29. Friedrich Nietzsche, *Beyond Good and Evil*, trans. R. J. Hollingdale (London: Penguin, 1973), sec. 154, 85.

30. See online appendix A, supplement 4: "Limitations of Teleological Unity."

31. Maurice Merleau-Ponty, *The Phenomenology of Perception*, trans. Colin Smith (Abingdon, UK: Routledge, 1989), xxii.

CHAPTER 1

1. See Nietzsche on Christianity as "Platonism for the people" in the preface to his *Beyond Good and Evil*. Friedrich Nietzsche, *Beyond Good and Evil*, ed. Rolf-Peter Horstmann and Judith Norman, trans. Judith Norman (Cambridge: Cambridge University Press, 2002). See also George Santayana, *Three Philosophical Poets* (New York: Charles Scribner's Sons, 1936); and Ralph Waldo Emerson, "Plato, or the Philosopher," in *Representative Men* (Boston: James R. Osgood and Company, 1875).

2. Plato, "Phaedo," in *Dialogues of Plato*, trans. Benjamin Jowett (Oxford: Clarendon Press, 1875), 97.b–99.d., 476–478.

3. Charles Hartshorne, *Divine Relativity: A Social Conception of God* (New Haven: Yale University Press, 1948), 116–158.

4. F. W. J. Schelling, *Philosophical Investigations into the Essence of Human Freedom* (Albany, NY: SUNY Press, 2006), 17; see also Schelling, *The Ages of the World (1811)*, trans. Joseph P. Lawrence (Albany, NY: SUNY Press, 2019); Schelling, *Historical-Critical Introduction to the Philosophy of Mythology*, trans. Mason Richey and Markus Zisselberger (Albany, NY: SUNY Press, 2007); Schelling, *Philosophy of Revelation (1841–42): And Related Texts*, trans. and intro. Klaus Ottmann (Thompson, NY: Spring Publications, 2020); and throughout his work.

5. I say "almost": there is undeniably a margin of ambiguity on this point in the Confucian tradition, as will be explored in online appendix B, and some influential Confucian thinkers, such as the Han ideologue Dong Zhongshu, were clearly groping toward something more robustly similar to a purposive model of Heaven and its role in human affairs by moving determinacy and purpose into a more primal position in the cosmos. I've explored elsewhere the ways in which the entailments of the raw materials of the tradition with which they had to work to construct such a system, in particular yin-yang conceptions, put severe limits on the success of this venture, and even undermined it. See Brook Ziporyn, *Ironies of Oneness and Difference: Coherence in Early Chinese Thought: Prolegomena to the Study of Li* (Albany, NY: SUNY Press, 2013), 250–255. Though this was a philosophical dead end within Chinese tradition, which was mainly ignored or disparaged by later Confucian thinkers, its political importance cannot be denied. The other sometimes-alleged exception to the primacy of indeterminacy, the notion of primordial Li in Zhu Xi's Neo-Confucianism, is, in my view, not an exception at all but rather still really a variant of it: Li is ultimately the presence in each thing of the Great Pivot (*taiji* 太極), which serves as the ultimate standard that defines determinate order, and primary is itself a form of indeterminacy between the contrasted determinations of yin and yang, hence also *wuji* 無極, which is the ultimate in nothingness, the complete lack of any standard. It is precisely the convertibility of these two terms that marks the beginning of Zhu Xi's metaphysics—which then stands as the standard of orthodoxy for about six hundred years, from 1313 to 1905.

6. See David Sedley, *Creationism and Its Critics in Antiquity* (Berkeley: University of California Press, 2007), 138.

7. Sedley, *Creationism*, 155–166.

8. Sedley, *Creationism*, 11–12; italics added.

9. Sedley, *Creationism*, 12; italics in the original.

10. A milder, slightly cheerier alternative version of this idea of love as union is put forth in the dialogue in the "love is harmony" theory of Erixymachos the physician. Here too there is a relativistic implication that Plato is eager to squash in what follows. The key point for any of these models, for our purposes here, is that, as Spinoza will say, we do not desire any particular thing *because* it is good; rather, we *call* it good *because* we desire it—and we desire it because we *happen* to be constituted in some particular way. This is the point of contention.

11. The same logic lives on in the Sermon on the Mount: "If thy hand offends thee, cut it off" (Matthew 5:30).

12. Plato, "Symposium," in *Great Dialogues of Plato*, trans. W. H. D. Rouse (New York: Mentor Books, 1956), 204D, 101.

13. See, again, online appendix A, supplement 8, "Monotheist Negative Theology, and Why It Doesn't Help Much."

14. For more on this, see, again, online appendix A, supplement 8: "Aristotle's Halfway House: Out of the Frying Pan and into the Fire," and supplement 2: "Monotheist Innovation as Backfiring Detheology."

15. Friedrich Nietzsche, *Human, All Too Human*, trans. Marion Faber with Stephen Lehmann (Lincoln: University of Nebraska Press, 1984), sec. 111, 81–82; italics in the original.

16. Baruch de Spinoza, *The Ethics and Selected Letters*, trans. Samuel Shirley (Indianapolis, IN: Hackett Publishing, 1982), 57–58.

17. Friedrich Nietzsche, *The Will to Power*, #524, from notes dated March–June 1888, trans. Anthony M. Ludovici (New York: Barnes & Noble, 2006), 304–305. Cf. Nietzsche, "On the Despisers of the Body," in *Thus Spoke Zarathustra: A Book for Everyone and No One*, trans. R. J. Hollingdale (New York: Penguin, 1961), 61–63.

18. Arthur Schopenhauer, *The World as Will and Representation*, vol. 2, trans. E. F. Payne (New York: Dover, 1958), 201.

19. Schopenhauer, *World as Will*, 247.

20. Friedrich Nietzsche, *The Gay Science*, trans. Walter Kaufmann (New York: Vintage Books, 1974), sec. 354.

21. Friedrich Nietzsche, *The Will to Power*, sec. 478, from notes dated March–June 1888, trans. Walter Kaufmann and R. J. Hollingdale (New York: Vintage Books, 1967), 264.

22. Friedrich Nietzsche, "The Antichrist," in *The Portable Nietzsche*, ed. and trans. Walter Kaufmann (New York: Penguin, 1954), 585–586.

23. Friedrich Nietzsche, *Beyond Good and Evil*, trans. R. J. Hollingdale (New York: Penguin, 1972), sec. 16, 27.

24. Friedrich Nietzsche, "'Reason' in Philosophy," in *Twilight of the Idols, or, How to Philosophize with the Hammer*, trans. Richard Polt (Indianapolis, IN: Hackett Publishing, 1997), sec. 5, 20.

25. Nietzsche, *Gay Science*, sec. 11, 84–85.

26. Confucius, *The Analects*, unpublished translation by Brook Ziporyn.

CHAPTER 2

1. Zhuangzi, *Zhuangzi: The Complete Writings*, trans. Brook Ziporyn (Indianapolis, IN: Hackett Publishing, 2020), 272; slightly modified.

2. E3p27 refers to *Ethics*, Part 3, Proposition 27. References to Spinoza's *Ethics* will be given in this format throughout this work. All Spinoza translations are from the works of Samuel Shirley. Baruch de Spinoza, *The Ethics: Treatise on the Emendation of the Intellect*, trans. Samuel Shirley (Indianapolis, IN: Hackett Publishing, 1992).

3. Ralph Waldo Emerson, "Spiritual Laws," in *The Complete Works of Ralph Waldo Emerson: His Essays, Lectures, Poems, and Orations* (London: Bell and Daldy, 1866), 59–60.

4. That is, *Ethics*, Part 2, Definition 7. Subsequent citations of this work will follow the same format.

5. Zhuangzi, *Zhuangzi: The Complete Writings*, 155; slightly modified.

6. Zhuangzi, *Zhuangzi: The Complete Writings*, 35; slightly modified.

7. "'Natural Law' as Global Incoherence," in Brook Ziporyn, *Being and Ambiguity: Philosophical Experiments with Tiantai Buddhism* (Chicago: Open Court Publishing, 2004).

8. The basic structure of this convenient A/B schema for organizing a coherent approach to the text, though not the conclusions drawn from it, is derived from A. C. Graham, *Disputers of the Tao: Philosophical Argument in Ancient China* (Chicago: Open Court, 1989).

9. See Chad Hansen, "Chinese Language, Chinese Philosophy, and 'Truth,'" *Journal of Asian Studies* 44, no. 3 (May 1985): 491–519.

10. Laozi, *Daodejing*, trans. Brook Ziporyn (New York: Liveright, 2023); slightly modified.

11. Laozi, *Daodejing*; slightly modified.

12. Laozi, *Daodejing*; slightly modified.

13. Friedrich Nietzsche, "Of the Compassionate," in *Thus Spoke Zarathustra: A Book for Everyone and No One*, trans. R. J. Hollingdale (New York: Penguin, 1961), 113.

14. A stricter and more literal rendering can be found in Zhuangzi, *Zhuangzi: The Complete Writings*, 29.

15. *Du* 督. In Chinese medicine, this term, which in other contexts means "controller," refers to the current of energy that runs vertically through the middle of the human back. The image of a flowing current connects to the opening trope of the chapter. This flow tends toward the central (hence, if left to itself, never going too far toward either good or evil), the unseen (hence opposed to "the knowing mind"), and the real controller (as opposed to the knowing mind's pretensions to control and direct life).

16. Unlike the Confucian thinker Mencius, Zhuangzi resists reading the motion of this river *toward the sea* or *downward* as an implicit direction or telos of the natural zigzag, thus giving a higher-level directionality to its apparent directionlessness. On the contrary, as in the *Daodejing*, water's downward flow is taken as an image of its moving *away* from all values—that is, toward the "low," the disvalued, the unseen, the unintended. But even in the Confucian reading, the "goodness" toward which the undirected flows is precisely *not* the deliberately willed or designed, as in the animistic *Noûs* as *Arché* idea; rather it too is Heaven as *wuwei*, nondeliberate and effortless; it is ultimately purposeless, or purposive only in the derivative sense in which purpose itself is reduced to something beyond purpose, for there is no conscious controlling mind behind the construction of the world. See online appendix B for a fuller discussion of this point.

17. Zhuangzi, *Zhuangzi: The Complete Writings*, 36; slightly modified.

18. Zhuangzi, *Zhuangzi: The Complete Writings*, 29–30; slightly modified.

19. Zhuangzi, *Zhuangzi: The Complete Writings*, 50; slightly modified.

CHAPTER 3

1. Zhuangzi, *Zhuangzi: The Complete Writings*, trans. Brook Ziporyn (Indianapolis, IN: Hackett Publishing, 2020), 159; slightly modified.

2. As *Laozi* 21 tells us, the Dao is itself *intrinsically* "vague," indistinct, indeterminate—this is its only determination, shape, image, the only thing guide or model it provides, the determination of indetermination that alone is what never vanishes: it is the undermining of all fixed determination. 孔德之容，唯道是從。道之為物，唯恍唯惚。忽兮恍兮，其中有象；恍兮忽兮，其中有物。窈兮冥兮，其中有精；其精甚真，其中有信。自古及今，其名不去，以閱衆甫。吾何以知衆甫之狀哉？以此。

3. Zhuangzi, *Zhuangzi: The Complete Writings*, 56; slightly modified. Some background might help interpreting this: "Yao" is a stock ancient Chinese paragon of virtue: think Gandhi. "Jie" is a stock example of extreme evil: think Hitler.

4. Zhuangzi, *Zhuangzi: The Complete Writings*, 56; slightly modified.

5. Ralph Waldo Emerson, "Love," in *Emerson's Essays: First and Second Series Complete in One Volume* (New York: Thomas Y. Crowell Company, 1926), 130.

6. Zhuangzi, *Zhuangzi: The Complete Writings*, 59; slightly modified.

7. Zhuangzi, *Zhuangzi: The Complete Writings*, 157; slightly modified.

8. Zhuangzi, *Zhuangzi: The Complete Writings*, 63; slightly modified.

9. Keiji Nishitani, *Religion and Nothingness*, trans. Jan Van Bragt (Berkeley: University of California Press, 1982), 42.

10. See online appendix A, supplement 6: "The Atheist Matrix of Polytheism."

11. For some of the implications of this when applied to the most well-known case, see online appendix A, supplement 7: "Why So Hard on Love Incarnate?"

12. Online appendix A, supplement 8, "Monotheist Negative Theology, and Why It Doesn't Help Much."

CHAPTER 4

1. Georges Bataille, *Erotism*, trans. Mary Dalwood (San Francisco: City Lights, 1986), 123.

2. Georges Bataille, *Theory of Religion*, trans. Robert Hurley (New York: Zone Books, 1989), 18–19.

3. Bataille, *Theory of Religion*, 23.

4. Bataille, *Theory of Religion*, 27.

5. Bataille, *Theory of Religion*, 29–30.

6. Bataille, *Theory of Religion*, 28–29.

7. Bataille, *Theory of Religion*, 31.

8. Bataille, *Theory of Religion*, 50–51.

9. Bataille, *Theory of Religion*, 51–52.

10. Bataille, *Theory of Religion*, 33.

11. Bataille, *Theory of Religion*, 34.

12. Bataille, *Theory of Religion*, 35.

13. Bataille, *Theory of Religion*, 35–37.

14. Bataille, *Theory of Religion*, 56. See also online appendix A, supplement 9: "Durkheim, Bataille, and Girard on Violence, Sacrifice, and the Sacred," for continuities and disparities, with some related reflections on these phenomena.

15. Bataille, *Theory of Religion*, 69–70.

16. Bataille, *Theory of Religion*, 71.

17. Bataille, *Theory of Religion*, 71.

18. Bataille, *Theory of Religion*, 80.

19. Georges Bataille, *Erotism* (New York: Walker and Company, 1962), 118.

20. Bataille, *Theory of Religion*, 80–81.

21. Bataille, *Theory of Religion*, 82–83.

22. Bataille, *Theory of Religion*, 83–84.

23. Bataille, *Theory of Religion*, 118.

24. Bataille, *Theory of Religion*, 118–119.

25. Bataille, *Theory of Religion*, 119.

26. Bataille, *Theory of Religion*, 119.

27. Bataille, *Theory of Religion*, 119–120.

28. Bataille, *Theory of Religion*, 110.

29. Bataille, *Theory of Religion*, 113. The capitalization is Bataille's.

30. Schopenhauer, Arthur. *On the Fourfold Root of the Principle of Sufficient Reasons and Other Writings*, trans. and ed. by David E. Cartwright, Edward E. Erdmann, and Christopher Janaway (Cambridge: Cambridge University Press), 2012, 479.

31. This focus on the PSR and what may lie outside it also can help us understand both the unexpected proximity of this view to certain other theories of religion and their profound differences. See, again, online appendix A, supplement 9: "Durkheim, Bataille, and Girard on Violence, Sacrifice, and the Sacred."

32. See Arthur Schopenhauer, *The World as Will and Representation*, vol. 1, trans. E. F. J. Payne (New York: Dover, 1958), sec. 3.38, 196.

33. Cf. Immanuel Kant, *Critique of Judgement*, translated by James Creed Merideth, revised, edited and introduced by Nicholas Walker (Oxford: Oxford World's Classics, 2007), sec. 11, 52.

34. See Nietzsche's "Preface to Wagner," in *Birth of Tragedy and Other Writings*, trans. Roland Speirs (Cambridge: Cambridge University Press, 1999), 13–14. His detailed account of the art as the metaphysics is to be found in the analysis of the Dionysian. Nietzsche, *Birth of Tragedy*, 28–33.

35. This is a deliberately opaque summary of Tiantai thinking, which I've tried to present more cogently and explicitly in other works on the subject. See, for example, Ziporyn, *Evil and/or/as the Good: Omnicentrism, Intersubjectivity, and Value Paradox in Tiantai Buddhist Thought* (Cambridge, MA: Harvard University Press, 2000); Ziporyn, *Being and Ambiguity: Philosophical Experiments with Tiantai Buddhism* (Chicago: Open Court Publishing, 2004); Ziporyn, *Beyond Oneness and Difference: Li and Coherence in Chinese Buddhist Thought and Its Antecedents* (Albany, NY: SUNY Press, 2014); and Ziporyn, *Emptiness and Omnipresence: An Essential Introduction to Tiantai Buddhism* (Bloomington: Indiana University Press, 2016). I ask the reader to consult those works for a fuller explanation; in this one I will assume their availability rather than trying to walk the reader through all the steps yet again.

36. See, for example, *Enneads* 6:9, "On the Good or the One," in Plotinus, *The Enneads*, trans. Stephen MacKenna (London: Penguin, 1991), 535–549 and throughout his works.

37. See, for example, Aristotle, *Metaphysics*, 1003b23–24, 1061a17–18.

38. See, for example, *Enneads* 5:1–5, "The Three Initial Hypostases," "The Origin and Order of the Beings Following on the First," "The Knowing Hypostases and the Transcendent," and "That the Intellectual Beings Are Not Outside the Intellectual Principle; and on the Nature of the Good." Plotinus, *The Enneads*, 347–405 and throughout.

39. See, for example, *Enneads* 2:4, secs. 11–16, "Matter." Plotinus, *The Enneads*, 92–107.

40. See, for example, *Enneads* 4:3–4, "Problems of the Soul [I]" and "Problems of the Soul [II]." Plotinus, *The Enneads*, 251–333.

41. See, again, online appendix A, supplement 8, "Monotheist Negative Theology, and Why It Doesn't Help Much."

42. See, for example, *Enneads* 6:4–5, "On the Integral Omnipresence of the Authentic Existent [I]" and "On the Integral Omnipresence of the Authentic Existent II," in Plotinus, *The Enneads*, 439–467.

43. Plotinus, *The Enneads*, 512–535.

44. Again, see online appendix A, supplement 5: "Aristotle's Halfway House: Out of the Frying Pan and into the Fire."

45. Here we may respond to and perhaps reverse an influential insight first clearly enunciated by Henri Bergson: we have been misconceiving time because we have been implicitly assimilating its structure to that of space. One of the crucial entailments of this mistaken spatialization of time, he thought, was that we had thought of *moments in time* as mutually exclusive, thereby making incomprehensible the experienced duration of time, the stretching of the past into the present and the present projecting into the future, which constitutes the very pith of all our experience. In doing so, we have made free will and accountable purposive activity (which was thought to be all that gave our lives their meaning) incomprehensible, reducing it to the mechanical causal effect of the discrete past on the discrete present. Understanding that past and present moments are not separate, static entities, as regions of space were thought to be, would change all that, he thought. Much of the most powerful twentieth-century philosophy, from Whitehead to Heidegger, has built impressively on this insight. But here we are suggesting that this conception of the mutual externality and static lifelessness of regions of space was itself a by-product of a particular model of temporality, which then rebounded as a model of time, leading to the mechanistic impasse. Bergson and those who followed in his footsteps sought to preserve the *one-sided, unidirectional* inclusiveness (future including past but not vice-versa) characteristic of purposive action, not seeing that this was itself the source of the mutual exclusivity that threatened it. For as will hopefully become increasingly clear in the pages that follow, it was our fanatical commitment to purposivity alone that inflicted bivalent mutual exclusivity on the ontological structure of both space and time—and on ourselves.

46. There is a sense in which "mind" can be understood in a more "spatial" way: not as intelligence, but as awareness of any and all mental states that arise, intentionally or unintentionally. We will see applications of this model to a very different understanding of the world as manifestations of an infinite "mind" in some of the Buddhist thinkers treated in online appendix B. We will also find there Confucians who develop the idea of "the Mind of Heaven and Earth," a nonintentional "Mindless Mind" correlated with a purposeless purposivity, aimed only at the omnitelic/nontelic telos of ceaseless generation of any and all new states, with a merely secondary and intermittent dispos-

itive intentionality. It should be clear already why neither sense should be mistaken for anything like the mind of God.

47. See online appendix A, supplement 10: "By-Products of God: Autonomy, Revolution, Nothingness, Finitude."

48. Again, see online appendix A, supplement 7: "Why So Hard on Love Incarnate?"

CHAPTER 5

1. That is, Spinoza's *Ethics*, Part 2, Axiom 3. Subsequent references to the *Ethics* in this chapter will utilize the same format. Baruch de Spinoza, *The Ethics: Treatise on the Emendation of the Intellect*, trans. Samuel Shirley (Indianapolis, IN: Hackett Publishing, 1992).

2. That is, Spinoza's *Principles of Cartesian Philosophy*, Part 2, Proposition 2. Subsequent references will utilize the same format. Baruch de Spinoza, *The Principles of Cartesian Philosophy and Metaphysical Thoughts*, trans. Samuel Shirley (Indianapolis, IN: Hackett Publishing, 1998).

3. See Shannon Dea, "The Infinite and the Indeterminate in Spinoza," *Dialogue* 50 (2011): 603–621, for the relevant citations in Spinoza and an overview of the scholarly disputes on this point in contemporary Spinoza literature. I share Dea's conclusion that *infinite* is precisely synonymous with *indeterminacy* in Spinoza, and that this is crucial for understanding him, for the reasons she adduces there in addition to others that will become apparent later in this chapter.

4. I suggest this as an interpretation of E1p16, tentatively, on the basis of item 7 on the last page of *Treatise on the Emendation of the Intellect*, where Spinoza refers to the "innumerable" ways in which any given mode (in this case, modes of Thought, any "idea that the intellect forms from other ideas") can be derived. In this reading, E1p16 means not only that each infinite Attribute produces infinite modes, such that each is produced "in infinite ways" in the sense of being a mode ("way") of an infinite number of Attributes, but also that every mode is an essence that can be produced through an infinite set of alternate chains of causality. Spinoza, *The Ethics: Treatise on the Emendation of the Intellect*.

5. Spinoza, Letters 35 and 36, in *Complete Works of Spinoza*, trans. Samuel Shirley (Indianapolis, IN: Hackett Publishing, 2002), 855–860.

6. That is, Spinoza, "Treatise on the Emendation of the Intellect," in Spinoza, *Complete Works of Spinoza*, sec. 36, 11.

7. In the scholium of the Proposition 9 of Book 3, Spinoza states this point in the following sentence. "It is clear from the above considerations that we do not endeavor, will, seek after or desire because we judge a thing to be good. On the contrary, we judge a thing to be good because we endeavor, will, seek after and desire it. Spinoza, *Ethics*, in *Complete Works of Spinoza*, 284.

8. Baruch de Spinoza, "Metaphysical Thoughts," app., 2.6., in *Spinoza, Complete Works of Spinoza*, 197.

9. Spinoza, *Ethics*, after 2p13, axiom 3, lemmas 4–7, and scholium.

10. Spinoza, *Ethics*, 1, app.

11. Martial Gueroult, "Spinoza's Letter on the Infinite," trans. Kathleen McLaughlin from M. Gueroult, *Spinoza*, vol. 1 (Paris: Aubier-Montaigne, 1968), app. 9, 500–528, repr. in *Spinoza: A Collection of Critical Essays*, ed. Marjorie Grene (Notre Dame, IN: University of Notre Dame Press, 1979), 195–196; italics in the original.

12. It could be objected that the stipulation about causality provides a realist crite-rion for dividing Nature at its real joints: where real causality occurs, whatever concurs in producing an effect is, ipso facto, to that extent a real individual—but where no real causality occurs, we are not at liberty to posit an individual. This is plausible, but I believe Gueroult's point is that Spinoza's insistence on infinite divisibility of modes trumps this consideration and tells us how it must be interpreted: the concurrence of individuals in causality is itself construable in infinitely various ways, and for this reason modes are infinitely divisible. Adequate causal explanation would still pertain, but only *within* any given way of dividing.

13. Gueroult, "Spinoza's Letter," 211–212.

14. Don Garrett, *Nature and Necessity in Spinoza's Philosophy* (New York: Oxford University Press, 2018), 255; italics in the original.

15. Ulysses Pinheiro, "Looking for Spinoza's Missing Mediate Infinite Modes of Thought," *Philosophical Forum* 46, no. 4 (2015): 363–376; https://doi.org/10.1111/phil .12083. A similar view is adopted by Christopher P. Martin in "The Framework of Es-sences in Spinoza's *Ethics*," *British Journal for the History of Philosophy* 16, no. 3 (2008): 489–509. Pinheiro and Martin both share Garrett's view that formal essences of finite modes are infinite and omnipresent, though via different arguments and with different implications. I share this view as well, but I differ from both Pinheiro and Martin. Like Martin but unlike Pinheiro, I hold that this applies to the formal essences of all finite modes without exception, without the distinction between the formal essences of the "simplest bodies," but like Pinheiro and unlike Martin, I do not view some of these essences as "speciesist" general essences and others as applying only to singular things.

16. Garrett, *Nature and Necessity*, 247–248.

17. Garrett, *Nature and Necessity*, 247–248.

18. *Attribute* is defined by Spinoza as a way of *correctly* identifying a thing—in this case, Substance. So each of the Attributes gives us the actual *essence of Substance*: each tells us correctly *what Substance is*. When there is only one Attribute, the Substance and the Attribute are actually synonyms, two names for the same thing. Spinoza compares the Substance/Attribute relationship to the relationship between the third Hebrew patriarch and one of his nicknames: "by Israel I mean the third patriarch, and by Jacob I mean the same individual, the latter name being given to him insofar as he grabbed his brother's heel." He gives another example: the terms "plane surface" and "white surface" from his other area of expertise (besides biblical philology), namely, optics: a plane surface is one that reflects all rays of light unchanged, and a white sur-face is the same surface "except that it is called white with respect to a person looking at it" (letter 9). Both terms refer to the same thing, but one, the Attribute name, refers to it in some particular relation, in some particular context or respect. Thus Substance just is all its Attributes; the difference being that each of them is only one, while it is all of them and their convertibility into each other, the unique form of unity pertaining to infinite Substance. In the case of the face and its characteristic look, they are one and the same thing: Brook's face is what it looks like to be Brook, but the latter is a way of referring to that face insofar as it is looked at. (That face may have other Attributes, i.e., the oiliness of that face as analyzed by a cosmetologist, say, or the flavor of that face after being sliced off and fried like a pancake by a cannibal—the face not in the Levi-nasian sense but as a piece of matter.) For our purposes, one Attribute is fine: we just want to illustrate the difference between the whole/part relation pertaining to infinite

and finite modes (the angry face and its elements) and the indivisibility and sameness-in-whole-and-part character pertaining, in contrast, to Attributes and modes.

19. "On the question of whole and parts, I consider things as parts of a whole to the extent that their natures adapt themselves to one another so that they are in the closest possible agreement. Insofar as they are different from one another, to that extent each one forms in our mind a separate idea and is considered a whole, not a part." Baruch de Spinoza, letter 32, in *Complete Works of Spinoza*, 848–851. Throughout the discussion. Spinoza is careful to say that we "consider" things whole and part "to the extent" that, and "insofar" as, we view them in a certain way, as having to do with how much they are in conflict with other things—beyond a certain point, we cease considering them parts and form a new idea of a whole. But it is clear that these are only aids to our imagination and not unambiguous facts about the world.

20. Spinoza, letter 32; italics added.

21. F. W. J. Schelling, proposition 40 in "Presentation of My System of Philosophy" (1801), in *The Philosophical Rupture between Fichte and Schelling: Selected Texts and Correspondence (1800–1802)*, trans. Michael G. Vater and David W. Wood (Albany: SUNY Press, 2012), 156.

22. Spinoza, *Treatise on the Emendation of the Intellect*, sections 99–102.

23. Spinoza, *Short Treatise*, first part, chapter 2, "Second Dialogue."

24. Spinoza, Letter 12, in Spinoza, *Spinoza: Complete Works*, 790.

25. Spinoza, "Metaphysical Thoughts," sec. 1.6.

26. Spinoza, *Complete Works*, 859.

27. Spinoza, *Principles of Cartesian Philosophy and Metaphysical Thoughts*, 104–105.

28. In *Ethics* 2, Spinoza sets forth a straightforward definition. "It is not in the nature of reason to regard things as contingent, but as necessary." As a Proof he also adds that "It is in the nature of reason to perceive things truly (Pr. 41, II), to wit (Ax. 6, I), as they are in themselves; that is (Pr. 29, I), not as contingent, but as necessary." Baruch Spinoza, *The Ethics and Selected Letters*, trans. Samuel Shirley (Indianapolis, IN: Hackett Publishing, 1982), 269.

29. See online appendix A, supplement 11: "Europe's Missed Exit to Atheist Mysticism: Spinoza Introduced by Schelling to Kant in the Mind of Hegel in 1801." See also online appendix B, supplement 7: "Intersubsumption of Purpose and Purposelessness, Theist and Atheist Versions: Hegel and Tiantai."

30. See online appendix A, supplement 12: "Spinoza or Hegel: The Inclusive and the Exclusive Oneness Redux."

31. Schopenhauer does actually give his own version of "the affirmation of the will-to-live" in book 4 of *Die Welt als Will und Vorstellungen*, a beautifully written overview of just the kind of vision of universal will and life that would fit in perfectly with Spinoza's vision, and Nietzsche's and Bataille's afterward: any evil and pain will be transformed by the very fact of their universalization in the beatific vision; when seen as unconditioned and eternal, all the hideous aspects of life are beautiful. But after his very thorough and poetic invocation of this position, Schopenhauer turns around and puts it all in the subjunctive: that's how things *would* look if one chose to affirm the universal will. But his point is: why would one do that? It's a horror show.

32. Ralph Waldo Emerson, "Nominalist and Realist," in *Emerson's Essays: First and Second Series Complete in One Volume* (New York: Thomas Y. Crowell Company, 1926), 425.

364   <   NOTES TO CHAPTER 6

CHAPTER 6

1. Friedrich Nietzsche, "Epigrams and Arrows," in *Twilight of the Idols, or, How to Philosophize with the Hammer*, trans. Richard Polt (Indianapolis, IN: Hackett Publishing, 1997), sec. 44, 11. See also "Attempt at a Critique of Christianity," in *The Antichrist*, in *The Portable Nietzsche*, ed. and trans. Walter Kaufmann (London: Penguin, 1954), sec. 1, 570.

2. Friedrich Nietzsche, *On the Genealogy of Morality*, ed. Keith Ansell-Pearson; trans. Carol Diethe (Cambridge: Cambridge University Press, 2006), third essay, 28.

3. Friedrich Nietzsche, "On War and Warrior-Peoples," in *Thus Spoke Zarathustra: A Book for Everyone and Nobody*, trans. Graham Parkes (Oxford: Oxford University Press, 2005), 42.

4. Gilles Deleuze, *Difference and Repetition*, trans. Paul Patton (New York: Columbia University Press, 1995), 50–51.

5. Others read Hegel otherwise. Alexandre Kojève claims that for Hegel, time itself is the Absolute, and Hegel does say at least that time is the Absolute in the form of immediate existence.

6. I take it this is the point of the enigmatic incident in "The Other Dance Song" in Part 4 of *Thus Spake Zarathustra*, at the very climax of the book. There, Zaruthustra, acknowledging that he is soon to leave Life, says, "Yes, but you also know that . . ." and whispers something into the ear of Life, who answers, "You *know* that, O Zarathustra? No one knows that—." *Thus Spoke Zarathustra: A Book for Everyone and Nobody*, trans. Parkes, 449; italics in the original.

7. Friedrich Nietzsche, *The Will to Power*, trans. Walter Kaufmann and R. J. Hollingdale (New York: Vintage Books, 1967), sec. 1067, 550.

8. "The ideal of the most high-spirited, alive, and world-affirming human being who has not only come to terms and learned to get along with whatever was and is, but who wants to have what was and is repeated into all eternity. . . . What? And this wouldn't be—circulus vitiosus deus?" Friedrich Nietzsche, *Beyond Good and Evil*, trans. Walter Kaufmann (New York: Vintage Books, 1967), sec. 3.56, 68.

9. See Friedrich Nietzsche, *Beyond Good and Evil*, trans. R. J. Hollingdale (Oxford: Penguin, 1986), sec. 19, 25–27. for Nietzsche's description of what *more* is involved in the idea of "willing," as opposed to that of desiring as such—most notably, the affects of command and obedience among the constituent parts of the self.

10. Friedrich Nietzsche, "On Redemption," *Thus Spoke Zarathustra: A Book for Everyone and Nobody*, trans. Parkes, 121–122; italics in the original.

11. Friedrich Nietzsche, "'Reason' in Philosophy," in *Twilight of the Idols: How to Philosophize with a Hammer*, in Nietzsche, *The Anti-Christ, Ecce Homo, Twilight of the Idols, and Other Writings*, ed. Aaron Ridley; trans. Judith Norman (Cambridge: Cambridge University Press, 2005), sec. 5.5, 169–170.

12. Nietzsche, *Twilight of the Idols*, trans. Norman, 181–182; italics in the original.

13. Friedrich Nietzsche, *The Will to Power*, trans. Walter Kaufmann and R. J. Hollingdale (New York: Vintage Books, 1967), sec. 55, 35–36.

14. Schopenhauer conceives of these Platonic forms, rather obscurely, as "adequate grades of objectification of the Will," and admits Forms only for elemental natural objects, not for manufactured individual objects as such. Architecture, for example, is a way of presenting the Forms not of this house or that tower (for there are no such Forms), but of gravity and stone and metal. As against Plato, however, the apprehen-

sion of Forms is the province of perception rather than thought, but perception that sees in the individual only the timeless and placeless universal or "species." Arthur Schopenhauer, *The World as Will and Representation*, trans. E. F. J. Payne (New York: Dover, 1958), 1:169–212.

15. Schopenhauer, *World as Will and Representation*, 1:195.
16. Schopenhauer, *World as Will and Representation*, 1:196.
17. Friedrich Nietzsche, "On Immaculate Perception," in *Thus Spoke Zarathustra: A Book for Everyone and Nobody*, trans. Parkes, 106–107; italics in the original.
18. Nietzsche, "On Immaculate Perception," 283–284; italics in the original.
19. Nietzsche, "On Immaculate Perception," 142–143; italics in the original.
20. Nietzsche, "On Immaculate Perception," 24; italics in the original.

CHAPTER 7

1. Friedrich Nietzsche, *The Anti-Christ, Ecce Homo, Twilight of the Idols and Other Writings*, ed. Aaron Ridley; trans. Judith Norman (Cambridge: Cambridge University Press, 2005), sec. 47, 45.
2. See Julian Young, *Nietzsche's Philosophy of Religion* (Cambridge: Cambridge University Press, 2006), for a different version of Nietzsche as intensely proreligion but antimonotheism.
3. Laozi, *Daodejing*, 40 and 78, respectively; slightly modified.
4. For example, consider its earliest uses in the *Iliad* 3.161: "But Priam bade her draw nigh. 'My child,' said he, 'take your seat in front of me that you may see your former husband, your kinsmen and your friends. I lay no responsibility [*aitia*] upon you, it is the gods, not you who are responsible [*aitioi*]. It is they that have brought about this terrible war with the Achaeans.'" *The Iliad of Homer and The Odyssey*, trans. Samuel Butler (Chicago: Encyclopædia Britannica, 1952).
5. Friedrich Nietzsche, *The Will to Power*, trans. Walter Kaufmann and R. J. Hollingdale (New York: Vintage Books, 1967), sec. 639, 341.
6. Note Spinoza's comment about geometric thinking, his model of Reason, which he credits above all with liberating him from teleological thinking (Ep1 app.). Baruch de Spinoza, *The Ethics: Treatise on the Emendation of the Intellect*, trans. Samuel Shirley (Indianapolis, IN: Hackett Publishing, 1992).
7. Georges Bataille, *Visions of Excess: Selected Writings, 1927–1939*, trans. Allan Stoekl with Carl R. Lovitt and Donald M. Leslie Jr. (Minneapolis: University of Minnesota Press, 1985), 15; italics in the original.
8. Bataille, *Visions of Excess*, 45.
9. Friedrich Nietzsche, "'Guilt,' 'Bad Conscience' and Related Matters," in *On the Genealogy of Morality*, ed. Keith Ansell-Pearson; trans. Carol Diethe (Cambridge: Cambridge University Press, 2006), second essay, sec. 7, 43.
10. Georges Bataille, *The Accursed Share*, trans. Robert Hurley (New York: Zone Books, 1991), 1:180–181.
11. Georges Bataille, *Erotism*, trans Mary Dalwood (San Francisco: City Lights Books, 1986), 11.
12. Nietzsche, *Thus Spoke Zarathustra: A Book for Everyone and Nobody*, trans. Graham Parkes (Oxford: Oxford University Press, 2005), 102.
13. Bataille, *Accursed Share*, 33–35; italics in the original.
14. The idea has important resonances with the idea of the nonsubordination of

each moment in Guo Xiang. See Brook Ziporyn, *The Penumbra Unbound*: The Neo-Taoist Philosophy of Guo Xiang (Albany, NY: SUNY Press, 2003).

15. Bataille's freewheeling metaphorical style can often be misleading. Trying to invoke the full incommensurability, he admirably dispels any equation of his notion of the anti-God realm with the vulgar conception of matter or with materialism. In contrast, Bataille's "base matter" is "external and foreign to ideal human aspirations" and "refuses to allow itself to be reduced to the great ontological machines resulting from these aspirations." Bataille, "Gnosticism and Base Materialism," *Visions of Excess*, 51. In another place he clarifies the implication of this conception: "Matter can only be defined as the *nonlogical difference* that represents in relation to the *economy* of the universe what *crime* represents in relation to the law." Bataille, "The Notion of Expenditure," *Visions of Excess*, 129. This is very fine and very illuminating. But we are in danger of attributing to him a certain crudity of conception when we come across his sometimes careless usages of terms like *formless* to describe the intimate oceanic universe that is beyond both matter and form in their ordinary sense. Actually, what he means by this term is not something completely lacking in form, but the type of temporary form "like a spider or an earthworm" that "has no rights in any sense and is squashed everywhere." As he puts it, "Affirming that the universe resembles nothing and is only formless amounts to saying the universe is something like a spider or spit." Bataille, "Formless," *Visions of Excess*, 31; italics in the original. Here at least he is not insisting on formlessness or meaninglessness as a separate state outside any form or meaning—as he sometimes seems to do elsewhere, thereby trapping himself in paradox after paradox. The point here is rather to highlight a conception of form that is itself free of both the full ontological constitution that grants it the rights and responsibilities of full membership in the teleological order of spirit/form/God but also few of granting the latter's implication that anything falling outside its grasp has, ipso facto, already vanished into nothingness. It is rather this form on the constant verge of nothingness that embodies for us the full convergence of form and formlessness, and for that matter spirit and spiritlessness, telos and atelos—and even points, as in our other atheist mystics, toward the immanent omniform and interform and omnitelos and intertelos of full-fledged mystical atheism.

16. Bataille, *Visions of Excess*, 235.

17. Bataille, *Visions of Excess*, 235–237.

18. Bataille, *Visions of Excess*, 237–240.

19. Georges Bataille, *Erotism*, trans Mary Dalwood (San Francisco: City Lights Books, 1986), 11.

20. See Brook Ziporyn, *Evil and/or/as the Good: Omnicentrism, Intersubjectivity, and Value Paradox in Tiantai Buddhist Thought* (Cambridge, MA: Harvard University Press, 2000), for a complete account of this episode, and Zhili's theoretical justifications for it.

21. Bataille, *Visions of Excess*, 37.

CONCLUSION

1. This is a bonus elaboration of Zhuangzi 1, which is not explicitly discussed in online appendix B. For more details on Guo Xiang's thought, see *The Penumbra Unbound: The Neo-Taoist Philosophy of Guo Xiang* (Albany, NY: SUNY Press, 2003).

2. See also item 7 in online appendix B: "Intersubsumption of Purpose and Pur-

poselessness, Theist and Atheist: Hegel and Tiantai," for a comparison of Tiantai's "Emulative Intersubsumptive Atheism" with its closest theistic analogue, Hegel's "Emulative Intersubsumptive Theism."

3. That is, Spinoza, *Ethics*, Part 3, Proposition 27, in Baruch de Spinoza, *Complete Works of Spinoza*, trans. Samuel Shirley (Indianapolis, IN: Hackett Publishing, 2002).

4. See G. W. F. Hegel, *The Science of Logic*, trans. George Di Giovanni (Cambridge: Cambridge University Press, 2010), 684–685.

5. Kisāgotamīsutta, *Saṃyukta Nikāya*, 5.3.

6. "A passive emotion ceases to be a passive emotion as soon as we form a clear and distinct idea of it."

7. "Among all the emotions that are related to the mind is so far as it is active, there are none that are not related to pleasure or desire."

8. Bataille, *Accursed Share*, 33–35; italics in the original.

9. Zhuangzi, *Zhuangzi: The Complete Writings*, trans. Brook Ziporyn (Indianapolis, IN: Hackett Publishing, 2020), 58; modified to cover the full range of implications in this context of the character *cheng* 成, occurring twice in the Chinese and rendered here with the English words "form," "shape," "complete," "become," and "consummation."

Bibliography

Assmann, Jan. *Of God and Gods: Egypt, Israel, and the Rise of Monotheism*. Milwaukee: University of Wisconsin Press, 2008; reprint, Milton Keynes: Lightning Source UK, 2015.

Bataille, Georges. *Erotism: Death and Sensuality*. Translated by Mary Dalwood. San Francisco: City Lights Books, 1986.

———. *Theory of Religion*. Translated by Robert Hurley. Brooklyn, NY: Zone Books, 1989.

———. *Visions of Excess: Selected Writings, 1927–1939*. Edited and with an introduction by Allan Stoekl. Translated by Allan Stoekl with Carl R. Lovitt and Donald M. Leslie Jr. Minneapolis: University of Minnesota Press, 1985.

Dawkins, Richard. *Unweaving the Rainbow: Science, Delusion and the Appetite for Wonder*. London: Penguin, 2016.

Dea, Shannon. "The Infinite and the Indeterminate in Spinoza." *Dialogue* 50, no. 3 (2011): 603–621. https://doi.org/10.1017/s0012217311000564.

Deleuze, Gilles. *Difference and Repetition*. Translated by Paul Patton. New York: Columbia University Press, 1995.

Emerson, Ralph Waldo. *The Complete Works of Ralph Waldo Emerson: His Essays, Lectures, Poems, and Orations*. London: Bell & Daldy, 1866.

———. *Representative Men*. Boston: James R. Osgood and Company, 1875.

Feuerbach, Ludwig. *The Fiery Brook: Selected Writings of L. Feuerbach*. Translated by Zawar Hanfi. Garden City, NY: Doubleday, 1972.

Freud, Sigmund. *The Origins of Religion: Totem and Taboo, Moses and Monotheism, and Other Works*. Edited by Albert Dickson. Translated by James Strachey. London: Penguin, 1985.

———. *The Standard Edition of the Complete Psychological Works of Sigmund Freud*. Translated by James Strachey and Anna Freud. New York: Norton, 1976.

Garrett, Don. *Nature and Necessity in Spinoza's Philosophy*. New York: Oxford University Press, 2018.

Graham, A. C. *Disputers of the Tao: Philosophical Argument in Ancient China*. Chicago: Open Court Publishing, 1989.

Grene, Marjorie, editor. *Spinoza: A Collection of Critical Essays*. South Bend, IN: University of Notre Dame Press, 1979.

Hansen, Chad. "Chinese Language, Chinese Philosophy, and 'Truth.'" *Journal of Asian Studies* 44, no. 3 (1985): 491–519. https://doi.org/10.2307/2056264.

Harris, Sam. *Waking Up: A Guide to Spirituality without Religion*. New York: Simon & Schuster Paperbacks, 2014.

Hartshorne, Charles. *The Divine Relativity: A Social Conception of God*. New Haven, CT: Yale University Press, 1948.

Hegel, Georg Wilhelm Friedrich. *The Science of Logic*. Translated by George Di Giovanni. Cambridge: Cambridge University Press, 2010.

Holy Bible: King James Version. Nashville, TN: Thomas Nelson, 2016.

Homer. *The Iliad of Homer and The Odyssey*. Translated by Samuel Butler. Chicago: Encyclopaedia Britannica, 1952.

Lacan, Jacques, and Jacques-Alain Miller. *The Seminar of Jacques Lacan, Book XI: The Four Fundamental Concepts of Psychoanalysis*. Translated by Alan Sheridan. New York: Norton, 1988. Original French edition, 1973.

Laozi. *Daodejung*. Translated by Brook Ziporyn. New York: Liveright, 2023.

Martin, Christopher P. "The Framework of Essences in Spinoza's *Ethics*." *British Journal for the History of Philosophy* 16, no. 3 (2008): 489–509. https://doi.org/10.1080/09608780802200489.

Merleau-Ponty, Maurice. *Phenomenology of Perception*. Translated by Colin Smith. London: Routledge, 1989.

Nancy, Jean-Luc. *Adoration: The Deconstruction of Christianity II*. Translated by John McKeane. New York: Fordham University Press, 2012.

Nancy, Jean-Luc, Gabriel Malenfant, and Michael B. Smith. *Dis-Enclosure: The Deconstruction of Christianity*. Translated by Bettina Bergo. New York: Fordham University Press, 2008.

Nietzsche, Friedrich W. *The Anti-Christ, Ecce Homo, Twilight of the Idols and Other Writings*. Edited by Aaron Ridley. Translated by Judith Norman. Cambridge: Cambridge University Press, 2005.

———. *Beyond Good and Evil: Prelude to A Philosophy of the Future*. Translated by R. J. Hollingdale. London: Penguin, 1973.

———. *Beyond Good and Evil: Prelude to a Philosophy of the Future*. Edited by Rolf-Peter Horstmann and Judith Norman. Translated by Judith Norman. Cambridge: Cambridge University Press, 2002.

———. *The Gay Science*. Translated by Walter Kaufmann. New York: Vintage Books, 1974.

———. *Human, All Too Human: A Book for Free Spirits*. Translated by Marion Faber with Stephen Lehmann. Lincoln: University of Nebraska Press, 1984.

———. *Nietzsche: "The Birth of Tragedy" and Other Writings*. Translated by Ronald Speirs. Cambridge: Cambridge University Press, 1999.

———. *On the Genealogy of Morality*. Edited by Keith Ansell-Pearson. Translated by Carol Diethe. Cambridge: Cambridge University Press, 2006.

———. *The Portable Nietzsche*. Edited and translated by Walter Kaufmann. London: Penguin, 1954.

———. *Thus Spoke Zarathustra: A Book for Everyone and No One*. Translated by R. J. Hollingdale. London: Penguin, 1961.

———. *Thus Spoke Zarathustra: A Book for Everyone and Nobody*. Translated by Graham Parkes. Oxford: Oxford University Press, 2005.

———. *Twilight of the Idols, or, How to Philosophize with the Hammer*. Translated by Richard Polt. Indianapolis, IN: Hackett Publishing, 1997.

———. *Twilight of the Idols, or, How to Philosophize with a Hammer*. Translated by Duncan Large. Oxford: Oxford University Press, 1998.

———. *The Will to Power*. Translated by Walter Kaufmann and R. J. Hollingdale. New York: Vintage Books, 1967.

———. *The Will to Power*. Translated by Anthony M. Ludovici. New York: Barnes & Noble, 2006.

Nishitani, Keiji. *Religion and Nothingness*. Translated by Jan Van Bragt. Oakland: University of California Press, 1982.

Pinheiro, Ulysses. "Looking for Spinoza's Missing Mediate Infinite Mode of Thought." *Philosophical Forum* 46, no. 4 (2015): 363–376. https://doi.org/10.1111/phil.12083.

Plato. *The Dialogues of Plato*. Translated by Benjamin Jowett. Oxford: Clarendon Press, 1875.

———. *The Great Dialogues of Plato*. New York: New American Library, 1956.

Plotinus. *The Enneads*. Translated by Stephen MacKenna. London: Penguin, 1991.

Santayana, George. *Three Philosophical Poets*. New York: Charles Scribner's Sons, 1936.

Schelling, F. W. J. *The Ages of the World (1811)*. Translated by Joseph P. Lawrence. Albany, NY: SUNY Press, 2019.

———. *Historical-Critical Introduction to the Philosophy of Mythology*. Translated by Mason Richey and Markus Zisselberger. Albany, NY: SUNY Press, 2008.

———. *Philosophical Investigations into the Essence of Human Freedom*. Albany, NY: SUNY Press, 2006.

———. *Philosophy of Revelation (1841–42): And Related Texts*. Translated and with an introduction by Klaus Ottmann. Thompson, CT: Spring Publications, 2020.

Schopenhauer, Arthur. *On the Fourfold Root of the Principle of Sufficient Reasons and Other Writings*. Translated and edited by David E. Cartwright, Edward E. Erdmann, and Christopher Janaway. Cambridge: Cambridge University Press, 2012.

———. *The World as Will and Representation*. Translated by E. F. J. Payne. New York: Dover Publications, 1958; reprint, 1966.

Sedley, D. N. *Creationism and Its Critics in Antiquity*. Oakland: University of California Press, 2007.

Spinoza, Baruch de. *Complete Works of Spinoza*. Translated by Samuel Shirley. Indianapolis, IN: Hackett Publishing, 2002.

———. *The Ethics: Treatise on the Emendation of the Intellect*. Translated by Samuel Shirley. Indianapolis, IN: Hackett Publishing, 1992.

———. *The Ethics and Selected Letters*. Translated by Samuel Shirley. Indianapolis, IN: Hackett Publishing, 1982.

———. *The Principles of Cartesian Philosophy and Metaphysical Thoughts*. Translated by Samuel Shirley. Indianapolis, IN: Hackett Publishing, 1998.

Tertullian, Quintus Sept. Flor. *Ante-Nicene Christian Library: Translations of the Writings of the Fathers down to A.D. 325. Vol. XV: The Writings of Tertullian Vol. 2*. Edinburgh: T. & T. Clark, 1870.

Young, Julian. *Nietzsche's Philosophy of Religion*. Cambridge: Cambridge University Press, 2006.

Zhuangzi. *Zhuangzi: The Complete Writings*. Translated by Brook Ziporyn. Indianapolis, IN: Hackett Publishing, 2020.

———. *Zhuangzi: The Essential Writings with Selections from Traditional Commentaries*. Translated by Brook Ziporyn. Indianapolis, IN: Hackett Publishing, 2009.

Ziporyn, Brook. *Being and Ambiguity: Philosophical Experiments with Tiantai Bud-dhism*. Chicago: Open Court Publishing, 2004.

———. *Beyond Oneness and Difference: Li and Coherence in Chinese Buddhist Thought and Its Antecedents*. Albany, NY: SUNY Press, 2014.

———. *Emptiness and Omnipresence: An Essential Introduction to Tiantai Buddhism*. Bloomington: Indiana University Press, 2016.

———. *Evil and/or/as the Good: Omnicentrism, Intersubjectivity, and Value Paradox in Tiantai Buddhist Thought*. Cambridge, MA: Harvard University Press, 2000.

———. *Ironies of Oneness and Difference: Coherence in Early Chinese Thought: Prole-gomena to the Study of Li*. Albany, NY: SUNY Press, 2013.

———. *The Penumbra Unbound: The Neo-Taoist Philosophy of Guo Xiang*. Albany, NY: SUNY Press, 2003.

Index

Abrahamic religions, 9, 12, 51, 61, 139, 140

Absolute, the, 35–36, 176, 178; God as, 27, 28, 166; halfway measure of "God" obstructing, 161–73; ineffability of, 179 (*see also* ineffability); moments of existence as modes of, 307; nature of, 5, 35, 135, 177, 179; Plotinus on, 179; PSR and, 166–67, 177, 178; and world, 187

absolute infinity, 134, 211, 249; of God, 237, 252–53; nature of, 206, 209–10, 240, 252–53

absolute intrinsic Goodness, 64

absoluteness, 198, 199. *See also specific topics*

absolutization, xvi–xvii, 26, 35, 133

accountability, 295. *See also* responsibility

accountable controller, 60, 116, 135–38. *See also* responsible controller

actually existing essences: formal essences and, 207, 243, 247, 248, 261; nature of, 207, 242, 243, 247, 248, 261. *See also* conatus; existent essence

addiction, religion as, 32–33

aesthetic experience, 167–68, 170, 277

aesthetics, 172, 282, 288, 297; as "real metaphysical activity of man" (Nietzsche), 172, 280, 282, 305. *See also* beauty

agápē and eros, 131, 132

agency, 7, 28, 71, 84, 147; divination of, 28; moral, 111; ontological ultimacy of, 25, 30. *See also* free will

agnosticism, 125, 328

alterity, 16

ambiguity, 23, 24, 44, 94. See also *Being and Ambiguity* (Ziporyn)

ambiguous appearance, 176

ambivalence, 23–26

Amis, Kingsley, xii

amor fati (love of necessity), 134, 293, 304, 343

Anaxagoras, 66, 68; *apeiron* (infinity) and, 52, 53, 58, 59, 189, 190; consciousness and, 164; *Noûs* (intelligence) and, xvi, 52, 53, 57–59, 61, 66–67, 170, 189, 226 (see also *Noûs* [intelligence]); on opposites, 58–59; Schopenhauer and, 170; Socrates and, 48, 52, 61

Anaximander, 52, 55, 58

Anaximenes, 53

animality and animate beings, 96–97

animals, 96; Bataille on, 143, 147–49, 312, 313, 336; PSR and conscious, 164; tool-making and, 96, 143, 147–49, 159

animism, 123; Bataille on roots of, 147; defined, 123; gone wild, 68–77; totalization of, 34; unity and, 34, 77

animistic hypothesis, 21

annihilation, 317–19, 321

antagonism, 90, 91

anti-God, 60, 125, 270, 366n15

apeiron (infinity), 52, 53, 58, 59. *See also* infinity

apophaticism, 29, 140, 141. *See also* negative theologies

Arché, 52; and elements, 52, 53; meanings and translations of, 52. See also *Noûs* as *Arché*

Aristophanes, 62–64, 66

unity (*continued*)
117–18, 122, 124; desire for, 62–63 (*see also* desire: inclusion and); exclusivity and, 35, 66, 122; finite, 124; goodness and, 50, 52, 325; infinity and, 41, 59, 171; monotheism and, 34, 35, 66; Nietzsche and, 74–75; *Noûs* and, 66, 181, 182; and the oceanic, 35; personhood and, 117–18, 122; Platonic Forms and, 181; Plotinus on, 181, 185, 325; purpose and, 50, 52, 76, 91, 112, 122, 168; Reason and, 11; teleology and, 34, 113, 171, 182; types of, 35, 76, 77, 91, 112, 122, 214, 234, 277. *See also* oneness
universal mind, 26; nature of, 227, 234; Spinoza on, 60, 203, 204, 225–27
universal mind-body, 203–5
universal Will, 363n31, 277; God as, 274; goodness and, 275, 277; as unreason, reason, and both, 274–78, 363n31. *See also* Will
universe: purpose, 126; what to do about, 128. *See also* cosmogonies
unmixedness. See *Noûs* (intelligence): as unmixed
unreal, all things as, 42

value, 84, 91, 99; intrinsic, 63, 64
valued and disvalued things, 103; asymmetry between, 100–101; Daoism and, 94–95, 97, 99–101; nature of, 94, 99–100. *See also* category A (valued things); category B (disvalued things)
valuelessness, 64, 91, 99–102
values, 91; absolutism concerning, 65. *See also* morality
vicious circles, 219, 288
violence, 153, 156–57, 277, 315, 318–20; Bataille and, 114, 146, 153–55, 157–61, 172, 317, 319–20, 340; and body, 151–52; boundaries and, 153, 154, 157, 158; Christianity and, 154–59; clear consciousness of, 161; disavowed, 154; eroticism, sex, and, 157, 159–61; forms of, 156; God and, 114, 153–59; intimacy and, 114, 146, 152–58, 161, 340; lawgiving and, 153; love and, 154, 158, 160, 340; monopoly on, 153; monotheism

and, xviii, 152, 153, 158; mystical form of, 340; and the oceanic, 146, 152–59; owning, 154; and the sacred, 153, 154, 156–57; self-, 161; sin and, 155–57; tools and, 152, 153, 156, 157; transgression and, 152, 158–60; violent usurpation of, 153; water and, 146, 153, 160; Will and, 277, 340
visionaries. See mystical visionaries
visualization, Bataille and, 317, 319–20

wants. See desire
war, 317, 318; Bataille on, 150, 319, 327, 343; chaos and, 319, 343; Nietzsche and, 279, 288
water, 127, 133, 357n15; bodies and, 226; flame and, 232, 265; flow of, 109, 129–31, 143, 357n16 (*see also* flow); nature of, 52, 111, 126, 127, 130, 232; and other elements, 52–54; violence and, 146, 153, 160; whirlpools and, 204, 226
water in water, 145, 146, 148, 150–53; animals as, 159; Bataille and, 133, 134, 143, 144, 157, 170; Emulative Atheism of, 157; intimacy of, 133, 143, 153; "like water in water," 134, 143, 145
whirlpools, 200–201, 203, 204, 226
whole, world as, 147, 322
whole/part relation, 231; Bataille and, 308–9; finite modes as not merely parts of the whole, 236–52; formal essences and, 248–49; God and, 198, 210, 239, 295, 308–9; infinity, finitude, and, 171, 189, 201, 205, 206, 237–41, 244, 245, 248–52, 255, 362n18; Nature and, 200, 238, 239, 244, 245, 249; Nietzsche and, 293, 295; omnipresence and, 179–80, 187–89, 341; pain and, 336; purpose, purposelessness, and, 88–89; Spinoza and, 171, 187, 200, 201, 203, 205, 206, 210, 213, 220, 238, 239, 249–50, 252, 264, 293, 306–7, 362–63nn18–19; Substance and, 237, 239–41, 244, 249–50; universal mind and, 203
Will, 283, 285, 292, 302, 343; Bataille and, 314, 319, 334, 340, 343; beauty and, 285, 289, 297–99, 301–2; chaos